THE INSTITUTE CLAUSES

THIRD EDITION

OTHER TITLES IN THIS SERIES:

Shipbuilding Contracts
SECOND EDITION
by Malcolm A. Clarke
1992

Time-Barred Actions
SECOND EDITION
Edited by Francesco Berlingieri
1993

Liability for Damage to the Marine Environment
Edited by Colin de la Rue
1993

The York-Antwerp Rules
SECOND EDITION
by N. Geoffrey Hudson
1996

Bill of Lading: A Document of Title to Goods
by Michael Bools
1997

Shipbrokers and the Law
by Andrew Jamieson
1997

Ship Arrest Handbook
Edited by Paul Smith
1997

Douglas & Geen on The Law of Harbours, Coasts and Pilotage
FIFTH EDITION
by Richard Douglas OBE, Peter Lane and Monica Peto
1997

Liability for Oil Pollution and Collisions
by Oya Özçayır
1998

Commencement of Laytime
THIRD EDITION
by Donald Davies
1998

Bills of Lading and Bankers' Documentary Credits
THIRD EDITION
by Paul Todd
1998

Forum Shopping
Edited by Carel J. H. Baron Van Lynden
1998

THE INSTITUTE CLAUSES

BY

N. GEOFFREY HUDSON AND J. C. ALLEN

THIRD EDITION EDITED BY

N. GEOFFREY HUDSON, M.A.

LLP

LONDON HONG KONG

1999

LLP Reference Publishing
69–77 Paul Street
London EC2A 4LQ

EAST ASIA
LLP Asia
Sixth Floor, Hollywood Centre
233 Hollywood Road
Hong Kong

First published in Great Britain, 1986
Second edition 1995
Third edition 1999

British Library Cataloguing in Publication Data
A catalogue record for this book is available from the British Library

ISBN 1-85978-677-4

Typeset in 10/12pt Plantin by
Interactive Sciences Limited, Gloucester
Printed in Great Britain by
WBC Limited,
Bridgend, Mid-Glamorgan

ACKNOWLEDGEMENTS

The author and the publishers are grateful to the International Underwriting Association of London and Witherby & Co. Ltd. for their permission to copy the text of the Institute Clauses referred to herein and to the Association of Average Adjusters for their authority to reproduce Advisory Committee and Special Committee reports together with a number of the Rules of Practice of the Association.

ABOUT THE AUTHORS

GEOFFREY HUDSON, M.A. (OXON) is a barrister and consultant average adjuster, having been for many years senior partner of Ernest Robert Lindley & Sons, one of the leading firms of international average adjusters. He has been both Chairman of the Association of Average Adjusters and President of the International Association of European Average Adjusters (A.I.D.E.). He is currently a Titulary Member of the Comité Maritime Internationale and a Vice-President of the British Maritime Law Association.

He has contributed to several publications including *Lloyd's Maritime and Commercial Law Quarterly*. He is the author of *The York-Antwerp Rules* (2nd ed.), and co-author of *The Institute Clauses* (2nd ed.) and *The Marine Claims Handbook* (5th ed.).

JEFF ALLEN F.C.I.I. is Joint Managing Director of the Richards Hogg Lindley Group. He is a member and past Chairman of the Association of Average Adjusters and is a member of the International Association of European Average Adjusters (A.I.D.E.). He is a frequent speaker at seminars and conferences, has contributed to several publications and is co-author of *The Marine Claims Handbook*, which is also published by LLP Limited.

CONTENTS

GLOSSARY

The following abbreviations are employed in the text:

A.A.A.	Association of Average Adjusters
A.I.D.E.	Association Internationale de Dispacheurs Européens
C.M.I.	Comité Maritime Internationale
C.T.L.	Constructive Total Loss
F.C. & S.	Free of Capture and Seizure
F.O.S.F.A.	Federation of Oils, Seeds and Fats Associations
F.P.A.	Free of Particular Average
I.C.C.	Institute Cargo Clauses
I.M.O.	International Maritime Organization
I.M.T.A.	International Meat Trade Association
I.T.C.	Institute Time Clauses
J.C.C.	Joint Cargo Committee
J.H.C.	Joint Hull Committee
L.O.F.	Lloyd's Open Form (of Salvage Agreement)
M.I.I.	Mortgagees' Interest Insurance
MAR	Marine Policy
P. & I.	Protection and Indemnity
R.D.C.	Running Down Clause
W.A.	With Average
Y.A.R.	York-Antwerp Rules

TABLE OF WORDS AND PHRASES

The following abbreviations are used for the forms of the Clauses:

Abbreviation	*Form of Clause*
ICC	Institute Cargo Clauses
IFFC	Institute Frozen Food Clauses
IBOC	Institute Bulk Oil Clauses
INRC	Institute Natural Rubber Clauses
FOSFA S(1)	Institute FOSFA Supplementary Clauses (1)
IMDC	Institute Malicious Damage Clause
ITP+N-DC	Institute Theft, Pilferage and Non-Delivery Clause
ITCH	Institute Time Clauses, Hulls
IFVC	Institute Fishing Vessel Clauses
IYC	Institute Yacht Clauses
ITCF	Institute Time Clauses, Freight
IAPC(H)	Institute Additional Perils Clauses, Hulls
IP+IC	Institute Protection and Indemnity Clauses, Hulls—Time
ICBR	Institute Clauses for Builders' Risks
IContC	Institute Container Clauses
IMIC	Institute Mortgagees' Interest Clauses
IWC(C)	Institute War Clauses (Cargo)
ISC(C)	Institute Strikes Clauses (Cargo)
IWSC(H)	Institute War and Strikes Clauses, Hulls

TABLE OF CASES

TABLE OF LEGISLATION AND RULES

PART I

INTRODUCTION TO THE NEW CLAUSES

1. THE QUIET REVOLUTION

In November 1978 the Secretariat of the United Nations Conference on Trade and Development (U.N.C.T.A.D.) distributed a document entitled "*Marine Insurance—Legal and Documentary Aspects of the Marine Insurance Contract*".[1]

This was a profound and well-researched study, the depth and objectivity of which were marred only by an unjustified assumption that commercial interests in the developing countries would prefer their contracts to be regulated in accordance with local, rather than international, rules.

Some of the observations made by the U.N.C.T.A.D. Secretariat appear ingenuous—perhaps deliberately so. Thus, the Secretariat found that "the entire marine insurance industry had evolved historically from, and had largely retained, practices and conditions of cover which were formulated by insurers from developed countries". They recognised the ascendancy of the United Kingdom as "the international market centre of marine insurance", and consequently, as stated in the report, the Secretariat concentrated a large part of its investigation on the English marine insurance regime. In the course of this analysis, bouquets and brickbats were bestowed with equal largesse. Although the Lloyd's form of policy (the S.G. form) and many of the current clauses were criticised as antiquated and liable to be misunderstood, it was recognised that "English conditions offer a sophisticated set of widely known clauses ready for immediate use".

It would be a gross exaggeration to say that this document exploded like a bombshell in the London insurance market, or in any other insurance market, for that matter. Nevertheless, as U.N.C.T.A.D. is an inter-governmental body, representatives of the British insurance industry were invited to make their views known to Her Majesty's Government, and the process of consultation began. No doubt, at the outset, there were those who asked: "who are these international civil servants, that they should interfere with the smooth running

1. U.N.C.T.A.D. document TD/B/C14/ISL/27.

of our market?" However, as we may now recognise, the last-ditchers were eventually persuaded by the advocates for reform.

Marine underwriters at Lloyd's are represented by a body called Lloyd's Underwriters' Association, whereas the vast majority of insurance companies writing marine business in the United Kingdom are members of the Institute of London Underwriters. When working together, these bodies form joint committees, so called since they represent both Lloyd's and company underwriters. As a result of the groundswell for reform, Lloyd's Underwriters' Association and the Institute of London Underwriters set up a joint working party to consider what might be done in order to counter the criticisms made in the U.N.C.T.A.D. Report and to drag the standard policy forms into the twentieth century. In the words of an official document—"as a result it was recommended that the Lloyd's S.G. form should be replaced with a new form and the introduction of new cargo clauses". Thus, with typical British understatement, the quiet revolution was announced.

In fact, the review of policy conditions is one of the responsibilities exercised at all times by the Joint Cargo Committee and the Joint Hull Committee. When there are proposals to amend or update any of the standard forms, the drafting is undertaken by yet another joint committee, called the Technical and Clauses Committee. These are the bodies which undertook the major revision of the standard clauses which are reviewed in this book.

This work has been accomplished in an extremely thorough and competent manner. In the first place, as the result of the abolition of the old Lloyd's S.G. form, it has been necessary to transplant into each of the new sets of clauses the Perils Clause, the Sue and Labour Clause and the Waiver Clause, and at the same time to rephrase them in modern and (so far as possible) unambiguous language. On the other hand, other parts of Lloyd's S.G. form, such as the Memorandum and the paragraphs relating to the duration of risk, were already so out-dated that their provisions had for many years been varied or over-ridden in the forms of clauses attached to the policy. In the course of transplantation, some of the time-honoured expressions have been cast aside and replaced with entirely new wording. The old "Sue and Labour Clause" appears in an entirely new guise as the "Duty of Assured Clause", although its intention has been carefully preserved. On the other hand, to take one example, the words "perils of the seas" remain, obdurately ambiguous for those who are unfamiliar with the many English law cases which define that term, even though, for the avoidance of one possible area of doubt, "the seas" have been joined by rivers, lakes or other navigable waters.

A great deal has, however, been done to render the new clauses more intelligible to an assured who enjoys only a nodding acquaintance with the English law relating to marine insurance. For example, the fact that the assured must have an insurable interest in the subject-matter insured at the time of the loss is expressly stated in the new forms of cargo clauses, although no attempt has been made to define what "insurable interest" means. Conversely, the effect of the expression "lost or not lost", as defined in Rule 1 of the Rules for Construction of Policy attached to the First Schedule to the Marine Insurance Act 1906, has been neatly reproduced for the assured to read and comprehend if he can. These and many other such provisions have been inserted into the new clauses for the sake of completeness and comprehension. Some critics might say that such additions to the new clauses are unnecessary, in view of the statement in all the new forms that the insurance "is subject to English law and practice", thereby importing the whole of the Marine Insurance Act 1906, as well as the effect of subsequent legal decisions, but there is no doubt in the mind of the editor that such declaratory provisions are valuable when the new clauses are employed in foreign markets.

Lastly, there are instances where the new clauses have introduced changes in the cover provided. There are many such instances—too many to mention in a general commentary—and the reader will have to delve further into this book to find out what they are.

2. THE MAR FORMS

With the abolition of Lloyd's S.G. form of policy, it was necessary to create a new formal document of contract. It was decided to do this in the simplest possible form of words consistent with the need to validate the existence of the contract and comply with the provisions of the Marine Insurance Act 1906.

Section 22 of the Marine Insurance Act provides:

> "Subject to the provisions of any statute, a contract of marine insurance is inadmissible in evidence unless it is embodied in a marine policy in accordance with this Act. The policy may be executed and issued either at the time when the contract is concluded or afterwards."

Section 23 used to set out a number of matters which the policy must specify by law, but now requires merely that the policy should specify the name of the assured, or of some person who effects the insurance on his behalf.[2]

Section 24(1) of the Act provides:

> "A marine policy must be signed by or on behalf of the insurer, provided that in the case of a corporation the corporate seal may be sufficient, but nothing in this section shall be construed as requiring the subscription of a corporation to be under seal."

The form of the Institute of London Underwriters—Companies Marine Policy—reads as follows:

2. The remainder of section 23, setting out other matters previously required to be specified was repealed in 1959, when stamp duty on marine insurance policies was abolished by the Finance Act 1959.

WE, THE COMPANIES, hereby agree, in consideration of the payment to us by or on behalf of the Assured of the premium specified in the Schedule, to insure against loss damage liability or expense in the proportions and manner hereinafter provided. Each Company shall be liable only for its own respective proportion. This insurance shall be subject to the exclusive jurisdiction of the English Courts, except as may be expressly provided herein to the contrary.

IN WITNESS whereof the General Manager and Secretary of the Institute of London Underwriters has subscribed his name on behalf of each Company.

....

General Manager and Secretary
The Institute of London Underwriters

This Policy is not valid unless it bears the embossment of the Policy Department of The Institute of London Underwriters.

MAR 91

Lloyd's Form of Marine Policy is similar, and provides that the liability of each underwriting member of any syndicate whose definitive number and proportion are set out in the list of syndicates forming part of the policy is limited to his share of that syndicate's proportion. The Lloyd's form is distinguished by the initial letters MAR in the bottom left hand corner, by reason of which these forms are now customarily referred to as the "MAR Forms".

"This insurance shall be subject to the exclusive jurisdiction of the English Courts . . ."

This paragraph was inserted in 1991 with the object of requiring an assured who wishes to sue on the policy to institute legal proceedings in England. The previous form of words—"This insurance is subject to English jurisdiction"—had been held not to constitute an exclusive jurisdiction clause, and to be merely declaratory, for the benefit of an assured, who might be foreign, that the rights which he had under the policy were capable of enforcement in the English Courts.[3]

The inclusion of this clause in the MAR form may be contrasted with the provision contained in each of the various Institute Clauses which we shall examine later in this book, to the effect that the insurance is "subject to English law and practice". The reason for this is that, whereas the MAR forms

3. *Berisford* v. *New Hampshire Insurance Co.* [1990] 1 Lloyd's Rep. 454.

will only be used when the contract is concluded in the United Kingdom, the Institute Clauses may also be used in conjunction with a policy of insurance issued abroad specifically providing for jurisdiction, exclusive or otherwise, in the country of issue.

On the second page of each MAR Form is a schedule with a number of printed headings, as shown overleaf:

SCHEDULE

POLICY NUMBER

NAME OF ASSURED

VESSEL

VOYAGE OR PERIOD OF INSURANCE

SUBJECT-MATTER INSURED

AGREED VALUE
(if any)

AMOUNT INSURED HEREUNDER

PREMIUM

CLAUSES, ENDORSEMENTS, SPECIAL CONDITIONS AND WARRANTIES

THE ATTACHED CLAUSES AND ENDORSEMENTS FORM PART OF THIS POLICY

3. CONSTRUCTION OF THE POLICY FORMS

It might be thought that the terms of Lloyd's S.G. form, having been entirely set aside, were now totally irrelevant to the construction of a policy of marine insurance comprising the MAR form with one of the new Institute Clauses attached. But this is not so.

Section 30 of the Marine Insurance Act 1906 provides:

> "(1) A policy may be in the form in the First Schedule to this Act.
> (2) Subject to the provisions of this Act, and unless the context of the policy otherwise requires, the terms and expressions mentioned in the First Schedule to this Act shall be construed as having the scope and meaning in that schedule assigned to them."

The "form in the First Schedule to this Act" is in fact Lloyd's S.G. form with certain (relatively minor) additions made up to 1906. Several of the more important words and expressions used in Lloyd's form are explained in the First Schedule to the Act in accordance with the Rules for Construction of Policy set out in that Schedule. Thus when the same expressions appear in the Institute Clauses, such as, for example "perils of the seas", they must likewise be interpreted in accordance with those Rules.[4]

Section 91(2) of the Act provides:

> "The rules of the common law including the law merchant, save in so far as they are inconsistent with the express provisions of this Act, shall continue to apply to contracts of marine insurance."

As we shall see hereafter, all the major forms of the Institute Clauses expressly provide:

> "This insurance is subject to English law and practice"

Where this is the case, or in any case where the proper law of the contract is English law,[5] then the rights and obligations of the parties have to be construed in accordance with the provisions of the Marine Insurance Act 1906, and by section 91(2) this brings in (save when inconsistent) all the English law precedents and authorities which make up the *corpus* of English mercantile and insurance law.

The above applies irrespective of the terms of any jurisdiction clause, or the selection by the parties of the Court or other tribunal having jurisdiction.

4. For "perils of the seas" see the commentary on Clause 6.1.1 of I.T.C. Hulls on p. 105.
5. See *The "Al Wahab"* [1983] 2 Lloyd's Rep. 365, discussed on p. 91.

PART II

MARINE CARGO FORMS

1. HISTORICAL PERSPECTIVE—CARGO INSURANCE FROM LLOYD'S FORM TO THE PRESENT DAY

The extent of cover provided

Until relatively recently all cargo insurance was written on restricted terms. Looking at the list of perils which the underwriters on Lloyd's S.G. form were "contented to bear and did take upon themselves", we find that they fall into two main categories:

Acts of God, but limited to perils "of the seas" and
Acts of men, but limited to:

- (i) Acts performed maliciously, malevolently, fraudulently or with a hostile intent. In such category were enemies, pirates, rovers and even the master and crew when acting barratrously, that is to say in fraud of their employers and in breach of their duties.
- (ii) General Average acts.

What is missing? The acts of men while performing their duties, however negligently they may have performed them.

The reason for this limitation on the extent of cover is not hard to seek. In the time when Lloyd's form of policy was being evolved, the carrier of the goods had full responsibility for the cargoes entrusted to his care and was answerable for all losses which might occur to those goods, other than those arising from acts of God, the action of enemies and like persons, or general average acts. From the consequences of these the carrier was exonerated by law and this therefore was the area in which the merchant required protection. For this protection the policy of insurance was evolved.

About 200 years ago it began to be asked whether the term "perils of the seas" comprehended those events such as stranding or collision which were brought about by some failure of the master or crew to perform their duties adequately, for example when they were negligent in navigation. The answer provided by the English courts was that if the loss or damage was caused "proximately" by the stranding or collision, as the case might be, the underwriter was liable to pay even though the stranding or collision was brought about by the negligence of master or crew. More or less concurrently with the unfolding of the doctrine of "proximate cause" came a clear elucidation of another important principle of insurance, namely that of subrogation, whereby in such an event the underwriter who had paid for the loss would be entitled to stand in the shoes of his assured and bring a legal action against the carrier for the consequences of his breach of the contract of carriage.

Later in the nineteenth century with the explosive expansion of commerce, and perhaps influenced also by the improvement in legal machinery, shipowners began to feel in need of some protection against their potential liabilities. To this end, in so far as they were permitted to do so within the principle of freedom of contract, they came to insert wide exoneration clauses in their bills of lading so as virtually to disclaim all responsibility for the goods in their care, and they also formed themselves into associations or clubs for their better protection and indemnity.

This brings us to the twentieth century, in which, despite the Hague Rules, the Hague-Visby Rules and even (despite their limited application) the Hamburg Rules, the merchant adventurer stands in need of better protection by wider and more refined insurance cover.

Restrictions upon the losses paid for

It was not only in the list of perils that the traditional marine insurance policy was restricted. There was also a considerable limitation upon the extent of the losses which would be paid for. This limitation was expressed in what was called the Memorandum to Lloyd's form of policy, which read:

> "N.B.—Corn, fish, salt, fruit, flour and seed are warranted free from average, unless general, or the ship be stranded; sugar, tobacco, hemp, flax, hides and skins are warranted free from average, under five pounds per cent; and all other goods, also the ship and freight, are warranted free from average, under three pounds per cent, unless general, or the ship be stranded, sunk or burnt."

The reasons for this limitation were no doubt the lack of capacity in a market in an early stage of development and a desire to cut out small or contentious claims, coupled with a very real practical problem as to the proof of loss by insured perils. For example, in the event of goods being discharged at destination damaged by sea water, who could say whether the wet in the hold and the deteriorated condition of the cargo were due to an inevitable percolation of water through leaky seams in the side of the ship, or a failure on the part of the crew regularly to pump the bilges, or to a violent incursion of sea water which occurred in a storm?

So, in the case of those goods particularly susceptible to sea water damage enumerated in the first section of the Memorandum, the underwriters would pay no partial loss. Likewise, in the case of other commodities, losses under five per cent or three per cent, as the case might be, were deemed to have come about through the normal incidents of the voyage and not by reason of perils of the seas. Only if the ship had stranded at some time during the voyage were underwriters prepared to take a generous view, and for this the reason is clear. The act of stranding places particular stresses on the hull of a wooden ship and even if on refloating she is found to have sustained no permanent damage, the very act of setting upon the ground would be likely to distort her timbers, disturb the caulking and open up the seams. Hence, if the ship had stranded during the voyage losses by sea peril would be payable irrespective of percentage.

The other significant exception to this limitation of underwriters' liability is in respect of general average contribution, which has always been responded for by underwriters on ships and cargoes.

Restricted conditions on the forms of 1.1.63: The Institute Cargo Clauses (W.A.) and the Institute Cargo Clauses (F.P.A.)

The initials stood for "with average" and "free of particular average" respectively.

These forms incorporated the "Memorandum" restrictions although with rather less severity than in the S.G. form. The assured had an option. He might elect to bear all the risk of partial loss (under the F.P.A. Clause), or the risk of small partial losses below three per cent or five per cent (the W.A. Clause), in either case except for those specified instances where the severity of the Memorandum wording was alleviated by the Average Clause.

The Average Clause (in the W.A. form) / The F.P.A. Clause (in the F.P.A. form)

By these clauses underwriters expressly agreed to pay certain classes of claim outside the average warranty. They were:

1. Claims for particular average irrespective of percentage for damage caused by any of the perils insured, if during the insured voyage the carrying vessel or craft was stranded, sunk or burnt. In the words of the old authorities these events "opened the warranty", and provided the insured goods were on board at the time of the event the assured was entitled to recover in full for any particular average damage sustained by insured perils whenever those perils had occurred—even if prior to the event which opened the warranty.
2. Packages totally lost in the course of loading, transhipment or discharge.
3. Loss or damage reasonably attributed to fire, explosion, collision or contact with an external substance (including ice).
4. Loss or damage reasonably attributed to discharging at a port of refuge or distress.

5. The F.P.A. Clause also covered special charges for landing, warehousing and forwarding to destination goods which had been discharged at an intermediate port subject to a proviso (rather curiously expressed) that the loss averted by such special charges would have been one which underwriters would be liable to pay under the W.A. Clause.

The area of additional cover granted by these exceptions to the average warranty was exactly the same in the F.P.A. Clause as in the W.A. Clause. Some of these extensions to underwriters' liability have now been transferred into the named risk sections of the new (B) and (C) Clauses.

The development of "All Risks" cover

About a hundred years ago, when iron and steel had largely displaced timber in the construction of the hulls of ships, and with other factors contributing to the safe carriage of goods by sea, underwriters were prepared to extend the area of cover which they granted to their assured. No doubt in the first instance such additions to the cover were made piecemeal, by adding such words as "including all risks of craft and/or lighterage to and from the ship", but for a merchant with a good claims record, who was prepared to pay a slightly higher rate of premium, the extra cover afforded by an "All Risks" insurance was—and still is—of great comfort.

2. INSTITUTE CARGO CLAUSES (A)—The "All Risks" form (1/1/82)

RISKS COVERED

The risks covered by this form are set out in Clauses 1, 2 and 3.

Clause 1—Risks Clause

1 This insurance covers all risks of loss of or damage to the subject-matter insured except as provided in Clauses 4, 5, 6 and 7 below.

"all risks"

The expression "all risks" comprehends any loss or damage occasioned fortuitously, but not that which occurs inevitably. In that respect, the cover provided is less wide than an insurance to cover, for example, "all loss and damage, howsoever caused".

The leading case is *Gaunt* v. *British & Foreign Marine Insurance Co. Ltd.*[1]

1. (1921) 26 Com.Cas. 247.

This was an insurance on bales of wool, subject to conditions "including . . . all risks from sheeps back . . . until safely delivered . . . ". On arrival it was found that many of the bales had been damaged by freshwater wetting, some of which must have occurred prior to shipment on the ocean steamer. The House of Lords held that the existence of fortuitous damage was sufficient evidence of a casualty, and that under an insurance against "all risks" it was not necessary to prove the exact nature of the casualty which had occasioned the loss. Lord Sumner said: "'All Risks' has the same effect as if all insurable risks were separately enumerated; for example, it includes the risk that when it happens to be raining the men who ought to use the tarpaulins to protect the wool may happen to be neglecting their duty. This concurrence is fortuitous; it is also the cause of loss by wetting."

Limitations on the expression "all risks"

In the same case Lord Sumner said: "There are, of course, limits to 'all risks'. They are risks and risks insured against. Accordingly the expression does not cover inherent vice or mere wear and tear or British capture. It covers a risk, not certainty; it is something, which happens to the subject-matter from without, not the natural behaviour of that subject-matter, being what it is, in the circumstances under which it is carried. Nor is it a loss which the assured brings about by his own act, for then he has not merely exposed the goods to the chance of injury, he has injured them himself."

Proof of loss

The onus of proof remains upon the assured to show that, on the evidence, some accidental or fortuitous loss or damage has occurred during the duration of the risk as expressed by the policy. In the words of Lord Sumner, when a claimant "avers loss by some risk coming within 'all risks', as used in this policy, he need only give evidence reasonably showing that the loss was due to a casualty, not to a certainty or to inherent vice or to wear and tear. That is easily done. I do not think he has to go further and pick out one of the multitude of risks covered, so as to show exactly how his loss was caused. If he did so he would not bring it any the more within the policy."

By contrast, damage caused by moisture in the atmosphere would normally not be considered to be fortuitous. See *Whiting* v. *New Zealand Insurance Co.*[2]

"loss of or damage to"

This expression comprehends all physical loss and damage to the goods. It does not include financial loss unaccompanied by any physical loss or damage,

2. (1932) 44 Ll.L.Rep. 179.

such as loss of market, even though the cause of the financial loss was a peril insured against.

Expense as such is not covered under this Clause 1, except for the charges customarily paid in the establishment of a claim upon the insurance. These comprise the expenses paid in order to ascertain the nature and extent of the loss and/or damage, e.g., stacking and sorting, separating sound and damaged lots and the cost of surveys and adjustment. (See Rule of Practice No. A9 of the Association of Average Adjusters.)

Certain classes of expenditure are however covered under Clauses 2, 3, 12 and 16.

"the subject-matter insured"

The Marine Insurance Act 1906 provides, by section 26:

> "(1) The subject-matter insured must be designated in a marine policy with reasonable certainty.
> (2) The nature and extent of the interest of the assured in the subject-matter insured need not be specified in the policy.
> (3) Where the policy designates the subject-matter insured in general terms, it shall be construed to apply to the interest intended by the assured to be covered.
> (4) In the application of this section regard shall be had to any usage regulating the designation of the subject-matter insured."

Provision is made for the declaration of the subject-matter insured in the schedule which is printed on the reverse of the MAR Policy Forms (see page 6). Although there might be some argument that the Rules for Construction of Policy, which form part of the First Schedule to the Marine Insurance Act, no longer apply to a policy consisting merely of the MAR Form and Institute Cargo Clauses, it is submitted that Rule 17 is a valid restatement of English law and, like the other Rules for Construction of Policy, continue to have effect, since the new wordings, although no longer incorporating Lloyd's S.G. form, constitute an "other like form".

Rule 17 states:

> "The term 'goods' means goods in the nature of merchandise, and does not include personal effects or provisions and stores for use on board.
>
> In the absence of any usage to the contrary, deck cargo and living animals must be insured specifically, and not under the general denomination of goods."

An example of a "usage to the contrary" would be "wood goods", meaning sawn timber, which by the custom of the trade is frequently carried on deck and which therefore need not be declared as "deck cargo".

Do packing materials form part of the subject-matter insured?

There is a "rule of thumb" in the London insurance market that, unless the description of the subject-matter of the insurance is so clearly worded as to include the packing materials or containers, underwriters will not respond to any claim for damage sustained to the packing materials or containers, even when caused by a peril insured against.[3]

Such law as there is does not appear wholly to justify this practice. In *Brown* v. *Fleming*[4] the insurance was expressed to be upon "228 cases whisky". Survey at destination disclosed that in a large number of cases the straw in which the bottles were packed was sodden and discoloured by sea water and that many of the labels on the bottles had been damaged. There was nothing wrong with the whisky. The cases subject to damage were sold and the assured claimed the loss which they had sustained thereby. The underwriters declined the claim on the ground that the damage to the straw and labels was not covered by the policy. Bigham J., giving judgment for the assured, said:

> "The straw in which the bottles were packed and the labels upon the bottles are part of the subject of the insurance just as are the bottles and corks. Damage to the labels affects the selling value of the whisky on the market just as much as damage to the corks would."

In *Berk* v. *Style*[5] the policy was on a quantity of kieselguhr which was carried in heavy paper bags on a voyage from North Africa to London. On arrival in London it was found that a number of bags had split and it was therefore necessary to rebag a quantity of kieselguhr in order to enable it to be discharged ex lighters. The assured claimed the cost of rebagging and the underwriters denied liability on the ground that the bags were inadequate, and this inadequacy amounted to inherent vice. In argument for the underwriters counsel conceded that "if this had been a loss by a peril insured against, what the plaintiffs did would have been suing and labouring within the clause in the policy". In relation to the argument whether or not the rebagging was done in order to avert loss or damage to the goods, Sellers J. said: "I prefer the view accepted and alleged by the underwriters that the subject-matter of the insurance was kieselguhr packed in paper bags . . . I think it must be taken that both parties to the insurance contemplated that the goods would be packed for carriage and would not be carried in bulk".

On the other hand, in *Vacuum Oil Company* v. *Union Insurance Society of Canton*[6] where the policy was on "10,000 tins of petroleum", Roche J. said: "Here I hold on the facts that the policy covered petroleum in tins. The thing insured was not the tins but the petroleum. In other words, if all the petroleum was lost and the tins arrived, I should hold there was an actual total loss. If on the other hand the petroleum could be saved, although it had to be saved in other tins, I should hold that there was no loss."

3. See *Arnould on Marine Insurance*, 16th edn. (British Shipping Laws), footnote 62 appearing at the end of Section 280.
4. (1902) 7 Com.Cas. 245.
5. [1955] 2 Lloyd's Rep. 383.
6. (1925) 24 Ll.L.Rep. 188.

It is submitted that this passage, which was obiter, is inconsistent with the principles followed in other cases.

It has been suggested that, in the absence of clear words to describe the subject-matter of insurance, the packing will not form part of the subject-matter where the goods can, and commonly do, travel unprotected. Thus in *Lysaght* v. *Coleman*,[7] where the policy was on "galvanised iron", Lord Esher said: "I think I ought to say also that it is clear that the insurance was on the iron, so that no claim could arise in respect of damaged packing cases".

This would not be inconsistent with the principle suggested by *Berk* v. *Style* that where good commercial practice requires a certain standard of packaging for the transit, such packing does form part of the subject-matter insured, even if not specifically mentioned.

Clause 2—General Average Clause

2 This insurance covers general average and salvage charges, adjusted or determined according to the contract of affreightment and/or the governing law and practice, incurred to avoid or in connection with the avoidance of loss from any cause except those excluded in Clauses 4, 5, 6 and 7 or elsewhere in this insurance.

Both general average and salvage charges are a species of ransom from total loss. Under English law, they are defined as follows:

General average

The Marine Insurance Act 1906, section 66(2) states:

> "There is a general average act where any extraordinary sacrifice or expenditure is voluntarily and reasonably made or incurred in time of peril for the purpose of preserving the property imperiled in the common adventure."

Section 66(3) states how the charges are dealt with:

> "Where there is a general average loss, the party on whom it falls is entitled, subject to the conditions imposed by Maritime Law, to a rateable contribution from the other parties interested and such contribution is called a general average contribution."

Salvage charges

The Marine Insurance Act, section 65(2) states:

> " 'Salvage charges' means the charges recoverable under Maritime Law by a salvor independently of contract. They do not include the expenses of services in the nature of salvage rendered by the assured or his agents, or any person employed for hire by them, for the purpose of averting a peril insured against. Such expenses, where properly incurred, may be recovered as particular charges or as a general average loss, according to the circumstances under which they were incurred."

7. (1895) 7 Asp.M.L.C. 552.

The chief distinction is that salvage charges have to do with the amount of the reward payable to a salvor, who is a "volunteer" from outside the common maritime adventure, whereas general average concerns the settlement of expenditure incurred and/or amounts made good for property sacrificed, as between the parties to the adventure *inter se*. Where the adjustment of general average is governed by the York-Antwerp Rules, Rule VI provides that the total of the payments made on account of salvage (including costs and other expenses incurred in connection therewith) will be admitted in general average whenever the salvage operation was undertaken for the common safety of all the interests at risk.

For a short summary of the similarities and differences between general average and salvage, see Hudson and Allen, *Marine Claims Handbook*, Part III.

"adjusted or determined"

It is submitted that the word "adjusted" must be read as applying to general average, whereas the word "determined" (which is meaningless in the context of general average) has to be read as applying to salvage charges.

"according to the contract of affreightment and/or the governing law and practice"

The corresponding words in the previous Institute Clauses of 1/1/63 were " . . . according to Foreign Statement or to York-Antwerp Rules if in accordance with the contract of affreightment".

Some expansion is required, over and above a mere undertaking to pay general average and salvage charges, since by virtue of English law and practice (see Clause 19) it is implicit that underwriters will respond, even under the simplest form of policy (e.g., Lloyd's S.G. form without any other additions), for general average contributions and the proportion of salvage charges attaching to the insured interest, but only for such amounts as would be recognised as general average or "salvage charges" by English law and practice.

The vast majority of general average adjustments are drawn up in accordance with the York-Antwerp Rules, by virtue of a clause in the bill of lading or charter-party stipulating for such adjustment according to the current version of those rules. It is probably to be regretted that this Clause 2 in its present form does not accord recognition to this virtually universal practice. However, the same effect is achieved by the use of the words "according to the contract of affreightment", with the added advantage to the assured that if the general average clause in the bill of lading or charter-party should stipulate either for some other rule to apply (for example, the so-called Peking (Beijing) Rules) then the underwriters will respond (subject to the rule regarding under-insurance) for the general average contribution payable by their assured in accordance with such other rules.

If the bill of lading or charter-party should be silent as to the manner in which any general average should be adjusted, the law of all maritime countries is that the adjustment should be prepared in accordance with the law and practice obtaining at the port where the ship and goods part company.[8]

The words "the governing law and practice" apply not only to protect this principle in regard to the adjustment of general average when there is no relevant provision in the contract of affreightment, but also, it is submitted, to the "determination" of salvage charges if the same are not, as explained above, brought into a general average adjustment under Rule VI of the York-Antwerp Rules. An example would be when the efforts of a salvor have been directed not to all the property at risk, but merely to save some particular interests.

"incurred to avoid or in connection with the avoidance of loss from any cause except those excluded"

Under the (A) Clauses these words are merely declaratory of the principle set out in section 66(6) of the Marine Insurance Act, which states:

> "In the absence of express stipulation, the insurer is not liable for any general average loss or contribution where the loss was not incurred for the purpose of avoiding, or in connection with the avoidance of, a peril insured against."

Compare the position under Institute Cargo Clauses (B) and (C), where the corresponding provision has greater significance.

Clause 3—"Both to Blame Collision" Clause

3 This insurance is extended to indemnify the Assured against such proportion of liability under the contract of affreightment "Both to Blame Collision" Clause as is in respect of a loss recoverable hereunder. In the event of any claim by shipowners under the said Clause the Assured agree to notify the Underwriters who shall have the right, at their own cost and expense, to defend the Assured against such claim.

In a collision action in the United States, the owners of cargo damaged by the collision may in principle proceed with their claim for damages against either the carrying vessel or the non-carrying vessel involved in the collision. Hence, if the carrier (as would be expected) is exempted from liability under the contract of carriage, the cargo owners will proceed to recover their losses in full from the owners of the non-carrying vessel, who can then in their turn claim as part of *their* damages the proportion of the claim they have paid to the cargo owners attaching to the degree of fault found against the carrying vessel. The "Both to Blame Collision Clause" has been inserted in bills of lading and charter-parties in an attempt to prevent this rule of American law from operating to saddle the owner of the carrying vessel with liability for the

8. In English law, this principle was stated in *Simonds* v. *White* (1824) 2 B. & C. 811.

collision damages sustained by the cargo on board his own ship. In the United States, a carrier seeking to avoid liability for the damages sustained by the cargo on board his own ship by pleading the "Both to Blame Collision Clause" would fail, since the Supreme Court has held such a clause to be invalid in bills of lading on the grounds of public policy.[9] The clause may, however, be valid in charter-parties,[10] and the possibility also exists that the parties involved in a collision might agree to the American rules of settlement without invoking the jurisdiction of the United States.

If underwriters have already paid for the loss or damage sustained to the goods in consequence of the collision, then the benefit of any legal proceedings commenced by the assured against the non-carrying vessel would accrue to them by virtue of the doctrine of subrogation, and any diminution of their recovery resulting from the owner of the carrying vessel pleading the "Both to Blame Collision Clause" would be for the underwriters' account. However, the policy clause covers the contingency of an assured, having sustained a loss or damage by collision, seeking to recover for his own account from the non-carrying vessel, and being met by a valid "Both to Blame Collision Clause" in the contract of affreightment.

EXCLUSIONS

The exclusions are contained in Clauses 4, 5, 6, and 7. Some of them, notably those referred to in Clauses 4.1, 4.2, 4.4 and 4.5, replicate what are sometimes called the "statutory exclusions" set out in section 55(2) of the Marine Insurance Act 1906.

Clause 4—General Exclusions Clause

4 In no case shall this insurance cover
 4.1 loss damage or expense attributable to wilful misconduct of the Assured

It is to be noted that *all* the exclusions apply to "expense" as well as to claims for loss or damage. Consequently a claim for the cost of forwarding charges under Clause 12, for example, would be defeated if the event giving rise to the need to forward arose through one of the exclusions.

"attributable to wilful misconduct of the Assured"

These words are a direct importation from the Marine Insurance Act, section 55(2)(*a*).

"*attributable to*" is intentionally wider than "caused by" (the words employed in all the other exclusion clauses). A loss proximately caused by a

9. *United States of America* v. *Atlantic Mutual Insurance Co.*, 1952 A.M.C. 659.
10. *American Union Transport Inc.* v. *United States of America*, 1976 A.M.C. 1480.

peril insured would therefore appear to be defeasible if the wilful misconduct of the assured was a remote, but nonetheless effective cause.

"*wilful misconduct*" means a course of action undertaken either deliberately, knowing it to be wrongful so far as others are concerned, or recklessly, without caring whether it is wrongful or not.[11]

"*the Assured*" means "the persons interested (in the subject-matter insured), the persons for whose benefit the insurance is made".[12]

Most of the English law cases on wilful misconduct concern ships which are allegedly cast away by their owners, and there have probably not been many instances where cargo underwriters have needed to avail themselves of this defence to a claim. It is, however, submitted that this exclusion would apply, for example, if a merchant insured goods, knowing that they were prohibited from importation in the country of destination, and they were destroyed or confiscated on the order of the customs authorities.

4.2 ordinary leakage, ordinary loss in weight or volume, or ordinary wear and tear of the subject-matter insured

"*Ordinary*" leakage or loss is to be contrasted with leakage or loss due to a fortuity, which would be covered within "all risks". It is submitted therefore that "ordinary" in its context means non-fortuitous or inevitable.

These exclusions, and that of wear and tear are, under English law, capable of being brought back within the policy cover by the use of express words. See Marine Insurance Act, section 55(2)(*c*).

"*Ordinary wear and tear of the subject-matter insured*". This exclusion was not expressed in the Institute Cargo Clauses (All Risks) of 1/1/63. However, the effect of inserting these words into the Institute Cargo Clauses of 1/1/82 is in fact to extend the cover granted to the assured, since the wear and tear excluded is limited to that "of the subject-matter insured" and does not extend to the wear and tear of the carrying vessel, barge or container.

4.3 loss damage or expense caused by insufficiency or unsuitability of packing or preparation of the subject-matter insured (for the purpose of this Clause 4.3 "packing" shall be deemed to include stowage in a container or liftvan but only when such stowage is carried out prior to attachment of this insurance or by the Assured or their servants)

"*insufficiency or unsuitability of packing*". Whether, in any particular case, the packing was insufficient or unsuitable is often a nice question of fact. The test is whether the packing was adequate "to endure the ordinary contemplated handling and carriage".[13] It is submitted that if the type of packing is in accordance with the normal custom of the trade, this would raise a strong presumption that it was adequate.

" . . . *stowage in a container or liftvan*". It is to be noted that loss or damage

11. See *Arnould on Marine Insurance*, 16th edn. (British Shipping Laws), Section 786.
12. See *Ocean Iron Steamship Insurance Association* v. *Leslie* (1887) 6 Asp.M.L.C. 226.
13. See *Berk* v. *Style* [1955] 2 Lloyd's Rep. 383, in which it was held that, when the packing is included in the subject-matter insured and is inadequate, this amounts to inherent vice.

due to bad stowage in a container or liftvan is not covered in two circumstances:

(a) When the stowage is carried out before the attachment of the insurance, or
(b) When it is the assured or his servants who carry out the stowage.

4.4 loss damage or expense caused by inherent vice or nature of the subject-matter insured.

A definition of inherent vice is: "the unfitness of the goods to withstand the ordinary incidents of the voyage, given the degree of care which the shipowner is required by the contract to exercise in relation to the goods".[14] Also—"a loss by inherent vice is one which is proximately caused by the natural behaviour of the subject-matter insured, being what it is, in the circumstances in which it was expected to be carried".[15]

In *Noten B.V.* v. *Harding*[16] four consignments of leather gloves shipped in cardboard boxes stuffed in containers at Calcutta were found on out-turn at Rotterdam to be wet, stained, mouldy and discoloured. The damage to the gloves was due to the moisture which they had absorbed prior to shipment being carried by convection to the roof of the container, where it condensed and fell as drops of water on the cartons below. The Court of Appeal held that the damage was proximately caused by the inherent vice of the subject-matter insured. Bingham L.J. said: "The goods deteriorated as a result of their natural behaviour in the ordinary course of the completed voyage, without the intervention of any fortuitous external accidents or casualty".

The exclusion is of considerable antiquity, and is recognised by the maritime law of all countries. In English law it is one of those events for which an underwriter will not be liable "unless the policy otherwise provides"—Marine Insurance Act, section 55(2)(*c*). For a case in which the policy did "otherwise provide" see *Soya G.m.b.H.* v. *White*[17] where the insurance was effected "to cover the risks of heat, sweat and spontaneous combustion only".

4.5 loss damage or expense proximately caused by delay, even though the delay be caused by a risk insured against (except expenses payable under Clause 2 above)

"*proximately caused by delay*". The word "proximately" is used in this clause, presumably in order to conform to section 55(2)(*b*) of the Marine Insurance Act, viz.:

> "Unless the policy otherwise provides, the insurer on ship or goods is not liable for any loss proximately caused by delay, although the delay be caused by a peril insured against."

14. *Scrutton on Charterparties*, 19th edn., art. 109.
15. *Per* Lord Sumner in *British & Foreign Marine Insurance Co.* v. *Gaunt* (1921) 7 Ll.L.Rep. 62, adapted by Scrutton L.J. in *Sassoon* v. *Yorkshire Insurance Co.* (1923) 16 Ll.L.Rep. 129 and approved by the Court of Appeal in *Soya G.m.b.H.* v. *White* [1982] 1 Lloyd's Rep. 136.
16. [1989] 2 Lloyd's Rep. 527; [1990] 2 Lloyd's Rep. 283.
17. [1983] 1 Lloyd's Rep. 122 (H.L.).

The leading English case is *Pink* v. *Fleming*.[18] In that case part of a cargo of fruit deteriorated owing to delay occasioned on the voyage by the ship requiring to be repaired on account of collision damage. In the United States, the rule is different,[19] and consequently a delay exclusion clause would be essential in a policy governed by American law if the underwriters wished to exclude a similar claim.

"*(except expenses payable under Clause 2 above)*". The only instance of claim for expenses consequent upon delay for which the insurers will respond arises when a ship has been detained in the circumstances envisaged in Rule XI of the York-Antwerp Rules or other similar provision affecting general average. In such a case, these words make it clear that the insurers will reimburse their assured for cargo's proportion of general average so settled, including the ship's detention expenses.

> **4.6** loss damage or expense arising from insolvency or financial default of the owners managers charterers or operators of the vessel

This clause was new in 1982 and its introduction caused a certain amount of resentment in some quarters. This clause was felt to bear particularly heavily upon the assured under an "all risks" policy, since it has been held that an unlawful detention of goods amounts to "conversion", thus founding a claim upon a policy against "all risks".[20]

In the light of the representations make to them, London Market underwriters agreed to ameliorate the severity of this clause in the standard forms which were negotiated with various trade associations.

"*insolvency or financial default*". A person is said to be insolvent when he is unable to pay all his debts in full. If that be the applicable definition in the context of this clause, "insolvency" would appear to be wider even than "financial default" and include the situation in which many shipowners or operators still manage to continue trading.

It appears that the intention of the draftsmen was to exclude all types of claim for recovery and forwarding of the goods arising from the abandonment of a voyage by shipowners or operators who run out of funds while the voyage was still in being.

> **4.7** loss damage or expense arising from the use of any weapon of war employing atomic or nuclear fission and/or fusion or other like reaction or radioactive force or matter.

"*use of any weapon of war*" presumably includes the testing of such weapons as well as their use in a war situation. If a ship and cargo were contaminated by fall-out from the test of a nuclear device intended to form the basis of a weapon, it is submitted the exclusion would apply. On the other hand, if the contamination occurred as a result of a radioactive emission owing to an

18. (1890) 25 Q.B.D. 396.
19. *Lanasa Fruit* v. *Universal Insurance Co. (The "Smaragd")*, 302 U.S. 556.
20. *London & Provincial Leather Processes* v. *Hudson* (1939) 64 Ll.L.Rep. 352.

accident at a nuclear power station, underwriters insuring on "All Risks" conditions would respond for the loss or damage so caused.

Clause 5—Unseaworthiness and Unfitness Exclusion Clause

5 5.1 In no case shall this insurance cover loss damage or expense arising from
unseaworthiness of vessel or craft,
unfitness of vessel craft conveyance container or liftvan for the safe carriage of the subject-matter insured,
where the Assured or their servants are privy to such unseaworthiness or unfitness, at the time the subject-matter insured is loaded therein.

5.2 The Underwriters waive any breach of the implied warranties of seaworthiness of the ship and fitness of the ship to carry the subject-matter insured to destination, unless the Assured or their servants are privy to such unseaworthiness or unfitness.

Logically, Clause 5.2 has to be considered first. In the absence of such a waiver of the implied warranty of seaworthiness, the assured would have no claim at all if his goods were loaded on to an unseaworthy ship, since the Marine Insurance Act, section 40(2), provides:

> "In a voyage policy on goods or other moveables there is an implied warranty that at the commencement of the voyage the ship is not only seaworthy as a ship, but also that she is reasonably fit to carry the goods or other moveables to the destination contemplated by the policy."

This rule bears very hard on an innocent assured, since very few owners of cargo are in a position to influence, still less control, the fitness of the carrying ship.

In previous editions of Institute Cargo Clauses underwriters' waiver of the implied warranty was expressed shortly by the words: "the seaworthiness of the vessel as between the Assured and Underwriters is hereby admitted".

It is submitted that the effect of Clause 5.2 is the same, since the fitness of the ship to carry the goods to destination is already imported into the definition of seaworthiness by section 40(2) of the Act, quoted above. The proviso—"unless the Assured or their servants are privy to such unseaworthiness or unfitness"—is new, and takes the place of a positive statement in the previous edition of Institute Cargo Clauses that in the event of loss the assured's right of recovery would not be prejudiced by the fact that the loss may have been attributable to the wrongful act or misconduct of the shipowners or their servants, committed without the assured's privity.

Clause 5.1 might appear at first sight to cover much the same ground as Clause 5.2, but the presumed intention of the draftsman was to clarify the position in regard to those cases where unseaworthiness of the ship or unfitness of the "vessel craft conveyance container or liftvan" for the safe carriage of the goods was the *cause* of the loss, in contrast to those cases where, but for the waiver of the implied warranty of seaworthiness, the underwriters would have had a defence, on the ground of breach of warranty, against *any* claim for loss, however caused.

"Privy"

To be "privy" to something involves having actual positive knowledge of it or, being suspicious of the true situation, "turning a blind eye" to it and refraining from enquiry.[21]

"the Assured or their servants"

This state of knowledge, or "turning a blind eye", about the condition of the ship or, for example, a container may be that of a cargo superintendent employed by the assured to supervise the operation of loading. In such a case, his knowledge would afford the underwriters a defence if he was employed by the assured, but not if he were employed by the assured's agents. On the other hand, the addition of the word "servants" broadens the scope of underwriters' defence beyond that provided for in the Marine Insurance Act in relation to a time policy on a ship, where, to afford underwriters a defence, the privity to the unseaworthiness has to be that of the assured personally or, in the case of a company, its *alter ego* or at least one of its top men.

The exclusion provided in Clause 5.1 is not likely in practice to apply very frequently in relation to the unseaworthiness of a ship, except in those instances where a shipowner or operator is loading goods for his own account. The exclusion does however place a heavy obligation upon the assured to ensure that the conveyances or containers into which the goods are loaded at the commencement of the transit are in a fit condition.

Clause 6—War Exclusion Clause

6 In no case shall this insurance cover loss damage or expense caused by

6.1 war civil war revolution rebellion insurrection, or civil strife arising therefrom, or any hostile act by or against a belligerent power

6.2 capture seizure arrest restraint or detainment (piracy excepted), and the consequences thereof or any attempt thereat

6.3 derelict mines torpedoes bombs or other derelict weapons of war.

This War Exclusion Clause replaces the old Free of Capture and Seizure (F.C. & S.) Clause, the wording of which had become extremely convoluted owing to amendments having been made to it in the course of its history.

A commentary on the risks excluded by the clause appears in Part VI of this book, where the various war risk covers are examined. However, two changes which were made in the 1/1/82 wording are particularly relevant to the cover afforded by the Institute Cargo Clauses (A):

"*Piracy*", by being excepted from the list of war exclusions, has been reinstated as a risk covered by Marine Underwriters when the (A) conditions apply. One definition of piracy, judicially approved,[22] is:

21. See the words of Lord Denning M.R. in *Compania Maritima San Basilio S.A.* v. *The Oceanus Mutual Underwriting Association (The "Eurysthenes")* [1976] 2 Lloyd's Rep. 171.

22. By Kennedy L.J. in *Republic of Bolivia* v. *Indemnity Mutual Marine Assurance Co.* (1909) 11 Asp.M.L.C. 218; 14 Com.Cas. 156.

"piracy is forcible robbery at sea, whether committed by marauders from outside the ship or by mariners or passengers within it. The essential element is that they violently dispossess the Master, and afterwards carry away the ship itself, or any of the goods, with a felonious intent."

Other old English law cases[23] have established that the term "pirates" includes passengers who mutiny and rioters who attack the ship from the shore (this being the partial definition contained in Rule for Construction of Policy No. 8 in Schedule 1 to the Marine Insurance Act).

In a more recent case, the judge considered the extent of force required to establish an act as piratical, and also the relevance of the place where the act was committed. He decided that the non-forcible entry of thieves on board a vessel moored in berth was not piracy, since the element of violence was absent, and the vessel was not "at sea".[24]

"derelict mines torpedoes bombs or other derelict weapons of war". Under previous editions of the Institute Clauses there was some doubt as to whether loss or damage caused by derelict weapons of war fell within Marine or War Risks.[25] Now the position has been clarified; such damage falls within the War Risks cover.

Clause 7—Strikes Exclusion Clause

7 In no case shall this insurance cover loss damage or expense
- **7.1** caused by strikers, locked-out workmen, or persons taking part in labour disturbances, riots or civil commotions
- **7.2** resulting from strikes, lock-outs, labour disturbances, riots or civil commotions
- **7.3** caused by any terrorist or any person acting from a political motive.

A fuller commentary is contained in the section of this book dealing with the Institute Strikes Clauses (see page 297).

However, it is worth noting in this context that claims which arise from the activity of terrorists or persons acting from a political motive (which may well include agitators and hijackers) have been transferred from the Marine Risks cover to the Strike Risks cover.

DURATION

Clause 8—Transit Clause

8 **8.1** This insurance attaches from the time the goods leave the warehouse or place of storage at the place named herein for the commencement of the transit, continues during the ordinary course of transit and terminates either
- **8.1.1** on delivery to the Consignees' or other final warehouse or place of storage at the destination named herein,

23. See *Naylor* v. *Palmer* (1854) 10 Exch. 382 (mutiny of passengers) and *Nesbitt* v. *Lushington* (1792) 4 T.R. 783 (rioters from shore).

24. *Athens Maritime Enterprises Corporation* v. *Hellenic Mutual War Risks Association (The "Andreas Lemos")* [1982] 2 Lloyd's Rep. 483, *per* Staughton J.

25. See *Costain-Blankevoort (U.K.) Ltd.* v. *Davenport (The "Nassau Bay")* [1979] 1 Lloyd's Rep. 395.

8.1.2 on delivery to any other warehouse or place of storage, whether prior to or at the destination named herein, which the Assured elect to use either

8.1.2.1 for storage other than in the ordinary course of transit or

8.1.2.2 for allocation or distribution,

or

8.1.3 on the expiry of 60 days after completion of discharge overside of the goods hereby insured from the oversea vessel at the final port of discharge,

whichever shall first occur.

8.2 If, after discharge overside from the oversea vessel at the final port of discharge, but prior to termination of this insurance, the goods are to be forwarded to a destination other than that to which they are insured hereunder, this insurance, whilst remaining subject to termination as provided for above, shall not extend beyond the commencement of transit to such other destination.

8.3 This insurance shall remain in force (subject to termination as provided for above and to the provisions of Clause 9 below) during delay beyond the control of the Assured, any deviation, forced discharge, reshipment or transhipment and during any variation of the adventure arising from the exercise of a liberty granted to shipowners or charterers under the contract of affreightment.

This Clause 8 has to be read in close conjunction with Clauses 9 and 10 (*q.v.*) as all three of them have to do with the duration of the risk.

Clause 8 is in fact the old "Warehouse to Warehouse" clause, as it used to be called in previous editions of Institute Cargo Clauses. It defines the points at which the risk attaches and terminates, and adds (in Clause 8.3) comfortable words as to the circumstances in which it remains in force notwithstanding certain events beyond the control of the assured.

Clauses 9 and 10, however, are in effect exceptions, and they set out circumstances in which the assured must give notice to the underwriters if he wishes the cover to remain in force.

Commencement of the transit

"*from the time the goods leave the warehouse*". "Leaving" involves physical movement of the goods with the intention to proceed on the transit. The mere loading into a lorry, which then remains on the premises, is not sufficient.

"*the place named herein for the commencement of the transit*". This may be anywhere in the interior, provided that the assured has accurately identified the place in his declaration, so that the same can be entered in the voyage description contained in the schedule to the MAR form.

Continuation of the transit

"*continues during the ordinary course of transit*". Though it may appear very hard on an innocent assured, cover will be suspended, even though the goods have been properly loaded on the vessel, craft or conveyance, if the "ordinary course of transit" has been interrupted. In *S.C.A. Freight Ltd.* v. *Gibson*,[26] a case under a Lloyd's Goods in Transit (C.M.R.) policy, the lorry containing the assured's goods overturned while being driven on a "joy-ride", i.e. a journey "unconnected with the furtherance of their carriage to

26. *S.C.A. Freight Ltd.* v. *Gibson* [1974] 2 Lloyd's Rep. 533.

[destination]"; it was held that this was not "whilst in the normal course of transit" and the underwriters were not liable to make good the loss sustained by the assured.

Termination of the transit

Three possibilities are envisaged by the clause, and the insured transit will terminate as soon as any one of them occurs, even though the assured may intend to continue the transit notwithstanding such occurrence. Consequently, if an assured becomes aware that the insurance may terminate prematurely (so far as he is concerned), he must give notice to the underwriters and request a special extension of the risk. The events, any one of which will terminate the risk, are:

Delivery to the consignees' or other final warehouse or place of storage at the destination named in the policy. This is self-explanatory.

Delivery to a place of storage, which the assured intends to use "other than in the ordinary course of transit or for allocation or distribution". An example would be delivery to a customs warehouse where the goods remain for some period of time because the assured, not being in urgent need of the goods, elects to defer payment of the customs duty.

Expiry of 60 days after completion of discharge from the ocean vessel at the conclusion of the sea-leg of the transit. This 60 days is a limit, and at the same time an automatic cut-off. Even if the intended overland transit to ultimate destination cannot possibly be performed within 60 days, the insurance will terminate unless the assured has been able to negotiate special terms for its continuation.

Clause 8.2 sets out another circumstance when the insurance will terminate, which may be prior to any of the three termini provided in Clause 8.1. This is when, after having been discharged from the ocean steamer, the goods are "forwarded to a destination other than that to which they are insured hereunder". This clause is intended to deal with the situation of a resale to a customer of the assured, and to make it quite clear which insurance would be in force (that of the original assured or his customer), the clause provides for termination of the original insurance at the time when the new transit commences. Although this Clause 8.2 is widely worded, it is not intended to deal with the situation where the final destination is changed by the assured, say by reallocation of the goods to a different point of distribution. Such a circumstance is covered by Clause 10 (*q.v.*).

Clause 8.3 sets out the circumstances in which the underwriters are content to maintain the cover, notwithstanding that the listed circumstances add to the risks initially contemplated at the time the insurance was placed. Thus the insurance remains in force, without any obligation on the part of the assured to give notice to the underwriters, during delay beyond the assured's control, any deviation, forced discharge, reshipment or transhipment during the voyage and any permitted variation of the contract of carriage (but not its termination, which is dealt with in Clause 9). The circumstances envisaged would include, for example, the resort of the carrying vessel to a port of refuge to repair accidental damage to the ship, when those repairs were necessary for the safe prosecution of the voyage. In such a case, it might be necessary to discharge the cargo and store it ashore in order to effect the repairs to the ship. In such circumstances, the insurance would remain in force and continue to cover against "all risks", including those ashore.

Clause 9—Termination of Contract of Carriage Clause

9 If owing to circumstances beyond the control of the Assured either the contract of carriage is terminated at a port or place other than the destination named therein or the transit is otherwise terminated before delivery of the goods as provided for in Clause 8 above, then this insurance shall also terminate *unless prompt notice is given to the Underwriters and continuation of cover is requested when the insurance shall remain in force, subject to an additional premium if required by the Underwriters,* either

9.1 until the goods are sold and delivered at such port or place, or unless otherwise specially agreed, until the expiry of 60 days after arrival of the goods hereby insured at such port or place, whichever shall first occur,

or

9.2 if the goods are forwarded within the said period of 60 days (or any agreed extension thereof) to the destination named herein or to any other destination, until terminated in accordance with the provisions of Clause 8 above.

This Clause 9 sets out one of the circumstances in which underwriters will require prompt notice to be given by the assured with a request for continuation of the cover, in order to maintain the insurance, subject to any additional premium that may be required. There are some small changes in the wording from that which applied in the previous edition of Institute Cargo Clauses, but the effect is the same. The clause contemplates either that the voyage is abandoned (with or without good cause) by the shipowner or other carrier, or that the adventure is frustrated, as for example occurred when ships were "locked in" the Suez Canal owing to its closure. However, the continuation of cover granted by the clause is fairly severely limited; it will end either when the goods are sold and delivered at the port or place where the transit has terminated, or on the expiry of 60 days if the goods have not been sold within that time, or, if the goods are forwarded within 60 days or any agreed extension of time, until delivery at either the original destination or a destination subsequently agreed to.

Clause 10—Change of Voyage Clause

10 Where, after attachment of this insurance, the destination is changed by the Assured, *held covered at a premium and on conditions to be arranged subject to prompt notice being given to the Underwriters.*

This clause is a good deal more restricted than its predecessor in the 1/1/63 edition of Institute Cargo Clauses. In that edition it read:

> "held covered at a premium to be arranged in case of change of voyage or of any omission or error in the description of the interest vessel or voyage".

What is a change of voyage? Section 45 of the Marine Insurance Act provides:

> "(1) Where, after the commencement of the risk, the destination of the ship is voluntarily changed from the destination contemplated by the policy, there is said to be a change of voyage.
>
> (2) Unless the policy otherwise provides, where there is a change of voyage, the insurer is discharged from liability as from the time of the change, that is to say, as from the time when the determination to change it is manifested, and it is immaterial that the ship may not in fact have left the course of the voyage contemplated by the policy when the loss occurs."

Since it is the shipowner or carrier who is most likely to order the carrying ship to sail to a different port, an innocent assured will be totally unable to influence the course of the voyage, and if it should be changed he may stand in even greater need of his insurance cover.

As we have seen, Clause 8.3 provides for continuation of the cover during any deviation of the ship (which is not the same thing as a "change of voyage"), and also during any "variation of the adventure" which the shipowners or charterers are permitted to undertake under the contract of affreightment. This Clause 10 appears only to apply when the destination is changed by the assured. It therefore appears to the editor that, by oversight or deliberately, there is now no provision in the Institute Cargo Clauses to hold the assured covered in the event of an illegal change of voyage by a shipowner or other carrier. It is submitted that if these circumstances should occur, an assured should none the less give notice to his underwriters, arguing that it would be equitable for them to hold him covered on the grounds that such a change of voyage by the shipowner or charterer was an event, like a deviation or even a termination of the contract of carriage, entirely beyond his control.

Another restriction in this clause is the absence of the agreement previously granted by underwriters to hold the assured covered if there was any omission or error in the description on the interest (i.e., the subject-matter insured), the name of the vessel or the voyage. In a case under the 1/1/63 clauses, it was held that this concession by the underwriters could only be granted to an innocent assured, and was certainly not available to an assured who had wilfully misdescribed the goods.[27] Now that the concession has been withdrawn in the 1/1/82 clauses, an assured and his broker have to be even more careful to describe accurately the subject-matter to be insured.

27. *Liberian Insurance Agency Inc.* v. *Mosse* [1977] 1 Lloyd's Rep. 560.

CLAIMS

Clause 11—Insurable Interest Clause

11 **11.1** In order to recover under this insurance the Assured must have an insurable interest in the subject-matter insured at the time of the loss.

11.2 Subject to 11.1 above, the Assured shall be entitled to recover for insured loss occurring during the period covered by this insurance, notwithstanding that the loss occurred before the contract of insurance was concluded, unless the Assured were aware of the loss and the Underwriters were not.

This clause closely follows section 6 of the Marine Insurance Act, which states:

> "(1) the assured must be interested in the subject-matter insured at the time of the loss though he need not be interested when the insurance is effected:
>
> Provided that where the subject-matter is insured 'lost or not lost', the Assured may recover although he may not have acquired his interest until after the loss, unless at the time of effecting the contract of insurance the Assured was aware of the loss, and the insurer was not.
>
> (2) Where the Assured has no interest at the time of the loss, he cannot acquire interest by any act or election after he is aware of the loss."

The leading case in English law is *Anderson* v. *Morice*.[28] This case concerned a cargo of rice which the plaintiff had contracted to buy on terms under which the property did not pass to him until the whole cargo had been shipped. When about three-quarters of the rice had been loaded the ship sprang a leak and sank. The House of Lords held that as the property in the rice which was lost had not passed to the plaintiff at the time of the loss, he had no insurable interest. Furthermore, he did not obtain an insurable interest by agreeing after the loss had occurred to pay the seller for the part quantity which had been shipped.

Clause 11.2 reproduces the meaning of the words "lost or not lost" which appeared in Lloyd's S.G. form. The positive statement contained in this clause, which follows closely the wording of the proviso to section 6(1) of the Act, makes the old phraseology unnecessary.

Clause 12—Forwarding Charges Clause

12 Where, as a result of the operation of a risk covered by this insurance, the insured transit is terminated at a port or place other than that to which the subject-matter is covered under this insurance, the Underwriters will reimburse the Assured for any extra charges properly and reasonably incurred in unloading storing and forwarding the subject-matter to the destination to which it is insured hereunder.

This Clause 12, which does not apply to general average or salvage charges, shall be subject to the exclusions contained in Clauses 4, 5, 6 and 7 above, and shall not include charges arising from the fault negligence insolvency or financial default of the Assured or their servants.

This clause recognises, as also does Clause 13, an important principle which has been expounded in a number of English law cases, namely, that what is insured is not merely the physical property in the goods, but also the voyage to which they are committed. In order to consider whether Clause 12 adds

28. (1876) 3 Asp.M.L.C. 290.

anything to the traditional cover, we should examine the circumstances in which underwriters would be liable to pay for forwarding charges on an insurance effected on Lloyd's S.G. form without any additional clauses attached:

1. If by the operation of an insured peril the voyage (what is now called the "insured transit") is terminated short of destination and the cost of recovering the goods, reconditioning them if necessary and forwarding them to destination would exceed their value on arrival, there is a constructive total loss. This proposition follows from the leading case of *Rosetto* v. *Gurney*,[29] and was put into statutory form in section 60(2)(iii) of the Marine Insurance Act 1906. This now appears as part of Clause 13 (Constructive Total Loss Clause).
2. If, owing to the operation of an insured peril, the insured transit is terminated short of destination and it is impossible or impractical to forward the goods to destination, there is likewise a constructive total loss of the goods even though they are in sound condition.

   This follows from the leading case of *Rodocanochi* v. *Elliott*,[30] in which cases of silk in transit from Shanghai to London were caught up in the Siege of Paris during the Franco-Prussian War of 1870. Even though the goods were undamaged and were non-perishable, it was held that the Restraint of Princes (in those days an included peril) was such as to destroy the object of the adventure and therefore the object of the insurance.

   Another example would be goods which remain quite undamaged on board a ship which has stranded in a position from which salvage is impossible, either of the ship or the cargo still in her holds.
3. If by operation of an insured peril the voyage is terminated short of destination and it is possible to forward the goods to destination at an expense less than their value on arrival, there can be no total loss and any claim upon the policy can only be of a partial loss nature. The area of protection afforded in these circumstances under the Suing and Labouring Clause was considered in three leading cases: *Great Indian Peninsular Railway* v. *Saunders*,[31] *Booth* v. *Gair*[32] and *Kidston* v. *Empire Marine Insurance Co.*[33] In all three cases the subject-matter was insured free of particular average and the decisions read together establish that the cost of forwarding cargo to destination will be recoverable under the clause only if incurred in order to avoid a risk of total loss.
4. If however the policy covered particular average in excess of a specified percentage, the cost of forwarding the cargo to destination after the

29. (1851) 11 C.B. 176.
30. (1874) 2 Asp.M.L.C. 399.
31. (1861) 2 B. & S. 266.
32. (1863) 33 L.J.C.P. 99.
33. (1866) L.R. 1 C.P. 535.

abandonment of the voyage on account of insured perils will be recoverable under the Suing and Labouring Clause if the loss averted (measured by the loss on sale at the intermediate port) would have amounted to the specified percentage.

The origin of the Forwarding Charges Clause

In order, therefore, to encourage assureds to take steps to minimise their loss, underwriters came to insert a forwarding clause in F.P.A. policies on goods by which they agreed: "Also to pay Special Charges for landing warehousing and forwarding if incurred at an intermediate port of call or refuge, for which underwriters would be liable under the standard form of English marine policy with the Institute Cargo Clauses (W.A.) attached."

By this wording underwriters granted cover which was additional to their liability under the Suing and Labouring Clauses to respond for Special Charges which averted a total loss. However, such a clause would have no effect and indeed would not be necessary under a policy of insurance which paid particular average irrespective of percentage.

Clause 12 in the (A) Clauses would therefore seem to be largely declaratory, and its chief virtue may be in drawing attention to the fact that in the event of the voyage being abandoned by the carrier, it is the duty of the assured as well as being in his own interest to forward the goods to destination if possible.

Clause 13—Constructive Total Loss Clause

13 No claim for Constructive Total Loss shall be recoverable hereunder unless the subject-matter insured is reasonably abandoned either on account of its actual total loss appearing to be unavoidable or because the cost of recovering, reconditioning and forwarding the subject-matter to the destination to which it is insured would exceed its value on arrival.

The clause closely follows English law as set out in section 60 of the Marine Insurance Act in that it provides that the subject-matter insured must be "reasonably abandoned" by reason of the circumstances specified in order to found a claim for a Constructive Total Loss. The circumstances specified are however more restrictively described than they are in the Act.

"abandoned"

The word "abandoned", as used in the Act, "denotes the voluntary cession by the assured to the insurer of whatever remains of the subject-matter insured, together with all proprietary rights and remedies in respect thereof".[34] It is submitted that it has the same meaning in Clause 12.

Section 62 of the Marine Insurance Act provides that "where the assured elects to abandon the subject-matter insured to the insurer he must give notice of abandonment. If he fails to do so the loss can only be treated as a partial

34. Chalmers' *Marine Insurance Act*, 9th edn., p. 95.

loss." While this requirement technically applies to any claim for a Constructive Total Loss under these clauses (because of Clause 19—the English Law and Practice Clause), it is submitted that there is a class of case, applicable only to policies of insurance on goods, when claims are settled as for a Constructive Total Loss, either without the necessity of notice of abandonment, or when the presentation of the claim constitutes such notice. This is the class of case known as a "salvage loss", when goods are sold or otherwise disposed of at a port or place short of destination, either because they are deteriorating to the extent that they would be worthless on arrival at destination, or because the cost of getting them to destination would exceed their value on arrival. Such claims are in practice settled on the basis of the insured value less the proceeds of sale.

The circumstances giving rise to a claim for Constructive Total Loss

By Clause 13 these circumstances are either:

> "on account of its actual total loss appearing to be unavoidable"

—an example would be the deterioration, by perils insured against, of a perishable commodity such that, by the time it was brought to market, it would either have no value or would cease to be a "thing of the kind insured". When such a commodity ceases to be merchantable as a thing of the kind originally insured, it is said to have lost its *specie*, and in those circumstances it has been held that there is an actual total loss of the goods.[35] Or

> "because the cost of recovering, reconditioning and forwarding the subject-matter to the destination to which it is insured would exceed its value on arrival."

This is a purely objective test which would, strictly speaking, have to be proved by figures showing that the estimated costs involved would be greater than what the goods were worth at their destination.

"*value on arrival*" also involves an estimation of what the goods would sell for in whatever condition they would be in on arrival at destination.

An additional circumstance (not mentioned in Clause 13) which may also found a claim for a Constructive Total Loss, is set out in section 60(2)(i) of the Marine Insurance Act: "where the assured is deprived of the possession of his ship or goods by a peril insured against, and (a) it is unlikely that he can recover the ship or goods . . . , or (b) the cost of recovering the ship or goods would exceed their value when recovered". While it is conceded that there may not be many cases in which these circumstances would apply (except under a War or Strikes Risks cover), the omission is regrettable. After all, conversion or other tortious detention of the goods by a third party is one of the perils which are protected by an insurance against "All Risks".

35. "Loss of specie"; see examples on p. 83.

Clause 14—Increased Value Clause

14 **14.1** If any Increased Value insurance is effected by the Assured on the cargo insured herein the agreed value of the cargo shall be deemed to be increased to the total amount insured under this insurance and all Increased Value insurances covering the loss, and liability under this insurance shall be in such proportion as the sum insured herein bears to such total amount insured.
In the event of claim the Assured shall provide the Underwriters with evidence of the amounts insured under all other insurances.

14.2 **Where this insurance is on Increased Value the following clause shall apply:**
The agreed value of the cargo shall be deemed to be equal to the total amount insured under the primary insurance and all Increased Value insurances covering the loss and effected on the cargo by the Assured, and liability under this insurance shall be in such proportion as the sum insured herein bears to such total amount insured.
In the event of claim the Assured shall provide the Underwriters with evidence of the amounts insured under all other insurances.

This clause did not appear in the 1/1/63 version of the Institute Cargo Clauses. While it appears to make good common sense, the real object of the clause is not to provide any additional advantage to the assured, but to regulate the position *inter se* between original and increased value underwriters, and to negate the unfortunate effect, under English law, of the judgment in the case of *Boag* v. *Standard Marine Insurance Co. Ltd.*[36] In that case the original underwriters had insured only part of the real value of the cargo, the balance being insured with Increased Value underwriters. During the voyage the shipment was jettisoned for the common safety, and the general average adjustment showed the whole amount to be made good in general average, less the contribution attaching to it. This calculation reduced the net credit balance to less than the amount insured by the original underwriters, and the court held that they were entitled to all of it. The intention of the draftsman is to ensure that all claims are divided *pro rata* over original and Increased Value underwriters, and that all recoveries shall be dealt with likewise.

Clause 15—Not to Inure Clause

15 This insurance shall not inure to the benefit of the carrier or other bailee.

This clause has been standard in Marine Cargo Insurance for many years. The object of the clause is to prevent a carrier or other bailee contracting out of his liability by inserting a clause in the contract of affreightment, or other agreement, claiming the benefit of insurance.

MINIMISING LOSSES

Clause 16—Duty of Assured Clause

16 It is the duty of the Assured and their servants and agents in respect of loss recoverable hereunder

16.1 to take such measures as may be reasonable for the purpose of averting or minimising such loss, and

16.2 to ensure that all rights against carriers, bailees or other third parties are properly preserved and exercised

36. (1937) 57 Ll.L.Rep. 83.

and the Underwriters will, in addition to any loss recoverable hereunder, reimburse the Assured for any charges properly and reasonably incurred in pursuance of these duties.

This clause seeks to amalgamate the wording of the "Bailee Clause" in previous editions of Institute Cargo Clauses with the time-honoured provisions of the Suing and Labouring Clause which appeared in Lloyd's S.G. form.

The words of the old Suing and Labouring Clause—once described by an enthusiast as "sheer poetry"—were:

> "And in case of any loss or misfortune it shall be lawful to the Assured, their factors, servants and assigns, to sue, labour, and travel for, in and about the defence, safeguards, and recovery of the said goods and merchandises, and ship, &c., or any part thereof, without prejudice to this insurance; to the charges whereof we, the assurers, will contribute each one according to the rate and quantity of his sum herein assured."

"Sue", incidentally, did not mean "commence legal proceedings"; neither did "travel" mean to go on a journey: it was in fact a transliteration of "travail".

There is authority[37] for the proposition that, when an insurance policy spells out the obligations of the assured to avert or minimise any loss which would otherwise fall upon the underwriters, it is implicit that the underwriters will be bound to reimburse the assured for the expense he has incurred. It will, of course, not be necessary to rely upon any such implied bargain under the Institute Cargo Clauses, since the obligation of the underwriters to reimburse the assured for any such expenses incurred by the assured, their servants or agents, is made quite explicit. Indeed, the draftsman is to be congratulated for restating in modern English the effect of the archaic wording in the Suing and Labouring Clause, and at the same time giving verbal expression to the provisions of section 78(1), (3) and (4) of the Marine Insurance Act. Given that the object was clarity of expression, it was necessary to draft the clause in such a way that its provisions could be read and acted upon without reference to section 78(1) of the Marine Insurance Act which is stated to apply "*where* the policy contains a Suing and Labouring Clause . . . "; for the reason that although this Clause 16 reproduces the effect of the Suing and Labouring Clause, it is *not* the Suing and Labouring Clause.

"the duty of the Assured and their servants and agents"

This expression is wider than appears at first sight. Under English law the master of a ship is invested with wide duties and responsibilities to take care of the goods entrusted to his charge. These duties derive in part under the law

37. *Emperor Goldmining Co. Ltd.* v. *Switzerland General Ins. Co.* [1964] 1 Lloyd's Rep. 348 (Sup.Ct. N.S.W.).

of bailment, since a shipowner who receives the goods for carriage is a bailee for reward and the master of the ship is the person responsible for exercising the duties of care which follow from that legal relationship. In some of the law cases dealing with this subject the master is said when exercising this authority to be acting as an "agent of necessity" for the owners of the property entrusted to his care.

In the event of a serious casualty, a shipowner may be responsible for the payment of substantial sums for the preservation and care of cargo, all of which (in the absence of his actionable fault) he will be entitled to recover as Special Charges on Cargo.[38]

"for the purpose of averting or minimising such loss"

This means a loss (or damage) for which the underwriters would respond under the policy, thus reproducing the effect of section 78(3) of the Marine Insurance Act, which states:

> "expenses incurred for the purpose of averting or diminishing any loss not covered by the policy are not recoverable under the Suing and Labouring Clause".

A case in the 1980s[39] concerned the measures taken by an assured to recover their property (containers) from the premises of their lessees who had gone bankrupt. The insurance was against all risks of loss or damage to the subject-matter insured, but the underwriters argued that the expense incurred by the assured had not been undertaken with the object of averting or minimising losses for which the insurers would have responded. The court held that when the lessees ceased to trade they were no longer capable of taking care as bailees of the plaintiff's property; consequently the plaintiff's containers "were exposed to the risk of theft, misuse, enforcement of a lien—in other words to the risk of loss or damage from some cause or another". The court considered the extent of the measures taken by the assured to recover their containers, and the probability that in the absence of those measures, a loss would have occurred, and found in favour of the assured on both points. The assured were thus entitled to recover the payments which they had made in respect of customs and storage charges in order to secure the release of containers, the cost of their transhipment from where they lay to their own depots, the travelling expenses of those engaged in this operation and legal fees incurred in the same connection.

38. See N. G. Hudson, "Special Charges on Cargo" [1981] L.M.C.L.Q. 315 (part 1) and 471 (part 2).

39. *Integrated Container Service Ltd.* v. *British Traders Insurance Co. Ltd.* [1981] 2 Lloyd's Rep. 460 and [1984] 1 Lloyd's Rep. 154.

"rights against carriers, bailees and other third parties"

On payment of a loss underwriters are by section 79 of the Marine Insurance Act subrogated to all rights and remedies of the assured in respect of the loss so paid for. However, owing to the lapse of time that may occur between the happening of the loss and the claim being paid, it is essential that rights and remedies against third parties should be preserved. Clause 16.2 (previously called the Bailee Clause) places a duty upon the assured to preserve and exercise the rights to which underwriters have, or will become entitled by subrogation. Expenses reasonably incurred by the assured in pursuance of this duty will be met by the underwriters, and this is now spelled out in the clause, even though the underwriters' obligation to reimburse the assured for such expenses is implicit.[40]

However, a breach or failure on the part of the assured under either section of the Duty of Assured Clause does not entitle the insurer to deny liability on that account. A failure of duty on the part of the assured would merely entitle the insurer to a counterclaim for damages.[41] In *Noble Resources* v. *Greenwood*[42] it was held that a mere failure to apply for a *Mareva* injunction against the shipowners in respect of a presumed recovery from hull underwriters did not, without more, establish a breach of Clause 16.2; the insurers would have to show that this was a step which a reasonable assured should in fact have taken: this the insurers were unable to do, and judgment was accordingly given in favour of the assured for their full claim.

Clause 17—Waiver Clause

17 Measures taken by the Assured or the Underwriters with the object of saving, protecting or recovering the subject-matter insured shall not be considered as a waiver or acceptance of abandonment or otherwise prejudice the rights of either party.

This clause has commonly been inserted in marine insurance policies for many years. Its purpose is to preserve the position of both assured and underwriter in the event of measures being taken to recover the property by either party after notice of abandonment has been given. Any steps taken by the assured "in saving, protecting or recovering the subject-matter insured" shall not constitute a waiver or withdrawal of the notice of abandonment which he has given; and similarly, the underwriters are free to take such steps

40. In *The Netherlands Insurance Co. Est. 1845* v. *Karl Ljunberg & Co.* [1986] 2 Lloyd's Rep. 19 the Judicial Committee of the Privy Council held that in the 1/1/63 edition of Institute Cargo Clauses a term must be implied in order to give business efficacy to the contract, that expenses incurred by an assured in performing his obligations under the second limb of the bailee clause shall be recoverable by him from the insurers in so far as they relate to the preservation or exercise of rights in respect of loss or damage for which the insurers are liable under the policy.

41. See *The "Gold Sky"* [1972] 2 Lloyd's Rep. 187; also n. 42, below.

42. *Noble Resources* v. *Greenwood* (*The "Vasso"*) [1993] 2 Lloyd's Rep. 309.

without their being regarded as an acceptance of the abandonment which had been previously declined.

AVOIDANCE OF DELAY

Clause 18—Reasonable Despatch Clause

18 It is a condition of this insurance that the Assured shall act with reasonable despatch in all circumstances within their control.

This clause is also of considerable antiquity and its purpose is self-evident.

LAW AND PRACTICE

Clause 19—English Law and Practice Clause

19 This insurance is subject to English law and practice.

This clause is common to all the new Institute Clauses issued from 1/1/82 onwards, except those intended to be attached to American Forms. As will be appreciated from the commentary on some of the more important clauses in this and other forms, the fact that these forms have to stand by themselves, instead of being attached to Lloyd's S.G. form of policy, means that, in several important particulars, the benefit of the interpretation pronounced in the U.K. Marine Insurance Act 1906 would be lost, if nothing were inserted in the new forms to preserve it. Hence the necessary rewording of many of the clauses to incorporate the more important provisions of the Marine Insurance Act; and hence, likewise, the reference to English law and practice in order to incorporate as much as possible of the body of case law which has been built up over many centuries.

That is the end of the numbered clauses. There then appears:

NOTE:—It is necessary for the Assured when they become aware of an event which is "held covered" under this insurance to give prompt notice to the Underwriters and the right to such cover is dependent upon compliance with this obligation.

This note appears at the foot of all Institute Clauses covering goods. It is not only sound advice: it also states the existing law, since it is an implied term of any contract of marine insurance that the assured will be unable to invoke a "held covered" provision unless within a reasonable time after knowing of the event he has given notice to the underwriter. As Scrutton L.J. said in *Hood* v. *West End Motor Car Parking Co.*[43]: "There is a tendency on the part of the assured to wait in order to see what may turn up, and he often omits to pay the extra premium until a loss has actually occurred. It is to meet that tendency that this implied term is introduced into the contract."

43. (1917) 23 Com.Cas. 112, following *Thames & Mersey Marine Insurance Co.* v. *Van Laun*, a case heard by the House of Lords in 1905, but not reported until *Hood*'s case.

3. INSTITUTE CARGO CLAUSES (B) and (C)—The restricted perils forms (1/1/82)

These are the new forms for restricted conditions which were issued at the same time as Institute Cargo Clauses (A) on 1/1/82. They may be said to replace the previous W.A. and F.P.A. Clauses, but with certain important differences. The W.A. and F.P.A. Clauses insured against the traditional risks enumerated in Lloyd's S.G. form (with some extensions set out in the Average Clause and F.P.A. Clause, respectively), but the quantum of recovery varied.[44] Under the (B) and (C) Clauses the restrictions apply to the list of the perils insured against, but in the event of loss or damage by one of the named perils the underwriters will pay any claim, however small it may be.

RISKS COVERED

The risks covered are set out in Clauses 1, 2 and 3.

Clause 1—Risks Clause

1 This insurance covers, except as provided in Clauses 4, 5, 6 and 7 below.
1.1 loss of or damage to the subject-matter insured reasonably attributable to
1.1.1 fire or explosion

"fire"

The expression "fire" includes damage by heat through proximity to something which is on fire, but it does not include deterioration due to the chemical changes involved in the heating up of some commodity by natural causes nor spontaneous combustion, both of which are excluded by Clause 4.4 as being caused by inherent vice or nature of the subject matter insured. Loss or damage reasonably attributable to fire also comprehends damage caused by the act of extinguishing fire or reasonably taken in order to avoid the spread of fire—see *Symington* v. *Union Insurance Society of Canton*[45] and in acts taken in anticipation of and to prevent the outbreak of fire—see *The "Knight of St. Michael"*.[46]

"explosion"

In the case of *Commonwealth Smelting Ltd.* v. *Guardian Royal Exchange Assurance*[47] the judge concluded that the word "explosion" in a policy of insurance denoted "an event that is violent, noisy and caused by a very rapid chemical

44. See Section 1, Historical Perspective, on p. 11.
45. (1928) 34 Com.Cas. 23.
46. (1888) 8 Asp.M.L.C. 360.
47. [1984] 2 Lloyd's Rep. 608.

or nuclear reaction, or the bursting out of gas or vapour under pressure". In that case it was held that the violent disintegration of a moving part revolving at high speed, causing fragments to fly outwards under considerable force and with a lot of noise, was not an explosion; it was centrifugal disintegration.

1.1.2 vessel or craft being stranded grounded sunk or capsized

These words are slightly wider than the corresponding words in the W.A. and F.P.A. Clauses. The addition of the word "grounded" makes it unnecessary to consider the limitations which were applied in a long series of law cases to the word "stranded" when it appeared alone in the Memorandum. "Stranded or grounded", read together, comprise any fortuitous taking of the ground by the carrying vessel or craft, for however short a period of time. It is also submitted that an intentional taking of the ground, for example in a mud berth where it is customary for ships to lie aground at low tide, will also be covered, if in consequence the insured goods sustain damage, since it is the causation of damage which constitutes the fortuity in what would otherwise have been a normal and uneventful situation.

The addition of the word "capsized" is new. It is submitted that the effect of its inclusion in the list of risks covered will mean that such a loss as took place in the case of *The "Stranna"*,[48] when goods fell into the sea as a result of the carrying ship taking a totally unexplained list whilst in port, will be settled by the underwriters.

1.1.3 overturning or derailment of land conveyance

This is an entirely new risk, which has not featured previously in any standard forms of policy covering restricted conditions. It is therefore to be expected that underwriters and claims practitioners will interpret both these words in their ordinary, everyday sense, without resorting to niceties of interpretation. It is, however, the opinion of the editor that, by use of the words "reasonably attributable to" in the preamble, the extent of loss or damage consequential upon these events should be afforded a reasonably wide construction. For example, if in consequence of derailment, the goods in the railway wagon have to be hurriedly unloaded and dumped by the side of the railway track in order to enable the wagon to be lifted back on to the rails, loss or damage caused by this operation should be responded for by the underwriters as well as the damage caused by the direct shock of the derailment.

1.1.4 collision or contact of vessel craft or conveyance with any external object other than water

The contact must be with something external to the carrying vessel, craft or conveyance. Hence, if goods fall to the quay or the ship's deck whilst slung from the ship's derrick, because the derrick boom hits a gantry on the quay, the consequent loss or damage will be recoverable under this section, but not if the derrick boom hits a part of the ship's superstructure. In that event, a total loss of an individual package will be recoverable as having been dropped

48. [1938] P. 69.

whilst loading or unloading within Clause 1.3 in the (B) Clauses, but if the assured has opted for the (C) Clauses, he will recover nothing.

Under the old Average Clause, the expression used was "any external substance (ice included) other than water", but it is suggested that this does not imply any change in meaning. The authors submit that contact with an iceberg or ice-floe is within the meaning of "any external object".

Collisions and contacts by vehicles on the land are included.

"Conveyance" in this clause (and also in Clause 1.2.3) comprehends any type of vehicle customarily used during the insured transit including, for example, a hovercraft or an amphibious vehicle.

1.1.5 discharge of cargo at a port of distress,

This is a relatively minor area of risk, since in practically every case where cargo is discharged at a port of refuge the cost of discharging the cargo is admissible in general average by virtue of Rule X(b) of the York-Antwerp Rules, and when that is the case any damage or loss of cargo caused in the process of discharging is likewise admitted under Rule XII. However in a small minority of instances the discharge of cargo at a port of refuge may be for a purpose unconnected with general average; for example for the purpose of examining the goods themselves for suspected damage or after the shipowner had validly abandoned the voyage, and in these circumstances it is reasonable that the assured should be similarly covered.

1.1.6 earthquake volcanic eruption or lightning,

These risks appear in the (B) Clauses but not in the (C) Clauses. They are a welcome addition to the cover.

1.2 loss or damage to the subject-matter insured caused by
1.2.1 general average sacrifice

This is merely declaratory. Any insurance subject to English law and practice (see Clause 19) will pay for general average, and in accordance with section 66(4) of the Marine Insurance Act 1906 an underwriter on property is liable to pay the whole of any general average loss without his assured having exercised his right to call for a general average contribution from other parties. Having paid the general average sacrifice in full, underwriters are then entitled under the doctrine of subrogation to require their assured to procure an adjustment of general average in order that he should be paid the contributions due from the other parties to the adventure. Under English law an owner of cargo sacrificed has the right to compel the shipowner to have the general average adjusted—see *Crooks* v. *Allan*.[49] Similar rights exist in most maritime countries, but it may well be that the English law and practice clause will similarly extend underwriters' subrogative rights when the policy is written outside the United Kingdom.

The next clause appears in different forms in the (B) and (C) Clauses.

49. (1880) 4 Asp.M.L.C. 216.

In the (B) form it reads:

> **1.2.2** jettison or washing overboard

In the (C) form it reads:

> **1.2.2** jettison.

Jettison is a peril specifically covered under the old Lloyd's S.G. form of policy. It means the lawful throwing overboard of goods whether in circumstances which make it general average or not. This could extend, for example, to the deliberate dumping overside of packages condemned as hazardous by a local authority, unless (by exclusion 4.1) the assured was guilty of wilful misconduct in shipping them. The deliberate damage exclusion (4.7) would not apply in such a case, since the throwing overboard would be entirely lawful. Washing overboard is a species of loss by sea peril and was covered under the W.A. and F.P.A. Clauses subject to the average warranty.

> **1.2.3** entry of sea lake or river water into vessel craft hold conveyance container liftvan or place of storage,

This appears in the (B) Clauses only. Most of the risk covered here was also covered, subject to average, as sea peril under the old clauses but the risk now clearly extends beyond the ocean transit. Suppose that during the overland leg of the transit a lorry driver loses his way and drives his lorry containing the insured goods into the middle of a river; underwriters will be liable for the damage due to their immersion.

The entry of sea water into the hold of a ship may also cause damage to one commodity, for example hides, which, becoming putrid, cause further damage to adjoining goods affected by taint or contagion. Under the authority of *Montoya* v. *London Assurance*,[50] the assured can recover the damage by taint.

> **1.3** total loss of any package lost overboard or dropped whilst loading on to, or unloading from, vessel or craft.

This appears in the (B) Clauses only. As it was in both the W.A. and F.P.A. Clauses, its exclusion from the (C) Clauses has to be recognised as a positive diminution of the cover.

Clause 2—General Average Clause

> 2 This insurance covers general average and salvage charges, adjusted or determined according to the contract of affreightment and/or the governing law and practice, incurred to avoid or in connection with the avoidance of loss from any cause except those excluded in Clauses 4, 5, 6 and 7 or elsewhere in this insurance.

The reference to the avoidance of loss from any cause except those specifically excluded in the insurance, which is merely declaratory under the (A) Clauses in view of section 66(6) of the Marine Insurance Act 1906, is necessary when the insurance is on restricted conditions, since otherwise general average contribution payable by the insured cargo would only be recoverable if the

50. (1851) 6 Exch. 451.

general average act were undertaken to avoid one of the limited named perils.

Take two packages, both insured with the (C) Clauses, being carried by a small schooner which is blown by a gale out of her course into waters infested with marauding pirates. One of the packages (the heavy one) is thrown overboard to lighten the schooner to enable her to escape from a pirate crew. This is a general average sacrifice. As such, and also as jettison, it is payable by the underwriters under the (C) Clauses. Piracy—the peril avoided—is not, however, covered; yet it is surely reasonable that the underwriters on the package saved should reimburse their assured for the general average contribution he has to pay towards the loss of the package jettisoned. And so they will, because the general average clause provides that the loss avoided shall be from any cause except those specifically excluded, and piracy—although not covered—is not specifically excluded.

Clause 3—"Both to Blame Collision" Clause

3 This insurance is extended to indemnify the Assured against such proportion of liability under the contract of affreightment "Both to Blame Collision" Clause as is in respect of a loss recoverable hereunder. In the event of any claim by shipowners under the said Clause the Assured agree to notify the Underwriters who shall have the right, at their own cost and expense, to defend the Assured against such claim.

The same as in the (A) Clauses—see commentary on page 18.

EXCLUSIONS

The exclusions are contained in Clauses 4, 5, 6 and 7.

Clause 4—General Exclusions Clause

4 In no case shall this insurance cover

4.1 loss damage or expense attributable to wilful misconduct of the Assured

4.2 ordinary leakage, ordinary loss in weight or volume, or ordinary wear and tear of the subject-matter insured

4.3 loss damage or expense caused by insufficiency or unsuitability of packing or preparation of the subject-matter insured (for the purpose of this Clause 4.3 "packing" shall be deemed to include stowage in a container or liftvan but only when such stowage is carried out prior to attachment of this insurance or by the Assured or their servants)

4.4 loss damage or expense caused by inherent vice or nature of the subject-matter insured

4.5 loss damage or expense proximately caused by delay, even though the delay be caused by a risk insured against (except expenses payable under Clause 2 above)

4.6 loss damage or expense arising from insolvency or financial default of the owners managers charterers or operators of the vessel

4.7 deliberate damage to or deliberate destruction of the subject-matter insured or any part thereof by the wrongful act of any person or persons

4.8 loss damage or expense arising from the use of any weapon of war employing atomic or nuclear fission and/or fusion or other like reaction or radioactive force or matter

All these exclusions, other than that contained in Clause 4.7, are the same as in the (A) Clauses—see commentary on pages 19 to 23.

On the other hand Clause 4.7, which does not appear in the (A) Clauses, is of some importance in the (B) and (C) Clauses. It excludes deliberate damage or deliberate destruction of the subject-matter insured by the wrongful act of any person. By this wording certain acts of man are excluded which would, under the traditional wording of Lloyd's S.G. form, have founded a legitimate claim; for example:

(a) barratry of the Master and crew, that is to say wrongful acts in prejudice of their employment and/or in breach of their duties,
(b) arson, or sabotage causing the ship to sink,
(c) scuttling of the carrying ship or craft by its owner in fraud of his insurers, and
(d) a jettison of the goods without reasonable cause.

However, this cover can be reinstated and extended, on payment of an additional premium, by attachment of a separate clause to the policy. This is the Institute Malicious Damage Clause (see page 79). It is, of course, not necessary when the goods are insured with the Institute Cargo Clauses (A).

Clause 5—Unseaworthiness and Unfitness Exclusion Clause

5 5.1 In no case shall this insurance cover loss damage or expense arising from
unseaworthiness of vessel or craft,
unfitness of vessel craft conveyance container or liftvan for the safe carriage of the subject-matter insured,
where the Assured or their servants are privy to such unseaworthiness or unfitness, at the time the subject-matter insured is loaded therein.

5.2 The Underwriters waive any breach of the implied warranties of seaworthiness of the ship and fitness of the ship to carry the subject-matter insured to destination, unless the Assured or their servants are privy to such unseaworthiness or unfitness.

The wording of the clause and its effect is the same as in the Institute Cargo Clauses (A). See commentary on pages 23 to 24.

Clause 6—War Exclusion Clause

6 In no case shall this insurance cover loss damage or expense caused by

6.1 war civil war revolution rebellion insurrection, or civil strife arising therefrom, or any hostile act by or against a belligerent power

6.2 capture seizure arrest restraint or detainment, and the consequences thereof or any attempt thereat

6.3 derelict mines torpedoes bombs or other derelict weapons of war.

The wording is similar to the War Exclusion Clause in the (A) Clauses, with one important exception. This is that, whereas in the (A) Clauses the risk of piracy is excepted from the list of war perils—"capture seizure arrest restraint or detainment"—listed in Clause 6.2, piracy is not so excepted under the (B) and (C) Clauses. The effect is that the merchant is protected against a loss by piracy if insured with the (A) Clauses, but he does not have this protection in the (B) or (C) Clauses. Moreover, since piracy is not included as one of the perils covered by the Institute War Clauses (Cargo)—see page 285—a merchant who opts for the (B) or (C) Clauses for marine perils plus the standard Clauses for War Risks will, perhaps to his astonishment, find himself unprotected against the risk of piracy.

Clause 7—Strikes Exclusion Clause

7 In no case shall this insurance cover loss damage or expense
7.1 caused by strikers, locked-out workmen, or persons taking part in labour disturbances, riots or civil commotions
7.2 resulting from strikes, lock-outs, labour disturbances, riots or civil commotions
7.3 caused by any terrorist or any person acting from a political motive.

This is the same as in the Institute Cargo Clauses (A). See commentary on page 25.

CLAUSES RELATING TO THE DURATION OF THE RISK

Clause 8—Transit Clause

8 8.1 This insurance attaches from the time the goods leave the warehouse or place of storage at the place named herein for the commencement of the transit, continues during the ordinary course of transit and terminates either
8.1.1 on delivery to the Consignees' or other final warehouse or place of storage at the destination named herein,
8.1.2 on delivery to any other warehouse or place of storage, whether prior to or at the destination named herein, which the Assured elect to use either
8.1.2.1 for storage other than in the ordinary course of transit or
8.1.2.2 for allocation or distribution,
or
8.1.3 on the expiry of 60 days after completion of discharge overside of the goods hereby insured from the oversea vessel at the final port of discharge,
whichever shall first occur.
8.2 If, after discharge overside from the oversea vessel at the final port of discharge, but prior to termination of this insurance, the goods are to be forwarded to a destination other than that to which they are insured hereunder, this insurance, whilst remaining subject to termination as provided for above, shall not extend beyond the commencement of transit to such other destination.
8.3 This insurance shall remain in force (subject to termination as provided for above and to the provisions of Clause 9 below) during delay beyond the control of the Assured, any deviation, forced discharge, reshipment or transhipment and during any variation of the adventure arising from the exercise of a liberty granted to shipowners or charterers under the contract of affreightment.

Clause 9—Termination of Contract of Carriage Clause

9 If owing to circumstances beyond the control of the Assured either the contract of carriage is terminated at a port or place other than the destination named therein or the transit is otherwise terminated before delivery of the goods as provided for in Clause 8 above, then this insurance shall also terminate *unless prompt notice is given to the Underwriters and continuation of cover is requested when the insurance shall remain in force, subject to an additional premium if required by the Underwriters*, either
9.1 until the goods are sold and delivered at such port or place, or, unless otherwise specially agreed, until the expiry of 60 days after arrival of the goods hereby insured at such port or place, whichever shall first occur,
or
9.2 if the goods are forwarded within the said period of 60 days (or any agreed extension thereof) to the destination named herein or to any other destination, until terminated in accordance with the provisions of Clause 8 above.

Clause 10—Change of Voyage Clause

10 Where, after attachment of this insurance, the destination is changed by the Assured, *held covered at a premium and on conditions to be arranged subject to prompt notice being given to the Underwriters.*

These Clauses 8, 9 and 10 are all the same as in the Institute Cargo Clauses (A). See commentary on pages 25 to 29.

CLAIMS

Clause 11—Insurable Interest Clause

11 **11.1** In order to recover under this insurance the Assured must have an insurable interest in the subject-matter insured at the time of the loss.

11.2 Subject to 11.1 above, the Assured shall be entitled to recover for insured loss occurring during the period covered by this insurance, notwithstanding that the loss occurred before the contract of insurance was concluded, unless the Assured were aware of the loss and the Underwriters were not.

This is the same as in the Institute Cargo Clauses (A). See commentary on page 30.

Clause 12—Forwarding Charges Clause

12 Where, as a result of the operation of a risk covered by this insurance, the insured transit is terminated at a port or place other than that to which the subject-matter is covered under this insurance, the Underwriters will reimburse the Assured for any extra charges properly and reasonably incurred in unloading storing and forwarding the subject-matter to the destination to which it is insured hereunder.

This Clause 12, which does not apply to general average or salvage charges, shall be subject to the exclusions contained in Clauses 4, 5, 6 and 7 above, and shall not include charges arising from the fault negligence insolvency or financial default of the Assured or their servants.

Whilst the wording of this clause is precisely the same as in the Institute Cargo Clauses (A), the effect of it is much more limited, by reason of the words "as a result of the operation of a risk covered by this insurance". As the Institute Cargo Clauses (A) cover All Risks, all the events which are likely to bring to an end the insured transit at an intermediate port or place are covered, except for some event arising from insolvency or financial default of the owners, managers, charterers or operators of the vessel (exclusion 4.6) or unseaworthiness of the vessel, to which the assured or their servants are privy at the time of loading the cargo (exclusion 5.1).

Under the Institute Cargo Clauses (B) and (C), however, the risks covered are limited to the named perils which we have considered under Clause 1. Under the laws of virtually all maritime countries relating to the carriage of goods by sea (and certainly under English law), the carrier is entitled to abandon the voyage without liability attaching to him if in consequence of excepted perils under the contract of carriage the ship has sustained such damage that the cost of making her fit to continue the voyage would exceed the value of the ship when repaired. While this would clearly constitute a risk insured under an "All Risks" policy, it would not, strictly speaking, be a risk covered under the Institute Cargo Clauses (B) or (C) except under Clauses 1.1.2 and 1.1.4 which in terms presuppose some damage sustained to the carrying vessel.

This construction, if correct, would render this Clause 12 under the (B) and (C) Clauses much narrower than the corresponding obligation to pay special charges for landing, warehousing and forwarding which were contained in the old W.A. and F.P.A. Clauses. Representatives of London market underwriters have, however, gone on record as saying that the intention of this Clause 12 is to provide coverage for forwarding charges which would correspond in practice with the cover previously granted. Such an interpretation would involve an implication (not expressly stated in the clauses) that the risks insured against included a loss of voyage by the carrying vessel arising from traditional sea perils.

In view of the uncertainty which exists as to the correct interpretation of this Clause 12, it is suggested that if there is a termination of the contract of carriage or of the insured transit at an intermediate port or place, the assured under Institute Cargo Clauses (B) or (C) should, at the same time as giving prompt notice to his underwriters requesting a continuation of the cover under Clause 9, also request that the underwriters will grant him a liberal interpretation of Clause 12 to cover any forwarding charges that he may reasonably incur.

Clause 13—Constructive Total Loss Clause

13 No claim for Constructive Total Loss shall be recoverable hereunder unless the subject-matter insured is reasonably abandoned either on account of its actual total loss appearing to be unavoidable or because the cost of recovering, reconditioning and forwarding the subject-matter to the destination to which it is insured would exceed its value on arrival.

While the wording of this clause is the same as in Institute Cargo Clauses (A), it will be appreciated that its effect is limited to those instances where the abandonment of the goods is reasonably made on account of one of the risks covered under Clause 1.

Clause 14—Increased Value Clause

14 14.1 If any Increased Value insurance is effected by the Assured on the cargo insured herein the agreed value of the cargo shall be deemed to be increased to the total amount insured under this insurance and all Increased Value insurances covering the loss, and liability under this insurance shall be in such proportion as the sum insured herein bears to such total amount insured.
In the event of claim the Assured shall provide the Underwriters with evidence of the amounts insured under all other insurances.

14.2 **Where this insurance is on Increased Value the following clause shall apply:**
The agreed value of the cargo shall be deemed to be equal to the total amount insured under the primary insurance and all Increased Value insurances covering the loss and effected on the cargo by the Assured, and liability under this insurance shall be in such proportion as the sum insured herein bears to such total amount insured.
In the event of claim the Assured shall provide the Underwriters with evidence of the amounts insured under all other insurances.

This is the same as in Institute Cargo Clauses (A). See commentary on page 34.

Clause 15—Not to Inure Clause

15 This insurance shall not inure to the benefit of the carrier or other bailee.

The wording and effect are the same as in Institute Cargo Clauses (A). See commentary on page 34.

Clause 16—Duty of Assured Clause

16 It is the duty of the Assured and their servants and agents in respect of loss recoverable hereunder

16.1 to take such measures as may be reasonable for the purpose of averting or minimising such loss, and

16.2 to ensure that all rights against carriers, bailees or other third parties are properly preserved and exercised

and the Underwriters will, in addition to any loss recoverable hereunder, reimburse the Assured for any charges properly and reasonably incurred in pursuance of these duties.

This clause is in the same terms as in Institute Cargo Clauses (A). However, because Clauses (B) and (C) are against the risks of named perils, it has to be borne in mind that "loss recoverable hereunder" is limited to any claim for loss or damage caused by those named perils.

As an example, if a package containing goods belonging to the assured falls overboard whilst being discharged from the carrying steamer at the port of destination, it will be the duty of the assured to try and recover it, and underwriters under the (B) Clauses will reimburse the assured for the cost of its recovery and safe landing, even if the contents are landed completely undamaged. No doubt a prudent assured under the (C) Clauses will also attempt to recover the package in the same circumstances, but in so doing he will be acting entirely for his own account as a "prudent uninsured owner" since the (C) Clauses afford no cover for loss in discharging, except at a port of distress.

Clause 17—Waiver Clause

17 Measures taken by the Assured or the Underwriters with the object of saving, protecting or recovering the subject-matter insured shall not be considered as a waiver or acceptance of abandonment or otherwise prejudice the rights of either party.

This clause and its effect are the same as under Institute Cargo Clauses (A). See commentary on page 37.

Clause 18—Reasonable Despatch Clause

18 It is a condition of this insurance that the Assured shall act with reasonable despatch in all circumstances within their control.

This is the same as in the (A) Clauses.

Clause 19—English Law and Practice Clause

19 This insurance is subject to English law and practice.

See the observations under the (A) Clauses on page 38.

NOTE:—It is necessary for the Assured when they become aware of an event which is "held covered" under this insurance to give prompt notice to the Underwriters and the right to such cover is dependent upon compliance with this obligation.

This is the standard form of note which appears at the foot of all Institute Clauses covering goods. The observations on page 38 also apply here.

COMPARISON IN THE COVER AFFORDED BY THE INSTITUTE CARGO CLAUSES (B) AND (C), 1/1/82 AND THE COVER PREVIOUSLY AVAILABLE UNDER THE INSTITUTE CARGO CLAUSES (W.A.) AND (F.P.A.), 1/1/63

The main change under the 1/1/82 clauses is that the risks insured have been limited to a number of named perils, and in return for that curtailment of the cover, the assured is entitled to claim for each and every loss which occurs during the insured transit as a result of those perils, however small such claims may be.

The perils no longer covered under the restricted conditions of Clauses (B) and (C) are:

1. Certain effects of "perils of the seas", viz.:
   (a) Damage resulting from the breaking of stowage due to heavy weather.
   (b) Damage consequential upon measures taken to avoid the effects of heavy weather, for example sweat damage through forced closure of ventilation—as in *Canada Rice Mills* v. *Union Marine*.[51]
   (c) Commixture and contagion damage, unless resulting from the entry of water into the hold or compartment in which the adjacent goods are stowed. (See Clause 1.2.3.)
2. Certain acts of man:
   (a) Theft, albeit only theft accompanied by violence, as previously covered in Lloyd's S.G. form.
   (b) "Takings at sea"—an expression of some antiquity whose limited meaning has now been established by the House of Lords in the case of *The "Salem"*.[52]
   (c) Barratry of the master and crew, that is to say wrongful acts in prejudice of their employment and/or breach of their duties.

COMPARISON IN THE COVER AFFORDED BY THE INSTITUTE CARGO CLAUSES (B) AND THE INSTITUTE CARGO CLAUSES (C)

The only difference consists in the list of the risks insured in Clause 1.

The following are the risks covered by the (B) Clauses which do *not* appear in the (C) Clauses:

1.1.6 earthquake, volcanic eruption or lightning,
1.2.2 (part), washing overboard,

51. [1941] A.C. 55.
52. *Shell International Petroleum* v. *Gibbs* [1983] 1 Lloyd's Rep. 342.

1.2.3 entry of sea, lake or river water into vessel, craft, hold, conveyance, container, liftvan or place of storage,

1.3 total loss of any package lost overboard or dropped whilst loading on to, or unloading from, vessel or craft.

4. INSTITUTE CLAUSES FOR PARTICULAR COMMODITIES

In certain instances, where noted, these clauses have been agreed with the trade associations concerned. In the commentary which follows, only those clauses are mentioned which differ from the standard Institute Cargo Clauses.

A. INSTITUTE FROZEN FOOD CLAUSES (A) (Excluding Frozen Meat) (1/8/82, re-issued 1/1/86)

Clause 1—Risks Clause

1 This insurance covers, except as provided in Clauses 4, 5, 6 and 7 below,

1.1 all risks of loss of or damage to the subject-matter insured, other than loss or damage resulting from any variation in temperature howsoever caused.

1.2 loss of or damage to the subject-matter insured resulting from any variation in temperature attributable to

1.2.1 breakdown of refrigerating machinery resulting in its stoppage for a period of not less than 24 consecutive hours

1.2.2 fire or explosion

1.2.3 vessel or craft being stranded grounded sunk or capsized

1.2.4 overturning or derailment of land conveyance

1.2.5 collision or contact of vessel craft or conveyance with any external object other than water

1.2.6 discharge of cargo at a port of distress.

It is to be noted that the Risks Clause is not quite as wide as "All Risks", since claims for loss or damage resulting from variation in temperature are limited to those attributable to the causes set out in Clauses 1.2.1 to 1.2.6.

Of the perils causing variation in temperature, the most important is:

> "1.2.1 breakdown of refrigerating machinery resulting in its stoppage for a period of not less than 24 consecutive hours."

It has been held that the expression "breakdown of machinery", by itself, does not necessarily involve the machinery coming to a full stop.[53] Hence the addition of the words "resulting in its stoppage" which has the effect of excluding claims arising from variation in temperature due to the mere malfunction of the refrigerating machinery. It is also to be noted that in order to found a claim under this clause the assured must be able to show, presumably by evidence obtained from the carrier, that the stoppage of the refrigerating machinery extended for a continuous period of not less than 24 hours.

The other listed perils from which "variation in temperature" claims may arise are the same as set out in Institute Cargo Clauses (C), Clause 1.1. These

53. *Giertsen* v. *Turnbull*, 1908 S.C. 1011.

are the same as in previous Frozen Food Clauses, but with the addition of the overturning or derailment of any land conveyance.

Clause 2—General Average Clause

Clause 3—"Both to Blame Collision" Clause

These clauses are the same as in the Institute Cargo Clauses.

Clause 4—General Exclusions Clause

4 In no case shall this insurance cover

4.1 loss damage or expense attributable to wilful misconduct of the Assured

4.2 ordinary leakage, ordinary loss in weight or volume, or ordinary wear and tear of the subject-matter insured

4.3 loss damage or expense caused by insufficiency or unsuitability of packing or preparation of the subject-matter insured (for the purpose of this Clause 4.3 "packing" shall be deemed to include stowage in a container or liftvan but only when such stowage is carried out prior to attachment of this insurance or by the Assured or their servants)

4.4 loss damage or expense caused by inherent vice or nature of the subject-matter insured (except loss damage or expense resulting from variation in temperature specifically covered under Clause 1.2 above)

4.5 loss damage or expense proximately caused by delay, even though the delay be caused by a risk insured against (except expenses payable under Clause 2 above)

4.6 loss damage or expense arising from insolvency or financial default of the owners managers charterers or operators of the vessel

4.7 loss damage or expense arising from the use of any weapon of war employing atomic or nuclear fission and/or fusion or other like reaction or radioactive force or matter

4.8 loss damage or expense arising from any failure of the Assured or their servants to take all reasonable precautions to ensure that the subject-matter insured is kept in refrigerated or, where appropriate, properly insulated and cooled space

4.9 any loss damage or expense otherwise recoverable hereunder unless prompt notice thereof is given to the Underwriters and, in any event, not later than 30 days after the termination of this insurance.

Exclusions 4.1, 4.2, 4.3, 4.4, 4.5, 4.6 and 4.7 correspond with (and carry the same numbering as) the exclusions contained in the Institute Cargo Clauses (A).

Exclusion 4.4—the Inherent Vice exclusion—differs from the usual form, the words in parenthesis being added to make it clear that underwriters will not raise this defence against any claim resulting from variation in temperature which has come about through one of the specific causes mentioned in Clause 1.2.

There follow two exclusions which are particular to the Frozen Food Clauses. They are:

Exclusion 4.8 which exempts the underwriters from liability for any claim arising from the failure of the assured, or the assured's servants, to take reasonable precautions to ensure that the goods are kept in properly refrigerated or cool and insulated spaces.

Exclusion 4.9 which is unusual. It provides in effect that no claim under the policy will be recoverable if prompt notice of it has not been given to the underwriters within 30 days after the termination of the insurance. Although a claims "cut-off" clause, such as this, is sometimes thought to be a harsh provision, it reinforces the good sense of the proposition which every dealer in frozen food would recognise, that it is prudent for the receiver to ascertain as soon as possible after arrival of the goods into his cold store that they are in proper condition.

Clause 5—Unseaworthiness and Unfitness Exclusion Clause

Clause 6—War Exclusion Clause

Clause 7—Strikes Exclusion Clause

These clauses are the same as the corresponding clauses, so numbered in the Institute Cargo Clauses—see pages 23 to 25 for commentary.

Clause 8—Transit Clause

8 8.1 This insurance attaches from the time the goods are loaded into the conveyance at freezing works or cold store at the place named herein for the commencement of the transit, continues during the ordinary course of transit and terminates either

8.1.1 on delivery to the cold store or place of storage at the destination named herein,

8.1.2 on delivery to any other cold store or place of storage, whether prior to or at the destination named herein, which the Assured elect to use either

8.1.2.1 for storage other than in the ordinary course of transit or

8.1.2.2 for allocation or distribution,

or

8.1.3 on the expiry of 5 days after discharge overside of the goods hereby insured from the oversea vessel at the final port of discharge,

whichever shall first occur.

8.2 If, after discharge overside from the oversea vessel at the final port of discharge, but prior to termination of this insurance, the goods are to be forwarded to a destination other than that to which they are insured hereunder, this insurance, whilst remaining subject to termination as provided for above, shall not extend beyond the commencement of transit to such other destination.

8.3 This insurance shall remain in force (subject to termination as provided for above and to the provisions of Clause 9 below) during delay beyond the control of the Assured, any deviation, forced discharge, reshipment or transhipment and during any variation of the adventure arising from the exercise of a liberty granted to shipowners or charterers under the contract of affreightment.

This clause differs in a number of respects from the corresponding clause in Institute Cargo Clauses, viz.:

(a) The insured transit commences at the time the goods are loaded into the conveyance, whatever it may be, for the first leg of the journey. This is one stage earlier than is provided in the Institute Cargo Clauses, under which the insurance does not attach until the time the goods leave the warehouse or place of storage. Thus a loss caused by insured perils which occurs after the goods have been loaded into a lorry while it remains on the premises where the goods were loaded and before it begins its journey, will be covered under the Institute Frozen Food Clauses, whereas it would not be covered under Institute Cargo Clauses.

(b) The words "warehouse or place of storage" are replaced in the Institute Frozen Food Clauses by "freezing works or cold store" to describe the location where the goods are loaded, and by "cold store or place of storage" at destination.

(c) The transit "cut-off" is a mere five days after discharge of the goods from the ocean steamer, instead of the period of 60 days which is provided in Institute Cargo Clauses.

Clause 9—Termination of Contract of Carriage Clause

9 If owing to circumstances beyond the control of the Assured either the contract of carriage is terminated at a port or place other than the destination named therein or the transit is otherwise terminated before delivery of the goods as provided for in Clause 8 above, then this insurance shall also terminate *unless prompt notice is given to the Underwriters and continuation of cover is requested when the insurance shall remain in force, subject to an additional premium if required by the Underwriters*, either

9.1 until the goods are sold and delivered at such port or place, or, unless otherwise specially agreed, until the expiry of 30 days after arrival of the goods hereby insured at such port or place, whichever shall first occur,

or

9.2 if the goods are forwarded within the said period of 30 days (or any agreed extension thereof) to the destination named herein or to any other destination, until terminated in accordance with the provisions of Clause 8 above.

This clause is in the same form as the corresponding clause, so numbered, in Institute Cargo Clauses, except that in the event of the termination of the contract of carriage in the circumstances set out in the clause, and subject to prompt notice being given to the underwriters requesting a continuation of cover, the period of time for which such extension may be granted (without any further extension being asked for) is *30 days*, instead of 60 days as provided in the Institute Cargo Clauses.

Clauses 10 to 19

Clauses 10 to 19 are the same as in Institute Cargo Clauses (A). So is the usual note which appears at the foot of the 1/8/82 form. See pages 28 to 38 for commentary.

An additional Special Note was added when the Institute Frozen Food Clauses were reissued on 1/1/86. It reads:

SPECIAL NOTE:—This insurance does not cover loss damage or expense caused by embargo, or by rejection prohibition or detention by the government of the country of import or their agencies or departments, but does not exclude loss of or damage to the subject-matter insured caused by risks insured hereunder and sustained prior to any such embargo rejection prohibition or detention.

The purpose of this note is to make it clear that, if the goods have sustained no loss or damage by insured perils, the fact that they may be rejected from importation by government regulation (for example, by not attaining some standard prescribed by a sanitary authority) or made subject to an embargo, will not give the assured a right to claim under the policy. In a word, there is no "Rejection" cover under this form.

B. INSTITUTE FROZEN FOODS CLAUSES (C) (Excluding Frozen Meat) (1/8/82, re-issued 1/1/86)

As the title implies, these are the restricted conditions clauses available for the frozen food trade.

Clause 1—The Risks Clause

This clause is in the same terms as the corresponding clause in Institute Cargo Clauses (C). See pages 39 to 42 for text and commentary.

Clause 4—General Exclusions Clause

This incorporates Clauses 4.1 to 4.8, the exclusions contained in Institute Cargo Clauses (C), together with the special exclusions 4.9 and 4.10 applying to the trade, which have been commented upon in connection with the Institute Frozen Food Clauses (A).

The following may be observed:

"4.4 loss damage or expense caused by inherent vice or nature of the subject-matter insured"

This exclusion is not limited by the exception of claims resulting from variation in temperature (as is the corresponding exclusion in the Institute Frozen Food Clauses (A)), since there is no specific reference to coverage in the Risks Clause for losses so caused. In the editor's opinion, this does not necessarily mean that every claim based upon deterioration of the frozen goods by reason of loss of refrigeration will be caught by the "nature of the subject matter insured" exclusion. The question whether the assured will be able to recover for such deterioration will depend upon the application of the doctrine of proximate cause to the circumstances of the loss. For example, if in consequence of a collision the refrigeration machinery is rendered totally inoperable, and the ship being disabled is unable to attain a port of refuge where the frozen goods could be discharged into a cold store until such time as the goods have deteriorated, it is submitted that there is an unbroken chain of causation between the collision and the consequential deterioration of the refrigerated goods.

"4.7 deliberate damage to or deliberate destruction of the subject-matter insured or any part thereof by the wrongful act of any person or persons"

This exclusion does not appear in the (A) form of the Institute Frozen Food Clauses. It does however appear in the Institute Cargo Clauses (C). See commentary on page 43.

Clause 8—Transit Clause

Clause 9—Termination of Contract of Carriage Clause

These clauses are in the same terms as the (A) form of the Institute Frozen Food Clauses. See above.

Clauses 2, 3, 5–7, 10–19, Note and Special Note

Clauses 2, 3, 5–7 inclusive, 10–19 inclusive and the Note at the foot of the form are the same as the Institute Cargo Clauses (C).

In the 1/1/86 form the Special Note printed at the foot of the form is the same as in the (A) form.

C. INSTITUTE COAL CLAUSES (1/10/82)

These clauses form a welcome addition to the Institute's portfolio. They replace an old (undated) non-Institute form entitled "Clauses on Coal Shipments", which contained some curious provisions and had become outdated.

Clause 1—Risks Clause

1 This insurance covers, except as provided in Clauses 4, 5, 6 and 7 below,
1.1 loss of or damage to the subject-matter insured reasonably attributable to
1.1.1 fire explosion or heating, even when caused by spontaneous combustion, inherent vice or nature of the subject-matter insured
1.1.2 vessel being stranded grounded sunk or capsized
1.1.3 collision or contact of vessel with any external object other than water
1.1.4 discharge of cargo at a port of distress
1.1.5 earthquake volcanic eruption or lightning,
1.2 loss of or damage to the subject-matter insured caused by
1.2.1 general average sacrifice
1.2.2 jettison or washing overboard
1.2.3 entry of sea lake or river water into vessel hold container or place of storage.

The risks covered are those contained in Institute Cargo Clauses (B) with the following notable differences:

> "1.1.1 Fire explosion or heating, even when caused by spontaneous combustion, inherent vice or nature of the subject-matter insured."

This express provision displaces the time-honoured rule of construction laid down in section 55(2)(*c*) of the Marine Insurance Act 1906 that the insurer is not liable for inherent vice or nature of the subject-matter insured. It is in line with, and the wording is an improvement upon, a similar provision in the Clauses on Coal Shipments.

This is an important extension of underwriters' liability, and its inclusion carries with it a number of substantial benefits to both assured and underwriters:

(i) It renders unnecessary, for the purpose of establishing whether there is claim upon the policy, any investigation into the cause of the heating or combustion. As was stated in *Soya G.m.b.H.* v. *White*,[54] a

54. *Per* Lloyd J. in the Commercial Court, [1980] 1 Lloyd's Rep. 491. The decision in this case was upheld in the Court of Appeal, [1982] 1 Lloyd's Rep. 136, and the House of Lords, [1983] 1 Lloyd's Rep. 122.

policy against the risk of heating is like an insurance against fire, in that evidence of heating is sufficient proof of the causality.

(ii) It precludes what would otherwise be an extremely difficult question of fact to be determined, namely, where in each case to draw the dividing line between the extent of deterioration caused by heat alone and the loss/deterioration caused by a subsequent fire.

(iii) It encourages the assured to take timely and active steps to prevent the heating of a cargo from getting out of hand. The case of *The "Knight of St. Michael"*[55] illustrates the necessity of prompt action to avert the outbreak of fire in a coal cargo which has become heated. Although the coal was never in a state of combustion, the vessel had properly put into a port of refuge, where part of the coal was discharged and sold, the remainder being carried on and delivered at destination. The claim was brought by the shipowners under their policy of insurance on freight for the loss which they sustained in respect of the part cargo sold at the port of refuge, and Barnes J. held that the underwriters were liable. He said: "I have found that fire did not actually break out, but it is reasonably certain that it would have broken out, and the condition of things was such that there was an existing state of peril by fire, and not merely a fear of fire. . . . The danger was present, and, if nothing were done, spontaneous combustion and fire would follow in natural course."

Because of the limited duration of the risk (see Clause 8 below), there is no need to bring into the Risks Clause the perils which may occur only when the cargo is on board craft or land conveyances. Hence the omission of the perils of overturning and derailment of land conveyance and stranding, etc., of craft, and the limitation of the perils of the entry of sea, lake or river water into the vessel, hold, container or place of storage. Furthermore, as we shall see, "place of storage" in the context of this insurance can mean only such storage as is arranged after a forced discharge of the cargo.

Clause 2—General Average Clause

Clause 3—"Both to Blame Collision" Clause

These clauses are the same as in Institute Cargo Clauses.

Clause 4—General Exclusions Clause

4 In no case shall this insurance cover

4.1 loss damage or expense attributable to wilful misconduct of the Assured

4.2 ordinary leakage, ordinary loss in weight or volume, or ordinary wear and tear of the subject-matter insured

55. (1888) 8 Asp.M.L.C. 360; 3 Com.Cas. 62.

4.3 loss damage or expense proximately caused by delay, even though the delay be caused by a risk insured against (except expenses payable under Clause 2 above)

4.4 loss damage or expense arising from insolvency or financial default of the owners managers charterers or operators of the vessel

4.5 deliberate damage to or deliberate destruction of the subject-matter insured or any part thereof by the wrongful act of any person or persons

4.6 loss damage or expense arising from the use of any weapon of war employing atomic or nuclear fission and/or fusion or other like reaction or radioactive force or matter.

The list of exclusions is shorter than that contained in Institute Cargo Clauses. There is no need to refer to "insufficiency of packing" since this is not relevant to a cargo of coal in bulk. The usual exclusion of inherent vice and nature of the subject-matter insured are also omitted, since these risks are included by Clause 1.1.1.

Clause 5—Unseaworthiness and Unfitness Exclusion Clause

This is in the same terms as in the Institute Cargo Clauses, although the references to craft, conveyance or container are unnecessary.

Clauses 6 and 7

Clauses 6 and 7 contain the War and Strikes Exclusions in the same terms as in the Institute Cargo Clauses.

Clause 8—Transit Clause

8 8.1 This insurance attaches as the subject-matter insured is loaded on board the oversea vessel at the port or place named herein for the commencement of the transit, continues during the ordinary course of transit and terminates as the subject-matter insured is discharged overside from the oversea vessel at the destination named herein.

8.2 This insurance shall remain in force (subject to termination as provided for above and to the provisions of Clause 9 below) during delay beyond the control of the Assured, any deviation, forced discharge, reshipment or transhipment and during any variation of the adventure arising from the exercise of a liberty granted to shipowners or charterers under the contract of affreightment.

It is to be noted that the duration of the risk is limited and, except when the cargo is forced discharged at a port of refuge, it extends only to the period of time that the cargo is on board the "oversea vessel". The risk attaches "as the subject-matter insured is loaded on board". The use of these words signifies that, if only part of the cargo has been loaded at the time of a loss, the risk will attach in respect of the cargo which is on board the oversea vessel, but not in respect of the part cargo which remains on the shore. Likewise, the risk terminates "as the subject-matter insured is discharged overside" at destination, and similar considerations apply.

If the cargo is forced discharged during the ocean transit, the "shore risks" will be covered by the insurance, subject to Clause 9 below.

Clause 9—Termination of Contract of Affreightment Clause

This is in similar terms to Clause 9 of Institute Cargo Clauses except that, in the event of prompt notice being given to the underwriters for a continuation of the cover after termination of the contract of affreightment, the period of time for which underwriters will agree to continue the cover (subject to any agreed extension) is limited to 15 days, compared with 60 days under Institute Cargo Clauses.

Clauses 10 to 19 and Note

Clauses 10 to 19 inclusive and the Note at the foot of the form are the same as in Institute Cargo Clauses.

D. INSTITUTE BULK OIL CLAUSES (1/2/83)

This is another new addition to the Institute portfolio of clauses. Previously, the only clauses available for oil cargoes was a form of Bulk Oil Clauses (SP—13C of January 1962) which had its origin in the United States. Although in terms of cover provided, it might be argued that the Institute Bulk Oil Clauses are less wide than the SP—13C Form, in terms of draftsmanship and clarity of expression they are infinitely superior.

Clause 1—Risks Clause

1 This insurance covers, except as provided in Clauses 4, 5, 6 and 7 below,
1.1 loss of or contamination of the subject-matter insured reasonably attributable to
1.1.1 fire or explosion
1.1.2 vessel or craft being stranded grounded sunk or capsized
1.1.3 collision or contact of vessel or craft with any external object other than water
1.1.4 discharge of cargo at a port or place of distress
1.1.5 earthquake volcanic eruption or lightning,
1.2 loss of or contamination of the subject-matter insured caused by
1.2.1 general average sacrifice
1.2.2 jettison
1.2.3 leakage from connecting pipelines in loading transhipment or discharge
1.2.4 negligence of Master Officers or Crew in pumping cargo ballast or fuel,
1.3 contamination of the subject-matter insured resulting from stress of weather.

This list of perils insured is generally in line with the provisions of Institute Cargo Clauses (B). However, the following variations may be noted:

(a) Where the Institute Cargo Clauses refer to damage, the Bulk Oil Clauses substitute "contamination".

(b) As will be seen from the clauses which define the duration of the risk, overland transit (other than by pipeline) is not provided for, and consequently there is no reference to "conveyance", other than by vessel or craft.

(c) Two additional perils are specifically included:

"*1.2.3 leakage from connecting pipelines in loading transhipment or discharge*".

The words used express two limitations upon the risk of "leakage": (i) the leakage must occur in the course of loading transhipment or discharge of the cargo, (ii) the leakage must be from "connecting pipelines". There is some ambiguity in this expression, but the authors submit that it must mean leakage from any of the pipelines which connect the shore tanks at the place of loading or discharging with the ship, thus excluding any leakage from an associated pipeline (not connected with the ship) which is simultaneously put "on flow" by the pumping operation.

"*1.2.4 negligence of Master Officers or Crew in pumping cargo ballast or fuel*".

It is to be noted that, in order to found a claim under this sub-clause, the loss or contamination has to be caused by the negligence of those concerned "in pumping". This expression imports a limitation similar to that conveyed by the words "accidents in loading discharging or shifting cargo or fuel" in Clause 6.1.8 of the Institute Time Clauses, Hulls—see page 108.

There is, of course, some overlap in the way in which these two perils are expressed, in that a leakage from a pipeline caused by the negligence of the crew in operating the ship's pump in the course of loading, shipment or discharge will be covered by both sub-clauses, but the leakages covered by Clause 1.2.3 will include those occurring through any cause in these operations, whereas Clause 1.2.4 covers not only loss, but also contamination caused by the ship's crew in any pumping, including transfers from tank to tank on board the ship.

(d) In place of "entry of sea water etc." in the Institute Cargo Clauses, the Bulk Oil Clauses covers "contamination . . . from stress of weather". This can include, e.g., claims for depreciation in value of an oil cargo of a specific quality which becomes contaminated with the residues which normally lie inert at the bottom of the ship's tanks, through abnormal movement of the ship in severe weather.

Clause 2—General Average Clause

Clause 3—"Both to Blame Collision" Clause

These are in the same terms as the clauses so numbered in the Institute Cargo Clauses.

Clause 4—General Exclusions Clause

4 In no case shall this insurance cover

4.1 loss damage or expense attributable to wilful misconduct of the Assured

4.2 ordinary leakage, ordinary loss in weight or volume, or ordinary wear and tear of the subject-matter insured

4.3 loss damage or expense caused by inherent vice or nature of the subject-matter insured

4.4 loss damage or expense proximately caused by delay, even though the delay be caused by a risk insured against (except expenses payable under Clause 2 above)

4.5 loss damage or expense arising from insolvency or financial default of the owners managers charterers or operators of the vessel

4.6 loss damage or expense arising from the use of any weapon of war employing atomic or nuclear fission and/or fusion or other like reaction or radioactive force or matter.

These exclusions correspond to those which are set out in Clauses 4.1, 4.2, 4.4, 4.5, 4.6 and 4.8 of the Institute Cargo Clauses (B). However, it may be noted:

(a) there is no exclusion in respect of insufficiency of packing, since this would clearly be irrelevant; and

(b) whereas Clause 4.7 of the Institute Cargo Clauses (B)—and, for that matter, all the other Institute Clauses providing for restricted cover —stipulate for the exclusion of "deliberate damage to or deliberate destruction of the subject-matter insured . . . by the wrongful act of any person or persons", this does not appear in the Bulk Oil Clauses. One is tempted to see in this omission a gesture of repentance on the part of underwriters, in favour of that part of the judgment in the case of *The "Salem"*,[56] under which underwriters were held liable to make good the loss of the remainder of the oil cargo which went down with the ship when she was scuttled by the deliberate act of the now infamous conspirators.

Clauses 5, 6 and 7

Clauses 5, 6 and 7—the Unseaworthiness and Unfitness Exclusion Clause and the War and Strikes Exclusion Clauses are the same as in the Institute Cargo Clauses.

Clause 8—Transit Clause

8 8.1 This insurance attaches as the subject-matter insured leaves tanks for the purpose of loading at the place named herein for the commencement of the transit, continues during the ordinary course of transit and terminates either

8.1.1 as the subject-matter insured enters tanks on discharge to place of storage or to storage vessel at the destination named herein,

or

8.1.2 on the expiry of 30 days after the date of arrival of the vessel at the destination named herein, whichever shall first occur.

8.2 If, after discharge from the oversea vessel into craft at the final port or place of discharge, but prior to the termination of this insurance under 8.1 above, the subject-matter insured or any part thereof is to be forwarded to a destination other than that to which it is insured hereunder, the insurance on the subject-matter insured or such part hereof shall not extend beyond the commencement of transit to such other destination, *unless otherwise agreed by the Underwriters upon receipt of prompt notice from the Assured.*

8.3 *Subject to prompt notice being given to the Underwriters and to an additional premium if required by them,* this insurance shall remain in force (until terminated under 8.1 or 8.2 above and subject to the provisions of Clause 9 below) during delay beyond the control of the Assured, any deviation, forced

56. *Shell International Petroleum* v. *Gibbs* [1983] 1 Lloyd's Rep. 342.

discharge, reshipment or transhipment and during any other variation of the adventure provided such other variation is beyond the control of the Assured.

The definition of the duration of the risk is of importance in insurances on bulk oil, for two reasons:

(a) because of the number of losses which occur during the operations of loading and discharging cargo, and
(b) because the assessment of any claim for shortage necessarily starts with the determination of the quantity of cargo at the risk of the assured at the commencement of the cover.

In short the duration of the risk is from shore tank to shore tank, although provision is impliedly made for part of the transit to be performed by lighters or vessels of smaller capacity than the ocean tanker.

"*leaves tanks for the purpose of loading*". These words are deliberately wide enough to cover the movement of oil from one or more initial storage tanks in the tank farm at the place of loading into another tank or tanks for the purpose of loading onto the ship.

The period of "cut-off" after the date of arrival of the vessel at the place of destination is 30 days, compared with 60 days as provided in the Institute Cargo Clauses.

Clause 9—Termination of Contract of Carriage Clause

This is in the same terms as the corresponding clause in Institute Cargo Clauses, except that in the event of the termination of the contract of carriage in the circumstances set out in the clause, and subject to prompt notice being given to the underwriters requesting a continuation of cover, the period of time for which such extension may be granted (without any further extension being asked for) is 30 days, compared with 60 days as provided in the Institute Cargo Clauses.

Clauses 10 to 14 and 16 to 20 and Note

Clauses 10 to 14 inclusive and 16 to 20 inclusive are the same as the clauses numbered 10 to 19 inclusive in the Institute Cargo Clauses. Likewise the Note at the foot of the form.

Clause 15—Adjustment Clause

15 Claims for leakage and shortage recoverable under this insurance are to be adjusted as follows:—

15.1 The amount recoverable shall be the proportionate insured value of the volume of oil lost, to be ascertained by a comparison of the gross volume certified as having left tanks for loading on to the vessel with the gross volume certified as having been delivered to tanks at the termination of the transit, except that where the contract of sale is based on weight and not on volume the amount recoverable may be calculated on a weight basis from such certified quantities.

The term "gross volume" in this Clause 15.1 means total volume without deduction of sediment and water content and free water, except to the extent that the amount of water can be shown by the

Assured to have increased abnormally during the insured transit as a result of the operation of a risk covered by this insurance.

15.2 Adjustment shall be made to the calculation under Clause 15.1 above to eliminate any change in volume caused by variation in temperature and any apparent change in quantity arising from the use of inconsistent procedures in determining the certified quantities.

15.3 Where this insurance provides for an excess to be applied to claims for leakage or shortage, such excess shall be deemed to include ordinary loss in weight or volume except when caused by variation in temperature or settling out of water. Where there is no such provision, the amount recoverable in accordance with Clauses 15.1 and 15.2 shall be subject to reduction for any ordinary loss excluded by Clause 4.2 above.

This clause has been designed to eliminate as far as possible claims for "paper losses" occurring as a result of the incompatibility of documents recording quantities loaded and discharged, and the well-known difficulties of measuring liquid cargoes. A typical claim for shortage, adjusted in accordance with the above clause would be as follows:

Facts

A quantity of 650,497 bbls Crude Oil is ascertained by meter readings to have been loaded from shore tanks to the vessel. Sediment and water content is established by analysis to be 340 bbls. A bill of lading is issued, based on shore tank figures, for 650,497 bbls gross—650,157 bbls nett.

The consignment is insured for U.S.$9,752,355 under Institute Bulk Oil Clauses, with claims for shortage subject to a deductible of 0.50 per cent on the whole shipment.

At destination, the quantity ascertained to have been discharged to shore tanks is:

	645,100 bbls
Water drained from shore tanks is	1,384 bbls
	643,716 bbls
S & W content by analysis is	324 bbls
Quantity of oil available to the Assured	643,392 bbls

The Assured might submit his claim as follows:

Shipped	650,157 bbls	
Received	643,392 bbls	
	6,765 bbls	
Less deductible 0.50% on 650,157 bbls	3,251 bbls	
Amount Claimed	3,514 bbls	*Insured Value*
		US$52,710

However, by reference to this Clause 15, the liability of underwriters is to be ascertained as follows:

Received from shore tanks, gross	650,497 bbls
Delivered to shore tanks, gross	645,100 bbls
	5,397 bbls
Less deductible 0.50% on *whole* shipment 650,497 bbls	3,252 bbls
Amount Recoverable	2,145 bbls
Insured Value	US$32,175

E. INSTITUTE COMMODITY TRADES CLAUSES (A)(B)(C) (5/9/83) Agreed with the Federation of Commodity Associations for the insurance of shipments of cocoa, coffee, cotton, fats and oils not in bulk, hides and skins, metals, oil seeds, refined sugar and tea.

These clauses are available in each of the (A)(B)(C) Forms. In each of these forms, Clause 1—Risks Clause—is in exactly the same terms as the corresponding Clause 1 of the Institute Cargo Clauses (A)(B) and (C). In fact the only difference between these clauses and the Institute Cargo Clauses is that underwriters have agreed to ameliorate the severity of the "insolvency clause" and the Unseaworthiness and Unfitness Exclusion Clause, viz.:

Clause 4.6—"insolvency clause"

In no case shall this insurance cover

4.6 loss damage or expense caused by insolvency or financial default of the owners managers charterers or operators of the vessel where, at the time of loading of the subject-matter insured on board the vessel, the Assured are aware, or in the ordinary course of business should be aware, that such insolvency or financial default could prevent the normal prosecution of the voyage.
This exclusion shall not apply where this insurance has been assigned to the party claiming hereunder who has bought or agreed to buy the subject-matter insured in good faith under a binding contract.

Clause 5—Unseaworthiness and Unfitness Exclusion Clause

5 **5.1** In no case shall this insurance cover loss damage or expense arising from

5.1.1 unseaworthiness of vessel or craft or unfitness of vessel or craft for the safe carriage of the subject-matter insured, where the Assured are privy to such unseaworthiness or unfitness, at the time the subject-matter insured is loaded therein

5.1.2 unfitness of container liftvan or land conveyance for the safe carriage of the subject-matter insured, where loading therein is carried out prior to attachment of this insurance or by the Assured or their servants.

5.2 Where this insurance has been assigned to the party claiming hereunder who has brought or agreed to buy the subject-matter insured in good faith under a binding contract, exclusion 5.1.1 above shall not apply.

5.3 The Underwriters waive any breach of the implied warranties of seaworthiness of the ship and fitness of the ship to carry the subject-matter insured to destination.

In comparison with the standard wording contained in Institute Cargo Clauses, there are three major concessions:

(a) The exclusion of loss damage or expense caused by insolvency or financial default of the owners, managers, charterers or operators of the ship is limited to instances where the assured was or should have been aware that there was a risk that the voyage might be frustrated or interrupted on that account.

(b) Both the "insolvency exclusion" (Clause 4.6) and the unseaworthiness and unfitness exclusion (Clause 5.1) are agreed not to apply to a purchaser in good faith under a binding contract, to whom the insurance has been assigned. This is, of course, particularly important in trades where it is customary to supply customers with goods under a c.i.f. contract.

(c) By Clause 5.3, the underwriters agree to waive any breach of the implied warranties of seaworthiness or "cargo-worthiness". This agreement used to be expressed in virtually all previous forms of cargo insurances by such words as "the seaworthiness of the vessel as between the assured and the underwriters is hereby admitted", the absence of which has been commented upon on page 23.

Conversely, under the Institute Commodity Trades Clauses, the assured undertakes a somewhat heavier obligation in regard to the fitness of containers, liftvans and land conveyances for the safe carriage of the goods. Under these clauses, any claim arising from such unfitness will be excluded if the goods have been loaded therein by the assured or his servants, whereas under Institute Cargo Clauses the exclusion only applies when the assured or his servants are privy to the unfitness.

F. INSTITUTE JUTE CLAUSES (1/1/84)

Clause 1—Risks Clause

1 This insurance covers, except as provided in Clauses 4, 5, 6 and 7 below.
1.1 loss of or damage to the subject-matter insured reasonably attributable to
1.1.1 fire or explosion
1.1.2 vessel or craft being stranded grounded sunk or capsized
1.1.3 overturning or derailment of land conveyance
1.1.4 collision or contact of vessel craft or conveyance with any external object other than water
1.1.5 discharge of cargo at a port of distress,
1.2 loss of or damage to the subject-matter insured caused by
1.2.1 general average sacrifice
1.2.2 jettison or washing overboard
1.2.3 entry of sea lake or river water into vessel craft hold conveyance container liftvan or place of storage,
1.3 total loss of any package lost overboard or dropped whilst loading on to, or unloading from, vessel or craft.

The list of perils insured under these clauses corresponds with the list of perils insured under Institute Cargo Clauses (B) except for the risk of earthquake, volcanic eruption and lightning (Clause 1.1.6 in the Institute Cargo Clauses (B)) which are omitted from the Institute Jute Clauses.

Clause 2—General Average Clause

Clause 3—"Both to Blame Collision" Clause

Both are the same as in the Institute Cargo Clauses.

Clause 4—General Exclusions Clause

Clause 5—Unseaworthiness and Unfitness Exclusion Clause

Both these clauses appear in the same form as the corresponding clauses in the Institute Commodity Trades Clauses (A). It may therefore be noted:

(a) The underwriters have agreed to the same concessions, ameliorating the severity of the "insolvency clause" (Clause 4.6) and the Unseaworthiness Clause (Clause 5.1), as we have noted above on page 63.

(b) Although the Institute Jute Clauses are on restricted conditions, the risks covered being slightly more limited than under Institute Cargo Clauses (B), they do not contain the "deliberate damage" exclusion common to virtually all the cargo forms on restricted conditions.

Clauses 6 and 7—War and Strikes Exclusion Clauses

These are the same as in the Institute Cargo Clauses.

Clause 8—Transit clause

Clause 9—Termination of Contract of Carriage Clause

These are the same as in the Institute Cargo Clauses, except that:

(a) The "cut-off" period after the completion of discharge of the goods at the final port of discharge is 30 days compared with 60 days under Institute Cargo Clauses,

(b) in the event of the termination of the contract of carriage in the circumstances set out in the clause, and subject to prompt notice being given to the underwriters requesting a continuation of cover, the period of time for which such extension may be granted (without any further extension being asked for) is 15 days, instead of 60 days as provided in the Institute Cargo Clauses.

Clauses 10 to 19 inclusive and Note

Clauses 10 to 19 inclusive and the Note at the foot of the form are the same as in Institute Cargo Clauses.

G. INSTITUTE NATURAL RUBBER CLAUSES (Excluding Liquid Latex) (1/1/84)

Clause 1—Risks Clause

1 This insurance covers, except as provided in Clauses 4, 5, 6 and 7 below.

1.1 loss of or damage to the subject-matter insured reasonably attributable to

1.1.1 fire or explosion

1.1.2 vessel or craft being stranded grounded sunk or capsized
1.1.3 overturning or derailment of land conveyance
1.1.4 collision or contact of vessel craft or conveyance with any external object other than water
1.1.5 discharge of cargo at a port of distress
1.1.6 earthquake volcanic eruption or lightning,
1.2 loss of or damage to the subject-matter insured caused by
1.2.1 general average sacrifice
1.2.2 jettison or washing overboard
1.2.3 water or condensation
1.2.4 hooks, spillings or leakage of any substance or liquid, other cargo (excluding rubber), or moisture from wet or damp dunnage
1.2.5 theft pilferage or non-delivery.

The list of perils corresponds with the list of the perils insured under Institute Cargo Clauses (B) from Clause 1.1 through Clause 1.2.2, inclusive. Clauses 1.2.3, 1.2.4, 1.2.5 are particular to the Natural Rubber Clauses.

"1.2.3 water or condensation"

It is to be noted that there is no limitation upon the nature or the cause of the water or condensation damage which may be recovered for under this clause. It is submitted that as in the risks of fire or heating, evidence of damage by wetting is sufficient that a casualty has occurred.

"1.2.4 hooks, spillings or leakage of any substance or liquid, other cargo (excluding rubber), or moisture from wet or damp dunnage"

"hooks"

Instances of damage by hooks used to be far more frequent in the days when the majority of packaged cargo was individually handled by stevedores, and it became common to add the risk of damage by hooks to the lists of perils insured in many cargo policies in order to displace the assumption (which was probably justified in many instances) that a certain amount of hook damage was either inevitable and/or excluded from recovery by reason of section 55(2)(*c*) of the Marine Insurance Act 1906, which excluded "ordinary leakage and breakage" as one of the risks for which the insurer was not liable in the absence of a specific provision in the policy.

"spillings or leakage of any substance or liquid"

"Leakage" is not used here in the normal sense of a loss of liquid by its escape from its container. What is intended to be covered by this expression is damage to rubber by its coming into contact with any liquid or substance which has leaked or spilled, and is, in effect, where it should not be.

"other cargo"

Damage by other cargo may result from direct physical contact, as, for example, when the rubber is overstowed by heavy goods, or indirectly, by its being affected in some other way, e.g. by leakage, moisture, heat, fumes, gas or any other form of emanation from the other cargo. It is not necessary that the two parcels of cargo should have been stowed next to each other.

The question may also arise whether damage sustained by the rubber through its being stowed on top of the remnants of previous cargoes should be considered as coming within the words "other cargo" in terms of this clause. The practice of adjusters is against so extending the meaning of the words "other cargo".

"1.2.5 theft pilferage or non-delivery"

These words import the terms of the Institute Theft, Pilferage and Non-delivery Clause which is set out and commented upon on pages 80 to 82.

Clause 2—General Average Clause

Clause 3—"Both to Blame Collision" Clause

These are in the same form as in Institute Cargo Clauses.

Clause 4—General Exclusions Clause

4 In no case shall this insurance cover
- 4.1 loss damage or expense attributable to wilful misconduct of the Assured
- 4.2 ordinary loss in weight or volume, or ordinary wear and tear of the subject-matter insured
- 4.3 loss damage or expense caused by insufficiency or unsuitability of packing or preparation of the subject-matter insured (for the purpose of this Clause 4.3 "packing" shall be deemed to include stowage in a container or liftvan but only when such stowage is carried out prior to attachment of this insurance or by the Assured or their servants)
- 4.4 loss damage or expense caused by inherent vice or nature of the subject-matter insured
- 4.5 loss damage or expense proximately caused by delay, even though the delay be caused by a risk insured against (except expenses payable under Clause 2 above)
- 4.6 loss damage or expense caused by insolvency or financial default of the owners managers charterers or operators of the vessel where, at the time of loading of the subject-matter insured on board the vessel, the Assured are aware, or in the ordinary course of business should be aware, that such insolvency or financial default could prevent the normal prosecution of the voyage
  This exclusion shall not apply where this insurance has been assigned to the party claiming hereunder who has bought or agreed to buy the subject-matter insured in good faith under a binding contract
- 4.7 loss damage or expense arising from the use of any weapon of war employing atomic or nuclear fission and/or fusion or other like reaction or radioactive force or matter.

The exclusions follow the standard pattern, but the following variations from the wording employed in Institute Cargo Clauses (B) should be noted:

(a) Clause 4.2 does not refer to "ordinary leakage" since the Natural Rubber Clauses are not intended for use for shipments of liquid latex.

(b) Clause 4.6 ("insolvency" clause) is in the modified form which we have already noted in connection with the Institute Commodity Trades Clauses (see pages 63 to 64).

(c) The Deliberate Damage Clause (Clause 4.7 in the Institute Cargo Clauses (B)) is omitted.

Clause 5—Unseaworthiness and Unfitness Exclusion Clause

5 5.1 In no case shall this insurance cover loss damage or expense arising from

5.1.1 unseaworthiness of vessel or craft or unfitness of vessel or craft for the safe carriage of the subject-matter insured, where the Assured are privy to such unseaworthiness or unfitness, at the time the subject-matter insured is loaded therein

5.1.2 unfitness of container liftvan or land conveyance for the safe carriage of the subject-matter insured, where loading therein is carried out prior to attachment of this insurance or by the Assured or their servants.

5.2 Where this insurance has been assigned to the party claiming hereunder who has bought or agreed to buy the subject-matter insured in good faith under a binding contract, exclusion 5.1.1 above shall not apply.

5.3 The Underwriters waive any breach of the implied warranties of seaworthiness of the ship and fitness of the ship to carry the subject-matter insured to destination.

This clause is in the modified form which we have already noted under the Institute Commodity Trades Clauses. See pages 63 to 64.

Clauses 6 and 7—War and Strikes Exclusion Clauses

These are in the same form as in the Institute Cargo Clauses.

Clause 8—Transit Clause

8 8.1 This insurance attaches from the time the goods leave the warehouse or place of storage at the port of shipment named herein for the commencement of the transit and continues during the ordinary course of transit until the goods are delivered to a warehouse or place of storage at the port of destination named herein and, provided it is not a manufacturer's warehouse or place of storage, whilst there for a period not exceeding 30 days.

8.2 If the goods are to be forwarded to a place outside the limits of the said port of destination the insurance continues until the goods are loaded on to a vessel, craft or conveyance or until the expiry of 30 days from midnight of the day on which the discharge overside of the insured goods from the oversea vessel at the said port of destination is completed, whichever shall first occur.

8.3 *By giving notice to the Underwriters before the insurance ceases the Assured may obtain an extension at a premium to be arranged to cover the goods beyond the limits in 8.1 and 8.2 above.*

8.4 This insurance shall remain in force (subject to termination as provided for above and to the provisions of Clause 9 below) during delay beyond the control of the Assured, any deviation, forced discharge, reshipment or transhipment and during any variation of the adventure arising from the exercise of a liberty granted to shipowners or charterers under the contract of affreightment.

It will be noted that, whereas the attachment of the risk is the same as under Institute Cargo Clauses, namely, from the time the goods leave the warehouse or place of storage of the port of shipment, the provisions of this clause relating to the termination of the risk are slightly more favourable to the assured. In the ordinary way, the risk continues until either

- — the goods are delivered to a manufacturer's warehouse or place of storage, or
- — the expiry of 30 days at a warehouse or place of storage at the port of destination.

There is a further extension to the benefit of the assured, in that if the goods are to be forwarded beyond the limits of the port of destination named in the policy, the insurance will continue until the goods are loaded onto the forwarding vessel, craft or conveyance, or until the expiry of 30 days after completion of discharge from the ocean steamer at the port of destination. An extension can be obtained by the assured in terms of Clause 8.3 if so desired.

Clauses 8.4, 9 and 10 and 11 to 14

Clauses 8.4, 9 and 10 are in the same form as in the Institute Cargo Clauses, as are Clauses 11 to 14 inclusive.

Clause 15—Arbitration Clause

15 In the event of a dispute between the Assured and the Underwriters' Surveyors as to the extent of the depreciation to be allowed on damaged rubber, samples shall be drawn by recognised samplers and forwarded together with the Survey Report to the Rubber Trade Association of London whose award shall be final and binding on all parties so far as concerns the extent of depreciation.

The purpose and effect of this clause are self-explanatory. Its inclusion in earlier forms of the Rubber Clauses, as well as in the present form, demonstrates the advantage of the close liaison between the members of the Rubber Trade Association of London and British market underwriters.

Clauses 16 to 20 and Note

Clauses 16 to 20 correspond to Clauses 15 to 19 in the Institute Cargo Clauses. There is also the usual Note at the foot of the form.

H. INSTITUTE F.O.S.F.A. TRADES CLAUSES (1/7/85) Agreed with the Federation of Oils, Seeds and Fats Associations

These clauses are available in forms (A) (B) (C). The clauses are an exact replica of the Institute Cargo Clauses (A) (B) and (C), except for:

— Clause 4.6: "the insolvency clause", and
— Clause 5: Unseaworthiness and Unfitness Exclusion Clause,

both of which are in the modified form which we have already noted in the Institute Commodity Trades Clauses (see pages 63 to 64).

There are also four sets of Supplementary Clauses available for use in the F.O.S.F.A. trades, likewise dated 1/7/85. They are as follows:

1. Institute F.O.S.F.A. Supplementary Clause (1) (for use in conjunction with Institute F.O.S.F.A. Trades Clause (B))

It is hereby agreed that this insurance shall also include

1 Loss of or damage to the subject-matter insured, due to breakdown or collapse of proper stow in vessel or craft caused by stress of weather, subject always to the exclusions contained in this insurance.

2 Institute Malicious Damage Clause 1/8/82.

Clause 1 of these Supplementary Clauses reintroduces a cause of loss or damage for which an assured obtained coverage (subject to the Memorandum percentage being attained) under the old Institute Cargo Clauses (W.A.). This is for a species of damage caused by a "peril of the sea", namely, heavy weather—in this clause called "stress of weather". So when goods, properly stowed in the carrying vessel or craft, have sustained loss or damage by the stowage being disturbed by the violent motion of the vessel or craft in heavy weather the underwriters will respond.

". . . breakdown or collapse of proper stow"

The use of the word "proper" in this context makes it clear that the assured has to exercise the burden of proving that the collapse of the stow was due to the violent motion of the vessel in a storm, and that such collapse or breakdown of stow would not have occurred in any event due to an improper or inadequate method of stowage.

Clause 2 imports the Institute Malicious Damage Clause. See page 79.

2. Institute F.O.S.F.A. Supplementary Clause (2) (for use in conjunction with Institute F.O.S.F.A. Trades Clause (C))

It is hereby agreed that this insurance shall also include

1 Total loss of any package lost overboard or dropped whilst loading on to, or unloading from, vessel or craft, subject always to the exclusions contained in this insurance.

2 Washing overboard of Containers, subject always to the exclusions contained in this insurance.

3 Institute Malicious Damage Clause 1/8/82.

The effect of Clauses 1 and 2 is to uplift the cover granted by the F.O.S.F.A. Trades Clauses (C) almost to the equivalent of the F.O.S.F.A. Trades Clauses (B).

The words of Clause 1—"total loss of any package etc. . . . "—are the same as an Institute Cargo Clauses (B), Clause 1.3.

Clause 2 adds the risk of loss or damage to the goods by reason of the container in which they are stowed being washed overboard. The reference to containers, which does not appear in the corresponding Clause (1.2.2) in the Institute Cargo Clauses (B), recognises that F.O.S.F.A. goods would not properly be carried on deck, except in containers.

Clause 3 imports the Institute Malicious Damage Clause. See page 79.

3. Institute F.O.S.F.A. Supplementary Clause (3): Ship Navigation & Management (for use in conjunction with Institute F.O.S.F.A. Trades Clauses (B) & (C))

In consideration of an additional premium, it is hereby agreed that this insurance covers, subject always to the exclusions contained in this insurance, loss of or damage to the subject-matter insured, whilst on the ship, caused by error, neglect or default of the carrier or his servants in the navigation or management of the ship, for which they are relieved from liability under the contract of carriage.

This clause gives added protection to an assured to cover, on payment of an additional premium, loss or damage caused to the goods whilst on the ship, for which the carrier would be exonerated from liability by virtue of Article IV, Rule 2(a) of the Hague Rules (and likewise the Hague-Visby Rules).

Article IV, Rule 2 of those Rules reads:

> "2. Neither the carrier nor the ship shall be responsible for loss or damage arising or resulting from—
> (a) Act, neglect or default of the Master, mariners, pilot or the servants of the carrier in the navigation or in the management of the ship:"

Examples are: want of proper attention to the ship's pumps; negligence in clearing the ship's decks of water; neglect in clearing a waste pipe, or in ascertaining the condition of tanks before filling them, have all been held to be faults in the management of the ship.[57]

However, a failure to take proper care of the cargo would not fall within the Hague Rules exception, nor within the cover provided by this Supplementary Clause.

It is to be noted that the cover is limited to loss or damage which is sustained by the goods whilst they are on board the ship. The reason for this is that both the Hague Rules and the Hague-Visby Rules spell out the rights and responsibilities of the carrier under Article II "in relation to the loading, handling, stowage, carriage, custody, care, and discharge" of the goods, and consequently the immunities granted by Article IV do not apply to responsibilities which the carrier may have to exercise prior to the loading of the goods or after their discharge from the ship.

It will be appreciated that this Supplementary Clause (3) provides a logical extension to the restricted cover accorded by the F.O.S.F.A. Trades Clauses (B) and (C), since the risks which are insured under those clauses are very much the same as those for which the carrier is exonerated from liability, for example those of fire, "perils, dangers and accidents of the sea or other navigable waters", Act of God, etc. As mentioned in the historical perspective on page 9, this is the area in which the merchant desires the protection of insurance.

4. Institute F.O.S.F.A. Supplementary Clause (4): Grade Clause (for use in conjunction with Institute F.O.S.F.A. Trades Clauses)

Held covered at a premium to be arranged in event of omission or error in description of grade, quality &/or other technical characteristics of the insured commodity, as named in the relevant FOSFA contract.

By this clause underwriters agree to hold the assured covered, at a premium to be arranged, in the event of any innocent misdescription of the subject-matter insured, in terms of the relevant F.O.S.F.A. contract. As noted above in the

57. Carver's *Carriage of Goods*, 13th edn. (British Shipping Laws), sections 192 to 194 and cases there cited.

commentary on Clause 10 of the Institute Cargo Clauses, this concession, previously available under virtually all forms of cargo insurance, was dropped from the standard marine cargo forms issued from 1/1/82 onwards.

I. INSTITUTE FROZEN MEAT CLAUSES (1/1/86)

Three basic forms are available:

Institute Frozen Meat Clauses (A)
Institute Frozen Meat Clauses (A)—24 Hours Breakdown
Institute Frozen Meat Clauses (C) and 24 Hours Breakdown

These forms are all sub-titled: "(Not suitable for chilled, cooled or fresh meat)".

There is also an additional clause available for attachment to the Institute Frozen Meat Clauses (A). See page 75.

Clause 1—Risks Covered

The (A) Clauses cover all risks of loss of or damage to the subject-matter insured except as provided in the Exclusion Clauses 4, 5, 6 and 7.

The (A)—24 Hours Breakdown form covers:

1 This insurance covers, except as provided in Clauses 4, 5, 6 and 7 below,
1.1 all risks of loss of or damage to the subject-matter insured, other than loss or damage resulting from any variation in temperature howsoever caused,
1.2 loss of or damage to the subject-matter insured resulting from any variation in temperature attributable to
1.2.1 breakdown of refrigerating machinery resulting in its stoppage for a period of not less than 24 consecutive hours
1.2.2 fire or explosion
1.2.3 vessel or craft being stranded grounded sunk or capsized
1.2.4 overturning or derailment of land conveyance
1.2.5 collision or contact of vessel craft or conveyance with any external object other than water
1.2.6 discharge of cargo at a port of distress.

These risks are precisely the same as those covered by the Institute Frozen Food Clauses (A), and similar observations apply. See page 50.

The (C) and 24 Hours Breakdown form covers:

1 This insurance covers, except as provided in Clauses 4, 5, 6 and 7 below,
1.1 loss of or damage to the subject-matter insured attributable to
1.1.1 fire or explosion
1.1.2 vessel or craft being stranded grounded sunk or capsized
1.1.3 overturning or derailment of land conveyance
1.1.4 collision or contact of vessel craft or conveyance with any external object other than water
1.1.5 discharge of cargo at a port of distress
1.1.6 breakdown of refrigerating machinery resulting in its stoppage for a period of not less than 24 consecutive hours
1.2 loss of or damage to the subject-matter insured caused by
1.2.1 general average sacrifice
1.2.2 jettison.

The risks covered are the same as in the Institute Cargo Clauses (C) but with the addition of loss or damage caused by the breakdown of refrigerating machinery resulting in its stoppage for a period of not less than 24 hours.

Clauses 2 and 3—General Average and "Both to Blame Collision" Clauses

These clauses are the same, in all three forms, as in the Institute Cargo Clauses.

Clause 4—Exclusions

In the (A) Clauses, exclusions 4.1, 4.2, 4.3, 4.5 and 4.7 are the same as in the Institute Cargo Clauses (A).

Exclusion 4.4—the "inherent vice" exclusion—excepts loss, damage or expense resulting from variation in temperature whilst this insurance is in force.

Exclusion 4.6—the "insolvency" exclusion—is in the modified form which we have noted in connection with the Institute Commodity Trades Clauses. See pages 63 to 64.

Exclusion 4.8 is unexpected in an All Risks insurance. It reads:

> "loss damage or expense on shore caused directly or indirectly by earthquake, volcanic eruption and/or fire resulting therefrom".

It is to be noted that this exclusion only applies when the goods are on land.

Exclusion 4.9 is:

> "loss damage or expense arising from any failure of the assured or their servants to take all reasonable precautions to ensure that the subject-matter insured is kept in refrigerated or, where appropriate, properly insulated and cooled space".

This is the same as we have noted under the Institute Frozen Food Clauses. See page 51.

In the (A)—24 Hours Breakdown form the exclusions are the same, except that the exception of 4.4—the "inherent vice" exclusion—is worded "except loss, damage or expense resulting from variation in temperature specifically covered under Clause 1.2 above".

In the (C) and 24 Hours Breakdown form there is an additional exclusion:

> "4.7 deliberate damage to or deliberate destruction of the subject-matter insured or any part thereof by the wrongful act of any person or persons".

This exclusion, as we have already noted, is customary when the insurance is on restricted conditions.

Clause 5—Unseaworthiness and Unfitness Exclusion Clause

In all three forms, Clause 5—Unseaworthiness and Unfitness Exclusion Clause—is in the modified form which we have noted in connection with the Institute Commodity Trades Clauses.

Clauses 6 and 7—War and Strikes Exclusion Clauses

Clauses 6 and 7—the War and Strikes Exclusion Clauses appear in the standard form.

Clause 8—Transit Clause

This clause is the same in all three forms:

8 8.1 This insurance attaches from the time

8.1.1 the goods pass into the cooling and/or freezing chambers of the works at the place named herein, provided that the period in such chambers prior to shipment on board the oversea vessel shall not exceed 60 days unless prompt notice be given to the Underwriters and an additional premium paid for each further period of 30 days or part thereof.

8.1.2 the goods are loaded into the conveyance at the freezing works or cold store at the place named herein for the commencement of the transit.

8.1.3 of loading of the goods into the oversea vessel.

DELETE SECTIONS NOT APPLICABLE

8.2 This insurance continues during the ordinary course of transit to and whilst in

8.2.1 cold store at the destination named herein

or

8.2.2 any other cold store which the Assured elect to use following discharge of the goods from the oversea vessel at the port of discharge either

8.2.2.1 for storage other than in the ordinary course of transit or

8.2.2.2 for allocation or distribution.

8.3 This insurance terminates

8.3.1 *for transit to a destination in the Continent of Europe (including Eire and the United Kingdom), U.S.A. or Canada* on the expiry of 30 days

8.3.2 *for transit to a destination elsewhere* on the expiry of 5 days

after final discharge of the goods from the oversea vessel at the port of discharge.

8.4 Any disposal of the goods other than by storage as in 8.2.1 or 8.2.2 above (except with the prior consent of the Underwriters) or any removal from cold store before the expiry of the relevant period in 8.3.1 or 8.3.2 above shall terminate the insurance on such goods.

8.5 If, after discharge overside from the oversea vessel at the final port of discharge, but prior to termination of this insurance, the goods are to be forwarded to a destination other than that to which they are insured hereunder, this insurance, whilst remaining subject to termination as provided for above, shall not extend beyond the commencement of transit to such other destination.

8.6 This insurance shall remain in force (subject to termination as provided for above and to the provisions of Clause 9 below) during delay beyond the control of the Assured, any deviation, forced discharge, reshipment or transhipment and during any variation of the adventure arising from the exercise of a liberty granted to shipowners or charterers under the contract of affreightment.

It is to be noted that there are three options available to the assured for the commencement of the risk, namely, as provided in Clause 8.1.1, 8.1.2 or 8.1.3. Furthermore, the time when the insurance terminates depends upon whether the transit is to a destination in Europe, the USA or Canada, in which event it expires 30 days after final discharge of the goods from the oversea vessel, or elsewhere in the world in which event the insurance terminates five days after final discharge of the goods. However, if the goods are removed from the cold store into which they have been placed after discharge from the ocean steamer, such removal will, by Clause 8.4, bring about a prior termination of the risk.

Clauses 8.5 and 8.6 are in the same terms as Clauses 8.2 and 8.3 of the Institute Cargo Clauses.

Clause 9—Termination of Contract of Affreightment Clause

This is in similar terms to Clause 9 of Institute Cargo Clauses, except that in the event of prompt notice being given to the underwriters for a continuation of the cover after termination of the contract of affreightment, the period of time for which underwriters will agree to continue the cover (subject to any agreed extension) is limited to 30 days, compared with 60 days under Institute Cargo Clauses.

Clauses 10 to 13

Clauses 10 to 13 are all the same as found in the Institute Cargo Clauses.

Clause 14—Adjustment Clause

14 Should the subject-matter insured or any part thereof not be shipped any claim in respect thereto shall be adjusted on the basis of its insured value less, where included, freight, duty and all charges not incurred.

The effect of this clause is that, in the event of any claim for loss or damage to the goods, or part of them, prior to their shipment on board the ocean steamer, the adjustment will be made on the basis of the proportion of the loss being applied not to the full value insured, but to that figure less any freight, duty or charges which the assured will not be liable to pay because of the loss or damage sustained to the goods.

Clauses 15 to 20, Note and Special Note

Clauses 15 to 20 correspond to Clauses 14 to 19 of the Institute Cargo Clauses. So likewise does the Note regarding prompt notice at the foot of the form. There is also a Special Note which reads:

SPECIAL NOTE:—This insurance does not cover loss damage or expense caused by embargo, or by rejection prohibition or detention by the government of the country of import or their agencies or departments, but does not exclude loss of or damage to the subject-matter insured caused by risks insured hereunder and sustained prior to any such embargo rejection prohibition or detention.

This note and its effect are the same as in the 1/1/86 version of the Institute Frozen Food Clauses. See page 53.

J. I.M.T.A. FROZEN MEAT EXTENSION CLAUSES 1/1/86 (For use only with the Institute Frozen Meat Clauses (A) 1/1/86)

Clause 1 and Clauses 4.4 and 4.5 of the attached Institute Frozen Meat Clauses (A) 1/1/86 are deemed to be deleted and replaced by:

1 Subject always to the goods being in sound condition at the time of attachment, this insurance covers, except as provided in Clauses 4, 5, 6 and 7 below, loss of, deterioration of, or damage to the subject-matter insured which shall arise during the currency of this insurance.

4 4.4 loss damage or expense arising from bone taint, salmonella, infection prior to attachment of this insurance, fault in preparation dressing cooling freezing wrapping or packing

4.5 claims arising from loss of market

Nevertheless, in the absence of prior notice to the Underwriters and agreement of any additional premium required by them, this insurance excludes any claim for deterioration of or damage to the subject-matter insured where the period in freezing works and in any cold store, before loading into the conveyance for commencement of the transit, exceeds 60 days.

As the title suggests, these clauses provide an extension to the cover granted by the Institute Frozen Meat Clauses (A) to which they have to be attached. As we have seen, the Frozen Meat Clauses (A) are on "All Risks" conditions. What could be wider than that?

Well, as we have seen from the commentary on page 13, there are limitations to the cover provided by the phrase "all risks". "The expression does not cover inherent vice or mere wear and tear . . . It covers a risk, not a certainty", and so on. But here, provided that the goods are in sound condition at the time the insurance attaches, we have coverage for any loss, deterioration or damage which arises during the currency of the insurance. This differs from an "all risks" cover in that it is not necessary for the assured to demonstrate that the loss, deterioration or damage has resulted from a casualty.

However, it will be necessary to prove that the frozen meat was in sound condition at the time the insurances attached—whichever of the three options has been selected from those listed in clause 8.1 (the Transit Clause) of the Institute Frozen Meat Clauses (A). This makes it even more important to hold a formal condition survey and/or carry out such form of inspection or certification as is required by the health authorities in the country of origin.

The other amelioration provided by these Extension Clauses concerns the list of exclusions. Clause 4.4 of the (A) Clauses, which replicates the statutory exclusions of inherent vice or nature of the subject-matter insured, is replaced by:

(a) a limited list of infections and
(b) "fault" (not merely insufficiency or unsuitability) "in preparation dressing cooling freezing wrapping or packing". Exactly how this exclusion fits in with the "insufficiency or unsuitability" test in regard to packing and preparation of the subject-matter insured—as provided by clause 4.3 of the Institute Frozen Meat Clauses (A)—is unfortunately unclear.

Clause 4.5 excluding any claim caused by delay is replaced by a more limited exclusion of any claim for loss of market—a situation which occurs quite frequently, though not always, in consequence of delay. However, although claims caused by delay (other than loss of market) will be paid for when the delay occurs after shipment, it is specifically provided in the last paragraph of these clauses that a delay in freezing works or cold store in excess of 60 days prior to shipment will automatically preclude any claim for deterioration or damage unless the assured have given the underwriters prior notice and have obtained their agreement to a continuation of the cover, with or without additional premium.

All the other exclusions provided in the Institute Frozen Meat Clauses (A), viz. clauses 4.1, 4.2, 4.3, 4.6, 4.7, 4.8 and 4.9, also apply to these Extension Clauses.

K. INSTITUTE TIMBER TRADE FEDERATION CLAUSES (Agreed with the Timber Trade Federation) (1/4/86)

Clause 1—Risks Clause

1 **Cargo whilst stowed on deck**

1.1 This insurance covers, except as provided in Clauses 4, 5, 6 and 7 below,

1.1.1 loss of or damage to the subject-matter insured whilst stowed on deck of the oversea vessel, or any part or item thereof whilst so stowed, reasonably attributable to

1.1.1.1 fire or explosion

1.1.1.2 vessel being stranded grounded sunk or capsized

1.1.1.3 collision or contact of vessel with any external object other than water

1.1.1.4 discharge of cargo at a port of distress,

1.1.2 loss of or damage to the subject-matter insured whilst stowed on deck of the oversea vessel, or any part or item thereof whilst so stowed, caused by

1.1.2.1 general average sacrifice

1.1.2.2 jettison or washing overboard

1.1.2.3 theft or non-delivery

1.1.2.4 malicious act.

Cargo whilst not stowed on deck

1.2 This insurance covers all risks of loss of or damage to the subject-matter insured excluding any part or item thereof whilst stowed on deck on the oversea vessel, except as provided in Clauses 4, 5, 6 and 7 below. Subject-matter insured or any part or item thereof stowed in poop, forecastle, deck house, shelter deck, other enclosed space, or in a container, shall be deemed to be subject-matter insured not stowed on deck.

Because of their high volume/weight ratio, timber cargoes are frequently carried on deck and are thus exposed to greater risks than cargo stowed under deck. This is therefore reflected in the terms of the insurance offered by underwriters on timber cargoes, and consequently when a ship has been chartered to carry a full cargo of wood goods, the cargo stowed under deck will be covered against "all risks", while the cargo stowed on deck is covered only against the named perils in Clause 1.1.

Timber stowed under cover or in a container (even though the container is itself stowed on deck) is given the advantage of the all risks cover as if it had been stowed under deck.

The specific perils insured for "on deck" cargo are, on the whole, wider than as provided in the Institute Cargo Clauses (C). Washing overboard, which is a very real hazard with deck cargoes, is specifically covered in Clause 1.1.2.2, as are theft or non-delivery by Clause 1.1.2.3, and any "malicious act". On the other hand, overturning or derailment of land conveyance is omitted from the list of perils insured, as is the risk of lighter or craft (but not, of course, the oversea vessel) being stranded, grounded, sunk, capsized or in collision or contact with any other object.

As already stated, cargo stowed under deck or in covered spaces or in a container is insured on "all risks" conditions.

Clause 2—General Average Clause

Clause 3—"Both to Blame Collision" Clause

These are in standard form.

Clause 4—General Exclusions Clause

Other than exclusion 4.6, which is in the modified form which we have noted under the Institute Commodity Trades Clauses, the list of exclusions 4.1 to 4.5 inclusive and 4.7 are in the same form as in the Institute Cargo Clauses (A).

Clause 5—Unseaworthiness and Unfitness Exclusion Clause

This clause is also in the modified form which we have noted in the Institute Commodity Trades Clauses.

Clauses 6 and 7—War and Strikes Exclusion Clauses

These are in standard form.

Clause 8—Transit Clause

8 **8.1** This insurance attaches on or after the loading of the goods insured hereunder on land and/or water conveyances or their floating at the mill, warehouse, factory, yard or premises wheresoever, from which the despatch to the oversea vessel is made, continues during the ordinary course of transit and terminates either

8.1.1 on delivery of the goods by land or water into the mill, warehouse, factory, yard or premises at their final destination, whether at the port of discharge of the oversea vessel or (further sea voyage excepted) elsewhere, and are there made available to the Assured or Receivers

8.1.2 on delivery to any other warehouse or place of storage which the Assured elect to use for storage other than in the ordinary course of transit

or

8.1.3 on the expiry of 60 days after completion of discharge overside of the goods hereby insured from the oversea vessel at the final port of discharge,

whichever shall first occur.

8.2 This insurance shall remain in force (subject to termination as provided for above and to the provisions of Clause 9 below) during delay beyond the control of the Assured, any deviation, forced discharge, reshipment or transhipment and during any variation of the adventure arising from the exercise of a liberty granted to shipowners or charterers under the contract of affreightment.

8.3 Each bill of lading to be deemed a separate insurance if required by the Assured at any time.

8.4 The provisions of Clause 8 shall apply notwithstanding that the description of the voyage in the body of the policy may state only the ports and places of shipment and discharge.

Clause 8.1 contains flexible provisions for the attachment of the risk. This may occur on loading the timber into land or water conveyances, wherever this takes place for the despatch to the ocean steamer. It may even be that logs are floated down river from the timber mill where they are prepared, in which event the insurance attaches at the time they are put into the water.

Termination of the risk is in accordance with either of Clauses 8.1.1, 8.1.2 or 8.1.3, whichever first occurs.

There is an interesting provision in Clause 8.3, which has been carried over from the previous version of the Timber Trade Federation Clauses (1/1/62). This is that each separate bill of lading may be deemed a separate insurance, if required by the assured. While this was relevant when the clauses were subject to an attainable franchise (as they were in the 1/1/62 form), it would not appear to be of any value to an assured under the current form, unless the insurance is specifically made subject either to an attainable franchise or to a deductible.

By Clause 8.4, an assured who requires to apply the flexible provisions of Clause 8.1, particularly as regards the attachment of the risk, will not be prejudiced by reason of his describing the voyage as from the port of shipment to the port of discharge. The reason for this concession is that, in the timber trade, it frequently happens that the exporter who arranges the insurance will not know from which mills or logging camps the pieces of timber will have started their journey to the port of loading.

The remainder of the clauses, viz. Clauses 9 to 19 and the Note at the end, are all in the same terms as in the Institute Cargo Clauses.

5. OCCASIONAL AND ADDITIONAL CLAUSES

A. INSTITUTE MALICIOUS DAMAGE CLAUSE (1/8/82)

In consideration of an additional premium, it is hereby agreed that the exclusion "deliberate damage to or deliberate destruction of the subject-matter insured or any part thereof by the wrongful act of any person or persons" is deemed to be deleted and further that this insurance covers loss of or damage to the subject-matter insured caused by malicious acts vandalism or sabotage, subject always to the other exclusions contained in this insurance.

The cover granted by this clause falls into two parts:

(a) The exclusion (by Clause 4.7 in Institute Cargo Clauses (B) and (C)) of "deliberate damage to or deliberate destruction of the subject-matter insured or any part thereof by the wrongful act of any person or persons" is deleted and
(b) positive cover is granted against loss or damage caused by "malicious acts vandalism or sabotage".

It will be appreciated that the extension of cover granted by this clause will benefit an assured whose goods are covered under restricted conditions but such extension will not be required when the goods are insured under "all risks" conditions.

A malicious act is one performed out of spite or ill-will, or something of the like. By that definition, vandalism and sabotage are merely examples of malicious acts.

Coverage against loss or damage caused by persons acting maliciously used to be provided by the Institute Strikes Clauses, but this is now not the case so far as cargo is concerned. See Part VI, pages 297 to 298. Instead, the current

Institute Strikes Clauses (Cargo) provides cover for loss or damage caused by "any terrorist or any person acting from a political motive", but this is not the same thing at all. Consequently, unless the assured has an "all risks" marine policy, he will need, in addition to the Institute War Clauses (Cargo) and the Institute Strikes Clauses (Cargo), the Institute Malicious Damage Clause to provide himself with all-round cover.

B. INSTITUTE THEFT, PILFERAGE AND NON-DELIVERY CLAUSE (For use only with Institute Clauses) (1/12/83)

In consideration of an additional premium, it is hereby agreed that this insurance covers loss of or damage to the subject-matter insured caused by theft or pilferage, or by non-delivery of an entire package, subject always to the exclusions contained in this insurance.

Once again, this additional clause will not be required by an assured who has taken out a policy on "all risks" conditions.

It is something of an open question whether three separate risks are covered by this clause, or whether they are merely three different species of the same genus. In *Middows Ltd.* v. *Robertson*,[58] Hilbery J. was invited at first instance to consider the non-delivery of a full cargo by reason of the carrying ship being diverted by order of the government in time of war. The insurance included a typed clause covering "damage by hook, oil, sweat, heat, fresh water and other cargo (liquid or solid), theft, pilferage and non-delivery". The judge said:

> "These general words 'non-delivery' following enumerated perils insured against cannot be divorced from what has gone before and treated as intended to denominate an entirely new risk. They are limited by the context in which they are found. Such words in such a context are to be construed not as creating a new or further risk but affecting the burden of proof. Where such words occur in such a context the insured need not prove loss by theft or pilferage; it is enough if he proves non-delivery and gives prima facie proof that the goods were not lost in any other way than by theft or pilferage. . . . The case I am deciding . . . is not a case which on its facts has anything to do with 'non-delivery' when those words are applied in the context in which they occur."

In the opinion of the editor, the context of the words "by theft or pilferage, or by non-delivery of an entire package" do not *by their context*, have to be construed *ejusdem generis*. On the contrary, it is considered that there are really two separate perils insured: (1) theft or pilferage, and, quite separately, (2) non-delivery of an entire package. This construction is supported by the comma which appears after the word "pilferage", and by the repetition of the words "or by" before "non-delivery".

"theft or pilferage"

In *Nishina Trading Co.* v. *Chiyoda Fire & Marine Insurance Co.*,[59] shipowners, in the erroneous belief that they had a valid lien on the cargo for arrears of

58. At first instance, (1940) 67 Ll.L.Rep. 484.
59. [1969] 1 Lloyd's Rep. 293, *per* Lord Denning M.R. at p. 298.

time-charter hire due to them from the time charterers, landed the goods at an intermediate port on the voyage and sold them there. Lord Denning M.R. said:

> "was there a 'theft' of cargo by the master? The word 'theft' is not used here in the strict sense of the criminal law. It does not bring in all the eccentricities of the law of larceny. It means only what an ordinary commercial man would consider to be theft: and before finding theft, the Court should be satisfied that it is an appropriate description of what took place. The Court need not be satisfied beyond reasonable doubt (as in the criminal law) but it should find on balance that there is sufficient to warrant the serious imputation of 'theft' ."

It was held by the Court of Appeal that the shipowners' action did not amount to theft.

"Pilferage" is a species of theft performed surreptitiously.

"non-delivery of an entire package"

Many cargo assured are under the impression that the inclusion of this risk in their policy entitles them to claim for any loss (of an entire package) which has occurred at any time, and from any cause, during the voyage. This is not so, as the following examples should make clear:

(a) A case of fireworks is short delivered at destination, and the carrier explains that it was seized by the Customs authorities at an intermediate port, as they considered it to be hazardous cargo. This is not a loss by non-delivery; it is a loss by "seizure", which is an excluded peril (Clause 6.2 of Institute Cargo Clauses).

(b) A case of fireworks is short delivered, but this time the carrier explains that the master ordered the case to be thrown overboard, since he considered it to be a danger to the other cargo on board. This is not a loss by non-delivery; it is a loss by jettison, and unless there was wilful misconduct on the part of the assured in shipping the fireworks, or in misdescribing them, there will be a claim under Institute Cargo Clauses without the addition of the Theft, Pilferage and Non-Delivery Clause.

(c) One package is short delivered and, after inquiry, the carrier "regrets that it may have been delivered to another consignee by mistake". This is a non-delivery as regards the bill of lading holder and, subject to his holding the carrier responsible as he is required to do by Clause 16.2 of the Institute Cargo Clauses, he will have a valid claim under the Institute Theft, Pilferage and Non-Delivery Clause.

(d) A case is short delivered and, after inquiry, it appears to have been over-carried to another port, and the ship's agent claims that he does not know what to do with it. In this case, although there has been a "non-delivery" in the ordinary sense of that word, there is no loss to the subject-matter insured, which is perfectly safe and sound. In fact it is the carrier's duty to ship it back at his own expense to the port to which it was consigned and there tender it to the bill of lading holder.

(e) A case is short delivered and, after inquiry, no one can offer any plausible explanation for its disappearance. This is a loss by non-delivery, in circumstances which suggest that the package may have been stolen, although there is insufficient evidence to prove it. This is the case where the cause of the loss is *ejusdem generis* with theft or pilferage, so whatever construction might be required of the words in the clause, the loss will be paid for by the underwriters.

C. INSTITUTE REPLACEMENT CLAUSE (1/1/34)

In the event of loss of or damage to any part or parts of an insured machine caused by a peril covered by the Policy the sum recoverable shall not exceed the cost of replacement or repair of such part or parts plus charges for forwarding and refitting, if incurred, but excluding duty unless the full duty is included in the amount insured, in which case loss, if any, sustained by payment of additional duty shall also be recoverable.

Provided always that in no case shall the liability of Underwriters exceed the insured value of the complete machine.

As will be appreciated from the date when this clause was first issued, the Institute Replacement Clause was not one of the new forms introduced as a result of the 1982 revolution; on the contrary, it has been in use for a considerable period of time. The object of the clause is to reduce the area of uncertainty and, one might add, contumely, in the event of an insured machine having suffered a partial loss by reason by sustaining loss or damage to one or more of its parts. This the clause achieves by substituting a measure of indemnity based upon the cost of repairs for one calculated by applying to the insured or insurable value the proportion of the loss established by the difference between the gross sound and damaged values at destination.[60]

Before the introduction of the Institute Replacement Clause, and even now when the Clause is not included in the policy conditions, it was (and is) the practice to limit the claim to the cost of replacement or repair (without reference to the insured value) when undertaken at an intermediate port during the voyage, this being consistent with the treatment in practice of reconditioning charges at such a port or place. To this extent the Institute Replacement Clause breaks new ground only as regards the measure of indemnity when the lost or damaged part(s) are replaced or repaired at the port of destination.

It is to be noticed that the Institute Replacement Clause can cut both ways. On the one side, the underwriters cannot complain if an assured has good reason to assert that his machine cannot be adequately repaired, i.e. placed in the same good condition as it was before the casualty, with anything less than a full replacement of the damaged part(s); on the other, an assured cannot claim that his machine has depreciated in value to an extent greater than the cost of repairing it.

60. See Marine Insurance Act 1906, s. 71(3).

Having said that, it has also to be borne in mind that the Institute Replacement Clause does not apply in a case where the assured has good grounds to claim for a total loss on account of the subject-matter ceasing "to be a thing of the kind insured".[61] In such a case, the subject-matter is said to have "lost its specie". That this can happen with manufactured goods, just as it can with commodities, is demonstrated by *Berger* v. *Pollock*,[62] in which second-hand industrial moulds, by reason of damage sustained on the voyage, could no longer be used for their intended purpose. Thus, in a case of substantial damage to a new ship's engine intended for fitting into a newbuilding (and so described in the policy of insurance), if the shipbuilder to whom it was consigned should be entitled to reject it even if repaired, the engine would no longer be a "thing of the kind insured", and the assured could claim for an actual total loss (less proceeds, of course, as scrap or for reconstruction as a second-hand engine).[63]

61. Marine Insurance Act 1906, s. 57(1).
62. *Berger* v. *Pollock* [1973] 2 Lloyd's Rep. 442.
63. This statement is based upon an actual case, so settled.

PART III

MARINE HULL FORMS

1. HISTORICAL PERSPECTIVE

Insurance for merchant adventurers and container operators

Lloyd's S.G. form catered for the merchant adventurer. The same form of policy was available to cover both the ship and the goods which the merchant adventurer—very often the owner or the master of the ship—had purchased or contracted to carry to distant parts of the world. On disposal of the outward cargoes at destination, the merchant adventurer would reckon to have the means, perhaps with something in hand, to purchase a homeward cargo, from the sale of which he would expect to be able to pay off his crew, refit and reprovision his ship and still be able to show a profit for himself and his co-adventurers.

For such an adventure a policy of insurance expressed to apply to a round voyage "out and home" was entirely adequate. Sometimes the voyage was a three-legged one, for example, from Plymouth to West Africa with home-produced produce, thence with a cargo of slaves to Barbados, and from there to the ship's home port with a cargo of sugar and rum.

If, during the course of such a voyage, the ship sustained damage by insured perils, it would not be possible to make an account of the same until she arrived back in her home port. No doubt the Master kept a careful note of any expenditure which he had had to incur for any repairs which had to be done at any of the outports, but since he had no means of presenting these bills to the underwriters until his return home, his account could not be presented until he had safely completed the voyage, at which time he would be able to call in shipwrights upon whose competence he could rely to make good any damage which the ship had sustained since leaving her home port many months before.

We have already noted that the "Memorandum" at the foot of Lloyd's form of policy stated that the ship and freight were "warranted free from Average under three per cent, unless general, or the ship be stranded". For the practical reasons which we have noted above, particular average losses occurring during the voyage were necessarily added together in order to ascertain whether the total cost of making good the damage exceeded the warranty percentage or not, and the practice of so doing was approved in the case of *Blackett* v. *Royal Exchange Assurance* in 1832.

With the expansion of commerce, ships began to engage upon regular liner trades, and also ventured further and wider in seeking cargoes. Hence the development of insurances on ship and freight, expressed not for a voyage, but for a period of time—usually 12 months. The question then arose—over what period could particular average losses occurring during the currency of a time policy be aggregated in order to ascertain whether the memorandum percentage had been attained? It was not until *Stewart* v. *Merchants' Marine Insurance Co.* (1885) that this question was answered. The Court of Appeal held that, although the policy was for a period of time, the aggregation of losses, for the purpose of ascertaining whether the stipulated percentage had been attained, should be limited, as in the case of a voyage policy, to those which had been sustained in the course of a round voyage. More or less simultaneously, the practice grew up of including a "voyage clause" in policies of insurance for time, whereby (as in the 1903 Time Clauses), "the warranty and conditions as to average under three per cent to be applicable to each voyage as if separately insured", and there followed detailed provisions as to how each voyage should be made up.

In the old days, the process of adjustment was fairly straightforward. There was but one custom of universal application, and that was that one-third was to be deducted from the cost of all repairs (unless the ship was engaged upon her first voyage), so as to protect the underwriter from having to pay any element of betterment or "improvement" in the value of the ship, by reason of replacing old material with new. With the advent of iron hulls, this practice (although, in the meantime, approved by the courts in *Aitchison* v. *Lohre* in 1879) ceased to be equitable, and in consequence underwriters began to insert in their policies of insurance a clause providing: "Average payable without deduction of thirds new for old, whether the average be particular or general".

As to liabilities, it was decided as long ago as 1836 in *De Vaux* v. *Salvador* that an underwriter on Lloyd's form of policy was not liable to indemnify a shipowner for the amount which he had been found liable to pay to another vessel in consequence of collision. As Lord Denman expressed it, "the obligation to pay was neither a necessary nor a proximate effect of perils of the sea, but growing out of an arbitrary provision of the law of nations". Yet within a few years, underwriters found it expedient to include a special clause in their policies, whereby in addition to any other claims which might be paid thereon up to the amount insured, they would indemnify their assured for three-fourths of such liabilities.

In yet another area underwriters were extremely prompt to close a gap exposed by the courts in the cover which they granted under traditional policy forms. In the well-known case of *The "Inchmaree" (Hamilton* v. *Thames and*

Mersey Marine Insurance Company) the underwriters agreed that the facts should be put up for consideration as a "test case" which was eventually decided by the House of Lords in 1887. The facts were that a rupture in an air-chamber in a donkey pump occurred through the negligence of engineers in failing to open the valve connecting the water-chamber with the boilers when the pump was put into operation. The House of Lords held that this could not be considered as the consequence of a peril of the sea or any cause *ejusdem generis* therewith. The immediate effect of this decision was the incorporation in policies of insurance of a new clause (thereafter known as the "Inchmaree" Clause) designed to add perils of this nature to those already covered by the traditional form of policy.

One might cite other instances where underwriters have been desirous of supplementing the cover which their policies provide, but instead we have to note that in the twentieth century the trend has been reversed. In particular, since 1969, the relatively generous provisions of the Voyage Clause have been swept away, and in its place, Clause 12 of the Institute Time Clauses, Hulls now provides for a deductible franchise to be applied to the aggregate of all claims arising out of each separate accident or occurrence. A number of other irksome provisions were introduced at the same time, many of which persist in the clauses which we will review hereafter.

2. INSTITUTE TIME CLAUSES, HULLS

Introduction to the Clauses of 1/10/83 and 1/11/95

The Institute Time Clauses, Hulls, 1/10/83 was the first of the modern comprehensive forms issued by the U.K. insurance market for the insurance of ships, all previous issues of Institute Time Clauses, Hulls, having been designed for attachment to Lloyd's S.G. form.[1] From 1/10/83 forward, therefore, we expect to find within the terms of the Institute Time Clauses, Hulls all the conditions which are needful to supplement, and in some instances to vary, the provisions of the Marine Insurance Act 1906.

It might therefore be thought that the terms of Lloyd's S.G. form, having been set aside entirely, were now totally irrelevant to the construction of a policy of marine insurance comprising the MAR form with Institute Time Clauses, Hulls, 1/10/83 or 1/11/95 attached. But this is not the case—at least, not entirely. The provisions of sections 30 and 91(2) of the Marine Insurance Act 1906 provide that:

(a) Certain terms and expressions used in Lloyd's S.G. form shall have the "scope and meaning" assigned to them in the First Schedule to

1. See commentary on the new clauses generally, pp. 2–3.

the Act.[2] Thus when the same expressions appear in the Institute Time Clauses, Hulls, such as, for example "perils of the seas", they must be interpreted in accordance with the Rules for Construction of Policy set out in that Schedule.[3]

(b) The rules of the common law including the law merchant shall continue to apply to contracts of marine insurance.[4]

The Clauses of 1/10/83

The changes made in the 1/10/83 version of Institute Time Clauses, Hulls, were therefore pretty far-reaching and involved a careful re-presentation of some of the basic material previously contained in Lloyd's S.G. form; and in particular:

(a) the "enumerated perils"—now clause 6 of I.T.C. Hulls, and
(b) the "sue and labour" clause—clause 13 of I.T.C. Hulls, 1/10/83 and clause 11 of I.T.C. Hulls, 1/11/95.

If the intention was to reproduce in modern language the effect of the time-honoured phraseology, then we must applaud the draftsmen in their efforts to reproduce the tenor and effect of the old Sue and Labour clause.[5] The re-drafting of the Perils Clause, on the other hand, has introduced two significant changes, one intentional—the omission of the "general words",[6] and the other, perhaps unintentional, affecting the incidence of loss upon consecutive policies of insurance.[7]

The Clauses of 1/11/95

The changes made in 1995 were by no means so far-reaching. Members of the Joint Hull Committee (J.H.C.), in introducing their proposals to prospective customers and marine insurance practitioners, explained that they had been influenced by two different factors:

Changes since 1983 in international maritime law

(1) The International Salvage Convention of 1989 came into effect in England on 1 January 1995.[8] In fact, the most important parts of the Conven-

2. Marine Insurance Act 1906 s. 30(2).
3. For "perils of the seas" see the commentary on Clause 6.1.1 of I.T.C. Hulls on p. 105.
4. Marine Insurance Act 1906, s. 91(2). These sections of the M.I.A. are set out and the subject discussed in more detail under the heading "Construction of the Policy" on p. 7.
5. For commentary on Clause 11 of I.T.C. Hulls, see pp. 131–135.
6. See commentary, p. 102.
7. See commentary, pp. 101–102.
8. Merchant Shipping (Salvage and Pollution) Act 1994.

tion had already been given practical effect by being incorporated into Lloyd's Form of Salvage Agreement 1990 or 1995.

(2) At an International Conference of the Comité Maritime International in 1994 the text of the York-Antwerp Rules had been thoroughly revised and several important changes made to it.

The report of the J.H.C. claimed that the changes which they proposed to make in the Institute Time Clauses, Hulls, 1/11/95 were, in respect to the above, merely of a clarificatory nature. In the commentary which follows we shall be obliged to examine whether this claim was justified.[9]

The decline in standards of ship operation and management

The aim of the J.H.C. in this regard was, according to its report, "to maintain and indeed increase the operational standards of vessel operations". This provided the motivation for two important changes in the Institute Time Clauses, Hulls, 1/11/95:

(1) The introduction as a permanent clause of universal application of the Classification Clause, based upon a similar clause for occasional use only, known as the Joint Hull Classification Clause. This new clause, while not so strict as the one it replaced, sets out fairly onerous duties upon the assured, owners and managers, for example to comply with any recommendations, requirements or restrictions imposed by the Classification Society in relation to the vessel's seaworthiness, and states that any breach thereof (other than as agreed to by the underwriters in writing) shall discharge the underwriters from liability as from the date of the breach.

(2) The extension of the "due diligence" proviso in clause 6.2. Under this proviso underwriters could previously avoid claims arising from the perils enumerated in clause 6.2 if they resulted from want of due diligence by the assured, owners or managers. As re-drafted in 1995, the want of due diligence on the part of a superintendent or any of the "onshore management" will also be fatal to a claim under clause 6.2.

The "Claims Cut-Off" provision

In addition to the above, a new provision was introduced in 1995 to the regular clause (cl. 11 of I.T.C. Hulls, 1/10/83; cl. 13 of I.T.C. Hulls, 1/11/95) relating to the notification of any event likely to result in a claim. The additional wording now requires that the notice must be given to the underwriters within 12 months of the date on which the assured, owners or managers became or should have become aware of the loss or damage, failing which

9. See pp. 126–130.

the underwriters will be automatically discharged from liability for any claim arising from such accident, loss or damage.

Reaction to the Clauses of 1/11/95

Not altogether surprisingly, the reactions of shipowners and market practitioners to the new clauses of 1/11/95 were almost universally unfavourable. There were a few commentators who applauded the boldness of the Joint Hull Committee in tackling head-on the problems associated with inadequate ship management and supervision, but the great majority of shipowners and managers were appalled that London market underwriters should henceforth seek to apply such a restrictive package to all their customers irrespective of their records.

At the time of writing (the summer of 1998) only a small proportion of hull insurances placed on the London insurance market are subject to Institute Time Clauses, Hulls, 1/11/95. Shipowners and managers operating quality tonnage and those with good records (who, after all, form the vast majority) have been able to negotiate their renewals with either the 1/10/83 version of Institute Time Clauses, Hulls, or with the American Institute Hull Clauses. Other shipowners have voted with their feet and have left the London market altogether.

Scheme of the commentary in this edition

In deference to the most recent issue of the Institute Time Clauses, Hulls, the commentary hereafter will follow the sequence of the 1/11/95 version (there having been some slight changes in this respect), but with emphasis supplied to the text in the form of underlining where it differs from the wording of the 1/10/83 version. Most of the observations which follow apply with equal force to both the 1/10/83 and 1/11/95 versions, but where there is something that applies only to the text of 1/11/95, this will be made quite clear.

3. INSTITUTE TIME CLAUSES, HULLS 1/10/83 AND 1/11/95

"This insurance is subject to English law and practice"

When underwriters were revising the Institute Time Clauses, Hulls, culminating in the 1/10/83 clauses, the representatives of the London market were conscious of the possibility that under the legislation of the European Economic Community British insurers could find themselves as defendants in an action before a court in another E.E.C. country, with that judgment being enforceable in the United Kingdom. This, coupled with the fact that the clauses had been drafted in the light of English law and practice and the Marine Insurance Act 1906, led to the inclusion of the above proviso.

However, whilst the clauses were drafted against this backcloth, they were also designed with a view to their adoption by the international insurance and shipping communities, and it was anticipated that they would be attached to foreign policy forms which would incorporate different jurisdiction clauses. Even in these circumstances it is still considered preferable for the above wording to be retained in the clauses so that the appropriate court has the benefit of the wealth of English law and practice on marine insurance, with the added advantage of consistency of interpretation.

The difference between the proper law of the contract and the correct jurisdiction was illustrated in the case of *The "Al Wahab"*[10] which went as far as the House of Lords. In this case neither the plaintiffs nor the defendant insurers were English and the policy had been issued in Kuwait. However, the policy form used was the Lloyd's S.G. form of policy scheduled to the Marine Insurance Act 1906 with the addition of standard Institute Clauses, the whole policy being in English. It was accepted by both sides that in Kuwait at the relevant time there was no indigenous law of marine insurance. The House of Lords held:

(1) It was not possible to interpret the policy or to determine what the mutual legal rights and obligations of the parties were except by reference to the Marine Insurance Act 1906 and its substantive provisions; the English rules of conflict of laws applied and the proper law of the contract embodied in the policy was English law.
(2) In the absence of an indigenous law of marine insurance in Kuwait, English law was the only system of private law by reference to which it was possible for a Kuwaiti court to give a sensible and precise meaning to the language that the parties had chosen to use in the policy.
(3) On the other hand, having no grounds for doubting that justice could be obtained in a Kuwaiti court there was no justification for compelling the defendants to submit to the jurisdiction of the English court.

Clause 1—Navigation

1 NAVIGATION

1.1 The Vessel is covered subject to the provisions of this insurance at all times and has leave to sail or navigate with or without pilots, to go on trial trips and to assist and tow vessels or craft in distress, but it is warranted that the Vessel shall not be towed, except as is customary or to the first safe port or place when in need of assistance, or undertake towage or salvage services under a contract previously arranged by the Assured and/or Owners and/or Managers and/or Charterers. This clause 1.1 shall not exclude customary towage in connection with loading and discharging.

The clause makes it clear that the vessel is covered at all times, including while sailing or navigating with or without pilots, undertaking trial trips and rendering assistance to other vessels or craft in distress. However, it is warranted that

10. [1983] 2 Lloyd's Rep. 365.

the vessel shall not be towed, except when in need of assistance, and then only to the first safe port or place. As to what is the first safe port or place, it is submitted that this has to be construed in the light of all the facts, and the "first safe port" may not necessarily be the nearest in mileage terms and should be construed as that port which, on the whole and in the actual circumstances, is the fittest place for receiving the ship in the light of the repair and other facilities required. The clause makes it clear that the warranty does not exclude "customary" towage, for example in or out of a port or dock or in connection with loading and discharging. The clause further warrants that the vessel will not undertake towage or salvage services under a prearranged contract.

1.2 This insurance shall not be prejudiced by reason of the Assured entering into any contract with pilots or for customary towage which limits or exempts the liability of the pilots and/or tugs and/or towboats and/or their owners when the Assured or their agents accept or are compelled to accept such contracts in accordance with established local law or practice.

1.3 The practice of engaging helicopters for the transportation of personnel, supplies and equipment to and/or from the Vessel shall not prejudice this insurance.

Both these clauses were new in 1995, although permissive clauses in similar terms were frequently inserted at the request of the assured or their brokers. It is of course well known that ship masters and ships' agents have generally no option but to accede to contracts for the engagement of pilots, tugs and helicopter services on terms which exempt or limit the liability of the service providers. The effect of entering into such contracts is to extinguish or curtail underwriters' subrogative rights, and these new sub-clauses are therefore to be welcomed since they make it clear that the position of the assured will not be prejudiced by reason of their acceptance of such contract terms.

1.4 In the event of the Vessel being employed in trading operations which entail cargo loading or discharging at sea from or into another vessel (not being a harbour or inshore craft) no claim shall be recoverable under this insurance for loss of or damage to the Vessel or liability to any other vessel arising from such loading or discharging operations, including whilst approaching, lying alongside and leaving, unless previous notice that the Vessel is to be employed in such operations has been given to the Underwriters and any amended terms of cover and any additional premium required by them have been agreed.

This clause, previously known unofficially as the "Mothership Clause", was introduced into the I.T.C. in 1969, and has continued to appear in all subsequent versions with only slight amendment. With the development of larger vessels which because of draft restrictions could not obtain entry to many ports, transhipment operations into smaller vessels became increasingly commonplace and underwriters began to experience correspondingly heavier claims resulting from ranging damage, collisions and contacts. There were also many practical problems in the adjustment of claims, the main difficulty being to assess the number of deductibles to be applied, for example, after a lengthy transhipment operation involving several other vessels, intermittently bad weather, with various minor collisions and periods of ranging having been logged.

The clause stipulates that if cover is required for cargo loading or discharging operations at sea from or into another vessel, previous notice must be given to underwriters and any amended terms of cover and any additional premium agreed. In the absence of such prior agreement, not only would any loss or damage sustained by the insured vessel as a result of the cargo operations (including whilst approaching, lying alongside and leaving) not be covered, but any liability to any other vessel arising from such operations would also be excluded. It should be noted that the clause only relates to employment of the vessel in "trading operations" and does not relate to emergency operations following a casualty, for example, jettison or transhipment/lightening of a stranded vessel. The clause is not intended to deal with the more routine and generally safer operations undertaken in port and consequently any claims arising from loading or discharging cargo, as customary, into harbour or inshore craft, even when undertaken at sea, are not excluded by the clause.

In practice, upon receiving prior notification of a cargo operation falling within this clause, underwriters will frequently suggest that the cover be amended to include one larger deductible, to be applied to the aggregate of all claims arising out of the whole cargo operation, with the payment of an additional premium where considered necessary. It is accordingly essential for any shipowner considering taking up a charter involving cargo operations of this kind to contact his broker to ensure that he is covered for the same and also to obtain details of the additional premium payable which will assist him in forecasting the likely profitability of the fixture.

1.5 In the event of the Vessel sailing (with or without cargo) with an intention of being (a) broken up, or (b) sold for breaking up, any claim for loss of or damage to the Vessel occurring subsequent to such sailing shall be limited to the market value of the Vessel as scrap at the time when the loss or damage is sustained, unless previous notice has been given to the Underwriters and any amendments to the terms of cover, insured value and premium required by them have been agreed. Nothing in this Clause 1.5 shall affect claims under Clauses 8 and/or 10.

First introduced in October 1983, this clause deals with the situation when the vessel sails with the intention of being broken up or sold for breaking up. In such circumstances the clause stipulates that, in the absence of prior notice having been given to underwriters and other terms having been agreed, any claim for loss of or damage to the vessel occurring subsequent to such sailing will be limited to the market value of the vessel as scrap at the time when the loss or damage is sustained. The clause expressly has no effect upon claims for collision liability or general average and salvage.

In the opinion of the editor this is one of the least satisfactory clauses in the I.T.C. A shipowner may well take up a charter which will leave the vessel in the area of one of the major scrapping centres. The shipowner may also have at the back of his mind the possibility of selling the vessel for scrap, depending upon several variable factors, such as the levels of scrap prices and freight rates. In such circumstances, when the vessel sails under the charter is she sailing with the intention of being broken up or being sold for breaking up? What is "the market value of the vessel as scrap at the time when the loss or damage is sustained" if a vessel sinks between two major scrapping centres, with widely disparate price levels? Common sense dictates that it should be the centre in the direction of which the vessel was proceeding at the time of the total loss even if at the time of the loss she is closer geographically to another centre. The abrogation of the agreed value when the clause is invoked could place a shipowner in breach of the insurance requirements laid down in his mortgage deed and great care needs to be exercised when undertaking any voyage which could be construed as falling within the terms of this clause.

Clause 2—Continuation

The 1995 wording is:

2 **CONTINUATION**
Should the Vessel at the expiration of this insurance be at sea and in distress or missing, she shall, provided notice be given to the Underwriters prior to the expiration of this insurance, be held covered until arrival at the next port in good safety, or if in port and in distress until the Vessel is made safe, at a pro rata monthly premium.

In 1983 and previously, the clause read:

2 **CONTINUATION**
Should the Vessel at the expiration of this insurance be at sea or in distress or at a port of refuge or of call, she shall, provided previous notice be given to the Underwriters, be held covered at a pro rata monthly premium to her port of destination.

The 1995 version of this clause introduces two restrictions upon the liberty previously available to the assured under the 1/10/83 and earlier versions of the I.T.C.H., whereby in fairly wide circumstances the ship could be held covered at a *pro rata* monthly premium under the terms of the existing hull policy from the date of its expiry until arrival of the ship at her port of destination. The new restrictions are:

(1) In order for the liberty to be available, the vessel must be missing at sea or in distress, either at sea or in port, at the time when the policy expires. Furthermore, since it is required that the assured gives previous notice to the underwriters, the vessel must *ex hypothesi* be missing or in distress at the time when the notice was given.

(2) Provided that notice is properly and timely given, the period for which the vessel will be held covered at a *pro rata* monthly premium will expire upon her arrival, if at sea, at the next port in good safety; or if in port, at the time she is made safe.

"in good safety"

This seemingly simple phrase has had a chequered history. It dates back to the days of Lloyd's S.G. form, when the duration of the insured risk was defined in terms of the ship's voyage, which continued not merely until arrival at the port of destination, but further "*upon the said ship, &c., until she hath moored at anchor twenty-four hours in good safety*".

Taking the old authorities[11] as our guide, a ship would not be considered to have arrived "in good safety" if she was so badly damaged on arrival that she could only be kept afloat by mooring her to a hulk, or if by reason of an existing embargo, she would be subject to seizure or confiscation as soon as she arrived.

Clause 3—Breach of Warranty

3 **BREACH OF WARRANTY**
Held covered in case of any breach of warranty as to cargo, trade, locality, towage, salvage services or date of sailing, provided notice be given to the Underwriters immediately after receipt of advices and any amended terms of cover and any additional premium required by them be agreed.

Other clauses contain various warranties and this clause provides for the breach of certain specified warranties to be held covered, subject to notice being given to underwriters immediately after receipt of advices and any amended terms and additional premium being agreed. It is important to note that only breaches of certain specified warranties are held covered and if the policy incorporates additional warranties, their breach may not be held covered under this clause.

There was no change in this clause in 1995.

Clause 4—Classification

4 **CLASSIFICATION**

4.1 It is the duty of the Assured, Owners and Managers at the inception of and throughout the period of this insurance to ensure that

4.1.1 the Vessel is classed with a Classification Society agreed by the Underwriters and that her class within that Society is maintained,

4.1.2 any recommendations requirements or restrictions imposed by the Vessel's Classification Society which relate to the Vessel's seaworthiness or to her maintenance in a seaworthy condition are complied with by the dates required by that Society.

4.2 In the event of any breach of the duties set out in Clause 4.1 above, unless the Underwriters agree to the contrary in writing, they will be discharged from liability under this insurance as from the date of the breach provided that if the Vessel is at sea at such date the Underwriters' discharge from liability is deferred until arrival at her next port.

4.3 Any incident condition or damage in respect of which the Vessel's Classification Society might make recommendations as to repairs or other action to be taken by the Assured, Owners or Managers must be promptly reported to the Classification Society.

4.4 Should the Underwriters wish to approach the Classification Society directly for information and/or documents, the Assured will provide the necessary authorization.

This clause was entirely new in 1995, at least so far as the Institute Time Clauses, Hulls, is concerned. By including it in the 1/11/95 form underwriters manifested their intention to place a duty on all assured to maintain their ships in a classification society and to comply with the "recommendations, requirements or restrictions" of that society. In so doing the London market wished to demonstrate their support for the efforts being made by the I.M.O. and the

11. *Shawe* v. *Felton* (1801) 2 East 109 (physical safety), *Minett* v. *Anderson* (1794) Peake N.P.R. 277 (political safety) and other cases cited in *Arnould* ss. 552/4.

International Association of Classification Societies to improve the standards of safety in shipping.

The clause was based upon the Joint Hull Classification Clause, which had previously been imposed by underwriters only on a limited number of assured who were felt by underwriters to be operating old and/or sub-standard tonnage. Now it was intended that all owners and operators should toe the line.

There are two major duties, and one of lesser importance, imposed by the clause on all "Assured, Owners and Managers". The duties of serious importance are:

— by sub-clause 4.1.1 to maintain the vessel at all times in a classification society approved by the underwriters, and
— by sub-clause 4.1.2 to comply with any "recommendations requirements or restrictions" imposed by that society in relation to the vessel's seaworthiness, and to do so within the time scale set by that society.

In the event of failure on the part of any of the assured, owners or managers to comply with either of these duties, the underwriters by sub-clause 4.2 have the right to treat the breach of duty as if it were a breach of a warranty,[12] i.e. to consider themselves to be discharged from all liability under the policy as from the time of the breach. However, they may relent, if advised by the assured in good time, in which case, as indicated in the wording of the clause, they may give their consent in writing to the situation which has arisen.

It is important to note, as has already been stated on underwriters' behalf, that in the event of a breach of either of these duties in relation to a ship insured on a fleet policy, the underwriters will consider themselves to be discharged from liability only in regard to that particular vessel, provided that there is a stipulation in the policy that each vessel is deemed to be a separate insurance.

The obligation of lesser importance is contained in sub-clause 4.3. which is to report promptly to the classification society any "incident condition or damage" in respect of which the society *might* make recommendations as to repairs or other action to be taken by the assured. The wording of this sub-clause is quite clearly unsatisfactory, probably in consequence of being drafted too hastily, without adequate consultation. By what criterion, for example, should it be inferred that a particular classification society *might* make a certain recommendation? In all cases where it has the power to make that recommendation?—or only in such cases where past experience indicates a likelihood?—or a probability?—that such and such a course of action will be recommended? Perhaps in the case of this sub-clause the lack of precision does not matter too much, since no sanction is provided in the event of non-

12. See Marine Insurance Act 1906, s. 33(3).

compliance by the assured. The present editor is left with the impression that the great majority of owners and managers will effectively comply with this sub-clause since it has always been their practice to inform the classification society of events which may affect the vessel's tradeworthiness, and to follow their recommendations, because that is the sensible and proper course to take.

Clause 5—Termination

5 **TERMINATION**

This Clause 5 shall prevail notwithstanding any provision whether written typed or printed in this insurance inconsistent therewith.

Unless the Underwriters agree to the contrary in writing, this insurance shall terminate automatically at the time of

5.1 change of the Classification Society of the Vessel, or change, suspension, discontinuance, withdrawal or expiry of her Class therein, or any of the Classification Society's periodic surveys becoming overdue unless an extension of time for such survey be agreed by the Classification Society, provided that if the Vessel is at sea such automatic termination shall be deferred until arrival at her next port. However where such change, suspension, discontinuance or withdrawal of her Class or where a periodic survey becoming overdue has resulted from loss or damage covered by Clause 6 of this insurance or which would be covered by an insurance of the Vessel subject to current Institute War and Strikes Clauses Hulls—Time such automatic termination shall only operate should the Vessel sail from her next port without the prior approval of the Classification Society or in the case of a periodic survey becoming overdue without the Classification Society having agreed an extension of time for such survey.

5.2 any change, voluntary or otherwise, in the ownership or flag, transfer to new management, or charter on a bareboat basis, or requisition for title or use of the Vessel, provided that, if the Vessel has cargo on board and has already sailed from her loading port or is at sea in ballast, such automatic termination shall if required be deferred, whilst the Vessel continues her planned voyage, until arrival at final port of discharge if with cargo or at port of destination if in ballast. However, in the event of requisition for title or use without the prior execution of a written agreement by the Assured, such automatic termination shall occur fifteen days after such requisition whether the Vessel is at sea or in port.

A pro rata daily net return of premium shall be made provided that a total loss of the Vessel, whether by insured perils or otherwise, has not occurred during the period covered by this insurance or any extension thereof.

In the 1/10/83 form this was Clause 4. The rubric printed in bold type is common to both sets of clauses and is intended to emphasise that this is akin to a Clause Paramount which will prevail notwithstanding anything in the policy to the contrary.

The clause provides that unless the underwriters have given their agreement in writing to maintain coverage, the insurance will automatically terminate in the event of either of two sets of circumstances. These are:

(1) Under the 1/10/83 clause 4.1 (now 5.1 under the 1/11/95 form):
- — a change of classification society, or any change, suspension, discontinuance, withdrawal or expiry of the vessel's class.

  Under the 1/11/95 form the terminating circumstances in Clause 5.1 have been extended to include overdue class surveys.

(2) Under both the 1/10/83 and 1/11/95 forms:
- — any change in ownership, flag, management, bareboat charter or requisition (whether for title or use).

Let us consider each of these sets of circumstances in a little more detail.

Clause 5.1—Change of classification society, etc.

At the time this clause was introduced, underwriters were concerned at the difference in the standards of maintenance acceptable to different classification societies; hence the importance to underwriters of the standing of the classification society in which the vessel is entered. Given the importance of the status of the vessel's classification at the time of proposal for insurance, it will be appreciated that if the vessel is allowed to fall out of classification during the currency of the policy, this would constitute an unacceptable variation of the risk.

It might be thought that under the 1/11/95 form, this Clause 5.1 had become largely pointless by reason of the more precise obligations imposed upon the assured under the new Classification Clause (Clause 4 of the I.T.C.H. 1/11/95), but London market underwriters stand convinced that this Clause 5.1 remains an essential weapon in their fight against sub-standard ship operators.

"change, suspension, discontinuance, withdrawal or expiry of her Class"

Although this precise wording has yet to be considered by an English court, a rather similar form of words was considered in the case of *The "Caribbean Sea"*.[13] In that case the vessel was insured with the American Institute Hull Clauses which provided that the policy would automatically terminate "if the Classification Society of the Vessel or her class therein be changed, cancelled or withdrawn". By the regulations of the Bureau Veritas, with which the vessel was classed, it was laid down that in the event of grounding the ship's classification certificate "loses its validity". The vessel had grounded but the Master had failed to inform the Bureau Veritas prior to the loss of the vessel from another cause. The underwriters raised this by way of defence, arguing that the policy had automatically terminated from the time of the grounding. Robert Goff J. held that the "loss of validity" of the classification certificate did not amount to a withdrawal of class.

This case to some extent alleviated the anxieties of a number of shipowners who had expressed concern at the form of Classification Clause then under discussion, and prior to the coming into effect of the I.T.C.H. 1/10/83, the rather drastic effect of the clause was further ameliorated in an effort to allay anxiety, but only in certain circumstances, viz.:

(a) If the event which triggers automatic termination occurs while the vessel is at sea, termination is deferred until arrival at her next port.

(b) If the cause of the alteration in the vessel's classification status is a

13. *Prudent Tankers Ltd. S.A.* v. *Dominion Insurance Co. (The "Caribbean Sea")* [1980] 1 Lloyd's Rep. 338.

result of damage covered by Clause 6 of the I.T.C., or under the current War and Strikes Clauses, the automatic termination only operates if the vessel sails from her next port without the prior approval of the classification society, or if a periodic survey has become overdue, without an extension of time having been agreed by the classification society.

It is interesting to note that the amelioration mentioned in (b) is only in respect of loss or damage covered by Clause 6 of the I.T.C., and not all loss or damage covered by the marine policy. Strictly speaking any change in the classification status brought about by damage covered by a supplementary clause, such as the Institute Additional Perils Clauses—Hulls, would result in automatic termination, but the editor would be extremely surprised if underwriters ever took this point. However, to be on the safe side, shipowners would be well advised to notify their underwriters of any such change.

Under the rules of certain classification societies there is provision for retrospective cancellation of class and in such circumstances the insurance could be deemed to be terminated automatically from the retrospective date of such suspension.

Clause 5.2—Change of ownership, flag, management, etc.

This deals with change of ownership, transfer to new management, change of flag, charter on a bare-boat basis, or requisition for title or use. The insurance terminates automatically at the time of any of these changes, unless underwriters have given their written agreement to the contrary. Once again the effect of the clause is ameliorated in certain circumstances, namely:

(a) If the vessel has commenced a cargo passage or is at sea in ballast, termination can be deferred, while the vessel continues her planned voyage, until arrival at her final port of discharge, or port of destination if in ballast. Such deferment continues only while the vessel is proceeding on her planned voyage so that if following requisition, the vessel is ordered on a different voyage, cover terminates automatically from the time of deviation from the original voyage.

(b) If the requisition was without the prior execution of a written agreement by the assured, the automatic termination is deferred until 15 days after the requisition.

It is only chartering the vessel on a bare-boat basis which is mentioned in the clause and time or voyage charters do not affect the cover.

It should be emphasised that it is any change, voluntary or otherwise, in the specified areas which can invoke automatic termination so that the action of a mortgagee bank, for example, in foreclosing and transferring the management, against the wishes of the assured, would give rise to automatic termination unless underwriters' written agreement to continue cover is obtained.

The American Institute Hull Clauses (2 June 1977) expressly state that the term "new management" refers only to the transfer of the management of the vessel from one form or corporation to another, and does not apply to internal changes within the offices of the assured. The drafters of the I.T.C. were advised that such clarification was unnecessary and this is why there is no equivalent wording in the I.T.C., although the construction of the term should be the same.

Finally, the clause provides for a pro rata daily net return of premium in the event of automatic termination of the cover, unless (under the 1/11/95 form) there has been a total loss of the vessel, whether caused by an insured peril or not, during the currency of the policy.

Clause 6—Perils

6 **PERILS**

6.1 This insurance covers loss of or damage to the subject-matter insured caused by
6.1.1 perils of the seas rivers lakes or other navigable waters
6.1.2 fire, explosion
6.1.3 violent theft by persons from outside the Vessel
6.1.4 jettison
6.1.5 piracy
6.1.6 contact with land conveyance, dock or harbour equipment or installation
6.1.7 earthquake volcanic eruption or lightning
6.1.8 accidents in loading discharging or shifting cargo or fuel.
6.2 This insurance covers loss of or damage to the subject-matter insured caused by
6.2.1 bursting of boilers breakage of shafts or any latent defect in the machinery or hull
6.2.2 negligence of Master Officers Crew or Pilots
6.2.3 negligence of repairers or charterers provided such repairers or charterers are not an Assured hereunder
6.2.4 barratry of Master Officers or Crew
6.2.5 contact with aircraft, helicopters or similar objects, or objects falling therefrom
provided that such loss or damage has not resulted from want of due diligence by the Assured, Owners, Managers or Superintendents or any of their onshore management.
6.3 Master Officers Crew or Pilots not to be considered Owners within the meaning of this Clause 6 should they hold shares in the Vessel.

The 1/11/95 wording set out above differs only slightly from the 1/10/83 text, which was as follows:

6 **PERILS**

6.1 This insurance covers loss of or damage to the subject-matter insured caused by
6.1.1 perils of the seas rivers lakes or other navigable waters
6.1.2 fire, explosion
6.1.3 violent theft by persons from outside the Vessel
6.1.4 jettison
6.1.5 piracy
6.1.6 breakdown of or accident to nuclear installations or reactors
6.1.7 contact with aircraft or similar objects, or objects falling therefrom, land conveyance, dock or harbour equipment or installation
6.1.8 earthquake volcanic eruption or lightning.
6.2 This insurance covers loss of or damage to the subject-matter insured caused by
6.2.1 accidents in loading discharging or shifting cargo or fuel
6.2.2 bursting of boilers breakage of shafts or any latent defect in the machinery or hull
6.2.3 negligence of Master Officers Crew or Pilots
6.2.4 negligence of repairers or charterers provided such repairers or charterers are not an Assured hereunder
6.2.5 barratry of Master Officers or Crew,
provided such loss or damage has not resulted from want of due diligence by the Assured, Owners or Managers

6.3 Master Officers Crew or Pilots not to be considered Owners within the meaning of this Clause 6 should they hold shares in the Vessel.

The differences between the 1/10/83 and 1/11/95 versions, although slight, are nevertheless sufficiently significant to be referred to in the commentary which follows. Particularly important, however, is the addition of "Superintendents" and "onshore management" to the list of persons whose exercise of "due diligence" is critical to the establishment of a claim for loss or damage caused by a peril under sub-clause 6.2.[14]

Consequences of the abolition of the traditional wording in Lloyd's S.G. form

The "adventures and perils" which, by Lloyd's S.G. form, the assurers were contented to bear and take upon themselves were:

> " . . . of the seas, men of war, fire, enemies, pirates, rovers, thieves, jettisons, letters of mart and countermart, surprisals, takings at sea, arrests, restraints and detainments of all kings, princes and people, of what nation, condition or quality soever, barratry of the master and mariners, and of all other perils, losses, and misfortunes, that have or shall come to the hurt, detriment, or damage of the said goods and merchandises, and ship, etc., or any part thereof."

Prior to 1983, the current version of Institute Time Clauses, Hulls was physically attached to Lloyd's S.G. form, and consequently it was not necessary to mention the traditional perils within the text of the I.T.C. On the other hand, it *was* necessary to mention a certain number of additional perils which had been added to the standard policy conditions in the late nineteenth century, following the famous case of *The "Inchmaree"*.[15] The additional cover so provided was introduced by such words as: "This insurance includes loss of or damage to the subject-matter insured directly caused by:—" followed by a list of the additional perils.[16]

One of the prime objects of the 1982/83 re-draft of the Institute Clauses was to consign Lloyd's S.G. form to the dustbin of history. This had two significant consequences so far as the named perils are concerned; one intentional and the other probably unintentional.

Let us consider the unintentional consequence first.

1. Incidence of loss under the policies

"This insurance covers loss of or damage to the subject-matter insured"

As we have seen, under the S.G. policy form with the previous editions of the I.T.C. attached, it was necessary to differentiate between:

14. See commentary on pp. 114–118.

15. *Hamilton, Fraser & Co.* v. *Thames & Mersey Ins. Co. (The "Inchmaree")* (1887) 6 Asp.M.L.C. 200; see commentary on pp. 108–109.

16. e.g. I.T.C. Hulls 1/10/70, Cl. 7.

(1) A claim under the body of the policy where the perils were covered *per se*, and
(2) the Inchmaree Clause contained in the I.T.C. where it was the "loss or damage" caused by the enumerated additional perils which was covered.

Some examples may illustrate the position.

If a vessel struck a submerged object two days before a change in policies but did not actually sink until after the next set of policies had incepted, the claim, which arose from a basic peril in the body of the policy (perils of the seas), would have fallen on the first set of policies which were current when the peril operated.

The incidence upon the policies of a claim under the Inchmaree Clause, where the cover is against "loss or damage caused by . . . ", had to be differentiated. Let us take as an example a claim resulting from the incorrect refitting of a propeller seal ring at a routine drydocking, resulting in corrosion during the next four years, which is only discovered at the next routine drawing of the tailshaft. Here the claim would be apportioned over all four policy years covering the period when the damage occurred (and not when the negligent act took place).

Since the I.T.C. 1/10/83, the clauses continue to include the perils which used to be found in the body of the S.G. policy, but instead of covering the perils *per se*, the insurance cover is against "loss of or damage to the subject-matter insured caused by", bringing it into line with the basis of cover provided by the Inchmaree Clause. The effect of this is that in all cases the policy (policies) which will respond for a claim for total loss or particular average will be that (or those) current at the time when the loss occurred or the damage was sustained.

2. The loss of the ejusdem generis wording

The basic perils in the S.G. policy were followed by the words "*and of all other perils, losses, and misfortunes, that have or shall come to the hurt, detriment, or damage of the said goods and merchandises, and ship, etc., or any part thereof*". This wording "includes only perils similar in kind to the perils specifically mentioned in the policy" (Rules for Construction of Policy, Schedule 1, Marine Insurance Act 1906). This is the *ejusdem generis* rule of construction, where specific words are followed and amplified by general words.

In the drafting of the Perils Clause these words have been dropped. There is no doubt that many assureds, who were not conversant with insurance law, found the wording to be misleading. Some commentators have argued that the decided cases in which the *ejusdem generis* wording covered losses which would not have been covered by the standard perils are few in number. Probably only one of them is noteworthy in the context of wording which has now been omitted: in *Phillips* v. *Barbour*[17] a ship in a graving dock was blown over by a violent gust of wind. This was held to be not a loss by a peril of the seas, but one which fell within the *ejusdem generis* wording.

We now continue our examination of the text:

Proximate cause

"caused by"

The Marine Insurance Act 1906, section 55 provides:

> "(1) Subject to the provisions of this Act, and unless the policy otherwise provides, the insurer is liable for any loss proximately caused by a peril insured against, but, subject as aforesaid, he is not liable for any loss which is not proximately caused by a peril insured against.
>
> (2) In particular,—
>
> (*a*) The insurer is not liable for any loss attributable to the wilful misconduct of the assured, but, unless the policy otherwise provides, he is liable for any loss proximately caused by a peril insured against, even though the loss would not have happened but for the misconduct or negligence of the master or crew;
>
> (*b*) Unless the policy otherwise provides, the insurer on ship or goods is not liable for any loss proximately caused by delay, although the delay be caused by a peril insured against;
>
> (*c*) Unless the policy otherwise provides, the insurer is not liable for ordinary wear and tear, ordinary leakage and breakage, inherent vice or nature of the subject-matter insured, or for any loss proximately caused by rats or vermin, or for any injury to machinery not proximately caused by maritime perils."

The Act does not define the expression "proximate cause", and for this we have to look at some of the cases which have come before the Courts, both before and after the passing of the Act. One of the most important cases prior to the Act was *Dudgeon* v. *Pembroke*,[18] in which a ship became a total loss after going aground for a combination of reasons, summarised by Blackburn J. as follows:

> "The ship perished because she went ashore on the coast of Yorkshire. The cause of her going ashore was partly that it was thick weather and she was making for Hull in distress, and partly that she was unmanageable because she was full of water. The cause of that cause, viz. her being in distress and full of water, was that when she laboured in the rolling sea she made water; and the cause of her making water was that when she left London she was not in so strong and staunch a state as she ought to have been . . . "

The case went to the House of Lords, which confirmed, *per* Lord Penzance, that there was no implied warranty of seaworthiness in a time policy and

17. *Phillips* v. *Barbour* (1821) B. & A. 161; but as for possible coverage under current policy wording, see Cl. 6.1.6 discussed on p. 107.
18. *Dudgeon* v. *Pembroke* (1874) L.R. 9 Q.B. at p. 595; (1877) 2 App.Cas. 284.

further, that a loss proximately caused by the sea, yet more remotely though "substantially" brought about by the condition of the ship itself was to be paid by underwriters as a loss by perils of the seas.

The leading case subsequent to the Act is *Leyland Shipping Co. Ltd.* v. *Norwich Union Insurance Co. Ltd. (The "Ikaria")*.[19] The ship was insured against marine risks, but "warranted free from all consequences of hostilities". She was torpedoed by a German submarine about 25 miles off Le Havre, but managed to reach port where she was ordered to a berth where she took the ground on each ebb tide and refloated on the flood. Finally, her bulkheads collapsed and she became a total loss. The House of Lords held that although not nearest in point of time, the torpedoing was the proximate cause of the loss. Lord Shaw said:

> "To treat proximate cause as the cause which is nearest in time is out of the question. Causes are spoken of as if they were as distinct from one another as beads in a row or links in a chain, but . . . this is not wholly so . . . Causation is not a chain but a net . . .
>
> What does 'proximate' here mean? . . . The cause which is truly proximate is that which is proximate in efficiency."

There was, however, an alternative line of reasoning, ignored by their lordships, which would have led to the same result, namely that where there are two contributing causes, both equal (or nearly equal) in efficiency, and one is a peril insured and the other is specifically excluded by the terms of the insurance, then the exclusion prevails.[20] This may be compared with the position which arises when there are two contributing causes, more or less equal in efficiency, one of which is a peril insured and the other a cause which, although not specifically excluded, is not covered by the terms of the policy.

This was the situation in *The "Miss Jay Jay"*[21]—a case which, although a little over 100 years later than *Dudgeon* v. *Pembroke*, is in effect its modern counterpart. The facts were that a motor cruiser of a new design with a fibreglass hull and laminated fibreglass topsides sustained quite substantial damage during a crossing of the English Channel in choppy, yet not particularly severe weather. The insurance was on a rather eccentric form of yacht policy, covering loss or damage "directly caused by external accidental means" and excluding "any part condemned solely in consequence of a latent defect or fault or error in design or construction". In the Commercial Court Mustill J. (as he then was) found as a fact that "*Miss Jay Jay*" was unseaworthy by reason of defects in her design and construction, but as this condition was not known to the assured, there was no breach of section 39(5) of the Marine Insurance Act 1906. For the purpose of construing the unusual Perils Clause, there was no material distinction to be made between "external accidental

19. *Leyland Shipping Co. Ltd.* v. *Norwich Union Insurance Co. Ltd.* [1918] A.C. 350.

20. *Wayne Tank & Pump Co. Ltd.* v. *Employers' Liability Assurance Corp.* [1974] Q.B. 57.

21. *J.J. Lloyd Instruments Ltd.* v. *Northern Star Insurance Co. (The "Miss Jay Jay")* [1985] 1 Lloyd's Rep. 264; [1987] 1 Lloyd's Rep. 32.

means" and the more familiar expression "perils of the seas". The judge summed up the position by saying: "The immediate cause [of the damage] was the action of adverse weather on an ill-designed and ill-made hull." The Court of Appeal concurred; since one of the two concurrent causes was expressly covered by the policy, and the other (whether referred to as "faulty design and/or construction" or as "unseaworthiness"), while equally efficient in causation, was not expressly excluded, the assured was entitled to recover.

We now turn to the individual perils set out in Clause 6:

"6.1.1 perils of the seas rivers lakes or other navigable waters"

With the disappearance of the *ejusdem generis* wording of "and of all other perils . . . ", it was decided to extend the wording to include rivers, lakes or other navigable waters.

The Rules for Construction of the Policy (Schedule 1 to the Marine Insurance Act 1906) state:

> "7. The term 'perils of the seas' refers only to fortuitous accidents or casualties of the seas. It does not include the ordinary action of the winds and waves."

Although attempts have been made over the years, no one has successfully produced a complete definition of the expression "perils of the seas". The word peril denotes that something fortuitous and accidental is envisaged; incursion of sea water into the vessel does not necessarily amount to a loss by perils of the seas. So that when due to the old and leaky condition of a storage hulk, sea water gained entry and damaged the cargo, this was not classed as a loss by perils of the seas. See *Sassoon* v. *Western Assurance Company.*[22] The policy only covers against accidents which may happen, not against events which must happen. Similarly, it does not include the deliberate action of the assured or his agents, for example in scuttling the vessel (*Samuel* v. *Dumas*[23]).

The term does not cover every accident or casualty which may happen to the subject-matter insured on the sea. It must be a peril "of" the sea. However, providing the elements of fortuity and "of the sea" are present, violence of the weather is not an essential pre-requisite so that if, for example, a vessel strands on the coast in fair weather, or as a result of negligence is involved in a collision with another vessel, the resulting loss would be attributable to "perils of the seas".

"6.1.2 fire, explosion"

Fire was one of the enumerated perils in the S.G. form of policy and "explosions on shipboard, or elsewhere" used to appear in the Inchmaree Clause.

22. (1912) 12 Asp.M.L.C. 206; 17 Com.Cas. 274.
23. [1924] A.C. 431.

Because of the due diligence provision in the Inchmaree Clause it was sometimes necessary to attempt to determine whether a loss was by fire or by explosion and this is frequently a difficult if not impossible exercise. The inclusion of both perils in the same clause, with neither subject to the due diligence proviso, is a logical and practical development. There is no explicit reference in the clauses to extinguishing damage; none is necessary under English law which recognises that any loss incurred to prevent a loss by an insured peril is recoverable as a loss by that peril. What constitutes an explosion was recently considered in *Commonwealth Smelting Ltd.* v. *Guardian Royal Exchange Assurance.*[24]

"6.1.3 violent theft by persons from outside the Vessel"

The equivalent peril in the S.G. form of policy was "thieves" with the Rules of Construction of Policy (Schedule 1, Marine Insurance Act 1906) providing that the term "does not cover clandestine theft or a theft committed by any one of the ship's company, whether crew or passengers". It has always been an accepted rule that simple theft is something which should be capable of prevention by the Master and as such is not a proper subject for insurance under the marine policy. The above words are intended to uphold this principle by stipulating that the theft must be:

(1) violent (in *Fabrique de Produits Chimiques* v. *Large*[25] it was held that violence towards persons was not essential to meet the definition; it was sufficient if the thieves had perpetrated violence towards property during the act of theft; *per* Bailhache J. "as when people go with crowbars and smash in doors and then steal the goods from a warehouse") and
(2) by persons from outside the vessel.

"6.1.4 jettison"

It is generally the cargo which is jettisoned at a time of danger but the vessel may be damaged as a result of such an operation or in extreme circumstances part of the ship's equipment may be jettisoned, in which case this would be recoverable as a general average sacrifice.

"6.1.5 piracy"

Since 1937 piracy had been in the war cover but in the 1983 revision of the clauses it was returned to the marine clauses. The Rules for Construction of Policy (Schedule 1, Marine Insurance Act 1906) provide that the term

24. [1984] 2 Lloyd's Rep. 608, see pp. 39–40.
25. (1923) 28 Com.Cas. 248; 16 Asp.M.L.C. 110.

"pirates" includes passengers who mutiny and rioters who attack the ship from the shore. However this definition is not exhaustive. In the case of *Republic of Bolivia* v. *Indemnity Mutual Marine Assurance Company Limited*,[26] the Court of Appeal held that the word "pirates" meant persons plundering indiscriminately for their own ends, and not persons simply operating, albeit illegally and criminally, against the property of a particular state for a political end.

In the 1/10/83 clauses the next stated peril was:

"6.1.6 breakdown of or accident to nuclear installations or reactors"

In previous editions the authors gave as a possible example of this peril the contamination of an insured vessel by radioactive material following its accidental emission from a nuclear power station, observing that if the clean-up costs were to exceed the insured value of the ship or if the vessel could not be made clear of the contamination, the assured's claim would be for a total loss.

This sub-clause does not appear in the 1/11/95 form. Instead we have:

"6.1.6 contact with land conveyance, dock or harbour equipment or installation"

In Institute Time Clauses, Hulls, 1/10/83, these perils were included with contact with aircraft etc. in Clause 6.1.7.

Traditionally, a contact between a ship or other floating subject-matter of insurance and an object attached to the land, such as a wharf or jetty, which takes place owing to the fact that the one is afloat on a moving surface whereas the other is static, has always been treated as having been caused by a peril of the sea; but what if a ship sustains damage while she is safely moored alongside the wharf or jetty, say in consequence of a shore crane falling on the ship's superstructure in a high wind? This is not a peril of the sea, but it is clearly the kind of incident for which the shipowner requires insurance, hence the addition of this list of perils to the standard form of cover.

Damage sustained by a ship toppling over whilst in a drydock is not recoverable as a loss arising from a peril of the sea (although under Lloyd's S.G. form it was held to be a loss recoverable under the *ejusdem generis* wording[27]). It is however submitted that provided the assured can demonstrate an element of fortuity, it would be recoverable under this clause as damage caused by contact with a dock installation.

26. (1909) 11 Asp.M.L.C. 218; 14 Com.Cas. 156.
27. *Phillips* v. *Barbour* (1821) B. & A. 161, see also p. 103.

"6.1.7 earthquake volcanic eruption or lightning"

In Institute Time Clauses, Hulls, 1/10/83, this sub-clause was numbered 6.1.8.

If a vessel were to be covered in volcanic dust following an eruption, this would constitute damage and the cost of cleaning the vessel would be recoverable under this clause. Apart from this, these perils speak for themselves and no special comment is necessary.

"6.1.8 accidents in loading discharging or shifting cargo or fuel"

In I.T.C. Hulls, 1/10/83, this sub-clause was numbered 6.2.1, having its origin as one of the perils incorporated into the Inchmaree Clause as a result of the decision in *Stott (Baltic) Steamers* v. *Marten*.[28] In this case the facts were as follows. Whilst lying in dock the vessel was taking on board a boiler from a floating crane. During the loading operation the boiler fouled the hatch coaming, the floating crane listed away from the vessel, and the crane tackle gave way, as a result of which the boiler fell into the lower hold damaging the ship, the claim on underwriters being for the cost of repairing the damage sustained by the vessel. The court held that an accident which might have happened in exactly the same way if the crane had been fixed on the quay could not be called a peril of the sea, or a peril, loss or misfortune of the same kind as a peril of the sea.

It is to be noted that it is only loss or damage caused by the accidents in the operations of loading, discharging or shifting cargo or fuel which is covered and not damage suffered by the vessel in consequence of the nature of the cargo loaded, for example damage to the hull plating from the loading (and carriage) of a corrosive cargo.

In I.T.C. Hulls, 1/10/83, recovery under this sub-clause was subject to the Clause 6.2 Proviso.[29] In the 1/11/95 form the sub-clause was relocated and released from the Proviso.

"6.2.1 bursting of boilers breakage of shafts or any latent defect in the machinery or hull"

In I.T.C. Hulls, 1/10/83, this sub-clause was numbered 6.2.2.

The perils set out in this sub-clause are those which were accepted by market underwriters and incorporated in standard policy forms in order to overcome the effect of the decision in the case of *The "Inchmaree"*.[30] In this case the claim was for the cost of replacing the air chamber of a donkey engine which burst due to a screw-valve, which should have been open, having been

28. (1914) 19 Com.Cas. 93.
29. The Clause 6.2 Proviso is discussed on pp. 114–118.
30. *Hamilton, Fraser & Co.* v. *Thames and Mersey Marine Ins. Co.* (1887) 6 Asp.M.L.C. 200.

accidentally or negligently left closed. The House of Lords held that damage had not been caused by one of the enumerated perils, or by a peril of a like kind under the *ejusdem generis* rule. It was impossible to say that the damage sustained was of a character to which a marine adventure is specially susceptible and therefore recoverable *ejusdem generis* with perils of the seas.

The policy only covers "loss or damage to the subject-matter insured caused by" and it is only the consequential damage which is covered and not the cost of repairing or replacing the latent defect itself. So that in the case of a boiler explosion or a shaft breakage, if there is no evidence that the original accident was caused by an insured peril, only the consequential damage is recoverable and there is no claim for the cost of repairing or replacing the damaged boiler or shaft. The construction of this clause has been the subject of a long line of law cases and in view of the importance of the clause the main authorities are summarised hereunder.

Oceanic Steamship Company v. *Faber*[31]: upon drawing the tailshaft for routine classification society survey, a fracture was discovered and it was condemned. It was subsequently proved that the fracture arose from a new end having been imperfectly welded on to the shaft some years before, it being accepted that this defect had not been visible at the previous Classification Society survey some two and a half years before and must have then constituted a latent defect. The court held that there had been no damage caused by a latent defect. It was nothing more than a latent defect becoming patent, which was not within the words of the Inchmaree Clause and there was therefore no claim.

Wills & Sons v. *The World Marine Insurance Co.*[32] illustrates the kind of consequential damage which the Inchmaree Clause was designed to cover. A link in the hoisting chain of the bucket ladder of a dredger gave way, resulting in the ladder and buckets falling and damaging the hull and machinery. It was held that the underwriters were liable under the clause for the consequential damage to the hull and machinery even though the latently defective link had been in that condition long before the commencement of the policy.

In *Hutchins Bros.* v. *The Royal Exchange Corporation*,[33] the assured had insured their vessel for a period of 12 months from December 1908 on conditions including the Inchmaree Clause. In 1909 and during the currency of the policies, a defect was discovered in the vessel's stern frame and it was condemned. It was found that the stern frame had contained a latent defect when it had been fitted during the building of the ship in 1906. The court of first instance found in favour of the underwriters and this judgment was affirmed in the Court of Appeal, *per* Scrutton L.J.:

31. (1907) 11 Com.Cas. 179; 13 Com.Cas. 28; 10 Asp.M.L.C. 303.
32. *The Times*, 14 March 1911.
33. (1911) 16 Com.Cas. 242; 12 Asp.M.L.C. 21.

"The only damage is the latent defect itself, which by wear and tear has become patent. But the latent defect did not arise during the currency of the policy; it existed in 1906; the only change is that a previous latent defect has by wear and tear become patent. It has not been constructively lost during the currency of the policy; it was constructively lost in 1906, if the true facts had been known; what has happened during the currency of the policy is the discovery of the true facts."

In *Scindia Steamship (London) Ltd.* v. *London Assurance*[34] the point at issue was one which had been left open in *Oceanic* v. *Faber*,[35] namely whether underwriters were liable for the cost of replacing a latently defective shaft which actually broke apart during the currency of the policy. The facts were very straightforward: during a routine drawing of the tailshaft as the propeller was being wedged off, the tailshaft broke owing to a latent defect in the shaft. The defendant underwriters, whilst admitting liability for the consequential damage sustained by the propeller when it fell to the dock floor, denied liability for the cost of replacing the latently defective tailshaft. Branson J. found in favour of the underwriters. He said:

"It seems to me that the proper reading [of the clause] is that the breakage of the shaft itself is not covered, nor can it properly be said that the breakage of the shaft is a loss or damage to machinery caused by the breakage of the shaft."

And later on:

"What I have said in regard to the breakage of the shaft and the necessity for there being some damage caused by the breakage of the shaft other than the breakage of the shaft itself, seems to me to apply also to the case of a latent defect."

The most recent case on the issue of latent defect is *The "Nukila"*.[36] This concerned fatigue cracks in the legs of an accommodation platform which during the period of insurance had developed to such a degree that extensive repairs were required. Analysis of the technical reports disclosed that the fractures had their origin in certain welds which had not been properly profiled; in these locations there had been a concentration of stress which over a period of time had caused the condition known as metal fatigue to arise. The bad welding amounted to a latent defect: the issue was whether the serious fractures which had developed from that condition amounted to damage to the hull of the vessel or, as argued on behalf of underwriters, a mere manifestation of the defect.

In the Commercial Court the judge said that the proposition of law which he derived from the leading cases (i.e. those reviewed above) was that "if all that has happened is that a latent defect has become patent, there is no cover under the Inchmaree Clause", and he concluded that in this case there was

34. (1937) 56 Ll.L.Rep. 136.
35. (1907) 11 Com.Cas. 179; 13 Com.Cas. 28; 10 Asp.M.L.C. 303.
36. *Promet Engineering (Singapore) Pte. Ltd.* v. *Sturge (The "Nukila")* [1997] 2 Lloyd's Rep. 146.

nothing which could be characterised as consequential damage to the vessel. In arriving at this conclusion the judge accepted the argument put forward by counsel for the underwriters that to found a claim under this part of the Inchmaree Clause there had to be some damage to a separate part of the hull or machinery (not merely to the defective part) and that "a part for this purpose was one which was physically separable and performed a separate function from the other part". This line of reasoning did not commend itself to the Court of Appeal, which held that the extensive fractures constituted damage to the hull of the vessel caused by the latent defects (the inadequate welds). The Court of Appeal specifically disapproved the "separate part" thesis; the word "part" does not appear in the Inchmaree Clause, and "provides no criterion for distinguishing what is and what is not damage".

The judgment of the Court of Appeal articulates a new approach to the interpretation of the phrase "damage . . . caused by . . . latent defect". Although there is a clear distinction on the facts between *The "Nukila"* and the earlier cases, it may be noted that the decision in the *Scindia* case, for example, can equally well be justified on the ground that in that case the tailshaft, even before the accident which brought about its final partition, was condemnable (or, as the old authorities used to say, "in a state of wreck") on account of its old flaw.

Latent defect compared with bad design

In *Jackson* v. *Mumford*[37] it was held that a "latent defect in the machinery" did not cover a weakness of design. *Per* Kennedy J.: "the phrase defect in machinery in a business document means a defect of material, in respect either of its original composition or in respect of its after acquired condition".

However, the relationship of latent defect to error or weakness of design was again considered in *The "Caribbean Sea"*.[38] In this case, which was considering the assured's claim for a total loss following the sinking of the vessel, the court found as a question of fact that the cause of the fatal ingress of sea water was the existence of fatigue cracks in a wedge shaped nozzle between a sea valve and the shell plating. The presence of these cracks was attributed to two factors—the manner in which the ship was designed (viz., the welding of gussets to the nozzle in proximity to another circumferential weld) and the effect upon the nozzle of the ordinary working of the ship. The court also found that these fractures must have been in existence at the inception of the policies current at the time of the total loss. In considering whether there was a defect in the hull and machinery which directly caused the loss, the judge held that the court is concerned with the actual state of the hull and machinery and not with the historical reason it has come about that the hull and

37. (1902) 8 Com.Cas. 61; 9 Com.Cas. 114; 52 W.R. 342.
38. *Prudent Tankers Ltd. S.A.* v. *Dominion Ins. Co. Ltd.* [1980] 1 Lloyd's Rep. 338.

machinery is in that state. He also held that the condition of the nozzle, which had arisen in part from the ordinary working of the ship, was not ordinary wear and tear and therefore was not excluded under section 55 of the Marine Insurance Act 1906.

Before leaving this clause we should return to the case of *Jackson* v. *Mumford*[39] which also considered what constituted a "shaft" within the meaning of the clause. Kennedy J. held that the breakage of a connecting rod of a main engine was not *ejusdem generis* with the breakage of a shaft:

> "A connecting rod and a shaft are always distinguished in the language of engineers . . . the functions really have a difference and that, while both rod and shaft alike transmit power, the connecting rod and the crankshaft transmit it by strains which are of an essentially different character".

It is not necessary in order to constitute a "breakage" of a shaft that there should be a complete partition of the shaft. A partial fracture will suffice, provided that it causes some consequential damage.

This sub-clause 6.2.1 and all those that follow are subject to the Clause 6.2 Proviso, discussed on pages 114 to 117.

"6.2.2 negligence of Master Officers Crew or Pilots"

In I.T.C. Hulls, 1/10/83, this sub-clause was numbered 6.2.3.

Negligence has been defined as:

> "The omission to do something which a reasonable man, guided by those considerations which ordinarily regulate the conduct of human affairs would do, or doing something which a prudent and reasonable man would not do."[40]

It is only loss or damage caused by the negligence of the Master, officers, crew or pilot which is covered, not the cost of effecting work which should have been carried out by the crew. For example, cases are sometimes experienced where, due to a negligent chief engineer, no routine maintenance and/or cleaning has been carried out for a considerable period. Any physical damage resulting from such neglect would be recoverable but there is no claim for the cost of catching up on the routine maintenance and cleaning which the ship's engineers should have, but failed to carry out. Any deliberate loss or damage resulting from wilful misconduct on the part of the crew may be recoverable under Clause 6.2.4 (6.2.5 in I.T.C.H. 1/10/83) which will be considered later.

"6.2.3 negligence of repairers or charterers provided such repairers or charterers are not an Assured hereunder"

In I.T.C. Hulls, 1/10/83, this sub-clause was numbered 6.2.4. In giving cover against loss or damage caused by negligence of repairers or charterers, under-

39. (1902) 8 Com.Cas. 61; 9 Com.Cas. 114; 52 W.R. 342.
40. *Blyth* v. *Birmingham Waterworks Co. Ltd.* (1856) 11 Ex. 784; 4 W.R. 294.

writers are conscious of the possibility of obtaining a recovery under their subrogated rights from the negligent party. This would not be possible if the repairers or charterers were named assureds in the policy and the cover is therefore subject to the proviso. To found a claim under this clause there must be physical loss or damage to the subject-matter insured as a consequence of the repairers' or charterers' negligence. If, for example, a shipowner discovers that a repairer has failed to undertake the replacement of parts for which he was contracted and paid for, there is no claim for the cost of purchasing and fitting the replacement parts, there being no consequential loss or damage as a result of the repairers' negligence.

"6.2.4 barratry of Master Officers or Crew"

In I.T.C. Hulls, 1/10/83, this sub-clause was numbered 6.2.5. The Rules for Construction of Policy (Schedule 1, Marine Insurance Act 1906) state:

> "The term 'barratry' includes every wrongful act wilfully committed by the Master or Crew to the prejudice of the owner, or, as the case may be, the charterer."

This definition is not exhaustive and barratry includes not only every type of fraud and malfeasance deliberately committed by the Master or crew for the intention of benefiting themselves at the expense of the shipowners, but every wilful act on the part of the Master or crew of illegality, corruption or criminal negligence, whereby the shipowners or the charterers are prejudiced.

"6.2.5 contact with aircraft, helicopters or similar objects, or objects falling therefrom"

In Institute Time Clauses, Hulls, 1/10/83 the perils of contact, other than with helicopters or objects falling from them, were lumped together with *land conveyance, dock or harbour equipment or installation* in sub-clause 6.1.7 and were not subject to the Clause 6.2 Proviso.

In Institute Time Clauses, Hulls, 1/11/95 these perils have been selected for transfer to Clause 6.2 and the due diligence Proviso applies to them. The only new peril in the list—that of contact with helicopters—was previously available only on brokers' wordings and is a welcome addition to the risks underwritten on standard clauses in view of the more frequent employment of helicopters in transporting men and equipment to and from many types of ship. Underwriters have recognised the utility of this form of transport not only by covering the risk but also by providing that the use of helicopters for this purpose shall not prejudice the insurance (Clause 1.3 of I.T.C. Hulls, 1/11/95), but their decision to make this part of the cover subject to the Clause 6.2 Proviso may reflect some anxiety that the engagement of helicopters by shore-based management may not always be prudent.

Prior to 1983, contact with aircraft was the only one of these risks covered by standard clauses, and the addition of *similar objects, or objects falling therefrom* was perceived as providing cover against the risk of vessels being damaged by satellites running out of control and/or pieces of aircraft or space debris falling to earth. Now, under the 1/11/95 wording, it might be argued that the addition of *helicopters* after *aircraft* has created a *genus* of objects from which, say, a piece of a spacecraft should be excluded. It is to be hoped that this argument would not prevail in the event (extremely unlikely, one would think) of this risk occurring.

The Clause 6.2 Proviso

In Institute Time Clauses, Hulls, 1/10/83 the text of the Proviso was:

". . . provided such loss or damage has not resulted from want of due diligence by the Assured, Owners or Managers"

In Institute Time Clauses, Hulls, 1/11/95 the following words were added after *Managers*:

". . . or Superintendents or any of their onshore management"

The first thing to be observed about this Proviso is that it is applicable only to the perils set out in Clause 6.2 and does not apply to any claim which can be brought within the perils enumerated in Clause 6.1.

Whether due diligence has been observed can only be a question of fact in each case. In the earlier editions of this book, referring to the 1/10/83 text of the Proviso, the authors surmised that the following circumstances were typical of the instances where underwriters might be expected to plead the Proviso as a defence to a claim for loss or damage:

(1) The bursting of a boiler which was found to have been beyond its due date for classification society survey at the time of the casualty.[41]
(2) A succession of crew negligence claims, where the evidence points to the crew employed being of insufficient calibre, perhaps coupled with inadequate management control checks on the crew's performance by the owners or managers.

In Institute Time Clauses, Hulls, 1/11/95 the list of persons whose failure to exercise due diligence will afford underwriters a defence to a claim has been extended to include "superintendents and any of their [assured's, owners' or managers'] onshore management". This change demonstrates the intention of London market underwriters to take a tougher line on claims involving bad management or poor maintenance. The object of the change is to supplement

41. The authors also remarked with uncanny prescience that in these circumstances underwriters might also wish to rely upon Clause 4.1 of I.T.C. Hulls, 1/10/83 by way of defence; now see Clause 5.1 of I.T.C. Hulls, 1/11/95.

the statutory defence of unseaworthiness which underwriters have recently found to be less than adequate for this purpose.

Unseaworthiness as a defence on time policies

The Marine Insurance Act 1906 provides by section 39(5):

> "In a time policy there is no implied warranty that the ship shall be seaworthy at any stage of the adventure, but where, with the privity of the assured, the ship is sent to sea in an unseaworthy state, the insurer is not liable for any loss attributable to unseaworthiness."

"with the privity of the assured"

The law on unseaworthiness goes back a long way, but for our purpose we shall begin with the definition of "privity" laid down by Lord Denning M.R. in the case of *The "Eurysthenes"*,[42] which incidentally, concerned a claim on a P. & I. policy. He said:

> "If the ship is sent to sea in an unseaworthy state, with the knowledge and concurrence of the assured personally, the insurer is not liable for any loss attributable to unseaworthiness, that is, unseaworthiness of which he knew and in which he concurred. To disentitle the shipowner he must, I think, have knowledge not only of the facts constituting the unseaworthiness but also knowledge that those facts rendered the ship unseaworthy, that is, not reasonably fit to encounter the ordinary perils of the sea. And when I speak of knowledge, I mean not only positive knowledge but also the sort of knowledge expressed in the phrase 'turning a blind eye . . . '."

Then, in answer to the question "who is the assured?" Lord Denning went on:

> "The knowledge must also be the knowledge of the shipowner personally, or his *alter ego*, or in the case of a company, of its head men or whoever may be considered their *alter ego*.
>
> But if the shipowner satisfied the Court that he did not know the facts or did not realise that they rendered the ship unseaworthy, then he ought not to be held privy to it, even though he was negligent in not knowing."

"any loss attributable to unseaworthiness"

Underwriters are relieved from liability only for such loss or damage as was caused by those aspects of the vessel's unseaworthiness to which the assured (as defined above) was privy. Likewise aspects of the vessel's unseaworthiness to which the assured was privy but which were not causative of the disputed claim are entirely irrelevant.

42. *The "Eurysthenes"* [1976] 2 Lloyd's Rep. 171.

All these factors were reviewed in the recent case of *The "Star Sea"*.[43] In that case the vessel became a constructive total loss in May 1990 in consequence of a fire which broke out in the engine room. Investigation showed that in three respects the vessel was unseaworthy as to her fire-fighting capability:

(a) the emergency fire pump did not work since the pipe supplying water to it had been cut and not repaired;
(b) the engine room could not be effectively sealed owing to inefficient dampers; and
(c) the Master was incompetent, in that he was totally ignorant of the proper way to employ the CO_2 system.

In the Commercial Court it was held that the fact that the fire pump was inoperative was irrelevant, since water would not have been used on a fire involving electric cables, but that the fire could have been extinguished if it had not been for both of the other two aspects of unseaworthiness; the persons to be regarded as the shipowners' *alter ego* were privy to these aspects of the vessel's unseaworthiness, and hence the plaintiff's claim for a constructive total loss failed. The Court of Appeal reviewed, *inter alia*, the separate but inter-related questions of unseaworthiness and privity. On unseaworthiness the findings of the Court below were upheld, but as to privity and "blind-eye" knowledge, Leggatt L.J., delivering the judgment of the Court of Appeal, held that in order for the underwriters to succeed, they would have to establish that one or other of the individuals identified as being the *alter ego* of the group of companies constituting the assured knew or at least "suspected that the master was incompetent in lacking the knowledge as to how to use CO_2 and that that rendered *Star Sea* unseaworthy, but . . . decided not to check for fear of having certain knowledge and allowed the ship to go to sea anyway". This had not been established on the facts and consequently the underwriters failed in their defence based upon section 39(5) of the Marine Insurance Act 1906.[44]

Now back to the Proviso. In the absence of any English legal decision directly on the interpretation of the Proviso, the practice under the 1/10/83 wording was to follow the reasoning of the "privity" cases and limit the persons whose lack of due diligence was to be considered that of "the Assured, Owners or Managers" to the *alter ego* or the head men of the companies concerned. Hence the amendment in the I.T.C. Hulls, 1/11/95 to extend the list of persons whose lack of due diligence will afford the underwriters a defence to claims under Clause 6.2. The wide expression "*any* of their on-shore management" is clearly designed to include persons or companies outside the named assured in the policy, such as managing agents, technical managers and the like, provided that they have been engaged by the assured,

43. *Manifest Shipping Co. Ltd.* v. *Uni-Polaris Insurance Co. Ltd. (The "Star Sea")* [1997] 1 Lloyd's Rep. 360.

44. The underwriters have applied for leave to appeal to the House of Lords, but at the time of writing it is not known whether leave will be granted.

owners or managers to perform supervisory or management functions which are relevant to the loss or damage which is the subject of the claim.

The I.S.M. Code in relation to the Proviso

The purpose of the I.S.M. Code is "to provide an international standard for the safe management and operation of ships and for pollution prevention". Its provisions are already mandatory in respect to tankers and bulk carriers (as from 1 June 1998) and will eventually apply to all cargo vessels exceeding 500 g.r.t. through flag state regulations and port state control by those countries who have acceded to or ratified the Convention. Responsibility for implementing those provisions of the Code having to do with the upkeep and management of ships rests with the "Company", which is defined as " . . . the owner of the ship or any other organisation or person such as the manager, or bareboat charterer, who has assumed the responsibility for the operation of the ship from the shipowner and who on assuming such responsibility has agreed to take over all the duties and responsibility imposed by the Code". In its turn the Company must designate a person ashore who has direct access to the highest level of management to ensure the safe operation of the ship and to provide a link between the Company and those on board.

The "Company" does not have to be the assured, nor does the "designated person" have to be at the highest level of management within the Company, but it appears fairly certain to the present editor that for the purpose of the Clause 6.2 Proviso the actions and omissions of the "designated person" will be open to scrutiny in attempting to ascertain whether due diligence has or has not been exercised by the owners' or managers' "onshore management". Conversely it may well be that when the "designated person" is within the highest level of management of the owning or operating company, evidence from him showing that a programme of preventive maintenance has been properly instituted and regularly reported upon will go a long way towards demonstrating that due diligence has been exercised.

"6.3 Master Officers Crew or Pilots not to be considered Owners within the meaning of this Clause 6 should they hold shares in the vessel"

It is not uncommon, particularly with smaller coasting type or fishing vessels, for the Master or crew to have shares in the vessel, and this clause is to cover this situation by making it clear that in such circumstances they will not be considered as owners within the meaning of the Proviso.

In the case of *The "Alastor"*,[45] which turned upon the question whether the owner was entitled to limit liability under the Merchant Shipping Acts, the Court of Appeal held that if the owner of a yacht decided to carry out his own

45. [1981] 1 Lloyd's Rep. 581.

maintenance and then did the maintenance negligently he would be acting as owner when he made the decision and it was impossible to say that the defendant's negligence in the doing of the maintenance was in his capacity as owner. The Court of Appeal decided that the question of capacity could be tested by asking: "If he had appointed an engineer, would the owner normally give instructions to the engineer as to what inspection should be made or would he leave it to the engineer?" and the answer was that, unless the engineer had shown himself to be negligent, or unless so long a period had elapsed and such circumstances had intervened that an inspection at a particular time was obviously necessary to any reasonable owner, then it was a matter which was to be left to the engineer.

Once it was accepted that an owner could combine the functions of owner and crew member there was no other way of ascertaining the capacity in which he acted than by a comparison with what the position would have been where the ownership and crew membership were separated.

Clause 7—Pollution Hazard

7 **POLLUTION HAZARD**

This insurance covers loss of or damage to the Vessel caused by any governmental authority acting under the powers vested in it to prevent or mitigate a pollution hazard, or damage to the environment, or threat thereof, resulting directly from damage to the Vessel for which the Underwriters are liable under this insurance, provided that such act of governmental authority has not resulted from want of due diligence by the Assured, Owners, or Managers to prevent or mitigate such hazard or damage, or threat thereof. Master Officers Crew or Pilots not to be considered Owners within the meaning of this Clause 7 should they hold shares in the Vessel.

Introduced into the I.T.C. in 1983, this clause had been in regular use as an additional clause since 1973, following major casualties involving pollution and governmental intervention such as the "*Torrey Canyon*" and the "*Amoco Cadiz*". The clause extends the insurance to cover loss of or damage to the vessel in the following circumstances:

(1) the loss or damage must be caused by a governmental authority when acting to prevent or mitigate damage to the environment or a real or threatened pollution hazard, and

(2) the damage to the environment or pollution hazard must result directly from damage to the vessel covered by the policy.

The reference to environmental damage was added in 1995.

The clause is subject to an important due diligence Proviso. The assured, owners or managers must be active in attempting to prevent or minimise the damage caused to the environment or the pollution hazard. They may not sit on their hands and do nothing until the government intervenes.

Clause 8—3/4ths Collision Liability

8 **3/4THS COLLISION LIABILITY**

8.1 The Underwriters agree to indemnify the Assured for three-fourths of any sum or sums paid by the

Assured to any other person or persons by reason of the Assured becoming legally liable by way of damages for

8.1.1 loss of or damage to any other vessel or property on any other vessel

8.1.2 delay to or loss of use of any such other vessel or property thereon

8.1.3 general average of, salvage of, or salvage under contract of, any such other vessel or property thereon,

where such payment by the Assured is in consequence of the Vessel hereby insured coming into collision with any other vessel.

8.2 The indemnity provided by this Clause 8 shall be in addition to the indemnity provided by the other terms and conditions of this insurance and shall be subject to the following provisions:

8.2.1 Where the insured Vessel is in collision with another vessel and both vessels are to blame then, unless the liability of one or both vessels becomes limited by law, the indemnity under this Clause 8 shall be calculated on the principle of cross-liabilities as if the respective Owners had been compelled to pay to each other such proportion of each other's damages as may have been properly allowed in ascertaining the balance or sum payable by or to the Assured in consequence of the collision.

8.2.2 In no case shall the Underwriters' total liability under Clauses 8.1 and 8.2 exceed their proportionate part of three-fourths of the insured value of the Vessel hereby insured in respect of any one collision.

8.3 The Underwriters will also pay three-fourths of the legal costs incurred by the Assured or which the Assured may be compelled to pay in contesting liability or taking proceedings to limit liability, with the prior written consent of the Underwriters.

EXCLUSIONS

8.4 Provided always that this Clause 8 shall in no case extend to any sum which the Assured shall pay for or in respect of

8.4.1 removal or disposal of obstructions, wrecks, cargoes or any other thing whatsoever

8.4.2 any real or personal property or thing whatsoever except other vessels or property on other vessels

8.4.3 the cargo or other property on, or the engagements of, the insured Vessel

8.4.4 loss of life, personal injury or illness

8.4.5 pollution or contamination, or threat thereof, of any real or personal property or thing whatsoever (except other vessels with which the insured Vessel is in collision or property on such other vessels) or damage to the environment, or threat thereof, save that this exclusion shall not extend to any sum which the Assured shall pay for or in respect of salvage remuneration in which the skill and efforts of the salvors in preventing or minimising damage to the environment as is referred to in Article 13 paragraph 1(b) of the International Convention on Salvage, 1989 have been taken into account.

Previously known as the R.D.C. or Running Down Clause, this is a marvellous example of how a clause initially introduced to fill a gap in the insurance cover has been developed and refined over the years to meet changing requirements. Although forms of a Running Down Clause had been in use since the early part of the nineteenth century its inclusion only became common-place following the case of *De Vaux* v. *Salvador*[46] in 1836 which decided that under the ordinary form of policy underwriters were not liable for the balance which the insured vessel had to pay to the other when both were to blame for a collision. The clause has subsequently been refined over the years in the light of the decisions of the courts and in recent years, with the increasing importance and magnitude of the liabilities arising from consequential risks such as pollution, the clause has been recast to differentiate quite clearly between the positive cover and the areas of exclusion, in particular those which are within the ambit of the P. & I. cover.

46. (1836) 5 L.J.K.B. 134.

Two cases which illustrate the development of the clause follow.

In *Xenos* v. *Fox*[47] the owners of the insured vessel successfully defended the claim of another ship which had sunk following a collision with the insured vessel. The assured claimed under the Sue and Labour Clause in the policy for the costs incurred in defending the other ship's claim. The claim was rejected by the court which held that the Sue and Labour clause applied only to the ordinary perils covered by the policy and did not extend to those covered by the Collision Clause, which was a supplemental agreement and did not contain any provision relating to costs. Following this decision the clause was amended to include a provision whereby underwriters would meet their due proportion of the costs, provided they had given their prior consent to the proceedings.

A further refinement took place following the case of *The "Balnacraig" (The London Steamship Owners' Mutual Insurance Association* v. *The Grampian Steamship Co)*.[48] The "*Balnacraig*" was involved in a collision for which both vessels were equally to blame. Due to the fact that the "*Balnacraig*" had sustained the greater damage, under the principle of single liability, which we shall consider later, there was a balance payable to the owners of the "*Balnacraig*" by the other vessel. The owners of the "*Balnacraig*" claimed under the Collision Clause in their policy for their liability towards the damage sustained by the other vessel, which had been set off against the other side's liability, thereby reducing the amount recovered by the "*Balnacraig*". The claim under the policy failed due to the fact that the assured had not actually paid anything to the owner of the other vessel. Following this decision the clause was extended to import the concept of "cross-liabilities" which we will consider in detail when we look at the actual provision in the present clause.

Turning to the clause in its present form, the salient points are as follows:

The agreement is to indemnify the assured for three-fourths of any sum or sums paid by the assured within the terms of the clause. The reason for coverage being limited to three-fourths is historical, it having been underwriters' original intention when introducing the clause to encourage care on the part of the assured by insisting upon one-fourth being self-insured. In practice, the remaining one-fourth is now invariably covered by entry in a Protection and Indemnity Association.

Payment must be made by the assured to give rise to a claim under the clause although in cases subject to the Third Parties (Rights Against Insurers) Act 1930 there could be circumstances in which a third party could invoke a direct claim against the policy. The payment must arise "by reason of the Assured becoming legally liable by way of damages" and the clause only covers

47. (1868) 38 L.J.C.P. 351; 17 W.R. 893.
48. (1890) 38 W.R. 651; 6 Asp.M.L.C. 506.

liabilities arising out of tort. So that when a shipowner entered into an agreement for the hire of a tug on terms that he should be liable for all damage to the tug, however caused, the payment made by the shipowner under the agreement, following a collision for which the tug was wholly to blame was held not to be recoverable under the clause (*Furness Withy & Co. Ltd.* v. *Duder*[49]).

The clause then specifies in 8.1.1 to 8.1.3 the various heads of claim of the other vessel or property thereon, liability for which is covered under the clause, and it is specified that such payment must be in consequence of the vessel insured "coming into collision with any other vessel". What constituted a collision with another "ship or vessel", which used to be the appropriate words in the Collision Clause, has been the subject of several judicial decisions, the leading ones of which were as follows.

An insured vessel collided with a pontoon crane which was permanently moored to a river bank in a naval dockyard. It was held that the pontoon was not a ship or vessel, the primary purpose for which it had been designed and adapted being to float and to lift, and not to navigate. The judge held that, whatever other qualities are attached to a ship or vessel, the adaptability for navigation and its uses for that purpose, are the most essential elements for bringing the craft within the definition (*Merchants' Marine Insurance Co.* v. *North of England Protecting and Indemnity Association*[50]).

The words can encompass part of a vessel's equipment, so that where a vessel struck the anchor of another vessel this was held to be a collision with the vessel (*Margetts* v. *Ocean Accident and Guarantee Corporation*[51]) but the fouling of nets attached to, but a mile distant from, a fishing vessel was not construed as a collision with another ship or vessel (*Bennett Steamship Co.* v. *Hull Mutual Steamship Protecting and Indemnity Association*[52]).

As to whether contact with a sunken vessel constitutes a collision with another ship or vessel depends upon the facts of each case but some guidance can be obtained from previous cases. In *Chandler* v. *Blogg*,[53] the insured vessel ran into a barge, which was lying half-submerged following a recent collision with another vessel; this was held to be a collision within the terms of the policy. In *Pelton Steamship Co.* v. *North of England Protecting and Indemnity Association*[54] the collision was with a vessel which had been sunk and was lying at the bottom of the sea, but salvage operations were in hand and the salvors had a reasonable expectation of raising her. This was held to be a collision with

49. (1936) 66 Ll.L.Rep. 52.
50. (1926) 32 Com.Cas. 165.
51. (1901) 49 W.R. 669; 9 Asp.M.L.C. 217.
52. (1914) 18 Com.Cas. 274.
53. [1898] 1 Q.B. 32; 67 L.J.Q.B. 436; 77 L.T. 524; 8 Asp.M.L.C. 349; 3 Com.Cas. 18.
54. (1925) 22 Ll.L.Rep. 510.

a ship or vessel within the terms of the Collision Clause. The test to be applied to any vessel which has sunk appears to be that if salvage operations have been abandoned, or were never contemplated, the wreck ceases to be a ship or vessel within the terms of the clause.

However, once there has been a collision with another vessel within the meaning of the clause, the assured is indemnified for all payments by way of damages for the categories of claims specified. So, for example, if insured vessel A is in collision with vessel B, which as a result is forced onto vessel C, any damages paid to vessel C would be recoverable under A's insurance, even though vessel A had not been in physical contact with vessel C.

Clause 8.2. makes it clear that the indemnity for collision liability is in addition to the indemnity provided by the other terms and conditions of the insurance and Clause 8.2.2 limits underwriters' total liability under Clauses 8.1 and 8.2 to three-fourths of the insured value in respect of any one collision. This means that, regardless of any other claim, the limit of liability for any claim under Clause 8 will be three-fourths of the insured value (with three-fourths of the costs payable in addition—see Clause 8.3).

Clause 8.2.1 imports the principle of cross-liabilities into the adjustment of claims under the clause. When two vessels are in collision and both are to blame, the respective liabilities are assessed, a set-off then occurs and there is a single payment by the vessel with the balance to pay (*The "Khedive"*[55]). This is known as Single Liability. Under the principle of cross-liabilities, imported into the policy by this clause, the claim upon underwriters is assessed as if each side actually made a payment to the other side of their respective liability. Some figures may illustrate the practical effect of the adoption of the cross-liabilities method for assessing the claim on the policy.

Vessels A and B are in collision, for which they are equally to blame, their respective losses being as follows:

A sustains damage to the extent of	£10,000
B sustains damage to the extent of	£ 6,000

The actual settlement between the vessels will be as follows:

B is liable for 50% of A's damage	£ 5,000
A is liable for 50% of B's damage	3,000
Single liability of B to A	£ 2,000

If this were the basis of the claims under the respective policies, the position (ignoring policy deductibles) would be as follows:

55. *Stoomvaart Maatschappij Nederland* v. *P. & O. Steam Navigation Company* (1882) 7 App. Cas. 795; 4 Asp.M.L.C. 567.

Vessel A—P.A. damage		£10,000
	Credit recovery from B	2,000
		£ 8,000

Vessel B—P.A. damage		£ 6,000
	Three-fourths of single liability payment	1,500
		£ 7,500

However, by reason of the cross-liabilities basis of adjustment the actual claims will be calculated as follows:

CLAIM UNDER A's POLICY

		P.A.	*3/4ths Collision Liability*	*Owners*
A's Damage		£10,000		
A's Notional Liability to B:				
50% of £6,000	£3,000		2,250	750
Credit:				
Notional recovery from B:		Cr.		
50% of £10,000		£5,000		
		£5,000	£2,250	£750

Claim under A's Policy

Particular Average (nett of notional recovery)	£5,000
3/4ths Collision Liability	£2,250
	£7,250

CLAIM UNDER B's POLICY

		P.A.	*3/4ths Collision Liability*	*Owners*
B's Damage:		£6,000		
B's Notional Liability to A:				
50% of £10,000	£5,000		3,750	1,250
Credit:				
Notional recovery from A:		Cr.		
50% of £6,000		£3,000		
		£3,000	£3,750	£1,250

Claim under B's Policy

Particular Average (nett of notional recovery)	£3,000
3/4ths Collision Liability	£3,750
	£6,750

There is an important limitation to the application of cross-liabilities, namely, when the liability of one or both vessels is limited by law. The reason for this is said to be that the limitation would distort the figures if cross-liabilities were applied. It should be mentioned in this connection that it is the Scandinavian practice for cross-liabilities to be applied even when one or both of the vessels has limited liability and the Norwegian Plan, for example, makes specific provision for this.

Following a collision the assured will invariably incur legal costs, the main areas of expense being:

(1) Determining and/or contesting liability.
(2) Instituting proceedings to limit liability.
(3) Any proportion of the other side's legal costs recoverable from the assured.
(4) Drawing up the claim of the insured vessel against the other side.
(5) Examining the claim received from the other side.

Although Clause 8.3 strictly only expressly deals with (1), (2) and (3), costs incurred under (5) are recoverable under the clause in practice as costs of defence, three-fourths of which are payable under the policy. Costs incurred in drawing up the claim of the insured vessel against the other side are "costs of recovery" or attempted recovery. They are apportioned between underwriters and the assured based upon their respective entitlement in the amount ranking for recovery. In practice, the apportionment of costs in collision cases is governed by Rule of Practice A8 of the Association of Average Adjusters which provides as follows:

> "APPORTIONMENT OF COSTS IN COLLISION CASES
> That when a vessel sustains and does damage by collision, and litigation consequently results for the purpose of testing liability, the technicality of the vessel having been plaintiff or defendant in the litigation shall not necessarily govern the apportionment of the costs of such litigation, which shall be apportioned between claim and counter-claim in proportion to the amount, excluding interest, which has been or would have been allowed in respect of each in the event of the claim or counter-claim being established; provided that when a claim or counter-claim is made solely for the purpose of defence, and is not allowed, the costs apportioned thereto shall be treated as costs of defence."

Under Clause 8.3, underwriters agree to pay three-fourths of the legal costs involved in testing liability or in limiting liability, provided that they were incurred with the prior written consent of underwriters. In practice, in addition to obtaining underwriters' initial consent it is recommended that underwriters be kept fully informed and their agreement obtained to every major step in any collision action.

It is interesting to note that the word "legal" has been inserted before "costs". The intention behind this has not, so far as the editor is aware, been the subject of any commentary elsewhere. It is submitted that it does not limit the recoverable costs to the fees and disbursements of members of the legal profession. Such a strict interpretation would exclude numerous properly claimable items examples of which are: P. & I. Club correspondents' fees; Master's travel expenses in connection with attendance at a hearing, etc. A more reasonable test, it is suggested, would be to examine whether the expenses would be accepted in principle by a Registrar or Taxing Master as party and party costs.

The exclusions detailed under Clause 8.4 are those liabilities which are customarily covered by a Protection and Indemnity Association and require no special comment, save that the exception under sub-clause 8.4.5 has been widened in the 1/11/95 form.

Clause 9—Sistership

9 **SISTERSHIP**
Should the Vessel hereby insured come into collision with or receive salvage services from another vessel belonging wholly or in part to the same Owners or under the same management, the Assured shall have the same rights under this insurance as they would have were the other vessel entirely the property of Owners not interested in the Vessel hereby insured; but in such cases the liability for the collision or the amount payable for the services rendered shall be referred to a sole arbitrator to be agreed upon between the Underwriters and the Assured.

If two vessels under the same ownership are in collision, there is no tortious liability between the two ships due to the fact that a person cannot bring an action against himself (*Simpson* v. *Thompson*[56]). If both vessels are insured, the shipowner can of course claim for the physical damage under his policies, subject to two policy deductibles; however he cannot recover any proportion of his loss of earnings which would have been recoverable if the colliding vessel had been in different ownership. Similarly, in the case of salvage services to a sister-ship, although the shipowner can claim salvage from the cargo (*Cargo ex "Laertes"*[57]) he is precluded under English law from claiming salvage in respect of the services to the ship and freight.

By this clause the assured is placed in the same position, when the insured vessel is in collision or receives salvage services from a vessel under the same ownership or management, as if the colliding or salving vessel belonged to entirely different owners. The clause also deals with the procedural manner in which liability for the collision or the amount payable for the salvage services is to be assessed. In practice these matters are often referred to an average adjuster for an independent opinion, which may be submitted to the leading underwriters and to the assured for their agreement.

There was no change to this clause in 1995.

56. (1877) 3 Asp.M.L.C. 567.
57. (1887) 6 Asp.M.L.C. 174.

Clause 10—General Average and Salvage

10 **GENERAL AVERAGE AND SALVAGE**

10.1 This insurance covers the Vessel's proportion of salvage, salvage charges and/or general average, reduced in respect of any under-insurance, but in case of general average sacrifice of the Vessel the Assured may recover in respect of the whole loss without first enforcing their right of contribution from other parties.

10.2 Adjustment to be according to the law and practice obtaining at the place where the adventure ends, as if the contract of affreightment contained no special terms upon the subject; but where the contract of affreightment so provides the adjustment shall be according to the York-Antwerp Rules.

10.3 When the Vessel sails in ballast, not under charter, the provisions of the York-Antwerp Rules, 1994 (excluding Rules XI(d), XX and XXI) shall be applicable, and the voyage for this purpose shall be deemed to continue from the port or place of departure until the arrival of the Vessel at the first port or place thereafter other than a port or place of refuge or a port or place of call for bunkering only. If at any such intermediate port or place there is an abandonment of the adventure originally contemplated the voyage shall thereupon be deemed to be terminated.

10.4 No claim under this Clause 10 shall in any case be allowed where the loss was not incurred to avoid or in connection with the avoidance of a peril insured against.

10.5 No claim under this Clause 10 shall in any case be allowed for or in respect of

10.5.1 special compensation payable to a salvor under Article 14 of the International Convention on Salvage, 1989 or under any other provision in any statute, rule, law or contract which is similar in substance

10.5.2 expenses or liabilities incurred in respect of damage to the environment, or the threat of such damage, or as a consequence of the escape or release of pollutant substances from the Vessel, or the threat of such escape or release.

10.6 Clause 10.5 shall not however exclude any sum which the Assured shall pay to salvors for or in respect of salvage remuneration in which the skill and efforts of the salvors in preventing or minimising damage to the environment as is referred to in Article 13 paragraph 1(b) of the International Convention on Salvage, 1989 have been taken into account.

In the 1/10/83 form this was Clause 11, and apart from referring to the 1974 version of the York-Antwerp Rules, the first four sub-clauses were the same.

Clauses 10.1 and 10.4 are in line with sections 66(4), 66(6) and 66(7) of the Marine Insurance Act 1906 which are as follows:

> "(4) Subject to any express provision in the policy, where the assured has incurred a general average expenditure, he may recover from the insurer in respect of the proportion of the loss which falls upon him; and, in the case of a general average sacrifice, he may recover from the insurer in respect of the whole loss without having enforced his right of contribution from the other parties liable to contribute.
>
> (6) In the absence of express stipulation, the insurer is not liable for any general average loss or contribution where the loss was not incurred for the purpose of avoiding, or in connexion with the avoidance of, a peril insured against.
>
> (7) Where ship, freight, and cargo, or any two of those interests, are owned by the same assured, the liability of the insurer in respect of general average losses or contributions is to be determined as if those subjects were owned by different persons."

There is a very interesting situation when there is a proportion of general average expenditure incurred by the shipowners which cannot be recovered from cargo because a subsequent casualty has diminished or extinguished the contributory value, or because the expenditure exceeds the total contributory values. The position under English law is quite clear: subject to the vessel being fully insured the insurers are liable to indemnify the assured against the proportion of his expenditure which remains to be borne by him, after taking into account contributions due from others (or as expressed in section 66(4) of the Marine Insurance Act 1906 "the proportion of the loss which falls upon him"): *Green Star Shipping Co.* v. *The London Assurance.*[58] Under Clause 10.1, however, the coverage is against only the *vessel's* proportion of salvage, salvage charges and/or general average, which should be differentiated from the proportion of loss which falls upon the *shipowner.* So far as the editor is aware, there was no intention when redrafting this clause to alter the position under English law, but this is one more example of where the deletion of the "English law and practice" provision[59] could give rise to a gap in the cover.

Under Clause 10.2 hull underwriters agree to the adjustment of general average according to either the York-Antwerp Rules, if so provided for in the contract of affreightment (as is the case in the majority of general averages) or, in the absence of any special terms in the contract of affreightment, according to the law and practice obtaining at the place where the adventure ends. In this context the "contract of affreightment" means:

(1) when the vessel is laden, the bill of lading or other document evidencing the terms under which the goods are being carried; or
(2) when the vessel is in ballast under a time and/or voyage charterparty, the relevant charterparty(ies).[60]

The York-Antwerp Rules are also stipulated by Clause 10.3 as the basis for the adjustment of general average when the vessel is in ballast and *not* under the charter (the voyage for this purpose being specifically defined), but there is a difference here between the 1/10/83 and 1/11/95 forms:

- The 1/10/83 form provides for the York-Antwerp Rules, 1974 (excluding Rules XX and XXI); whereas
- The 1/11/95 form provides for the York-Antwerp Rules, 1994 (excluding Rules XI(d), XX and XXI).

Rules XX and XXI are the rules which provide for the addition of commission and interest; Rule XI(d) sets out the circumstances when the cost of measures taken to prevent or minimise damage to the environment are allowable in general average.

The 1995 limitations on general average allowances

In addition to the limitation provided by Clause 10.3 (the exclusion of Rule XI(d) of the Y.A.R. 1994 when the general average occurs when the ship is in ballast and not under charter), Clause 10.5 excludes *any claim for*:

58. (1933) 36 Com.Cas. 258; 39 Ll.L.Rep. 213; 18 Asp.M.L.C. 225.
59. See pp. 90–91.
60. See A.A.A. Rule of Practice B26, reproduced below on pp. 232–233; but note that the Rule only applies to "British policies of insurance".

- Special Compensation payable to a salvor under Article 14 of the International Convention on Salvage, 1989, or any similar provision, and
- Expenses or liabilities incurred in respect of damage to the environment, or the threat of such damage, or as a consequence of the escape or release of pollutant substances from the vessel, or the threat of such escape or release.

The Clause 10.5 exclusions only apply to the proportion of general average payable by the interest insured; in the case of Institute Time Clauses, Hulls, the ship (and any other property insured on the same policy, e.g. with the Leased Equipment or Passenger Equipment Clauses[61]), and do not in any way affect the liability of other interests, e.g. cargo, to their proportions of general average as adjusted.

We will now consider these limitations individually:

1. The exclusion of Rule XI(d) when the vessel is in ballast, not under charter

Rule XI(d) sets out the circumstances in which the cost of measures undertaken to prevent or minimise damage to the environment are allowable in general average; which are, in summary, whenever those measures form part of a general average act. Rule XI(d) was introduced into the York-Antwerp Rules in 1994 as part of a package on the environmental issue, the other part of the package being the addition in Rule C of a new paragraph excluding from general average "any allowance for losses, damages or expenses incurred in respect of damage to the environment or in consequence of the escape or release of pollutant substances from the property involved on the common maritime adventure". At the Sydney Conference of the C.M.I. in October, 1994, these proposals were received without favour by delegates representing the opposing views of market underwriters and P. & I. Clubs, each of which claimed that the compromise was weighted in favour of the other. In fact the main purpose for spelling out in detail in Rule XI(d) the circumstances in which environmental damage avoidance measures could be allowed was to achieve uniformity; an A.I.D.E. survey having established a considerable variation in practice between different countries on this subject.[62]

However, this raises a problem: what is the effect of "excluding" Rule XI(d)? Is it:

(a) to treat the offending sub-Rule as if it were not there? We should then have to reinstate the different practices as they existed under the 1974 Rules, subject to the new Rule C (which in any event, by reason

61. For these clauses, see p. 223.

62. For the findings of the A.I.D.E. survey as to these differences in practice, see Hudson, *The York-Antwerp Rules* (2nd ed., 1996) pp. 183–187.

of the Rule of Interpretation, would not apply to any allowances governed by Rules X and XI), or

(b) to reverse the plain meaning of the text and disallow what under the 1974 Rules had previously been allowed?

Hypothesis (b) is that which underwriters probably intended; whereas (a) appears to the present editor to be the more correct and acceptable interpretation.

2. Clause 10.5.1. Special compensation under art. 14 of the International Convention on Salvage, 1989

This sub-clause states in formal manner what has long been agreed upon between market underwriters and P. & I. Clubs, namely that "traditional" salvage rewards will be paid by property underwriters, whereas special payments in consideration of efforts made to avoid environmental damage, whether under the "safety net" provided in L.O.F. 1980 or subject to article 14 of the International Convention on Salvage, 1989 (or any similar provision), will fall outside the market cover and will have to be picked up by the P. & I. Clubs. The form of words is clearly modelled upon the exclusion to the same effect which was brought into Rule VI of the York-Antwerp Rules in 1990 at the request of the International Maritime Organisation. This sub-clause does not present any problem.

3. Clause 10.5.2. Expenses or liabilities incurred in respect of damage to the environment, or the threat of such damage, or as a consequence of the escape or release of pollutant substances from the vessel, or the threat of such escape or release

The same cannot be said about this sub-clause. Although the majority of the exclusions contemplated here have already been taken outside the ambit of general average by operation of Rule C of the York-Antwerp Rules, 1994, it seems that underwriters' intention has been to create a separate and wider area of exclusion, so far as their liability for ship's proportion of general average is concerned. This decision has been criticised on a number of grounds:

(a) International polity. Only the London hull market has taken this attitude; cargo underwriters worldwide and other hull insurers may have grumbled, but have not been disposed to rock the boat of international uniformity in order to make such a small ripple.

(b) Interpretation. The wording of the sub-clause introduces a new and vague concept which has nothing to do with the adjustment of general average.

"incurred in respect of damage to the environment, or the threat of such damage, or as a consequence of the escape or release of pollutant substances . . . or the threat of such escape or release"

The criterion for allowance in general average is the *purpose* for which an action is undertaken or an expense incurred, and where any specific measure forms part of a total operation, it is the operation as a whole which is looked at. Thus, when an oil boom is placed around a ship which is stranded and in a position of peril, as a reasonable precaution prior to making an attempt to refloat, the cost of so doing would, under English practice, always be allowed in general average, whatever régime governed the adjustment. Now, under Clause 10.5.2, is one to apply a different test in order to examine whether the cost of that measure was "incurred *in respect of a threat* of damage to the environment or *as a consequence of a threat* of the escape of [oil]", and if so what is that different test? At the time of writing, there can be no certainty, but the present editor submits that if there is some indication of leakage at the time the decision is taken to put out the boom, then the clause applies, but not when the "anti-pollution measure" is a mere precaution, which would be undertaken in any event.

(c) Uncertainty. The introduction of a new concept which is alien to general average will mean additional time and trouble will have to be expended by the average adjuster when applying the claim for ship's proportion of general average to the hull policy and will create a new area of uncertainty likely to cause delay in settlement of the claim.

It is however fair to mention that not all the members of the Joint Hull Committee were in favour of adding this Clause 10.5.2 to the text of Institute Time Clauses, Hulls, 1/11/95, and consequently the market issued, as at the same date, a clause entitled the *Institute General Average—Pollution Expenditure Clause*[63] by which, for an additional premium, underwriters agree to reinstate allowances in general average under Rule XI(d) which would be cut out by Clause 10.5.2, provided the contract of affreightment provides for the York-Antwerp Rules, 1994.

Clause 10.6 makes it clear that notwithstanding the exclusions provided in Clause 10.5, underwriters will continue to respond for ship's proportion of any salvage reward under article 13 of the International Convention on Salvage, 1989, including any enhancement by reason of the skill and efforts of the salvors in preventing or minimising damage to the environment.

63. For the text of this clause, see p. 221.

Clause 11—Duty of Assured (Sue and Labour)

11 **DUTY OF ASSURED (SUE AND LABOUR)**

11.1 In case of any loss or misfortune it is the duty of the Assured and their servants and agents to take such measures as may be reasonable for the purpose of averting or minimising a loss which would be recoverable under this insurance.

11.2 Subject to the provisions below and to Clause 12 the Underwriters will contribute to charges properly and reasonably incurred by the Assured their servants or agents for such measures. General average, salvage charges (except as provided for in Clause 11.5), special compensation and expenses as referred to in Clause 10.5 and collision defence or attack costs are not recoverable under this Clause 11.

11.3 Measures taken by the Assured or the Underwriters with the object of saving, protecting or recovering the subject-matter insured shall not be considered as a waiver or acceptance of abandonment or otherwise prejudice the rights of either party.

11.4 When expenses are incurred pursuant to this Clause 11 the liability under this insurance shall not exceed the proportion of such expenses that the amount insured hereunder bears to the value of the Vessel as stated herein, or to the sound value of the Vessel at the time of the occurrence giving rise to the expenditure if the sound value exceeds that value. Where the Underwriters have admitted a claim for total loss and property insured by this insurance is saved, the foregoing provisions shall not apply unless the expenses of suing and labouring exceed the value of such property saved and then shall apply only to the amount of the expenses which is in excess of such value.

11.5 When a claim for total loss of the Vessel is admitted under this insurance and expenses have been reasonably incurred in saving or attempting to save the Vessel and other property and there are no proceeds, or the expenses exceed the proceeds, then the insurance shall bear its pro rata share of such proportion of the expenses, or of the expenses in excess of the proceeds, as the case may be, as may reasonably be regarded as having been incurred in respect of the Vessel, excluding all special compensation and expenses as referred to in Clause 10.5; but if the Vessel be insured for less than its sound value at the time of the occurrence giving rise to the expenditure, the amount recoverable under this clause shall be reduced in proportion to the under-insurance.

11.6 The sum recoverable under this Clause 11 shall be in addition to the loss otherwise recoverable under this insurance but shall in no circumstances exceed the amount insured under this insurance in respect of the Vessel.

This was Clause 13 in the Institute Time Clauses, Hulls, 1/10/83. Apart from the exclusions referred to in sub-clause 2, the text is the same.

Before looking at this clause in detail, it will be worth while to examine the traditional wording of the Sue and Labour Clause as it appeared in Lloyd's S.G. form of policy, once described by an enthusiastic maritime lawyer as "sheer poetry"[64]:

> "and in case of any loss or misfortune it shall be lawful to the assured, their factors, servants and assigns, to sue, labour, and travel for, in and about the defence, safeguards, and recovery of the said goods and merchandises, and ship, &c., or any part thereof, without prejudice to this insurance; to the charges whereof we, the assurers, will contribute each one according to the rate and quantity of his sum herein assured."

Section 78 of the Marine Insurance Act 1906 states the following:

> "(1) Where the policy contains a suing and labouring clause, the engagement thereby entered into is deemed to be supplementary to the contract of insurance, and the assured may recover from the insurer any expenses properly incurred pursuant to the clause, notwithstanding that the insurer may have paid for a total loss, or that the subject-matter may have been warranted free from particular average, either wholly or under a certain percentage.
>
> (2) General average losses and contributions and salvage charges, as defined by this Act, are not recoverable under the suing and labouring clause.

64. The late Donald O'May, in a private paper.

(3) Expenses incurred for the purpose of averting or diminishing any loss not covered by the policy are not recoverable under the suing and labouring clause.

(4) It is the duty of the assured and his agents, in all cases, to take such measures as may be reasonable for the purpose of averting or minimising a loss."

Clauses 11.1 and 11.2 express, rather neatly, in modern language the old Sue and Labour Clause.

"in case of any loss or misfortune"

It is necessary to found a claim under the clause that as the result of the operation of insured perils the subject-matter of the insurance has been brought into such danger that without unusual or extraordinary labour and/or expense a loss will probably fall on the underwriters. This is an essential pre-requisite to avoid claims for expenses reasonably and prudently incurred by the assured before any loss or danger had been experienced but without which a loss might well have occurred. Such expenses are part of the cost of owning and operating the insured property and in the absence of an insured peril creating a loss or danger of loss, are outside the ambit of insurance.

"it is the duty of the Assured and their servants and agents to take such measures as may be reasonable"

This imposes a positive duty upon the assured and their agents to take such measures as may be reasonable (and necessary). As to whose expenditure is recoverable under the clause, it should be noted that it is only those expenses which are incurred by the assured, their servants or agents. The case of *Uzielli* v. *Boston Marine Insurance Company*[65] illustrated one limitation of these words. In this case A, an underwriter, had reinsured with B, who in turn had reinsured with C. A, having paid the original assured for a total loss, himself incurred expenses in salving the vessel, which he recovered from B. B, however could not recover those expenses from C because A was not the "factor, servant or assign" (as the wording then was) of B.

"for the purpose of averting or minimising a loss which would be recoverable under this insurance"

These words do no more than restate the position under English law. In considering whether the measures undertaken were for the purpose of averting or minimising a loss which would be recoverable under the insurance two aspects have to be considered. The first is that the peril must be one that is covered by the policy. The second is that there must have been the danger of a loss which would have been covered by the policy so that if the only danger had been of a partial loss under a policy which covered total loss only, there

65. (1884) 5 Asp.M.L.C. 405.

would be no claim for any sue and labour expenses incurred (*Great Indian Peninsula Railway Company* v. *Saunders*[66] and *Booth* v. *Gair*[67]).

"Subject to the provisions below and to Clause 12"

The "provisions below" are those dealing with reduction of the claim for sue and labour charges in the event of under-insurance (which is in derogation of English law) together with provisions dealing with the adjustment of the expenses in the event of a total loss. The reference to Clause 12 is due to the fact that claims under Clause 11 are subject to the policy deductible unless, as provided in Clause 12, the claim under Clause 11 is associated with a claim for a total or constructive total loss of the vessel.

"the Underwriters will contribute to charges properly and reasonably incurred"

On account of these words, which reflect the phraseology of the old Sue and Labour Clause in Lloyd's S.G. form, a claim under this clause is not limited to items of expense. As was said by Phillips L.J. in *Royal Boskalis* v. *Mountain*[68]: "a generous construction [is] to be given to the word[s] 'charges . . . incurred' in the clause so that it covers both expenditure and the quantified loss consequent upon sacrifice."

"General average, salvage charges (except as provided for in Clause 11.5) special compensation and expenses as referred to in Clause 10.5 and collision defence or attack costs are not recoverable under this Clause 11"

As we have already seen the Marine Insurance Act 1906 provides (section 78(2)) that general average losses and contributions and salvage charges are not recoverable under the Sue and Labour Clause. The exclusion of salvage charges is based upon the leading case of *Aitchison* v. *Lohre*[69] which held that a distinction had to be drawn between salvage proper, which gave the salvors a lien on the property, and salvors working under special contract to the assured or the assured's agents. As we have already seen, the case of *Xenos* v. *Fox*[70] decided that the Sue and Labour Clause did not extend to the Running Down Clause. Clause 11 accordingly provides that collision costs, which fall for consideration under Clause 8, are not recoverable under the Duty of Assured Clause.

66. (1862) 6 L.T. 297; 10 W.R. 520.
67. (1863) 9 L.T. 286; 12 W.R. 106.
68. *Royal Boskalis Westminster N.V.* v. *Mountain* [1997] L.R.L.R. 523 at p. 637 col. 1.
69. (1879) 4 Asp.M.L.C. 168.
70. (1868) 17 W.R. 893.

In the 1995 form, by way of locking the already bolted door, it is also provided that expenses of a kind which underwriters will not accept under Clause 10 covering general average and salvage will likewise not be recoverable under this Clause 11.

Clause 11.3 is a redrafting of the Waiver Clause in the S.G. form of policy and makes it clear that if the assured or the underwriters undertake any measures with the object of saving, protecting or recovering the insured property such measures shall not be construed as a waiver or acceptance of abandonment or be allowed to prejudice the rights of either party *inter se*.

Whereas English law, as codified in the Marine Insurance Act 1906, makes provision for reduction in the measure of indemnity for general average contributions and salvage charges in the event of under-insurance, there is no similar provision for sue and labour charges. Clause 11.4 puts sue and labour charges on to a similar basis, the measure of indemnity being assessed by comparing the amount insured under the policy with either the insured value or the sound value of the vessel at the time of the occurrence giving rise to the expenditure, if that value is higher than the insured value. The effect of the clause is ameliorated where a claim for total loss has been admitted under the policy, when it is only the excess of the expenses over and above the proceeds, which is subjected to reduction to take account of any under-insurance.

Clause 11.5 deals with the situation when a claim for total loss has been admitted under the policy and the assured has incurred expenses in saving or attempting to save the vessel and other property and there are no proceeds, or the expenses exceed the proceeds. A simple example can perhaps best illustrate the type of expenditure contemplated by this clause.

Suppose a vessel with cargo on board is badly stranded. Having found that due to the gravity of the position none of the available tugs is willing to undertake the refloating of the vessel on a "no cure—no pay" basis, the shipowner is forced to enter into a contract for the hire of a tug on a daily basis. He is therefore committed to paying the cost of hiring the tug regardless of success. If the ship and cargo are successfully salved there is no problem as the cost of hiring the tug is included with the subsequent expenditure as general average. But what happens when the tug's services prove abortive; either nothing is saved or the cost of hiring the tug exceeds the proceeds of the property salved. Where does the shipowner recover the cost of hiring the tug? It is quite properly general average expenditure but cannot be recovered under that heading; the contributory values are nil and there is no liability upon hull underwriters after they have paid for a total loss. It is not salvage, being a charge incurred under contract, nor is it sue and labour expenditure, having been incurred to benefit both the ship and cargo and not solely the insured property. In such circumstances hull underwriters have always accepted that they should be liable for the proportion of the expenditure attaching to the ship but, in practice, the difficulty has been to determine what that proportion should be. The clause quite sensibly leaves the position open by providing that the hull policy shall bear its proportion of the expenses as may reasonably be regarded as having been incurred in respect of the vessel. This then leaves it for the average adjuster to investigate the facts of the particular case and make an equitable division.

Finally, Clause 11.5 provides for the reduction of any claim thereunder in the event of under-insurance. Clause 11.6 stipulates that any claim under Clause 11 is payable over and above any other loss recoverable under the policy, subject to the limit of the amount insured.

Clause 12—Deductible

12 **DEDUCTIBLE**

12.1 No claim arising from a peril insured against shall be payable under this insurance unless the aggregate of all such claims arising out of each separate accident or occurrence (including claims under Clauses 8, 10 and 11) exceeds the deductible amount agreed in which case this sum shall be deducted. Nevertheless the expense of sighting the bottom after stranding, if reasonably incurred specially for that purpose, shall be paid even if no damage be found. This Clause 12.1 shall not apply to a claim for total or constructive total loss of the Vessel or, in the event of such a claim, to any associated claim under Clause 11 arising from the same accident or occurrence.

12.2 Claims for damage by heavy weather occurring during a single sea passage between two successive ports shall be treated as being due to one accident. In the case of such heavy weather extending over a period not wholly covered by this insurance the deductible to be applied to the claim recoverable hereunder shall be the proportion of the above deductible that the number of days of such heavy weather falling within the period of this insurance bears to the number of days of heavy weather during the single sea passage. The expression "heavy weather" in this Clause 12.2 shall be deemed to include contact with floating ice.

12.3 Excluding any interest comprised therein, recoveries against any claim which is subject to the above deductible shall be credited to the Underwriters in full to the extent of the sum by which the aggregate of the claim unreduced by any recoveries exceeds the above deductible.

12.4 Interest comprised in recoveries shall be apportioned between the Assured and the Underwriters, taking into account the sums paid by the Underwriters and the dates when such payments were made, notwithstanding that by the addition of interest the Underwriters may receive a larger sum than they have paid.

Apart from the internal references to other clauses which have been renumbered, no amendment was made to this clause in 1995.

Until the revision of the I.T.C. in 1969, hull insurance had almost invariably been subject to a franchise applicable to each voyage as defined in some detail; the effect of this was that once the franchise had been attained, the claim was recoverable in full. Since 1969 the I.T.C. has incorporated a deductible, the exact figure to be specified, which is applied to "the aggregate of all such claims arising out of each separate accident or occurrence". Due to the multifarious situations which can be encountered when dealing with ships, these words created a problem of interpretation.

At the General Meeting of the Association of Average Adjusters, May 1971, the following resolution was passed:

> "That a Special Committee, including representatives of Underwriters and Shipowners, be appointed to consider the interpretation of the expression 'each separate accident or occurrence' in the Institute Time Clauses, Hulls, with particular regard to progressive damages, and to issue a statement of agreed lines of approach towards such interpretation."

The Committee first considered the interpretation of the relevant part of Clause 12 in the light of papers presented by members of the Committee which tended to show that "accident or occurrence" required a wider interpretation than "accident" alone, and that the word "separate" suggested that in some instances involving more than one accident or occurrence, only one deductible might be applicable when those accidents or occurrences formed a connected set of events.

The Committee appointed a working party consisting of the four average adjusters on the Committee to examine this interpretation with reference to multi-accident situations and to report to the Committee thereon.

The working party reported on 10 January 1972. Thirty cases of multi-accident situations were considered and the working party presented a summary of facts and a short commentary in each case, leading to the question whether one or more deductible should be applied. These cases and commentary, preceded by an analysis of the working party's conclusions, are set out as an Appendix to the Committee's report which is included in the Report of the Association of Average Adjusters' General Meeting, May 1972.

The working party confirmed that the provisional interpretation given to Clause 12 provided a reasonable basis in most of the cases considered for deciding whether one or more deductibles should be applied, but observed that in certain instances a strict interpretation of the clause could in practice lead to results which were inequitable. The working party suggested therefore that in these cases a reasonable and practical approach might be preferred to a strict interpretation of the clause.

At its second meeting, the Committee discussed the report of the working party and considered the following questions:

"1. Were any of the following factors material in determining how many deductibles should be applied:

(a) The fact that there were different heads of claim, e.g., particular average, general average contribution and 3/4ths collision liability, arising out of the accident or occurrence.

(b) The fact that certain items of claim might be recoverable under different principles if the policy conditions were varied by the attachment of other clauses, i.e., the 'Liner' Negligence and Additional Perils Clause.

(c) The fact that in certain instances of progressive damage the claim might be divisible over more than one policy period.

(d) The fact that a repair of part of the damage may have been effected prior to the ascertainment of other damage arising out of the same accident or occurrence.

In the opinion of the Committee none of these factors was in any way relevant to the interpretation of Clause 12.

2. What general line of approach should be adopted to the interpretation of Clause 12? In the opinion of the Committee the interpretation of Clause 12, giving each word its due weight and significance in its context, requires that:

(a) One deductible is to be applied when either:

(i) there is only one accident or occurrence from which the claims arise, or

(ii) even though there is more than one accident or occurrence, these accidents or occurrences are not separate but form a connected set of events from which the claims arise.

(b) On the other hand, if one or more of the events from which the claims arise are the result of a new cause, not directly connected with the previous events, i.e., that which would be considered in law a *novus actus interveniens*, then more than one deductible is to be applied to the claims.

3. What weight should be attached to the examples of multi-accident situations considered by the working party and the commentary thereon? The Committee considered that these examples provided guidelines to a reasonable interpretation of the clause in multi-accident situations, although they should not be considered as binding any party to a particular solution. In a number of cases the underwriters' representatives indicated that they did not agree with the comments of the working party. The Committee recognised that in practice the determination of the number of deductibles to be applied will depend upon a close consideration of the facts in each case.

4. What solution could be suggested in respect to the difficulties of interpretation in those instances where a strict interpretation of the clause could in practice lead to results which were inequitable, namely:

(i) Cases of a sequence of events where a strict interpretation suggests the application of only one deductible, but the working party considers that it would be more reasonable to apply more than one deductible.

(ii) Cases of a sequence of events where a strict interpretation suggests the application of more than one deductible, but the working party considered that it would be more reasonable to apply only one deductible.

At the suggestion of the average adjusters on the Committee, consideration was given to the question whether it would be reasonable in such cases for shipowners and underwriters respectively to forgo a strict interpretation of the clause, in the interest of avoiding dispute and simplifying the adjustment of claims. It was appreciated that such a solution would involve some 'give and take' on both sides, and that the effect of such an approach would have to be studied with care. In the meantime, the Committee expressed the hope that in such cases effect will be given to the clause in a sense which is both reasonable and practical."

The clause specifies that the aggregate of all claims includes claims for collision liability, general average, salvage and sue and labour charges. No deductible, however, is to be applied to a claim for a total or constructive total loss, or in the event of such a claim, any expenses claimable under Clause 11 (which includes sue and labour charges).

Stuck rather oddly in the middle of Clause 12.1 is the old Sighting Bottom Clause, which provides that underwriters will pay for the cost of sighting the bottom after a stranding, even if no damage is found, provided that the expense was reasonably incurred specially for that purpose, any claim thereunder being payable without application of the policy deductible.

The difficulty, referred to earlier, of deciding what constitutes a separate accident or occurrence can be particularly problematical in claims for heavy weather or ice damage. Clause 12.2 stipulates that all heavy weather (or ice) occurring during a single sea passage between two successive ports shall be treated as due to one accident. There is also detailed provision for the apportionment of the deductible when a period of heavy weather or ice extends over a period not wholly covered by the insurance. This is perhaps best illustrated by an example.

A vessel encounters floating ice during one passage, over the period 20.12.85 to 10.1.86, the relevant policies attaching for the periods of 12 months commencing 1.1.85 (deductible £6,000) and 1.1.86 (deductible £12,000), respectively.

The number of days of floating ice recorded in the vessel's deck log book amount to five, two of which occurred in 1985 and three in 1986 (there are no specific areas of damage recorded on any of the days in question).

The total cost of repairs amounted to £10,000.

The claim and the application of the Clause 12 deductible will be as follows:

1985 Policy Year

		Claim
Cost of repairs	£10,000	
Of which applying to this policy 2/5ths		£4,000
Less: Policy deductible 2/5ths × £6,000		2,400
		£1,600

1986 Policy Year

Cost of repairs	£10,000	
Of which applying to this policy 3/5ths		£6,000
Less: Policy deductible 3/5ths × £12,000		7,200
		NO CLAIM

The effective deductible unit in the case of heavy weather or ice claims is a single sea passage between two successive ports and for this purpose a call at any port, be it for bunkering only or even as a port of refuge, will terminate that passage in so far as the clause is concerned.

Recoveries

The rights of an insurer upon payment of a claim for a partial loss are laid down in section 79(2) of the Marine Insurance Act 1906 as follows:

> "Subject to the foregoing provisions, where the insurer pays for a partial loss, he acquires no title to the subject-matter insured, or such part of it as may remain, but he is thereupon subrogated to all rights and remedies of the assured in and in respect of the subject-matter insured as from the time of the casualty causing the loss, in so far as the assured has been indemnified, according to this Act, by such payment for the loss."

English law, as codified in the above section, proceeds upon the basis that "the assured has been indemnified, according to this Act . . . ". With the advent of policy deductibles, the basis of indemnification was substantially altered.

Where, by reason of the application of the policy deductible, the amount paid by the underwriter is less than an indemnity, English practice, in the absence of any policy provision to the contrary, is to divide the amount recovered rateably between the assured and the insurers in proportion to the net claim paid by the insurers and the policy deductible borne by the assured. Under the American Institute Hull Clauses, 2 June 1977, this principle of subrogation is specifically incorporated into the insurance conditions.

Clause 12.3, however, lays down a quite different basis upon which recoveries against any claim which has been subject to a deductible are to be adjusted; the recovery (excluding interest) is credited to underwriters in full until the sum which they have paid is fully reimbursed. It is only after this point is reached that the assured may participate in the sum recovered.

The method of dividing interest comprised in recoveries between underwriters and the assured is laid down in Clause 12.4. The crucial information needed to make such an apportionment is:

(1) The sums ranking for recovery.
(2) The interest recovered thereon, including information as to the period and rates of interest.
(3) The amounts and dates of underwriters' settlements (including any interim payments on account).

Clause 13—Notice of Claim and Tenders

13 **NOTICE OF CLAIM AND TENDERS**

13.1 In the event of accident whereby loss or damage may result in a claim under this insurance, notice must be given to the Underwriters promptly after the date on which the Assured, Owners or Managers become or should have become aware of the loss or damage and prior to survey so that a surveyor may be appointed if the Underwriters so desire.

If notice is not given to the Underwriters within twelve months of that date unless the Underwriters agree to the contrary in writing, the Underwriters will be automatically discharged from liability for any claim under this insurance in respect of or arising out of such accident or the loss or damage.

13.2 The Underwriters shall be entitled to decide the port to which the Vessel shall proceed for docking or repair (the actual additional expense of the voyage arising from compliance with the Underwriters' requirements being refunded to the Assured) and shall have a right of veto concerning a place of repair or a repairing firm.

13.3 The Underwriters may also take tenders or may require further tenders to be taken for the repair of the Vessel. Where such a tender has been taken and a tender is accepted with the approval of the Underwriters, an allowance shall be made at the rate of 30% per annum on the insured value for time lost between the despatch of the invitations to tender required by the Underwriters and the acceptance of a tender to the extent that such time is lost solely as the result of tenders having been taken and provided that the tender is accepted without delay after receipt of the Underwriters' approval.

Due credit shall be given against the allowance as above for any amounts recovered in respect of fuel and stores and wages and maintenance of the Master Officers and Crew or any member thereof, including amounts allowed in general average, and for any amounts recovered from third parties in respect of damages for detention and/or loss of profit and/or running expenses, for the period covered by the tender allowance or any part thereof.

Where a part of the cost of the repair of damage other than a fixed deductible is not recoverable from the Underwriters the allowance shall be reduced by a similar proportion.

13.4 In the event of failure by the Assured to comply with the conditions of Clauses 13.2 and/or 13.3 a deduction of 15% shall be made from the amount of the ascertained claim.

In Institute Time Clauses, Hulls, 1/10/83, this clause was numbered 10. Apart from sub-clause 1, which was changed to its present form in 1995, the text was not altered.

When an accident has occurred which may give rise to a claim upon the policy, it is natural that underwriters will wish to be informed as quickly as possible so that they may make arrangements for an early survey of the damage. So in these circumstances the 1983 text stipulated by Clause 10.1 that when an accident giving rise to a potential claim had occurred, notice should be given to underwriters and also, if the vessel were abroad, to the nearest Lloyd's Agent.

In Institute Time Clauses, Hulls, 1/11/95, the obligation upon the assured has become more onerous. The notice has to be given to the underwriters promptly after the date on which the assured, owners or managers became aware *or should have become aware* of the loss or damage, and if not given within 12 months of that date, then unless underwriters have agreed to the contrary in writing, they will be discharged from liability so far as concerns that loss or damage. This new provision is intended to reduce the number of unrecorded damage claims which used to be a regular feature when ships, particularly older vessels, were examined for Special Survey, and certainly the better the systems established by owners' and managers' operations and superintendence departments for recording accidents and other untoward happenings, the less frequently their insurance managers will have to seek underwriters' agreement to waive the 12-month cut-off.

Under Clause 13.2 underwriters have the right to decide to which port the vessel shall proceed for the damage drydocking and/or repair and they reserve the right of veto concerning a place of repair or a repairing firm. When underwriters elect to nominate a port of repair they agree to refund to the assured the additional expense of the voyage arising from compliance with their instructions.

Clause 13.3 gives underwriters the right to take tenders or to require further tenders to be taken. When underwriters invoke their rights under this clause an allowance is payable by underwriters at the rate of 30 per cent *per annum* on the insured value. The conditions of this allowance are:

(1) It is only for the period between the despatch of the invitation to tender required by underwriters and the acceptance of a tender.

(2) The time lost under (1) must result solely as a result of tenders having been taken and the tender must have been accepted without undue delay, following receipt of underwriters' approval. In previous versions of Institute Time Clauses, Hulls, there was no provision for any allowance when tenders were required on underwriters' instructions but were taken directly by the assured. Now, in the event that one of the tenders originally taken by the assured proves to be the

most reasonable and is accepted with the approval of the underwriters, the allowance will be made.

The period of any allowance under Clause 13.3 may also attract admissions in general average or be subject to a recovery from a third party, and in such circumstances credit has to be given against the allowance for any such recoveries. A final qualification to Clause 13.3 is that when part of the cost of the damage repair (other than a fixed deductible) is not recoverable, the allowance has to be reduced proportionately.

It is very unusual for underwriters to invoke the provisions of Clause 10.3. Although this must to a large extent be due to underwriters' satisfaction in the vast majority of cases with the repair arrangements made by their assured, when one considers that on a typical insured value of U.S.$10,000,000 the allowance works out at U.S.$8,219 per day this may well be another important reason.

There is a fixed penalty for non-compliance with the conditions of this clause and this is specified as a 15 per cent deduction from the ascertained claim (the ascertained claim being the net claim after the policy deductible).

Clause 14—New for Old

14 **NEW FOR OLD**
Claims payable without deduction new for old.

This clause was not changed in 1995. A contract of marine insurance is a contract of indemnity and when old parts of the vessel which have been lost or damaged through the operation of insured perils are replaced by new parts there is an element of betterment. However the practical difficulties of calculating the appropriate deduction to be made in respect of what is frequently only a notional improvement is simply not warranted and for many years hull insurances have provided for claims to be payable without being subject to "new for old" deductions.

Clause 15—Bottom Treatment

15 **BOTTOM TREATMENT**
In no case shall a claim be allowed in respect of scraping gritblasting and/or other surface preparation or painting of the Vessel's bottom except that

15.1 gritblasting and/or other surface preparation of new bottom plates ashore and supplying and applying any "shop" primer thereto,

15.2 gritblasting and/or other surface preparation of:

the butts or area of plating immediately adjacent to any renewed or refitted plating damaged during the course of welding and/or repairs,
areas of plating damaged during the course of fairing, either in place or ashore,

15.3 supplying and applying the first coat of primer/anti-corrosive to those particular areas mentioned in 15.1 and 15.2 above,

> shall be allowed as part of the reasonable cost of repairs in respect of bottom plating damaged by an insured peril.

The clause which appeared in the I.T.C. until the 1983 revision was as follows: "no claim shall in any case be allowed in respect of scraping or painting the Vessel's bottom".

The above clause had remained unchanged for close on a century and it was increasingly felt that it had become outdated due to the dramatic advance in the qualities and expected life of bottom coatings and the changes in the surface preparation required. At the Annual General Meeting of the Association of Average Adjusters in May 1978 a resolution was approved appointing a special committee which would include representatives of shipowners and underwriters to consider the treatment of modern bottom coatings damaged by an insured peril in the context of Clause 14. Following the report of this special committee a new Rule of Practice (D8) of the Association of Average Adjusters was drawn up and this is now incorporated in the I.T.C. as Clause 15. The clause is of necessity of a fairly technical nature and the adjustment of any claims thereunder is generally left to the average adjuster and his technical consultant. For any readers who wish to have more background information on this clause reference should be made to the Association of Average Adjusters' report of the General Meeting held on 10 May 1979 which includes the report of the special committee on the treatment of modern bottom coatings.

This clause was not changed in 1995.

Clause 16—Wages and Maintenance

> 16 WAGES AND MAINTENANCE
> No claim shall be allowed, other than in general average, for wages and maintenance of the Master, Officers and Crew, or any member thereof, except when incurred solely for the necessary removal of the Vessel from one port to another for the repair of damage covered by the Underwriters, or for trial trips for such repairs, and then only for such wages and maintenance as are incurred whilst the Vessel is under way.

This clause was not changed in 1995. The wages and maintenance of crew may under certain circumstances be allowed in general average, in which event the ship's proportion may form a claim under Clause 10. As to whether there is any liability under English law for wages and maintenance of the crew as part of a claim for particular average is highly questionable, but over the years the practice had grown up for appropriate allowances to be made in particular average for either the whole or part crew on removal passages and whilst engaged on such practices as docking and undocking the vessel and acting as shipkeepers during average repairs. This practice had been so long-standing that shipowners had become accustomed to receive such allowances for wages and maintenance of crew as a part of their indemnity. Hull underwriters had long been of the view that the wages and maintenance were not a proper item to be included in a particular average claim: they contended that in the absence of the operation of an insured peril and the damage resulting therefrom the shipowners would still have been liable for the wages and maintenance of the crew. In 1969 a clause was introduced excluding claims for the wages and maintenance of the crew other than in general average or other limited circumstances. Looking at the present wording in detail:

"No claim shall be allowed, other than in general average, for wages and maintenance of the Master, Officers and Crew"

The exclusion only relates to the wages and maintenance and would not preclude a claim for overtime and/or special payments made to the crew in appropriate circumstances, for example, assisting on damage repairs, tank cleaning etc. The terms "wages and maintenance" and "crew" were considered by the Advisory Committee of the Association of Average Adjusters.[71] The following are its recommendations as to the reasonable interpretation of the clause with the object of achieving uniformity of interpretation in practice:

"1. Wages and Maintenance

(a) Wages
The term 'wages' comprises the gross amount of all those payments made by the Shipowners to the members of the crew on a monthly, weekly or other periodic basis including leave pay, overseas allowance etc., and the employers' contribution to State and other Insurance and/or Pension Schemes which relate to those payments, and also payments of overtime to the crew in pursuance of their normal watchkeeping and/or other duties which may loosely be termed regular overtime.

However, when a vessel is in need of repair, whether at sea or in port, and the members of the crew are called upon to assist in those repairs, any payment for such services additional to wages as described above does not fall within the definition of the word because it is not earned on a regular periodic basis. This applies whether the payment is due under the terms of the contract of employment or whether it is a special payment made to the crew for additional services, the quantum of which is determined without reference to the crew basic wage or overtime structure.

(b) Maintenance
The term 'maintenance' comprises the cost of provisions, laundry etc., for the crew, together with the cost of providing accommodation on shore in certain circumstances.

2. Crew
The term 'crew' comprises those members of the ship's complement of sea-going rank engaged under articles and/or entered in the Master's portage bill or harbour wage account."

71. Advisory Committee Report No. 35 dated 15.9.71.

"except when incurred solely for the necessary removal of the vessel from one port to another for repair of damage covered by the underwriters"

It should be noted that the limitation to the exclusion only applies when the wages and maintenance have been incurred solely for the necessary removal of the vessel for damage repairs. So that if the removal was for both average and owners' repairs, no wages and maintenance are in practice paid by underwriters under this clause.

"or for trial trips for such repairs"

If following, say, a main engine damage, which forms a claim under the policy, the vessel goes out for a trial trip the wages and maintenance of the crew for the period whilst under way on trials will be claimable.

"and then only for such wages and maintenance as are incurred whilst the vessel is under way"

An allowance can only be made for the period whilst the vessel is actually under way, so that any period spent at anchor outside a port for example would be excluded.

Clause 17—Agency Commission

17 AGENCY COMMISSION
In no case shall any sum be allowed under this insurance either by way of remuneration of the Assured for time and trouble taken to obtain and supply information or documents or in respect of the commission or charges of any manager, agent, managing or agency company or the like, appointed by or on behalf of the Assured to perform such services.

This clause was not changed in 1995. The editor thinks that underwriters would be the first to admit that this is undoubtedly the worst piece of drafting in the I.T.C. Although the exclusion expressly relates only to "time and trouble taken to obtain and supply information or documents", and by implication should not exclude any claim for time and trouble taken in say arranging for salvage services or repairs, in practice underwriters have made it clear that their intention was to exclude all claims for remuneration by the assured, their managers or agents for time and trouble incurred on any aspect of a claim. In practice, underwriters will now only accept those expenses which fall within the terms of the Association of Average Adjusters Rule of Practice A3 which reads as follows:

> "That, in practice, neither commission (excepting bank commission) nor any charge by way of agency or remuneration for trouble is allowed to the ship-owner

in average, except in respect of services rendered on behalf of cargo when such services are not involved in the contract of affreightment."

Finally it should be mentioned that the clause does not exclude the fees and charges of an agent at a port of call, which can still be recoverable under certain circumstances with the other port charges as part of the cost of repairs.

Clause 18—Unrepaired Damage

18 UNREPAIRED DAMAGE

18.1 The measure of indemnity in respect of claims for unrepaired damage shall be the reasonable depreciation in the market value of the Vessel at the time this insurance terminates arising from such unrepaired damage, but not exceeding the reasonable cost of repairs.

18.2 In no case shall the Underwriters be liable for unrepaired damage in the event of a subsequent total loss (whether or not covered under this insurance) sustained during the period covered by this insurance or any extension thereof.

18.3 The Underwriters shall not be liable in respect of unrepaired damage for more than the insured value at the time this insurance terminates.

The wording of this clause was not changed in 1995. Before looking at this clause it would be as well to consider English law on this subject. The Marine Insurance Act 1906, section 69(3) states:

> "Where the ship has not been repaired, and has not been sold in her damaged state during the risk, the assured is entitled to be indemnified for the reasonable depreciation arising from the unrepaired damage, but not exceeding the reasonable cost of repairing such damage."

It will be noted at once that the subsection is not exhaustive, since it excludes the case where the vessel has been sold in damaged condition during the currency of the policies, which will be referred to shortly.

The subsection was subject to judicial interpretation in *Irvin* v. *Hine*.[72] In interpreting the subsection, there were two main questions:

(a) What was the reasonable cost of repairs?

In determining this, Devlin J. held that the cost is to be taken at the time when repairs would, in the particular circumstances of the case, have been effected, and not at the time of loss.

(b) What was the reasonable depreciation?

Having found that the sound value of the trawler in question was £3,000 and with the proceeds of sale having been agreed at £685 the question then became one of law; for the purpose of the Act was the reasonable depreciation:

72. (1950) 83 Ll.L.Rep. 162; [1949] 2 All E.R. 1089.

(1) The sound value less proceeds, that is £3,000 less £685 = £2,315, or
(2) The proportion of the insured value which the figure produced in the last calculation bore to the actual sound value, that is £2,315/3,000ths of the insured value, £9,000 = £6,945, or
(3) The insured value less proceeds, that is £9,000 less £685 = £8,315.

The learned judge held that the reasonable depreciation was not to be arrived at by the first of these calculations, and further than that he did not go, since the result produced by either of the alternatives exceeded the sum which he had previously found to be the reasonable cost of repairing the damage.

Although *Irvin* v. *Hine* was the first, and indeed the only, case in which the English courts have been called upon to give effect to section 69(3) of the Marine Insurance Act, it was not the first case in which the subsection had been the subject of judicial pronouncement. This is due to the fact that in an earlier case, *Elcock* v. *Thompson*[73] the words of section 69(3) were referred to by Morris J. as affording him guidance in a fire insurance case. In that case the learned judge held that where in a fire insurance policy provision was made for "reasonable depreciation", this was taking into account any agreed valuation in the policy. It was perhaps unfortunate that the attention of Devlin J. in *Irvin* v. *Hine* was not called to the case of *Elcock* v. *Thompson*, which had been heard very shortly before. Perhaps if the previous case had been mentioned by counsel, Devlin J.'s judgment might have been framed rather differently.

If the law rested there, it is submitted that it would be unreasonable to extract any certain rule from these two cases, since in *Irvin* v. *Hine* it was not necessary to establish the principle in order to reach the correct decision, and in *Elcock* v. *Thompson* the statement of principle was not, strictly speaking, in point in a non-marine case.

The matter does not rest there, for subsequently in 1954, the District Court of New York considered the matter in *Compania Maritima Astra S.A.* v. *Archdale*.[74] Whilst it is true that American decisions do not bind the English courts, nevertheless they are of considerable persuasive authority and particularly in a case such as this when the American law is founded on English law. In applying section 69(3) of the Marine Insurance Act, Rabin J. considered both *Elcock* v. *Thompson* and *Irvin* v. *Hine* and held that the formula to apply to determine the reasonable depreciation was the proportion of the insured value that the difference between the sound and damaged values bore to the sound value. The figure arrived at using this formula proved to be higher than the estimated cost of repairs and accordingly judgment was given for this lesser sum.

As mentioned previously, there is one situation which is not covered by the

73. [1949] 2 All E.R. 381; 82 Ll.L.Rep. 892.
74. 1954 A.M.C. 1674; [1954] 2 Lloyd's Rep. 95.

Marine Insurance Act, namely, where the ship has been sold in damaged condition during the currency of the policy. This case is governed by the well known decision in *Pitman* v. *The Universal Marine Insurance Company*.[75] In this case the learned judge held that the correct mode of ascertaining the proportion of loss to be made good by the underwriters is to compare the value of the sound ship at port of distress with her value there when damaged, and to apply this proportion to her real value at the commencement of the risk if the policy be opened, or to her agreed value, if, as in the case under consideration the policy be valued.

It is therefore submitted that in both cases, that is whether the ship has been sold during the currency of the risk or not, the principle of indemnity under English law remains the same. The assured is entitled to recover the proportion of the insured or insurable value, as the case may be, as the difference between the sound and damaged values bears to the sound value, but always with the proviso that where the shipowner could have repaired the damage for a lesser sum the liability of underwriters shall not exceed the estimated cost of repairs.

Clause 18 makes a radical alteration in the basis for assessing claims for unrepaired damage. Clause 18.1 lays down the measure of indemnity in respect of claims for unrepaired damage, namely, "the reasonable depreciation in the market value of the vessel at the time this insurance terminates arising from such unrepaired damage, but not exceeding the reasonable cost of repairs". As will be seen, there is no reference to the insured value in the clause and the indemnity is based upon the depreciation in the market value. The depreciation is to be assessed at the time when the insurance terminates, and this is in line with section 69(3) of the Marine Insurance Act 1906 which deals with those cases where the vessel has not been sold in her damaged state during the risk. Similarly, where the vessel is sold during the risk the insurance would terminate automatically in accordance with Clause 4 of the I.T.C. and this would then be the relevant date under the clause for assessing the reasonable depreciation in the market value of the vessel. In fact, providing there were no other factors affecting the sale price obtained, a comparison of the actual price realised with a valuers' estimate as to the value of the vessel if she had been in sound condition would be *prima facie* evidence of the depreciation arising from the unrepaired damage. In line with English law the measure of indemnity for unrepaired damage is limited to the estimated reasonable cost of repairs if this figure is less than the depreciation in the market value of the vessel.

Clause 18.2 is a restatement of the position under English law as codified by section 77(2) of the Marine Insurance Act 1906, which provides as follows:

75. (1882) 30 W.R. 900; 4 Asp.M.L.C. 544.

"Where, under the same policy, a partial loss, which has not been repaired or otherwise made good, is followed by a total loss, the assured can only recover in respect of the total loss."

The reason for these provisions is that in the event of a subsequent total loss any unrepaired damage becomes merged in the total loss and the assured has lost nothing by reason of the unrepaired damage. Two important points should be noted regarding any subsequent total loss:

(1) It does not matter whether the total loss is covered under the policy. See *British & Foreign Marine Insurance Company* v. *Wilson Shipping Company Limited*[76] where the vessel was insured, as customary, under separate policies against marine and war risks, respectively. Having sustained some damage which was left unrepaired and gave rise to a potential claim under the marine policy she was subsequently a total loss as the result of being torpedoed by a submarine (a risk covered under the war policy). The unrepaired partial loss was deemed to have been merged in the subsequent total loss and could not be recovered under the marine policy.

(2) The subsequent total loss must have occurred during the period covered by the insurance, or any extension thereof, as for example under Clause 2, so that a total loss during the currency of a subsequent policy would not affect any claim(s) for unrepaired damage under previous policies.

Under Clause 18.3 underwriters set an overall limit for their liability in respect of unrepaired damage, which is set at the insured value at the time when the insurance terminates.

Clause 19—Constructive Total Loss

19 CONSTRUCTIVE TOTAL LOSS

19.1 In ascertaining whether the Vessel is a constructive total loss, the insured value shall be taken as the repaired value and nothing in respect of the damaged or break-up value of the Vessel or wreck shall be taken into account.

19.2 No claim for constructive total loss based upon the cost of recovery and/or repair of the Vessel shall be recoverable hereunder unless such cost would exceed the insured value. In making this determination, only the cost relating to a single accident or sequence of damages arising from the same accident shall be taken into account.

This clause was not changed in 1995.

The relevant sections of section 60 of the Marine Insurance Act 1906 are as follows:

"60. Constructive Total Loss defined

(1) Subject to any express provision in the policy, there is a constructive total loss where the subject-matter insured is reasonably abandoned on account of its actual total loss appearing to be unavoidable, or because it could not be preserved

76. (1919) 4 Ll.L.Rep. 371; 26 Com.Cas. 13.

from actual total loss without an expenditure which would exceed its value when the expenditure had been incurred.

(2) In particular, there is a constructive total loss—

(i) . . .

(ii) In the case of damage to a ship, where she is so damaged by a peril insured against, that the cost of repairing the damage would exceed the value of the ship when repaired.

In estimating the cost of repairs, no deduction is to be made in respect of general average contributions to those repairs payable by other interests, but account is to be taken of the expense of future salvage operations and of any future general average contributions to which the ship would be liable if repaired; . . . "

As will be seen, section 60 is subject to any express provision in the policy and Clause 19.1 does contain the express provision that the insured value shall be taken as the repaired value. This means quite simply that it is the insured value which forms the point of reference when determining whether the vessel is a constructive total loss and against which the estimated cost of repairing the damage must be compared. Under English law there has been considerable controversy over the years as to whether the value of the wreck should be included in the cost of repairs, but this matter is put beyond doubt by the second section of Clause 19.1 which stipulates that nothing in respect of the damaged or breakup value of the vessel or wreck shall be taken into account in the computation. The clause only deals with the basis of calculating the figures and does not affect the question who may be entitled to exercise proprietary rights in the wreck.

The first part of Clause 19.2 is a clearly worded restatement of the position that arises out of the stipulations contained in Clause 19.1 when read in conjunction with the provisions of the Marine Insurance Act 1906. The simple test is whether the cost of recovery and/or repair of the vessel exceeds the insured value. If it does, the assured has the choice of either claiming for a constructive total loss or, alternatively, the assured may exercise his option of repairing the vessel and claiming for a 100 per cent partial loss. The latter course would be to the advantage of an assured who wished to retain the vessel.

The second part of Clause 19.2 deals with another point which is a grey area under English law, by stipulating that in assessing the cost of recovery and/or repair only the cost relating to a single accident or sequence of damages arising from the same accident may be taken into account.

Clause 20—Freight Waiver

20 **FREIGHT WAIVER**
In the event of total or constructive total loss no claim to be made by the Underwriters for freight whether notice of abandonment has been given or not.

This clause was not changed in 1995.

Section 63(2) of the Marine Insurance Act 1906 provides as follows:

"Upon the abandonment of a ship, the insurer thereof is entitled to any freight in course of being earned, and which is earned by her subsequent to the casualty causing the loss, less the expenses of earning it incurred after the casualty; and, where the ship is carrying the owner's goods, the insurer is entitled to a reasonable remuneration for the carriage of them subsequent to the casualty causing the loss."

Under Clause 20 underwriters give up their rights to any freight in the course of being earned when the vessel is a total or constructive total loss, so that it remains the property of the shipowner.

Clause 21—Assignment

21 **ASSIGNMENT**

No assignment of or interest in this insurance or in any moneys which may be or become payable thereunder is to be binding on or recognised by the Underwriters unless a dated notice of such assignment or interest signed by the Assured, and by the assignor in the case of subsequent assignment, is endorsed on the Policy and the Policy with such endorsement is produced before payment of any claim or return of premium thereunder.

This was Clause 5 in I.T.C. Hulls, 1/10/83. There was no change of wording in 1995.

Assignment of the policies is dealt with in sections 50–51 of the Marine Insurance Act 1906 as follows:

"50.—(1) A marine policy is assignable unless it contains terms expressly prohibiting assignment. It may be assigned either before or after loss.

(2) Where a marine policy has been assigned so as to pass the beneficial interest in such policy, the assignee of the policy is entitled to sue thereon in his own name; and the defendant is entitled to make any defence arising out of the contract which he would have been entitled to make if the action had been brought in the name of the person by or on behalf of whom the policy was effected.

(3) A marine policy may be assigned by indorsement thereon or in other customary manner.

51. Where the assured has parted with or lost his interest in the subject-matter insured, and has not, before or at the time of so doing, expressly or impliedly agreed to assign the policy, any subsequent assignment of the policy is inoperative;

Provided that nothing in this section affects the assignment of a policy after loss."

Clause 21 does not prohibit assignment but merely lays down the steps which must be undertaken by the assured, and any subsequent assignors, before an assignment will be recognised by underwriters and become binding upon them. This is a reasonable precaution on the part of underwriters and enables them to ascertain that any claims are paid to the correct party. There is one very important limitation to the assured's right of assignment and this arises not out of Clause 21 but Clause 5, the Termination Clause. If the assured sells the vessel he is precluded from assigning the policy to the new owner by reason of the automatic termination of the insurance cover operative under Clause 5 in the event of change of ownership.

Clause 22—Disbursements Warranty

22 **DISBURSEMENTS WARRANTY**

22.1 Additional insurances as follows are permitted:

22.1.1 *Disbursements, Managers' Commissions, Profits or Excess or Increased Value of Hull and Machinery.* A sum not exceeding 25% of the value stated herein.

22.1.2 *Freight, Chartered Freight or Anticipated Freight, insured for time.* A sum not exceeding 25% of the value as stated herein less any sum insured, however described, under 22.1.1.

22.1.3 *Freight or Hire, under contracts for voyage.* A sum not exceeding the gross freight or hire for the current cargo passage and next succeeding cargo passage (such insurance to include, if required, a preliminary and an intermediate ballast passage) plus the charges of insurance. In the case of a voyage charter where payment is made on a time basis, the sum permitted for insurance shall be calculated on the estimated duration of the voyage, subject to the limitation of two cargo passages as laid down herein. Any sum insured under 22.1.2 to be taken into account and only the excess thereof may be insured, which excess shall be reduced as the freight or hire is advanced or earned by the gross amount so advanced or earned.

22.1.4 *Anticipated Freight if the Vessel sails in ballast and not under Charter.* A sum not exceeding the anticipated gross freight on next cargo passage, such sum to be reasonably estimated on the basis of the current rate of freight at time of insurance plus the charges of insurance. Any sum insured under 22.1.2 to be taken into account and only the excess thereof may be insured.

22.1.5 *Time Charter Hire or Charter Hire for Series of Voyages.* A sum not exceeding 50% of the gross hire which is to be earned under the charter in a period not exceeding 18 months. Any sum insured under 22.1.2 to be taken into account and only the excess thereof may be insured, which excess shall be reduced as the hire is advanced or earned under the charter by 50% of the gross amount so advanced or earned but the sum insured need not be reduced while the total of the sums insured under 22.1.2 and 22.1.5 does not exceed 50% of the gross hire still to be earned under the charter. An insurance under this Section may begin on the signing of the charter.

22.1.6 *Premiums.* A sum not exceeding the actual premiums of all interests insured for a period not exceeding 12 months (excluding premiums insured under the foregoing sections but including, if required, the premium or estimated calls on any Club or War etc. Risk insurance) reducing pro rata monthly.

22.1.7 *Returns of Premium.* A sum not exceeding the actual returns which are allowable under any insurance but which would not be recoverable thereunder in the event of a total loss of the Vessel whether by insured perils or otherwise.

22.1.8 *Insurance irrespective of amount against:* Any risks excluded by Clauses 24, 25, 26 and 27 below.

22.2 Warranted that no insurance on any interests enumerated in the foregoing 22.1.1 to 22.1.7 in excess of the amounts permitted therein and no other insurance which includes total loss of the Vessel P.P.I., F.I.A., or subject to any other like term, is or shall be effected to operate during the currency of this insurance by or for account of the Assured, Owners, Managers or Mortgagees. Provided always that a breach of this warranty shall not afford the Underwriters any defence to a claim by a Mortgagee who has accepted this insurance without knowledge of such breach.

This was Clause 21 in I.T.C. Hulls, 1/10/83. There was no material change in wording in 1995.

The clause was originally introduced following the case of *The "Gunford"* (*Thames and Mersey Marine Insurance Company* v. *"Gunford" Ship Company*).[77] In this case the vessel was insured on a valuation which was in excess of the insurable value, and the freight was insured under a valued policy for a sum in excess of the gross amount at risk. In addition, the shipowners had effected a valued policy on disbursements. In examining the list of payments which were alleged by the assured to be the subject-matter of the disbursements policy, the court found that they were items which were already covered by either the freight or the ship policies. It was accordingly held that the disbursements policy constituted an over-insurance by double insurance and the assured was not entitled to any sum in excess of the indemnity permitted by law. One of the Law Lords took the opportunity to condemn disbursements policies which are

77. (1911) 16 Com.Cas. 270; 12 Asp.M.L.C. 49.

duplications of insurances on freight as "a gamble, discountenanced by sound principle and not enforceable by law".

Apart from the element of gambling, there are sound underwriting reasons for prohibiting excessive insurances on disbursements. In assessing the rate of premium, the underwriter is basing his calculations in part upon the assumption that the insured value represents the full value of the subject-matter insured. In the absence of any restriction upon the amount of additional insurances allowed, it would be possible for an assured to cover his vessel on full conditions for a valuation which he judged sufficient to cover most partial losses and he could then arrange additional cover on "total loss only" conditions at a lower rate of premium in order to bring the cover up to the full value required. Such an insurance programme would result in the first insurance becoming a first loss policy and would distort the premium/loss ratio figures.

It was for the above reasons that the Disbursements Clause was introduced with a view to limiting the amount of such ancillary insurances which can be effected.

The clause commences by listing the additional insurances which are permitted. Little comment is necessary upon the types of additional insurance listed which are self-explanatory. It should be noted that the limits under several sub-clauses are related to the sums insured under certain previous sub-clauses. As an example, the limit for freight, chartered freight or anticipated freight, insured for time (under Clause 22.1.2) must be calculated taking into account any sum insured under Clause 22.1.1. In practice the assured has the choice, subject to the rules of insurable interest, of apportioning the 25 per cent additional insurances allowed between the different types of insurances as set out in the clause as he sees fit and to suit his individual circumstances.

Clause 22.2 contains the express warranty against any insurances in excess of the amounts permitted in Clauses 22.1.1 to 22.1.7 and any other insurance which includes total loss of the vessel P.P.I. (policy proof of interest), F.I.A. (full interest admitted) or subject to any other like term. It is only P.P.I. insurances which include total loss of the vessel which are caught by the express warranty so that any other P.P.I. policies would not be in breach of the warranty.

To protect the position of an innocent mortgagee who has accepted the hull insurance in ignorance of a breach of the warranty,[78] underwriters waive the right to set up this defence against a claim by such a mortgagee.

Clause 23—Returns for Lay-Up and Cancellation

23 **RETURNS FOR LAY-UP AND CANCELLATION**

23.1 To return as follows:

23.1.1 pro rata monthly net for each uncommenced month if this insurance be cancelled by agreement,

78. As to what constitutes an "acceptance" of the insurance for the purpose of the proviso to this Clause 22.2, see *Outhwaite* v. *Commercial Bank of Greece* [1987] 1 Lloyd's Rep. 372.

23.1.2 for each period of 30 consecutive days the Vessel may be laid up in a port or in a lay-up area provided such port or lay-up area is approved by the Underwriters

(a)...................... per cent net not under repair

(b)...................... per cent net under repair.

23.1.3 The Vessel shall not be considered to be under repair when work is undertaken in respect of ordinary wear and tear of the Vessel and/or following recommendations in the Vessel's Classification Society survey, but any repairs following loss of or damage to the Vessel or involving structural alterations, whether covered by this insurance or otherwise shall be considered as under repair.

23.1.4 If the Vessel is under repair during part only of a period for which a return is claimable, the return shall be calculated pro rata to the number of days under 23.1.2 (a) and (b) respectively.

23.2 PROVIDED ALWAYS THAT

23.2.1 a total loss of the Vessel, whether by insured perils or otherwise, has not occurred during the period covered by this insurance or any extension thereof

23.2.2 in no case shall a return be allowed when the Vessel is lying in exposed or unprotected waters, or in a port or lay-up area not approved by the Underwriters

23.2.3 loading or discharging operations or the presence of cargo on board shall not debar returns but no return shall be allowed for any period during which the Vessel is being used for the storage of cargo or for lightering purposes

23.2.4 in the event of any amendment of the annual rate, the above rates of return shall be adjusted accordingly

23.2.5 in the event of any return recoverable under this Clause 23 being based on 30 consecutive days which fall on successive insurances effected for the same Assured, this insurance shall only be liable for an amount calculated at pro rata of the period rates 23.1.2(a) and/or (b) above for the number of days which come within the period of this insurance and to which a return is actually applicable. Such overlapping period shall run, at the option of the Assured, either from the first day on which the Vessel is laid up or the first day of a period of 30 consecutive days as provided under 23.1.2(a) or (b) above.

In I.T.C. Hulls, 1/10/83, this clause was numbered 22. In the 1/11/95 form two changes were made, which are mentioned in the commentary below.

The clause provides for returns of premium in two circumstances:

(1) If the insurance is cancelled by agreement a return is due of the pro rata monthly net premium for each uncommenced month.

(2) If the vessel is laid up in a port or in a lay-up area approved by underwriters a return of premium is due for each period of 30 consecutive days, at the specified rates which have to be entered into the clause, different rates applying depending on whether the vessel is under repair or otherwise. For those periods ranking for a return of premium when the vessel is under repair for only part of the period, the return of premium is calculated in proportion to the number of days under each category. In I.T.C. Hulls, 1/11/95, a new sub-clause 23.1.3 was added differentiating between different kinds of repair work, for the purpose of determining whether or not the vessel shall be considered to be "under repair".

The returns are subject to the following provisos:

(a) If a total loss of the vessel occurs during the period of the policy (or any extension thereto) no return of premium is due. This is the case regardless of whether the total loss resulted from insured perils or otherwise.

(b) As we have already seen, returns are only payable whilst the vessel is laid up if she is in a port or lay-up area which has been approved by underwriters. This was emphasised in both the 1983 and 1995 versions of I.T.C. Hulls by stating that in no case shall a return be allowed when the vessel is lying in exposed or unprotected waters. In I.T.C. Hulls, 1/10/83, underwriters granted a concession that provided such non-approved lay-up area is within the vicinity of the approved port or lay-up area, the period spent in the non-approved lay-up area may be added to the period spent in the approved lay-up area to calculate a minimum ranking period of 30 consecutive days, although the return of premium was due only for the proportion of such period during which the vessel was actually laid up in the approved port or lay-up area. This concession was withdrawn under the form of 1/11/95.

(c) Clause 23.2.3 makes it clear that loading or discharging operations or the presence of cargo on board will not prejudice returns of premium, where appropriate, but when the vessel is being used for the storage of cargo or for lightering purposes no return will be allowed for any period spent on such operations.

(d) If the annual rate of premium is adjusted it is only equitable that the rates of return should be adjusted accordingly and this is provided for by Clause 23.2.4.

(e) A return of premium may be due based on 30 consecutive days which fall on successive policies and in these circumstances Clause 23.2.5 sets out the basis for the calculation, giving the assured the option to decide the date from which the overlapping period shall run. This option can of course be of considerable benefit to the assured when there is a difference in the rate of return due under the different policies.

Clause 23 stipulates for the return of premium in two specified circumstances but it should be realised that under English law there can be other grounds for a return of premium. These are set out in section 84 of the Marine Insurance Act 1906 as follows:

"(1) Where the consideration for the payment of the premium totally fails, and there has been no fraud or illegality on the part of the assured or his agents, the premium is thereupon returnable to the assured.

(2) Where the consideration for the payment of the premium is apportionable and there is a total failure of any apportionable part of the consideration, a proportionate part of the premium is, under the like conditions, thereupon returnable to the assured.

(3) In particular—

(*a*) Where the policy is void, or is avoided by the insurer as from the commencement of the risk, the premium is returnable, provided that there has been no fraud or illegality on the part of the assured; but if the risk is not apportionable, and has once attached, the premium is not returnable.

(*b*) Where the subject-matter insured, or part thereof, has never been imperilled, the premium, or, as the case may be, a proportionate part thereof, is returnable;

Provided that where the subject-matter has been insured "lost or not lost" and has arrived in safety at the time when the contract is concluded, the premium is not returnable unless, at such time, the insurer knew of the safe arrival.

(*c*) Where the assured has no insurable interest throughout the currency of the risk, the premium is returnable, provided that this rule does not apply to a policy effected by way of gaming or wagering;

(*d*) Where the assured has a defeasible interest which is terminated during the currency of the risk, the premium is not returnable;

(*e*) Where the assured has over-insured under an unvalued policy, a proportionate part of the premium is returnable;

(*f*) Subject to the foregoing provisions, where the assured has over-insured by double insurance, a proportionate part of the several premiums is returnable;

Provided that, if the polices are effected at different times, and any earlier policy has at any time borne the entire risk, or if a claim has been paid on the policy in respect of the full sum insured thereby, no premium is returnable in respect of that policy, and when the double insurance is effected knowingly by the assured no premium is returnable."

Clauses 24, 25, 26—War, Strikes and Malicious Acts Exclusions

The following clauses shall be paramount and shall override anything contained in this insurance inconsistent therewith.

24 **WAR EXCLUSION**

In no case shall this insurance cover loss damage liability or expense caused by

24.1 war civil war revolution rebellion insurrection, or civil strife arising therefrom, or any hostile act by or against a belligerent power

24.2 capture seizure arrest restraint or detainment (barratry and piracy excepted), and the consequences thereof or any attempt thereat

24.3 derelict mines torpedoes bombs or other derelict weapons of war.

25 **STRIKES EXCLUSION**

In no case shall this insurance cover loss damage liability or expense caused by

25.1 strikers, locked-out workmen, or persons taking part in labour disturbances, riots or civil commotions

25.2 any terrorist or any person acting from a political motive.

26 **MALICIOUS ACTS EXCLUSION**

In no case shall this insurance cover loss damage liability or expense arising from

26.1 the detonation of an explosive

26.2 any weapon of war

and caused by any person acting maliciously or from a political motive.

In Institute Time Clauses, Hulls, 1/10/83 these clauses were numbered 23, 24 and 25. There was no change in wording in 1995.

These clauses are expressed to be paramount and to override anything contained in the policy inconsistent therewith. They replace the old F.C. & S. (Free of Capture and Seizure) Warranty, which we shall consider when we look at the positive cover afforded by the War and Strikes Risks forms (Part VI). Consequently only a limited amount of comment is required on the exclusions.

As we have already seen when examining the perils covered by Clause 6, in the redrafting of the I.T.C. the opportunity was taken to transfer piracy from the war to the marine cover. Both piracy and barratry can result in the "seizure or arrest restraint or detainment of the vessel", for example seizure of the vessel by pirates or the impounding of the vessel by customs authorities following smuggling by the crew.[79] It is for this reason that the exclusion of claims caused by capture, seizure, arrest, restraint or detainment is expressed to be "barratry and piracy excepted".

For some years the debate continued whether claims resulting from derelict mines etc., which could arise decades after the cessation of hostilities, should more properly fall upon the marine policies, as being no more than a "peril of the seas" rather than the war policies. The matter is now placed beyond doubt by Clause 24.3 which excludes such claims from the marine policies.

Before the Malicious Acts Exclusion (Clause 26) can apply, it is necessary to establish not only that the claim arises from the detonation of an explosive or any weapon of war but also that it was caused by a person acting maliciously or from a political motive. A claim resulting from the accidental explosion of a cargo of explosives would not be affected by the exclusion and would still be covered under Clause 6.1.2.

Clause 27—Radioactive Contamination Exclusion

27 **RADIOACTIVE CONTAMINATION EXCLUSION CLAUSE**
In no case shall this insurance cover loss damage liability or expense directly or indirectly caused by or contributed to by or arising from

27.1 ionising radiations from or contamination by radioactivity from any nuclear fuel or from any nuclear waste or from the combustion of nuclear fuel

27.2 the radioactive, toxic, explosive or other hazardous or contaminating properties of any nuclear installation, reactor or other nuclear assembly or nuclear component thereof

27.3 any weapon of war employing atomic or nuclear fission and/or fusion or other like reaction or radioactive force or matter.

In I.T.C. Hulls, 1/10/83, Clause 26 excluded loss, damage, liability or expense arising from any atomic or nuclear weapon in the same terms set out above as Clause 27.3 of the 1/11/95 form. Sub-clauses 27.1 and 27.2 were newly incorporated in I.T.C. Hulls, 1/11/95, although an Institute Radioactive Contamination Exclusion Clause had regularly been attached to London market policies since 1990.

4. INSTITUTE TIME CLAUSES, HULLS—RESTRICTED CONDITIONS

Not all shipowners require insurance on full conditions; the saving in premium obtained by opting for restricted conditions may be the governing factor; for older vessels the shipowner may have no choice if underwriters are not willing to offer insurance on full conditions.

79. See *Cory* v. *Burr* (1883) 5 Asp.M.L.C. 109.

There are at present three sets of Institute Time Clauses, Hulls, issued under date 1/11/95, which are available for the insurance of ships on restricted conditions. They are:

(1) Institute Time Clauses, Hulls—Restricted Perils.
(2) Institute Time Clauses, Hulls—Total Loss, General Average and 3/4ths Collision Liability (including Salvage, Salvage Charges and Sue and Labour).
(3) Institute Time Clauses, Hulls—Total Loss Only (including Salvage, Salvage Charges and Sue and Labour).

Many of the individual clauses in these forms are the same, word for word, as they are in the parent set—the Institute Time Clauses, Hulls, 1/11/95—and consequently, to avoid duplication, we shall set out and comment upon only those clauses which differ.

1. Institute Time Clauses, Hulls—Restricted Perils 1/11/95

The only difference between these clauses and the Institute Time Clauses, Hulls, 1/11/95, is in Clause 6, the Perils Clause, which reads:

6 **PERILS**
6.1 This insurance covers loss of or damage to the subject-matter insured caused by
6.1.1 perils of the seas rivers lakes or other navigable waters
6.1.2 fire, explosion
6.1.3 violent theft by persons from outside the Vessel
6.1.4 jettison
6.1.5 piracy
6.1.6 contact with land conveyance, dock or harbour equipment or installation
6.1.7 earthquake volcanic eruption or lightning
6.1.8 accidents in loading discharging or shifting cargo or fuel.
6.2 This insurance covers loss of or damage to the subject-matter insured caused by
6.2.1 any latent defect in the machinery or hull
6.2.2 negligence of Pilots provided such Pilots are not a Master, Officer or Member of the Crew of the Vessel
6.2.3 negligence of repairers or charterers provided such repairers or charterers are not an Assured hereunder
6.2.4 contact with aircraft, helicopters or similar objects, or objects falling therefrom
provided that such loss or damage has not resulted from want of due diligence by the Assured, Owners, Managers or Superintendents or any of their onshore management.
6.3 Masters Officers Crew or Pilots not to be considered Owners within the meaning of this Clause 6 should they hold shares in the Vessel.

The perils omitted are:

ex sub-clause 6.2.1—"bursting of boilers" and "breakage of shafts"
ex sub-clause 6.2.2—"negligence of Master, Officers and crew"
per sub-clause 6.2.4 in I.T.C. Hulls—"barratry of Master, Officers and crew".

The omission of "bursting of boilers" and "breakage of shafts" from sub-clause 6.2.1 will not have the effect of excluding all claims which are consequential upon those events, since the boiler may burst or the shaft fracture because of a latent defect, for which coverage is retained. See the commentary on "latent defect" on pages 108 to 112.

It may also be noted that although there is no change in the wording of sub-clause 5.1, the omission of the above perils from the coverage provided by Clause 6 will have the effect of reducing the instances where automatic termination of the insurance will be deferred, as provided in sub-clause 5.1, on account of the vessel's class position having changed owing to loss or damage sustained by insured perils. See this subject discussed on pages 98 to 99.

For short commentaries on "negligence" and "barratry" of Master, Officers and crew, see pages 112 to 113.

2. Institute Time Clauses, Hulls—Total Loss, General Average and 3/4ths Collision Liability (including Salvage, Salvage Charges and Sue and Labour) 1/11/95

Unlike the Restricted Perils form reviewed above, this form and the one that follows reduces the coverage granted by the policy, not by restricting the list of perils insured, but by striking out certain classes of claim—in this case Particular Average claims.

The following clauses in list A are those which in this form are (apart from numbering) the same as in the Institute Time Clauses, Hulls, 1/11/95 (correspondingly numbered as in list B):

Title of Clause	List A	List B
Navigation	1	1
Continuation	2	2
Breach of Warranty	3	3
Classification	4	4
3/4ths Collision Liability	8	8
Sistership	9	9
Duty of Assured (Sue and Labour)	11	11
Agency Commission	15	17
Constructive Total Loss	16	19
Freight Waiver	17	20
Assignment	18	21
Disbursements Warranty	19	22
Returns for Lay-up and Cancellation	20	23
Exclusions for War, Strikes, Malicious Acts and Radioactive Contamination	21/24	24/27

The clauses which differ are:

Clause 5—Termination

5 **TERMINATION**

This Clause 5 shall prevail notwithstanding any provision whether written typed or printed in this insurance inconsistent therewith.

Unless the Underwriters agree to the contrary in writing, this insurance shall terminate automatically at the time of

5.1 change of the Classification Society of the Vessel, or change, suspension, discontinuance, withdrawal or expiry of her Class therein, or any of the Classification Society's periodic surveys becoming overdue unless an extension of time for such survey be agreed by the Classification Society, provided that if the Vessel is at sea such automatic termination shall be deferred until arrival at her next port. However where such change, suspension, discontinuance or withdrawal of her Class or where a periodic survey becoming overdue has resulted from loss or damage covered by Clause 6 of this insurance or which would be covered by an insurance of the Vessel subject to current Institute Time Clauses—Hulls or Institute War and Strikes Clauses Hulls—Time such automatic termination shall only operate should the Vessel sail from her next port without the prior approval of the Classification Society or in the case of a periodic survey becoming overdue without the Classification Society having agreed an extension of time for such survey,

5.2 any change, voluntary or otherwise, in the ownership or flag, transfer to new management, or charter on a bareboat basis, or requisition for title or use of the Vessel, provided that, if the Vessel has cargo on board and has already sailed from her loading port or is at sea in ballast, such automatic termination shall if required be deferred, whilst the Vessel continues her planned voyage, until arrival at final port of discharge if with cargo or at port of destination if in ballast. However, in the event of requisition for title or use without the prior execution of a written agreement by the Assured, such automatic termination shall occur fifteen days after such requisition whether the Vessel is at sea or in port.

A pro rata daily net return of premium shall be made provided that a total loss of the Vessel, whether by insured perils or otherwise, has not occurred during the period covered by this insurance or any extension thereof.

The difference lies in the second sentence of sub-clause 5.1 which sets out the circumstances in which underwriters are prepared to defer automatic termination of the insurance until the vessel may have sailed from her "next port" after the change of classification society or "change, suspension, discontinuance, withdrawal or expiry of her Class therein". In Institute Time Clauses, Hulls, 1/11/95 those circumstances are when the change, suspension, etc. or the becoming overdue of a periodic survey has resulted from loss or damage "covered by . . . this insurance" or a war risk. Under this restricted form of insurance covering only total loss and (to a limited extent) general average, these words would not do; hence in sub-clause 5.1 of this form the circumstances are expressed as being when the change, suspension etc. or the becoming overdue of a periodical survey has resulted from loss or damage "covered by . . . Clause 6 of this insurance or which would be covered by an insurance . . . subject to current Institute Time Clauses—Hulls or Institute War and Strikes Clauses Hulls—Time".

Clause 6—Perils

6 **PERILS**

6.1 This insurance covers total loss (actual or constructive) of the subject-matter insured caused by

6.1.1 perils of the seas rivers lakes or other navigable waters

6.1.2 fire, explosion

6.1.3 violent theft by persons from outside the Vessel

6.1.4 jettison

6.1.5 piracy

6.1.6 contact with land conveyance, dock or harbour equipment or installation
6.1.7 earthquake volcanic eruption or lightning
6.1.8 accidents in loading discharging or shifting cargo or fuel.
6.2 This insurance covers total loss (actual or constructive) of the subject-matter insured caused by
6.2.1 bursting of boilers breakage of shafts or any latent defect in the machinery or hull
6.2.2 negligence of Master Officers Crew or Pilots
6.2.3 negligence of repairers or charterers provided such repairers or charterers are not an Assured hereunder
6.2.4 barratry of Master Officers or Crew
6.2.5 contact with aircraft, helicopters or similar objects, or objects falling therefrom
provided that such loss or damage has not resulted from want of due diligence by the Assured, Owners, Managers or Superintendents or any of their onshore management.
6.3 Master Officers Crew or Pilots not to be considered Owners within the meaning of this Clause 6 should they hold shares in the Vessel.

The perils insured against are the same as those listed in the Institute Time Clause, Hulls, 1/11/95, but in this form the cover is expressed to be limited to "total loss (actual or constructive) of the subject-matter insured caused by" those perils.

Clause 7—Pollution Hazard

7 **POLLUTION HAZARD**
This insurance covers total loss (actual or constructive) of the Vessel caused by any governmental authority acting under the powers vested in it to prevent or mitigate a pollution hazard, or damage to the environment, or threat thereof, resulting directly from damage to the Vessel for which the Underwriters are liable under this insurance, provided that such act of governmental authority has not resulted from want of due diligence by the Assured, Owners or Managers to prevent or mitigate such hazard or damage, or threat thereof. Master Officers Crew or Pilots not to be considered Owners within the meaning of this Clause 7 should they hold shares in the Vessel.

Once again, the risk covered by this clause is limited to total loss (actual or constructive).

Clause 10—General Average and Salvage

10 **GENERAL AVERAGE AND SALVAGE**
10.1 This insurance covers the Vessel's proportion of salvage, salvage charges and/or general average, reduced in respect of any under-insurance.
10.2 **This insurance does not cover partial loss of and/or damage to the Vessel except for any proportion of general average loss or damage which may be recoverable under Clause 10.1 above.**
10.3 Adjustment to be according to the law and practice obtaining at the place where the adventure ends, as if the contract of affreightment contained no special terms upon the subject; but where the contract of affreightment so provides the adjustment shall be according to the York Antwerp Rules.
10.4 When the Vessel sails in ballast, not under charter, the provisions of the York Antwerp Rules, 1994 (excluding Rules XI(d), XX and XXI) shall be applicable, and the voyage for this purpose shall be deemed to continue from the port or place of departure until the arrival of the Vessel at the first port or place thereafter other than a port or place of refuge or a port or place of call for bunkering only. If at any such intermediate port or place there is an abandonment of the adventure originally contemplated the voyage shall thereupon be deemed to be terminated.
10.5 No claim under this Clause 10 shall in any case be allowed where the loss was not incurred to avoid or in connection with the avoidance of a peril insured against.
10.6 No claim under this Clause 10 shall in any case be allowed for or in respect of
10.6.1 special compensation payable to a salvor under Article 14 of the International Convention on Salvage, 1989 or under any other provision in any statute, rule, law or contract which is similar in substance
10.6.2 expenses or liabilities incurred in respect of damage to the environment, or the threat of such damage, or as a consequence of the escape or release of pollutant substances from the Vessel, or the threat of such escape or release.

10.7 Clause 10.6 shall not however exclude any sum which the Assured shall pay to salvors for or in respect of salvage remuneration in which the skill and efforts of the salvors in preventing or minimising damage to the environment as is referred to in Article 13 paragraph 1(b) of the International Convention on Salvage, 1989 have been taken into account.

Clause 10.1 gives positive cover against vessel's proportion of salvage, salvage charges and/or general average (reduced in respect of any under-insurance). Clause 10.2 emphasises that the policy does not cover partial loss of and/or damage to the vessel, except for any proportion of general average loss or damage which may be recoverable under Clause 10.1. The practical effect of these clauses is that the assured is covered for any proportion of salvage, salvage charges and/or general average attaching to the vessel, including ship's proportion of any general average sacrifice of the ship, subject to reduction in respect of any under-insurance. This alters the position under English law which is codified by section 66(4) of the Marine Insurance Act 1906 which provides as follows:

> "Subject to any express provision in the policy, where the assured has incurred a general average expenditure, he may recover from the insurer in respect of the proportion of the loss which falls upon him; and in the case of a general average sacrifice he may recover from the insurer in respect of the whole loss without having enforced his right of contribution from the other parties liable to contribute."

Clause 12—Deductible

12 **DEDUCTIBLE**

12.1 No claim arising from a peril insured against shall be payable under this insurance unless the aggregate of all such claims arising out of each separate accident or occurrence (including claims under Clauses 8, 10 and 11) exceeds the deductible amount agreed in which case this sum shall be deducted. This Clause 12.1 shall not apply to a claim for total or constructive total loss of the Vessel or, in the event of such a claim, to any associated claim under Clause 11 arising from the same accident or occurrence.

12.2 Excluding any interest comprised therein, recoveries against any claim which is subject to the above deductible shall be credited to the Underwriters in full to the extent of the sum by which the aggregate of the claim unreduced by any recoveries exceeds the above deductible.

12.3 Interest comprised in recoveries shall be apportioned between the Assured and the Underwriters, taking into account the sums paid by the Underwriters and the dates when such payments were made, notwithstanding that by the addition of interest the Underwriters may receive a larger sum than they have paid.

The first sentence of sub-clause 12.1—which provides for a deductible to be applied to the aggregate of all claims "arising out of each separate accident or occurrence"—is identical to the wording of the Institute Time Clauses, Hulls. The sub-clause goes on to say—in common with all Institute Clauses on Hulls—that the deductible is not applied to any claim for a total or constructive total loss, or any associated claim under the Suing and Labouring Clause. The practical effect of this wording is that the deductible will be applied to the aggregate of all partial loss claims, i.e. those for general average, salvage (however described), sue and labour charges and 3/4ths collision liability arising out of any one "accident or occurrence".[80]

80. For the interpretation of the phrase "each separate accident or occurrence", see the commentary on pp. 135–138.

Since this form of policy does not cover particular average claims, the sentence providing for the payment of the expense of sighting the vessel's bottom after stranding is omitted, as is the sub-clause in the Institute Time Clauses, Hulls, defining what constitutes an accident in cases of heavy weather or ice damage.

The remaining sub-clauses dealing with recoveries are re-numbered.

Clause 13—Notice of Claim

13 **NOTICE OF CLAIM**

In the event of accident whereby loss or damage may result in a claim under this insurance, notice must be given to the Underwriters promptly after the date on which the Assured, Owners or Managers become or should have become aware of the loss or damage and prior to survey so that a surveyor may be appointed if the Underwriters so desire.

If notice is not given to the Underwriters within twelve months of that date unless the Underwriters agree to the contrary in writing, the Underwriters will be automatically discharged from liability for any claim under this insurance in respect of or arising out of such accident or the loss or damage.

The wording of this clause is identical with sub-clause 13.1 in the Institute Time Clauses, Hulls, 1/11/95. The provisions dealing with tenders, which appear as sub-clauses 13.2, .3 and .4 in the Institute Time Clauses, Hulls, do not have any place here, as they concern only claims for particular average.

Clause 14—New for Old

14 **NEW FOR OLD**

General Average payable without deduction new for old.

A policy in this form does not pay for any hull damage, other than total or constructive total loss and ship's proportion of general average sacrifice of ship: hence the "new for old" clause relates solely to repairs of general average sacrificial damage.

Clauses omitted

The following clauses which appear in the Institute Time Clauses, Hulls are omitted here, as they relate solely to claims for particular average:
15. Bottom Treatment; 16. Wages and Maintenance; 18. Unrepaired Damage.

3. Institute Time Clauses, Hulls—Total Loss Only (including Salvage, Salvage Charges and Sue and Labour) 1/11/95

This form is very similar to the one we have just reviewed, but as well as omitting all claims for particular average, this form also strikes out any claims for general average and collision liability.

The following clauses in list A are those which in this form (apart from numbering) are the same as in the Institute Time Clauses, Hulls, 1/11/95 (correspondingly numbered as in list B):

Title of Clause	List A	List B
Continuation	2	2
Breach of Warranty	3	3
Classification	4	4
Duty of Assured (Sue and Labour)	9	11
Constructive Total Loss	12	19
Freight Waiver	13	20
Assignment	14	21
Disbursements Warranty	15	22
Returns for Lay-up and Cancellation	16	23
Exclusions for War, Strikes, Malicious Acts and Radioactive Contamination	17/20	24/27

The clauses which differ are:

Clause 1—Navigation

1 **NAVIGATION**

1.1 The Vessel is covered subject to the provisions of this insurance at all times and has leave to sail or navigate with or without pilots, to go on trial trips and to assist and tow vessels or craft in distress, but it is warranted that the Vessel shall not be towed, except as is customary or to the first safe port or place when in need of assistance, or undertake towage or salvage services under a contract previously arranged by the Assured and/or Owners and/or Managers and/or Charterers. This Clause 1.1 shall not exclude customary towage in connection with loading and discharging.

1.2 This insurance shall not be prejudiced by reason of the Assured entering into any contract with pilots or for customary towage which limits or exempts the liability of the pilots and/or tugs and/or towboats and/or their owners when the Assured or their agents accept or are compelled to accept such contracts in accordance with established local law or practice.

1.3 The practice of engaging helicopters for the transportation of personnel, supplies and equipment to and/or from the Vessel shall not prejudice this insurance.

1.4 In the event of the Vessel being employed in trading operations which entail cargo loading or discharging at sea from or into another vessel (not being a harbour or inshore craft) no claim shall be recoverable under this insurance for loss of or damage to the Vessel from such loading or discharging operations, including whilst approaching, lying alongside and leaving, unless previous notice that the Vessel is to be employed in such operations has been given to the Underwriters and any amended terms of cover and any additional premium required by them have been agreed.

1.5 In the event of the Vessel sailing (with or without cargo) with an intention of being (a) broken up, or (b) sold for breaking up, any claim for loss of or damage to the Vessel occurring subsequent to such sailing shall be limited to the market value of the Vessel as scrap at the time when the loss or damage is sustained, unless previous notice has been given to the Underwriters and any amendments to the terms of cover, insured value and premium required by them have been agreed. Nothing in this Clause 1.5 shall affect claims under Clause 8.

The only differences between this clause and the Navigation Clause in the Institute Time Clauses, Hulls, 1/11/95 are:

— in sub-clause 1.4 the reference made in I.T.C. Hulls to "liability to any other vessel" is omitted from the non-recoverable consequences of loading or discharging cargo at sea without prior notice given and amended terms agreed;

— the provisions of sub-clause 1.5 (the "scrapping voyage" clause) are stated not to affect claims under Clause 8, i.e. for salvage and salvage charges, only.

Clause 5—Termination

5 **TERMINATION**

This Clause 5 shall prevail notwithstanding any provision whether written typed or printed in this insurance inconsistent therewith.

Unless the Underwriters agree to the contrary in writing, this insurance shall terminate automatically at the time of

5.1 change of the Classification Society of the Vessel, or change, suspension, discontinuance, withdrawal or expiry of her Class therein, or any of the Classification Society's periodic surveys becoming overdue unless an extension of time for such survey be agreed by the Classification Society, provided that if the Vessel is at sea such automatic termination shall be deferred until arrival at her next port. However where such change, suspension, discontinuance or withdrawal of her Class or where a periodic survey becoming overdue has resulted from loss or damage covered by Clause 6 of this insurance or which would be covered by an insurance of the Vessel subject to current Institute Time Clauses Hulls or Institute War and Strikes Clauses Hulls—Time such automatic termination shall only operate should the Vessel sail from her next port without the prior approval of the Classification Society or in the case of a periodic survey becoming overdue without the Classification Society having agreed an extension of time for such survey,

5.2 any change, voluntary or otherwise, in the ownership or flag, transfer to new management, or charter on a bareboat basis, or requisition for title or use of the Vessel, provided that, if the Vessel has cargo on board and has already sailed from her loading port or is at sea in ballast, such automatic termination shall if required be deferred, whilst the Vessel continues her planned voyage, until arrival at final port of discharge if with cargo or at port of destination if in ballast. However, in the event of requisition for title or use without the prior execution of a written agreement by the Assured, such automatic termination shall occur fifteen days after such requisition whether the Vessel is at sea or in port.

A pro rata daily net return of premium shall be made provided that a total loss of the Vessel, whether by insured perils or otherwise, has not occurred during the period covered by this insurance or any extension thereof.

The only difference lies in the second sentence of sub-clause 5.1 whereby the circumstances when underwriters are prepared to defer automatic termination have been re-stated to be when the change, suspension etc. of the vessel's class or the coming overdue of a periodic survey has resulted from loss or damage "covered by Clause 6 of this insurance or which would be covered by an insurance . . . subject to current Institute Time Clauses Hulls or War and Strikes Clauses Hulls—Time".

Clause 6—Perils

6 **PERILS**

6.1 This insurance covers total loss (actual or constructive) of the subject-matter insured caused by

6.1.1 perils of the seas rivers lakes or other navigable waters

6.1.2 fire, explosion

6.1.3 violent theft by persons from outside the Vessel

6.1.4 jettison

6.1.5 piracy

6.1.6 contact with land conveyance, dock or harbour equipment or installation

6.1.7 earthquake volcanic eruption or lightning

6.1.8 accidents in loading discharging or shifting cargo or fuel.

6.2 This insurance covers total loss (actual or constructive) of the subject-matter insured caused by

6.2.1 bursting of boilers breakage of shafts or any latent defect in the machinery or hull

6.2.2 negligence of Master Officers Crew or Pilots
6.2.3 negligence of repairers or charterers provided such repairers or charterers are not an Assured hereunder
6.2.4 barratry of Master Officers or Crew,
6.2.5 contact with aircraft, helicopters or similar objects, or objects falling therefrom

provided that such loss has not resulted from want of due diligence by the Assured, Owners, Managers or Superintendents or any of their onshore management.

6.3 Masters Officers Crew or Pilots not to be considered Owners within the meaning of this Clause 6 should they hold shares in the Vessel.

The perils insured are the same as those listed in the Institute Time Clauses, Hulls, 1/11/95, but in this form the cover is expressed to be limited to "total loss (actual or constructive) of the subject-matter insured caused by" those perils.

Clause 7—Pollution Hazard

7 **POLLUTION HAZARD**

This insurance covers total loss (actual or constructive) of the Vessel caused by any governmental authority acting under the powers vested in it to prevent or mitigate a pollution hazard or damage to the environment, or threat thereof, resulting directly from damage to the Vessel caused by a peril covered by this insurance, provided that such act of governmental authority has not resulted from want of due diligence by the Assured, Owners or Managers to prevent or mitigate such hazard or damage, or threat thereof. Master Officers Crew or Pilots not to be considered Owners within the meaning of this Clause 7 should they hold shares in the Vessel.

Once again, the risk covered by this clause is limited to total loss (actual or constructive).

Clause 8—Salvage

8 **SALVAGE**

8.1 This insurance covers the Vessel's proportion of salvage and salvage charges, reduced in respect of any under-insurance.

8.2 No claim under this Clause 8 shall in any case be allowed where the loss was not incurred to avoid or in connection with the avoidance of a peril insured against.

8.3 No claim under this Clause 8 shall in any case be allowed for or in respect of

8.3.1 special compensation payable to a salvor under Article 14 of the International Convention on Salvage, 1989 or under any other provision in any statute, rule, law or contract which is similar in substance

8.3.2 expenses or liabilities incurred in respect of damage to the environment, or the threat of such damage, or as a consequence of the escape or release of pollutant substances from the Vessel, or the threat of such escape or release.

8.4 Clause 8.3 shall not however exclude any sum which the Assured shall pay to salvors for or in respect of salvage remuneration in which the skill and efforts of the salvors in preventing or minimising damage to the environment as is referred to in Article 13 paragraph 1(b) of the International Convention on Salvage, 1989 have been taken into account.

It is first to be noted that this clause occupies the slot usually taken up by a clause covering both general average and salvage, but since this policy form excludes general average, we have here a clause which deals only with salvage and salvage charges.

Sub-clauses 8.1 and 8.2 re-state the effect of section 65(1) of the Marine Insurance Act 1906; likewise sub-clause 8.3.1 reflects Article 14 of the International Convention on Salvage, 1989. Sub-clause 8.3.2, on the other hand, has no authority to support it, and certainly can have no effect whenever the salvage remuneration has been fixed in accordance with Article 13 of the Convention referred to above (which also forms part of English law).

Clause 10—Sistership

10 **SISTERSHIP**
Should the Vessel hereby insured receive salvage services from another vessel belonging wholly or in part to the same Owners or under the same management, the Assured shall have the same rights under this insurance as they would have were the other vessel entirely the property of Owners not interested in the Vessel hereby insured; but in such cases the amount payable for the services rendered shall be referred to a sole arbitrator to be agreed upon between the Underwriters and the Assured.

Under the majority of hull insurances the Sistership Clause refers to both salvage and collision liability; here, of course, the Clause is effective only in the event of salvage services being rendered by a sister vessel.

Clause 11—Notice of Claim

11 **NOTICE OF CLAIM**
In the event of accident whereby loss or damage may result in a claim under this insurance, notice must be given to the Underwriters promptly after the date on which the Assured, Owners or Managers becomes or should have become aware of the loss or damage and prior to survey so that a surveyor may be appointed if the Underwriters so desire.
If notice is not given to the Underwriters within twelve months of that date unless the Underwriters agree to the contrary in writing, the Underwriters will be automatically discharged from liability for any claim under this insurance in respect of or arising out of such accident or the loss or damage.

The wording of this clause is identical with sub-clause 13.1 in the Institute Time Clauses, Hulls, 1/11/95. The provisions dealing with tenders, which appear as sub-clauses 13.2, .3 and .4 in the Institute Time Clauses, Hulls, do not have any place here, as they concern only claims for partial losses, which are excluded by this form of insurance.

Clauses omitted

The following clauses which appear in the Institute Time Clauses, Hulls are omitted here, as they are not relevant to an insurance against total loss only. **8. 3/4ths Collision Liability; 14. New for Old; 15. Bottom Treatment; 16. Wages and Maintenance; 17. Agency Commission; 18. Unrepaired Damage.**

5. INSTITUTE VOYAGE CLAUSES, HULLS

Whereas in the early days of insurance virtually all policies effected were for a round voyage, the reverse is now the case and the vast majority of insurances are effected on a time basis. For the minority of cases where an insurance is required for a voyage, two sets of main clauses are available. They are

Institute Voyage Clauses, Hulls
Institute Voyage Clauses, Hulls—Total Loss, General Average and 3/4ths

Collision Liability (including Salvage, Salvage Charges and Sue and Labour).

We set out below the full text of the first set, followed by a commentary which, to avoid duplication, will mention only the differences between the Voyage Clauses and the Institute Time Clauses, Hulls.

Institute Voyage Clauses, Hulls 1/11/95

This insurance is subject to English law and practice

1 **NAVIGATION**

1.1 The Vessel is covered subject to the provisions of this insurance at all times and has leave to sail or navigate with or without pilots, to go on trial trips and to assist and tow vessels or craft in distress, but it is warranted that the Vessel shall not be towed, except as is customary or to the first safe port or place when in need of assistance, or undertake towage or salvage services under a contract previously arranged by the Assured and/or Owners and/or Managers and/or Charterers. This Clause 1.1 shall not exclude customary towage in connection with loading and discharging.

1.2 This insurance shall not be prejudiced by reason of the Assured entering into any contract with pilots or for customary towage which limits or exempts the liability of the pilots and/or tugs and/or towboats and/or their owners when the Assured or their agents accept or are compelled to accept such contracts in accordance with established local law or practice.

1.3 The practice of engaging helicopters for the transportation of personnel, supplies and equipment to and/or from the Vessel shall not prejudice this insurance.

1.4 In the event of the Vessel being employed in trading operations which entail cargo loading or discharging at sea from or into another vessel (not being a harbour or inshore craft) no claim shall be recoverable under this insurance for loss of or damage to the Vessel or liability to any other vessel arising from such loading or discharging operations, including whilst approaching, lying alongside and leaving, unless previous notice that the Vessel is to be employed in such operations has been given to the Underwriters and any amended terms of cover and any additional premium required by them have been agreed.

2 **CHANGE OF VOYAGE**

Held covered in case of deviation or change of voyage or any breach of warranty as to towage or salvage services, provided notice be given to the Underwriters immediately after receipt of advices and any amended terms of cover and any additional premium required by them be agreed.

3 **CLASSIFICATION**

3.1 It is the duty of the Assured, Owners and Managers at the inception of and throughout the period of this insurance to ensure that

3.1.1 the Vessel is classed with a Classification Society agreed by the Underwriters and that her class within that Society is maintained,

3.1.2 any recommendations requirements or restrictions imposed by the Vessel's Classification Society which relate to the Vessel's seaworthiness or to her maintenance in a seaworthy condition are complied with by the dates required by that Society.

3.2 In the event of any breach of the duties set out in Clause 3.1 above, unless the Underwriters agree to the contrary in writing, they will be discharged from liability under this insurance as from the date of the breach provided that if the Vessel is at sea at such date the Underwriters' discharge from liability is deferred until arrival at her next port.

3.3 Any incident condition or damage in respect of which the Vessel's Classification Society might make recommendations as to repairs or other action to be taken by the Assured, Owners and Managers must be promptly reported to the Classification Society.

3.4 Should the Underwriters wish to approach the Classification Society directly for information and/or documents, the Assured will provide the necessary authorization.

4 **PERILS**

4.1 This insurance covers loss of or damage to the subject-matter insured caused by

4.1.1 perils of the seas rivers lakes or other navigable waters

4.1.2 fire, explosion

4.1.3 violent theft by persons from outside the Vessel

4.1.4 jettison

4.1.5 piracy

4.1.6 contact with land conveyance, dock or harbour equipment or installation

4.1.7 earthquake volcanic eruption or lightning

4.1.8 accidents in loading discharging or shifting cargo or fuel.

4.2 This insurance covers loss of or damage to the subject-matter insured caused by

4.2.1 bursting of boilers breakage of shafts or any latent defect in the machinery or hull
4.2.2 negligence of Master Officers Crew or Pilots
4.2.3 negligence of repairers or charterers provided such repairers or charterers are not an Assured hereunder
4.2.4 barratry of Master Officers or Crew
4.2.5 contact with aircraft, helicopters or similar objects, or objects falling therefrom

provided such loss or damage has not resulted from want of due diligence by the Assured, Owners, Managers or Superintendents or any of their onshore management.

4.3 Master Officers Crew or Pilots not to be considered Owners within the meaning of this Clause 4 should they hold shares in the Vessel.

5 **POLLUTION HAZARD**

This insurance covers loss of or damage to the Vessel caused by any governmental authority acting under the powers vested in it to prevent or mitigate a pollution hazard or damage to the environment, or threat thereof, resulting directly from damage to the Vessel for which the Underwriters are liable under this insurance, provided that such act of governmental authority has not resulted from want of due diligence by the Assured, Owners or Managers to prevent or mitigate such hazard, damage, or threat thereof. Master Officers Crew or Pilots not to be considered Owners within the meaning of this Clause 5 should they hold shares in the Vessel.

6 **3/4THS COLLISION LIABILITY**

6.1 The Underwriters agree to indemnify the Assured for three-fourths of any sum or sums paid by the Assured to any other person or persons by reason of the Assured becoming legally liable by way of damages for

6.1.1 loss of or damage to any other vessel or property on any other vessel
6.1.2 delay to or loss of use of any such other vessel or property thereon
6.1.3 general average of, salvage of, or salvage under contract of, any such other vessel or property thereon,

where such payment by the Assured is in consequence of the Vessel hereby insured coming into collision with any other vessel.

6.2 The indemnity provided by this Clause 6 shall be in addition to the indemnity provided by the other terms and conditions of this insurance and shall be subject to the following provisions:

6.2.1 where the insured Vessel is in collision with another vessel and both vessels are to blame then, unless the liability of one or both vessels becomes limited by law, the indemnity under this Clause 6 shall be calculated on the principle of cross-liabilities as if the respective Owners had been compelled to pay to each other such proportion of each other's damages as may have been properly allowed in ascertaining the balance or sum payable by or to the Assured in consequence of the collision,

6.2.2 in no case shall the Underwriters' total liability under Clauses 6.1 and 6.2 exceed their proportionate part of three-fourths of the insured value of the Vessel hereby insured in respect of any one collision.

6.3 The Underwriters will also pay three-fourths of the legal costs incurred by the Assured or which the Assured may be compelled to pay in contesting liability or taking proceedings to limit liability, with the prior written consent of the Underwriters.

EXCLUSIONS

6.4 Provided always that this Clause 6 shall in no case extend to any sum which the Assured shall pay for or in respect of

6.4.1 removal or disposal of obstructions, wrecks, cargoes or any other thing whatsoever
6.4.2 any real or personal property or thing whatsoever except other vessels or property on other vessels
6.4.3 the cargo or other property on, or the engagements of, the insured Vessel
6.4.4 loss of life, personal injury or illness
6.4.5 pollution or contamination, or threat thereof, of any real or personal property or thing whatsoever (except other vessels with which the insured Vessel is in collision or property on such other vessels) or damage to the environment, or threat thereof, save that this exclusion shall not extend to any sum which the Assured shall pay for or in respect of salvage remuneration in which the skill and efforts of the salvors in preventing or minimising damage to the environment as is referred to in Article 13 paragraph 1(b) of the International Convention on Salvage, 1989 have been taken into account.

7 **SISTERSHIP**

Should the Vessel hereby insured come into collision with or receive salvage services from another vessel belonging wholly or in part to the same Owners or under the same management, the Assured shall have the same rights under this insurance as they would have were the other vessel entirely the property of Owners not interested in the Vessel hereby insured; but in such cases the liability for the collision or the amount payable for the services rendered shall be referred to a sole arbitrator to be agreed upon between the Underwriters and the Assured.

8 **GENERAL AVERAGE AND SALVAGE**

8.1 This insurance covers the Vessel's proportion of salvage, salvage charges and/or general average, reduced in respect of any under-insurance, but in case of general average sacrifice of the Vessel the Assured may recover in respect of the whole loss without first enforcing their right of contribution from other parties.

8.2 Adjustment to be according to the law and practice obtaining at the place where the adventure ends, as if the contract of affreightment contained no special terms upon the subject; but where the contract of affreightment so provides the adjustment shall be according to the York-Antwerp Rules.

8.3 When the Vessel sails in ballast, not under charter, the provisions of the York-Antwerp Rules, 1994 (excluding Rules XI(d), XX and XXI) shall be applicable, and the voyage for this purpose shall be deemed to continue from the port or place of departure until the arrival of the Vessel at the first port or place thereafter other than a port or place of refuge or port or place of call for bunkering only. If at any such intermediate port or place there is an abandonment of the adventure originally contemplated the voyage shall thereupon be deemed to be terminated.

8.4 No claim under this Clause 8 shall in any case be allowed where the loss was not incurred to avoid or in connection with the avoidance of a peril insured against.

8.5 No claim under this Clause 8 shall in any case be allowed for or in respect of

8.5.1 special compensation payable to a salvor under Article 14 of the International Convention on Salvage, 1989 or under any other provision in any statute, rule, law or contract which is similar in substance

8.5.2 expenses or liabilities incurred in respect of damage to the environment, or the threat of such damage, or as a consequence of the escape or release of pollutant substances from the Vessel, or the threat of such escape or release.

8.6 Clause 8.5 shall not however exclude any sum which the Assured shall pay to salvors for or in respect of salvage remuneration in which the skill and efforts of the salvors in preventing or minimising damage to the environment as is referred to in Article 13 paragraph 1(b) of the International Convention on Salvage, 1989 have been taken into account.

9 **DUTY OF ASSURED (SUE AND LABOUR)**

9.1 In case of any loss or misfortune it is the duty of the Assured and their servants and agents to take such measures as may be reasonable for the purpose of averting or minimising a loss which would be recoverable under this insurance.

9.2 Subject to the provisions below and to Clause 10 the Underwriters will contribute to charges properly and reasonably incurred by the Assured their servants or agents for such measures. General average, salvage charges (except as provided for in Clause 9.5), special compensation and expenses as referred to in Clause 8.5, and collision defence or attack costs are not recoverable under this Clause 9.

9.3 Measures taken by the Assured or the Underwriters with the object of saving, protecting or recovering the subject-matter insured shall not be considered as a waiver or acceptance of abandonment or otherwise prejudice the rights of either party.

9.4 When expenses are incurred pursuant to this Clause 9 the liability under this insurance shall not exceed the proportion of such expenses that the amount insured hereunder bears to the value of the Vessel as stated herein, or to the sound value of the Vessel at the time of the occurrence giving rise to the expenditure if the sound value exceeds that value. Where the Underwriters have admitted a claim for total loss and property insured by this insurance is saved, the foregoing provisions shall not apply unless the expenses of suing and labouring exceed the value of such property saved and then shall apply only to the amount of the expenses which is in excess of such value.

9.5 When a claim for total loss of the Vessel is admitted under this insurance and expenses have been reasonably incurred in saving or attempting to save the Vessel and other property and there are no proceeds, or the expenses exceed the proceeds, then this insurance shall bear its pro rata share of such proportion of the expenses, or of the expenses in excess of the proceeds, as the case may be, as may reasonably be regarded as having been incurred in respect of the Vessel, excluding all special compensation and expenses as referred to in Clause 8.5; but if the Vessel be insured for less than its sound value at the time of the occurrence giving rise to the expenditure, the amount recoverable under this clause shall be reduced in proportion to the under-insurance.

9.6 The sum recoverable under this Clause 9 shall be in addition to the loss otherwise recoverable under this insurance but shall in no circumstances exceed the amount insured under this insurance in respect of the Vessel.

10 **DEDUCTIBLE**

10.1 No claim arising from a peril insured against shall be payable under this insurance unless the aggregate of all such claims arising out of each separate accident or occurrence (including claims under Clauses 6, 8 and 9) exceeds the deductible amount agreed in which case this sum shall be deducted. Nevertheless the expense of sighting the bottom after stranding, if reasonably incurred specially for that purpose shall be paid even if no damage be found. This Clause 10.1 shall not apply to a claim for total or constructive total loss of the Vessel or, in the event of such a claim, to any associated claim under Clause 9 arising from the same accident or occurrence.

10.2 Claims for damage by heavy weather occurring during a single sea passage between two successive ports shall be treated as being due to one accident. In the case of such heavy weather extending over a period not wholly covered by this insurance the deductible to be applied to the claim recoverable hereunder shall be the proportion of the above deductible that the number of days of such heavy weather falling within the period of this insurance bears to the number of days of heavy weather during the single sea passage. The expression "heavy weather" in this Clause 10.2 shall be deemed to include contact with floating ice.

10.3 Excluding any interest comprised therein, recoveries against any claim which is subject to the above deductible shall be credited to the Underwriters in full to the extent of the sum by which the aggregate of the claim unreduced by any recoveries exceeds the above deductible.

10.4 Interest comprised in recoveries shall be apportioned between the Assured and the Underwriters, taking into account the sums paid by the Underwriters and the dates when such payments were made, notwithstanding that by the addition of interest the Underwriters may receive a larger sum than they have paid.

11 **NOTICE OF CLAIM AND TENDERS**

11.1 In the event of accident whereby loss or damage may result in a claim under this insurance, notice must be given to the Underwriters promptly after the date on which the Assured, Owners or Managers become or should have become aware of the loss or damage and prior to survey and so that a surveyor may be appointed if the Underwriters so desire.

If notice is not given to the Underwriters within twelve months of that date, unless the Underwriters agree to the contrary in writing, the Underwriters will be automatically discharged from liability for any claim under this insurance in respect of or arising out of such accident or the loss or damage.

11.2 The Underwriters shall be entitled to decide the port to which the Vessel shall proceed for docking or repair (the actual additional expense of the voyage arising from compliance with the Underwriters' requirements being refunded to the Assured) and shall have a right of veto concerning a place of repair or a repairing firm.

11.3 The Underwriters may also take tenders or may require further tenders to be taken for the repair of the Vessel. Where such a tender has been taken and a tender is accepted with the approval of the Underwriters, an allowance shall be made at the rate of 30% per annum on the insured value for time lost between the despatch of the invitations to tender required by the Underwriters and the acceptance of a tender to the extent that such time is lost solely as the result of tenders having been taken and provided that the tender is accepted without delay after receipt of the Underwriters' approval.

Due credit shall be given against the allowance as above for any amounts recovered in respect of fuel and stores and wages and maintenance of the Master Officers and Crew or any member thereof, including amounts allowed in general average, and for any amounts recovered from third parties in respect of damages for detention and/or loss of profit and/or running expenses, for the period covered by the tender allowance or any part thereof.

Where a part of the cost of the repair of damage other than a fixed deductible is not recoverable from the Underwriters the allowance shall be reduced by a similar proportion.

11.4 In the event of failure by the Assured to comply with the conditions of Clauses 11.2 and/or 11.3 a deduction of 15% shall be made from the amount of the ascertained claim.

12 **NEW FOR OLD**

Claims payable without deduction new for old.

13 **BOTTOM TREATMENT**

In no case shall a claim be allowed in respect of scraping gritblasting and/or other surface preparation or painting of the Vessel's bottom except that

13.1 gritblasting and/or other surface preparation of new bottom plates ashore and supplying and applying any "shop" primer thereto,

13.2 gritblasting and/or other surface preparation of:

the butts or area of plating immediately adjacent to any renewed or refitted plating damaged during the course of welding and/or repairs,

areas of plating damaged during the course of fairing, either in place or ashore,

13.3 supplying and applying the first coat of primer/anti-corrosive to those particular areas mentioned in 13.1 and 13.2 above,

shall be allowed as part of the reasonable cost of repairs in respect of bottom plating damaged by an insured peril.

14 **WAGES AND MAINTENANCE**

No claim shall be allowed, other than in general average, for wages and maintenance of the Master Officers and Crew or any member thereof, except when incurred solely for the necessary removal of the Vessel from one port to another for the repair of damage covered by the Underwriters, or for trial trips for such repairs, and then only for such wages and maintenance as are incurred whilst the Vessel is under way.

15 **AGENCY COMMISSION**

In no case shall any sum be allowed under this insurance either by way of remuneration of the Assured for time and trouble taken to obtain and supply information or documents or in respect of the commission or charges of any manager, agent, managing or agency company or the like, appointed by or on behalf of the Assured to perform such services.

16 **UNREPAIRED DAMAGE**

16.1 The measure of indemnity in respect of claims for unrepaired damage shall be the reasonable depreciation in the market value of the Vessel at the time this insurance terminates arising from such unrepaired damage, but not exceeding the reasonable cost of repairs.

16.2 In no case shall the Underwriters be liable for unrepaired damage in the event of a subsequent total loss (whether or not covered under this insurance) sustained during the period covered by this insurance or any extension thereof.

16.3 The Underwriters shall not be liable in respect of unrepaired damage for more than the insured value at the time this insurance terminates.

17 **CONSTRUCTIVE TOTAL LOSS**

17.1 In ascertaining whether the Vessel is a constructive total loss, the insured value shall be taken as the repaired value and nothing in respect of the damaged or break-up value of the Vessel or wreck shall be taken into account.

17.2 No claim for constructive total loss based upon the cost of recovery and/or repair of the Vessel shall be recoverable hereunder unless such cost would exceed the insured value. In making this determination, only the cost relating to a single accident or sequence of damages arising from the same accident shall be taken into account.

18 **FREIGHT WAIVER**

In the event of total or constructive total loss no claim to be made by the Underwriters for freight whether notice of abandonment has been given or not.

19 **ASSIGNMENT**

No assignment of or interest in this insurance or in any moneys which may be or become payable thereunder is to be binding on or recognised by the Underwriters unless a dated notice of such assignment or interest signed by the Assured, and by the assignor in the case of subsequent assignment, is endorsed on the Policy and the Policy with such endorsement is produced before payment of any claim or return of premium thereunder.

20 **DISBURSEMENTS WARRANTY**

20.1 Additional insurances as follows are permitted:

20.1.1 *Disbursements, Managers' Commissions, Profits or Excess or Increased Value of Hull and Machinery.* A sum not exceeding 25% of the value stated herein.

20.1.2 *Freight, Chartered Freight or Anticipated Freight, insured for time.* A sum not exceeding 25% of the value as stated herein less any sum insured, however described, under 20.1.1.

20.1.3 *Freight or Hire, under contracts for voyage.* A sum not exceeding the gross freight or hire for the current cargo passage and next succeeding cargo passage (such insurance to include, if required, a preliminary and an intermediate ballast passage) plus the charges of insurance. In the case of a voyage charter where payment is made on a time basis, the sum permitted for insurance shall be calculated on the estimated duration of the voyage, subject to the limitation of two cargo passages as laid down herein. Any sum insured under 20.1.2 to be taken into account and only the excess thereof may be insured, which excess shall be reduced as the freight or hire is advanced or earned by the gross amount so advanced or earned.

20.1.4 *Anticipated Freight if the Vessel sails in ballast and not under Charter.* A sum not exceeding the anticipated gross freight on next cargo passage, such sum to be reasonably estimated on the basis of the current rate of freight at time of insurance plus the charges of insurance. Any sum insured under 20.1.2 to be taken into account and only the excess thereof may be insured.

20.1.5 *Time Charter Hire or Charter Hire for Series of Voyages.* A sum not exceeding 50% of the gross hire which is to be earned under the charter in a period not exceeding 18 months. Any sum insured under 20.1.2 to be taken into account and only the excess thereof may be insured, which excess shall be reduced as the hire is advanced or earned under the charter by 50% of the gross amount so advanced or earned but the sum insured need not be reduced while the total of the sums insured under 20.1.2 and 20.1.5 does not exceed 50% of the gross hire still to be earned under the charter. An insurance under this Section may begin on the signing of the charter.

20.1.6 *Premiums.* A sum not exceeding the actual premiums of all interests insured for a period not exceeding 12 months (excluding premiums insured under the foregoing sections but including, if required, the premium or estimated calls on any Club or War etc. Risk insurance) reducing pro rata monthly.

20.1.7 *Returns of Premium.* A sum not exceeding the actual returns which are allowable under any insurance but which would not be recoverable thereunder in the event of a total loss of the Vessel whether by insured perils or otherwise.

20.1.8 *Insurance irrespective of amount against:* Any risks excluded by Clauses 21, 22, 23 and 24 below.

20.2 Warranted that no insurance on any interests enumerated in the foregoing 20.1.1 to 20.1.7 in excess of the amounts permitted therein and no other insurance which includes total loss of the Vessel P.P.I., F.I.A., or subject to any other like term, is or shall be effected to operate during the currency of this insurance by or for account of the Assured, Owners, Managers or Mortgagees. Provided always that a breach of this warranty shall not afford the Underwriters any defence to a claim by a Mortgagee who has accepted this insurance without knowledge of such breach.

The following clauses shall be paramount and shall override anything contained in this insurance inconsistent therewith.

21 **WAR EXCLUSION**

In no case shall this insurance cover loss damage liability or expense caused by

21.1 war civil war revolution rebellion insurrection, or civil strife arising therefrom, or any hostile act by or against a belligerent power

21.2 capture seizure arrest restraint or detainment (barratry and piracy excepted), and the consequences thereof or any attempt thereat

21.3 derelict mines torpedoes bombs or other derelict weapons of war.

22 **STRIKES EXCLUSION**

In no case shall this insurance cover loss damage liability or expense caused by

22.1 strikers, locked-out workmen, or persons taking part in labour disturbances, riots or civil commotions

22.2 any terrorist or any person acting from a political motive.

23 **MALICIOUS ACTS EXCLUSION**

In no case shall this insurance cover loss damage liability or expense arising from

23.1 the detonation of an explosive

23.2 any weapon of war

and caused by any person acting maliciously or from a political motive.

24 **RADIOACTIVE CONTAMINATION EXCLUSION CLAUSE**

In no case shall this insurance cover loss damage liability or expense directly or indirectly caused by or contributed to by or arising from

24.1 ionising radiations from or contamination by radioactivity from any nuclear fuel or from any nuclear waste or from the combustion of nuclear fuel

24.2 the radioactive, toxic, explosive or other hazardous or contaminating properties of any nuclear installation, reactor or other nuclear assembly or nuclear component thereof

24.3 any weapon of war employing atomic or nuclear fission and/or fusion or other like reaction or radioactive force or matter.

Clause 1—Navigation

The text follows sub-clauses 1, 2, 3 and 4 as they appear in the Institute Time Clauses, Hulls, 1/11/95. However, sub-clause 1.5 of the I.T.C. Hulls is omitted, since this deals with the situation on a scrapping voyage, which is not required on a voyage insurance. Obviously the details and nature of the intended voyage are material facts which must be disclosed before the contract is concluded (see Marine Insurance Act 1906, section 18), and the underwriter on a voyage policy would therefore have ample opportunity to impose any special conditions considered necessary at the time of the negotiations for the placing of the risk.

Clause 2—Change of voyage

This clause takes the place of the Continuation and Breach of Warranty Clauses which appear in the I.T.C. Hulls, 1/11/95, since those clauses would not be relevant to a voyage insurance.

The relevant law as to insurances for voyage is laid out in sections 42–49 inclusive of the Marine Insurance Act 1906, which provide as follows:

> "**Implied condition as to commencement of risk**
>
> **42**.—(1) Where the subject-matter is insured by a voyage policy 'at and from' or 'from' a particular place, it is not necessary that the ship should be at that place when the contract is concluded, but there is an implied condition that the adventure shall be commenced within a reasonable time, and that if the adventure be not so commenced the insurer may avoid the contract.

(2) The implied condition may be negatived by showing that the delay was caused by circumstances known to the insurer before the contract was concluded, or by showing that he waived the condition.

Alteration of port of departure

43. Where the place of departure is specified by the policy, and the ship instead of sailing from that place sails from any other place, the risk does not attach.

Sailing for different destination

44. Where the destination is specified in the policy, and the ship, instead of sailing for that destination, sails for any other destination, the risk does not attach.

Change of voyage

45.—(1) Where, after the commencement of the risk, the destination of the ship is voluntarily changed from the destination contemplated by the policy, there is said to be a change of voyage.

(2) Unless the policy otherwise provides, where there is a change of voyage, the insurer is discharged from liability as from the time of change, that is to say, as from the time when the determination to change it is manifested; and it is immaterial that the ship may not in fact have left the course of voyage contemplated by the policy when the loss occurs.

Deviation

46.—(1) Where a ship, without lawful excuse, deviates from the voyage contemplated by the policy, the insurer is discharged from liability as from the time of deviation, and it is immaterial that the ship may have regained her route before any loss occurs.

(2) There is a deviation from the voyage contemplated by the policy—

(*a*) Where the course of the voyage is specifically designated by the policy, and that course is departed from; or

(*b*) Where the course of the voyage is not specifically designated by the policy, but the usual and customary course is departed from.

(3) The intention to deviate is immaterial; there must be a deviation in fact to discharge the insurer from his liability under the contract.

Several ports of discharge

47.—(1) Where several ports of discharge are specified by the policy, the ship may proceed to all or any of them, but, in the absence of any usage of sufficient cause to the contrary, she must proceed to them, or such of them as she goes to, in the order designated by the policy. If she does not there is a deviation.

(2) Where the policy is to 'ports of discharge,' within a given area, which are not named, the ship must, in the absence of any usage or sufficient cause to the contrary, proceed to them, or such of them as she goes to, in their geographical order. If she does not there is a deviation.

Delay in voyage

48. In the case of a voyage policy, the adventure insured must be prosecuted throughout its course with reasonable dispatch, and, if without lawful excuse it is not so prosecuted, the insurer is discharged from liability as from the time when the delay became unreasonable.

Excuses for deviation or delay

49.—(1) Deviation or delay in prosecuting the voyage contemplated by the policy is excused—

(*a*) Where authorised by any special term in the policy; or
(*b*) Where caused by circumstances beyond the control of the master and his employer; or
(*c*) Where reasonably necessary in order to comply with an express or implied warranty; or
(*d*) Where reasonably necessary for the safety of the ship or subject-matter insured; or
(*e*) For the purpose of saving human life, or aiding a ship in distress where human life may be in danger; or
(*f*) Where reasonably necessary for the purpose of obtaining medical or surgical aid for any person on board the ship; or
(*g*) Where caused by the barratrous conduct of the master or crew, if barratry be one of the perils insured against.

(2) When the cause excusing the deviation or delay ceases to operate, the ship must resume her course, and prosecute her voyage, with reasonable dispatch."

The Change of Voyage Clause ameliorates the position under English law very substantially and holds the assured covered in cases of deviation or change of voyage or any breach of warranty as to towage or salvage services. This is subject to the proviso that the accused gives notice to underwriters immediately he becomes aware of the facts and that any amended terms of cover and additional premium are agreed. The importance of complying with the proviso to give prompt notice in accordance with Clause 2 of the Institute Voyage Clauses, Hulls is illustrated by the recent case of *Fraser Shipping Ltd.* v. *Colton*.[81] In that case the assured delayed giving notice until the vessel had arrived at her alternative port, by which time that port was threatened by a typhoon. The brokers, not having been told by the assured that the port was unsafe, obtained the underwriters' apparent endorsement to an (admittedly late) change of voyage notice, but this was of no avail when the case came to trial, since the judge held that the underwriters were entitled to avoid the policy on the ground of non-disclosure.

Clauses 3 to 24 inclusive

The text of these clauses is the same, word for word (apart from numbering) as their counterparts in the Institute Time Clauses, Hulls, 1/11/95.

However, in addition to the Termination and Breach of Warranty Clauses

81. *Fraser Shipping Ltd.* v. *Colton (The "Shakir III")* [1997] 1 Lloyd's Rep. 586.

already mentioned, the following clauses appearing in the I.T.C. Hulls are omitted, since they are not required in an insurance for voyage:

— Termination Clause
— Returns for Lay-up and Cancellation

Institute Voyage Clauses, Hulls—Total Loss, General Average and 3/4ths Collision Liability (Including Salvage, Salvage Charges and Sue and Labour) 1/11/95

The following clauses in list A are those which in this form (apart from numbering) are the same as in the Institute Voyage Clauses, Hulls, 1/11/95 (correspondingly numbered as in list B):

Title of Clause	List A	List B
Navigation	1	1
Continuation	2	2
Classification	3	3
3/4ths Collision Liability	6	6
Sistership	7	7
Duty of Assured (Sue and Labour)	9	9
Agency Commission	13	15
Constructive Total Loss	14	17
Freight Waiver	15	18
Assignment	16	19
Disbursements Warranty	17	20
Exclusions for War, Strikes, Malicious Acts and Radioactive Contamination	18/21	21/24

The clauses which differ are:

Clauses 4 and 5—Perils and Pollution Hazard

The perils insured are the same as those set out in the Institute Voyage Clauses, Hulls, 1/11/95, but the cover in each case is limited to "total loss (actual or constructive)".

Clause 8—General Average and Salvage

The position here is the same as in Clause 10 of the Institute Time Clauses, Hulls—Total Loss, General Average and Sue and Labour, 1/11/95 (see pages

160 to 161); i.e. sacrifice of ship is payable only for ship's proportion, along with ship's proportion of salvage, general average expenditure and the contribution payable in general average to the losses of other parties.

Clauses 10, 11 and 12—Deductible, Notice of Claim and New for Old

These clauses are amended to reflect the fact that the cover is restricted to exclude claims for particular average. These clauses are the same, word for word, as the corresponding clauses in hull insurances for time (see pages 161 to 162).

Clauses omitted

The following clauses which appear in the Institute Voyage Clauses, Hulls are omitted here, as they relate solely to claims in particular average:
13. Bottom Treatment; 14. Wages and Maintenance; 16. Unrepaired damage.

6. INSTITUTE TIME CLAUSES, HULLS—PORT RISKS

These forms are available, at a reduced premium, to owners of vessels whose operations are restricted geographically to a closely defined area. This intended area of operation (or non-operation) is disclosed early in the negotiations prior to attachment of the insurance, and when defined and agreed, will be set out in the schedule to the MAR forms (see page 6) or otherwise attached to the policy.

In general terms, therefore, the Port Risk forms are appropriate to cover the risks attaching to:

- — vessels, such as tugs, pilot boats, dredgers, etc whose operations are confined to an agreed location
- — vessels laid up within an agreed location.

Institute Time Clauses Hulls—Port Risks 20/7/87

This insurance is subject to English law and practice.

See the commentary on these words on pages 90 to 91.

1 **NAVIGATION**
The Vessel has leave to proceed to and from any wet or dry docks harbours ways cradles and pontoons, within the limits specified in this insurance.

It will be noted that within the limits "specified in this insurance", i.e., negotiated prior to attachment, the vessel has leave to proceed to and from wet and dry docks, etc. Any trading outside the agreed limits, of course, requires separate negotiation.

2 **TERMINATION**
This Clause 2 shall prevail notwithstanding any provision whether written typed or printed in this insurance inconsistent therewith.
Unless Underwriters agree to the contrary in writing, this insurance shall terminate automatically at the time of
2.1 change of the Classification Society of the Vessel, or change, suspension, discontinuance, withdrawal or expiry of her Class therein. However where such change, suspension, discontinuance or withdrawal of her Class has resulted from loss or damage covered by Clause 4 of this insurance or which would be covered by an insurance of the Vessel subject to current Institute War and Strikes Clauses Hulls Time such automatic termination shall not operate—
2.2 any change, voluntary or otherwise, in the ownership or flag, transfer to new management, or charter on a bareboat basis, or requisition for title or use of the Vessel. However, in the event of requisition for title or use without the prior execution of a written agreement by the Assured, such automatic termination shall occur fifteen days after such requisition whether the Vessel is in port or at sea.

The wording in bold type emphasises that this is a clause paramount which prevails notwithstanding any contrary provision in the policy. The terms of the clause are similar to Clause 4 of the I.T.C. Hulls, except that there is no provision for the deferment of automatic termination of the policy when the vessel is at sea, since it is not expected that a vessel will be at sea during the currency of a Port Risks policy.

3 **ASSIGNMENT**
No assignment of or interest in this insurance or in any moneys which may be or become payable thereunder is to be binding on or recognised by the Underwriters unless a dated notice of such assignment or interest signed by the Assured, and by the assignor in the case of subsequent assignment, is endorsed on the Policy and the Policy with such endorsement is produced before payment of any claim or return of premium thereunder.

This is the same as Clause 21 in the Institute Time Clauses, Hulls. See commentary on page 150.

4 **PERILS**
4.1 This insurance covers loss of or damage to the subject-matter insured caused by
4.1.1 perils of the seas rivers lakes or other navigable waters
4.1.2 fire lightning explosion
4.1.3 violent theft by persons from outside the Vessel
4.1.4 jettison
4.1.5 piracy
4.1.6 breakdown of or accident to nuclear installations or reactors
4.1.7 contact with aircraft or similar objects, or objects falling therefrom, land conveyance, dock or harbour equipment or installation
4.2 This insurance covers loss of or damage to the subject-matter insured caused by
4.2.1 accidents in loading discharging or shifting cargo or fuel
4.2.2 bursting of boilers breakage of shafts or any latent defect in the machinery or hull
4.2.3 negligence of Master Officers Crew or Pilots
4.2.4 negligence of repairers or charterers provided such repairers or charterers are not an Assured hereunder
4.2.5 barratry of Master Officers or Crew
provided such loss or damage has not resulted from want of due diligence by the Assured, Owners or Managers.
4.3 Master Officers Crew or Pilots not to be considered Owners within the meaning of this Clause 4 should they hold shares in the Vessel.

5 **EARTHQUAKE AND VOLCANIC ERUPTION EXCLUSION**
In no case shall this insurance cover loss damage liability or expenses caused by earthquake or volcanic eruption. This exclusion applies to all claims including claims under Clauses 7, 9, 11 and 13.

It will be observed that the list of the perils insured is not the same as in the Institute Time Clauses, Hulls. The effect of the change is that, whereas lightning is included in Clause 4.1.2, earthquake and volcanic eruption is specifically excluded by Clause 5. The present editor can think of no rational explanation for this limitation of the cover, unless it be that underwriters wish to charge an additional premium for volcanic activity.

6 POLLUTION HAZARD

This insurance covers loss of or damage to the Vessel caused by any governmental authority acting under the powers vested in it to prevent or mitigate a pollution hazard, or threat thereof, resulting directly from damage to the Vessel for which the Underwriters are liable under this insurance, provided such act of governmental authority has not resulted from want of due diligence by the Assured, the Owners, or Managers of the Vessel or any of them to prevent or mitigate such hazard or threat. Master, Officers, Crew or Pilots not to be considered Owners within the meaning of this Clause 6 should they hold shares in the Vessel.

This clause is the same as that introduced into the Institute Time Clauses, Hulls in 1983. See commentary on page 118.

7 COLLISION LIABILITY

7.1 The Underwriters agree to indemnify the Assured for any sum or sums paid by the Assured to any other person or persons by reason of the Assured becoming legally liable by way of damages for

7.1.1 loss of or damage to any other vessel or property on any other vessel

7.1.2 delay to or loss of use of any such other vessel or property thereon

7.1.3 general average of, salvage of, or salvage under contract of, any such other vessel or property thereon,

where such payment by the Assured is in consequence of the Vessel hereby insured coming into collision with any other vessel.

7.2 The indemnity provided by this Clause 7 shall be in addition to the indemnity provided by the other terms and conditions of this insurance and shall be subject to the following provisions:

7.2.1 Where the insured Vessel is in collision with another vessel and both vessels are to blame then, unless the liability of one or both vessels becomes limited by law, the indemnity under this Clause 7 shall be calculated to the principle of cross-liabilities as if the respective Owners had been compelled to pay to each other such proportion of each other's damages as may have been properly allowed in ascertaining the balance or sum payable by or to the Assured in consequence of the collision.

7.2.2 In no case shall the Underwriters' total liability under Clauses 7.1 and 7.2 exceed their proportionate part of the insured value of the Vessel hereby insured in respect of any one such collision.

7.3 The Underwriters will also pay the legal costs incurred by the Assured or which the Assured may be compelled to pay in contesting liability or taking proceedings to limit liability, with the prior written consent of the Underwriters.

EXCLUSIONS

7.4 Provided always that this Clause 7 shall in no case extend to any sum which the Assured shall pay for or in respect of

7.4.1 removal or disposal of obstructions, wrecks, cargoes or any other thing whatsoever

7.4.2 any real or personal property or thing whatsoever except other vessels or property on other vessels

7.4.3 the cargo or other property on, or the engagements of, the insured Vessel

7.4.4 loss of life, personal injury or illness

7.4.5 pollution or contamination of any real or personal property or thing whatsoever (except other vessels with which the insured Vessel is in collision or property on such other vessels).

This clause differs from the corresponding clause in the Institute Time Clauses, Hulls, in that under the Port Risks clauses, the underwriters agree to bear the whole of the liability of the assured for collision, damages and costs, rather than the three-fourths which they are prepared to accept for vessels engaged in deep-sea trading. This extension, together with the cover provided by Clause 9—the Protection and Indemnity clause—makes it possible for an assured to obtain under one policy all the cover he requires, both for loss and damage to his vessel and for his potential liabilities.

Other than the extension from 3/4ths to 4/4ths, the detailed provisions and exclusions in this Clause 7 are the same as in the Running Down clause in the I.T.C. Hulls, 1/10/83. See commentary on pages 118 to 125.

8 **SISTERSHIP**
Should the Vessel hereby insured come into collision with or receive salvage services from another vessel belonging wholly or in part to the same Owners or under the same management, the Assured shall have the same rights under this insurance as they would have were the other vessel entirely the property of Owners not interested in the Vessel hereby insured; but in such cases the liability for the collision or the amount payable for the services rendered shall be referred to a sole arbitrator to be agreed upon between the Underwriters and the Assured.

The sistership clause is in the same terms as in the I.T.C. Hulls.

9 **PROTECTION AND INDEMNITY**
9.1 The Underwriters agree to indemnify the Assured for any sum or sums paid by the Assured to any other person or persons by reason of the Assured becoming legally liable, as owner of the Vessel, for any claim, demand, damages and/or expenses, where such liability is in consequence of any of the following matters or things and arises from an accident or occurrence during the period of this insurance.
9.1.1 loss of or damage to any fixed or movable object or property or other thing or interest whatsoever, other than the Vessel, arising from any cause whatsoever in so far as such loss or damage is not covered by Clause 7
9.1.2 any attempted or actual raising, removal or destruction of any fixed or movable object or property or other thing, including the wreck of the Vessel, or any neglect or failure to raise, remove, or destroy the same
9.1.3 liability assumed by the Assured under contracts of customary towage for the purpose of entering or leaving port or manoeuvering within the port during the ordinary course of trading
9.1.4 loss of life, personal injury, illness or payments made for life salvage
9.1.5 liability under Clause 1(a) of the current Lloyd's Standard Form of Salvage Agreement in respect of unsuccessful, partially successful, or uncompleted services if and to the extent that the salvor's expenses plus the increment exceed any amount otherwise recoverable under the Agreement.
9.2 The Underwriters agree to indemnify the Assured for any of the following arising from an accident or occurrence during the period of this insurance:
9.2.1 the additional cost of fuel, insurance, wages, stores, provisions and port charges reasonably incurred solely for the purpose of landing from the Vessel sick or injured persons or stowaways, refugees, or persons saved at sea
9.2.2 additional expenses brought about by the outbreak of infectious disease on board the Vessel or ashore
9.2.3 fines imposed on the Vessel, on the Assured, or on any Master Officer crew member or agent of the Vessel who is reimbursed by the Assured, for any act or neglect or breach of any statute or regulation relating to the operation of the Vessel, provided that the Underwriters shall not be liable to indemnify the Assured for any fines which result from any act neglect failure or default of the Assured their agents or servants other than Master Officer or crew member
9.2.4 the expenses of the removal of the wreck of the Vessel from any place owned, leased or occupied by the Assured
9.2.5 legal costs incurred by the Assured, or which the Assured may be compelled to pay, in avoiding, minimising or contesting liability with the prior written consent of the Underwriters.
EXCLUSIONS
9.3 Notwithstanding the provisions of Clauses 9.1 and 9.2 this Clause 9 does not cover any liability cost or expense arising in respect of:
9.3.1 any direct or indirect payment by the Assured under workmen's compensation or employers' liability acts and any other statutory or common law, general maritime law or other liability whatsoever in respect of accidents to or illness of workmen or any other persons employed in any capacity whatsoever by the Assured or others in on or about or in connection with the Vessel or her cargo, materials or repairs
9.3.2 liability assumed by the Assured under agreement expressed or implied in respect of death or illness of or injury to any person employed under a contract of service or apprenticeship by the other party to such agreement
9.3.3 punitive or exemplary damages, however described
9.3.4 cargo or other property carried, to be carried or which has been carried on board the Vessel but this Clause 9.3.4 shall not exclude any claim in respect of the extra cost of removing cargo from the wreck of the Vessel
9.3.5 property, owned by builders or repairers or for which they are responsible, which is on board the Vessel
9.3.6 liability arising under a contract or indemnity in respect of containers, equipment, fuel or other property on board the Vessel and which is owned or leased by the Assured
9.3.7 cash, negotiable instruments, precious metals or stones, valuables or objects of a rare or precious nature, belonging to persons on board the Vessel, or non-essential personal effects of any Master, Officer or crew member

9.3.8 fuel, insurance, wages, stores, provisions and port charges arising from delay to the Vessel while awaiting a substitute for any Master, Officer or crew member

9.3.9 fines or penalties arising from overloading or illegal fishing

9.3.10 pollution or contamination of any real or personal property or thing whatsoever (This Clause 9.3.10 shall not exclude any amount recoverable under Clause 9.1.5)

9.3.11 general average, sue and labour and salvage charges, salvage, and/or collision liability to any extent that they are not recoverable under Clauses 7, 11 and 13 by reason of the agreed value and/or the amount insured in respect of the Vessel being inadequate.

9.4 The indemnity provided by this Clause 9 shall be in addition to the indemnity provided by the other terms and conditions of this insurance.

9.5 Where the Assured or the Underwriters may or could have limited their liability the indemnity under this Clause 9 in respect of such liability shall not exceed Underwriters' proportionate part of the amount of such limitation.

9.6 In no case shall the Underwriters' liability under this Clause 9 in respect of each separate accident or occurrence or series of accidents arising out of the same event, exceed their proportionate part of the insured value of the Vessel.

9.7 PROVIDED ALWAYS THAT

9.7.1 prompt notice must be given to the Underwriters of every casualty event or claim upon the Assured which may give rise to a claim under this Clause 9 and of every event or matter which may cause the Assured to incur liability costs or expense for which he may be insured under this Clause 9.

9.7.2 the Assured shall not admit liability for or settle any claim for which he may be insured under this Clause 9 without the prior written consent of the Underwriters.

Protection and indemnity risks

Like the Running Down clause, the Protection and Indemnity clause creates a separate additional obligation on the part of underwriters to respond for certain deemed liabilities up to 100 per cent of the insured value of the vessel (see Clauses 9.4 and 9.6).

The detailed provisions of the Protection and Indemnity clause are set out and commented upon in Part IV of this book, on pages 240 to 249.

10 NOTICE OF CLAIM AND TENDERS

10.1 In the event of accident whereby lose or damage may result in a claim under this insurance, notice shall be given to the Underwriters prior to survey and also, if the Vessel is abroad, to the nearest Lloyd's Agent so that a surveyor may be appointed to represent the Underwriters should they so desire.

10.2 The Underwriters shall be entitled to decide the port to which the Vessel shall proceed for docking or repair (the actual additional expense of the voyage arising from compliance with the Underwriters' requirements being refunded to the Assured) and shall have a right of veto concerning a place of repair or a repairing firm.

10.3 The Underwriters may also take tenders or may require further tenders to be taken for the repair of the Vessel. Where such a tender has been taken and a tender is accepted with the approval of the Underwriters, an allowance shall be made at the rate of 30% per annum on the insured value for time lost between the despatch of the invitations to tender required by Underwriters and the acceptance of a tender to the extent that such time is lost solely as the result of tenders having been taken and provided that the tender is accepted without delay after receipt of the Underwriters' approval.

Due credit shall be given against the allowance as above for any amounts recovered in respect of fuel and stores and wages and maintenance of the Master Officers and Crew or any member thereof, including amounts allowed in general average, and for any amounts recovered from third parties in respect of damages for detention and/or loss of profit and/or running expenses, for the period covered by the tender allowance or any part thereof.

Where a part of the cost of the repair of damage other than a fixed deductible is not recoverable from the Underwriters the allowance shall be reduced by a similar proportion.

10.4 In the event of failure to comply with the conditions of this Clause 10, a deduction of 15% shall be made from the amount of the ascertained claim.

This clause is in the form current from 1983 until its revision in 1995. The provisions as to notice in sub-clause 10.1 are considerably less stringent than those which have been inserted in the Institute Time Clauses, Hulls 1/11/95.

Sub-clauses 10.2, 10.3 and 10.4 are however the same. See commentary on Clause 13 of I.T.C. Hulls on pages 139 to 141.

11 GENERAL AVERAGE AND SALVAGE

11.1 This insurance covers the Vessel's proportion of salvage, salvage charges and/or general average, reduced in respect of any under-insurance, but in case of general average sacrifice of the Vessel the Assured may recover in respect of the whole loss without first enforcing their right of contribution from other parties.

11.2 Adjustment to be according to the law and practice obtaining at the place where the adventure ends, as if the contract of affreightment contained no special terms upon the subject; but where the contract of affreightment so provides the adjustment shall be according to the York-Antwerp Rules.

11.3 No claim under this Clause 11 shall in any case be allowed where the loss was not incurred to avoid or in connection with the avoidance of a peril insured against.

The provisions for general average and salvage are the same as contained in the I.T.C. Hulls, 1/10/83, except that no provision is made for the situation where the vessel sails in ballast, not under charter. In these circumstances under the I.T.C. Hulls—Port Risks, the adjustment of general average will have to be made according to the law and practice obtaining at the place where the adventure ends; an assured wishing to have the advantage of an adjustment in accordance with the York-Antwerp Rules in these circumstances will have to negotiate this as a special term of the insurance.

12 DEDUCTIBLE

12.1 No claim arising from a peril insured against shall be payable under this insurance unless the aggregate of all such claims arising out of each separate accident or occurrence (including claims under Clauses 7, 9, 11 and 13) exceeds .... in which case this sum shall be deducted. Nevertheless the expense of sighting the bottom after stranding, if reasonably incurred specially for that purpose, shall be paid even if no damage be found. This Clause 12.1 shall not apply to a claim for total or constructive total loss of the Vessel or, in the event of such a claim, to any associated claim under Clause 13 arising from the same accident or occurrence.

12.2 Excluding any interest comprised therein, recoveries against any claim which is subject to the above deductible shall be credited to the Underwriters in full to the extent of the sum by which the aggregate of the claim unreduced by any recoveries exceeds the above deductible.

12.3 Interest in recoveries shall be apportioned between the Assured and the Underwriters, taking into account the sums paid by the Underwriters and the dates when such payments were made, notwithstanding that by the addition of interest the Underwriters may receive a larger sum than they have paid.

The deductible clause is in the same terms as in the I.T.C. Hulls, save that there is no provision for claims for damage by heavy weather or ice being treated as due to one accident if occurring during a single sea passage between two successive ports, for the simple reason that an insurance for port risks does not contemplate the vessel making any sea passage at all. Of course, ice damage can certainly occur to vessels in port, and in these circumstances it is necessary to revert to general principles in order to determine what is due to "each separate accident or occurrence"; see the commentary on pages 135 to 138.

13 DUTY OF ASSURED (SUE AND LABOUR)

13.1 In case of any loss or misfortune it is the duty of the Assured and their servants and agents to take such measures as may be reasonable for the purpose of averting or minimising a loss which would be recoverable under this insurance.

13.2 Subject to the provisions below and to Clause 12 the Underwriters will contribute to charges properly and reasonably incurred by the Assured their servants or agents for such measures. General average, salvage charges (except as provided for in Clause 13.5) collision defence or attack costs and costs incurred by the Assured in avoiding, minimising or contesting liability covered by Clause 9 are not recoverable under this Clause 13.

13.3 Measures taken by the Assured or the Underwriters with the object of saving, protecting or recovering the subject-matter insured shall not be considered as a waiver or acceptance of abandonment or otherwise prejudice the rights of either party.

13.4 When expenses are incurred pursuant to this Clause 13 the liability under this insurance shall not exceed the proportion of such expenses that the amount insured hereunder bears to the value of the Vessel as stated herein, or to the sound value of the Vessel at the time of the occurrence giving rise to the expenditure if the sound value exceeds that value. Where the Underwriters have admitted a claim for total loss and property insured by this insurance is saved, the foregoing provisions shall not apply unless the expenses of suing and labouring exceed the value of such property saved and then shall apply only to the amount of the expenses which is in excess of such value.

13.5 When a claim for total loss of the Vessel is admitted under this insurance and expenses have been reasonably incurred in saving or attempting to save the Vessel and other property and there are no proceeds, or the expenses exceed the proceeds, then this insurance shall bear its pro rata share of such proportion of the expenses, or of the expenses in excess of the proceeds, as the case may be, as may reasonably be regarded as having been incurred in respect of the Vessel; but if the Vessel be insured for less than its sound value at the time of the occurrence giving rise to the expenditure, the amount recoverable under this clause shall be reduced in proportion to the under-insurance.

13.6 The sum recoverable under this Clause 13 shall be in addition to the loss otherwise recoverable under this insurance but shall in no circumstances exceed the amount insured under this insurance in respect of the Vessel.

This clause is in very similar terms to the Suing and Labouring Clause contained in the Institute Time Clauses, Hulls, 1/10/83, save that there is here an important proviso in sub-clause 13.2 that costs incurred by the assured in defending himself against liabilities covered by the P. & I. Clause are not recoverable under this Clause 13.

14 **NEW FOR OLD**

Claims payable without deduction new for old.

15 **BOTTOM TREATMENT**

In no case shall a claim be allowed in respect of scraping gritblasting and/or other surface preparation or painting of the Vessel's bottom except that

15.1 gritblasting and/or other surface preparation of new bottom plates ashore and supplying and applying any "shop" primer thereto

15.2 gritblasting and/or other surface preparation of:
the butts or area of plating immediately adjacent to any renewed or refitted plating damages during the course of welding and/or repairs,
areas of plating damaged during the course of fairing, either in place or ashore,

15.3 supplying and applying the first coat of primer/anti-corrosive to those particular areas mentioned in 15.1 and 15.2 above

shall be allowed as part of the reasonable cost of repairs in respect of bottom plating damaged by an insured peril.

16 **WAGES AND MAINTENANCE**

No claim shall be allowed, other than in general average, for wages and maintenance of the Master, Officers and Crew, or any member thereof, except when incurred solely for the necessary removal of the Vessel, with the agreement of the Underwriters, from one port to another for the repair of damage covered by the Underwriters, or for trial trips for such repairs, and then only for such wages and maintenance as are incurred whilst the Vessel is under way.

17 **AGENCY COMMISSION**

No claim shall be allowed under this insurance either by way of remuneration of the Assured for time and trouble taken to obtain and supply information or documents or in respect of the commission or charges of any manager, agent, managing or agency company or the like, appointed by or on behalf of the Assured to perform such services.

18 **UNREPAIRED DAMAGE**

18.1 The measure of indemnity in respect of claims for unrepaired damage shall be the reasonable depreciation in the market value of the Vessel at the time this insurance terminates arising from such unrepaired damage, but not exceeding the reasonable cost of repairs.

18.2 In no case shall the Underwriters be liable for unrepaired damage in the event of a subsequent total loss (whether or not covered under this insurance) sustained during the period covered by this insurance or any extension thereof.

18.3 The Underwriters shall not be liable in respect of unrepaired damage for more than the insured value at the time this insurance terminates.

19 CONSTRUCTIVE TOTAL LOSS

19.1 In ascertaining whether the Vessel is a constructive total loss, the insured value shall be taken as the repaired value and nothing in respect of the damaged or break-up value of the Vessel or wreck shall be taken into account.

19.2 No claim for constructive total loss based upon the cost of recovery and/or repair of the Vessel shall be recoverable hereunder unless such cost would exceed the insured value. In making this determination only the cost relating to a single accident or sequence of damages arising from the same accident shall be taken into account.

Clauses 14 to 19 inclusive are in precisely the same terms as the corresponding clauses in Institute Time Clauses, Hulls. There is, however, no freight waiver clause, for the reason that a vessel operating under Port Risks conditions is unlikely to earn freight. On the other hand, this reasoning does not apply to the disbursements warranty, which reads as follows:

20 DISBURSEMENTS WARRANTY

20.1 Additional insurances as follows are permitted:

20.1.1 *Disbursements, Managers' Commissions, Profits or Excess or Increased Value of Hull and Machinery.* A sum not exceeding 25% of the value stated herein.

20.1.2 *Earnings or Anticipated Freight, insured for time.* A sum not exceeding 25% of the value as stated herein less any sum insured, however described, under 20.1.1.

20.1.3 *Freight or Hire, under contracts for voyage.* A sum not exceeding the gross freight or hire of the first passage and next succeeding cargo passage plus the charges of insurance. In the case of a voyage charter where payment is made on a time basis, the sum permitted for insurance will be calculated on the estimated duration of the voyage, subject to the limitation of two cargo passages as laid down herein. Any sum insured under 20.1.2 to be taken into account and only the excess thereof may be insured.

20.1.4 *Time Charter Hire or Charter Hire for Series of Voyages.* A sum not exceeding 50% of the gross hire which is to be earned under the charter in a period not exceeding 18 months. Any sum insured under 20.1.2 to be taken into account and only the excess thereof may be insured. An insurance under this Section may begin on the signing of the charter.

20.1.5 *Premiums.* A sum not exceeding the actual premiums of all interests insured for a period not exceeding 12 months (excluding premiums insured under the foregoing sections but including, if required, the premium or estimated calls on any Club or War etc. Risk insurance) reducing pro rata monthly.

20.1.6 *Returns of Premium.* A sum not exceeding the actual returns which are allowable under any insurance but which would not be recoverable thereunder in the event of a total loss of the Vessel whether by insured perils or otherwise.

20.1.7 *Insurance irrespective of amount against:*
Any risks excluded by Clauses 5, 22, 23, 24 and 25.

20.2 Warranted that no insurance on any interests enumerated in the foregoing 20.1.1 to 20.1.6 in excess of the amounts permitted therein and no other insurance which includes total loss of the Vessel P.P.I., F.I.A., or subject to any other like term, is or shall be effected to operate during the currency of this insurance by or for account of the Assured, Owners, Managers or Mortgagees. Provided always that a breach of this warranty shall not afford the Underwriters any defence to a claim by a Mortgagee who has accepted this insurance without knowledge of such breach.

See the commentary on pages 151 to 152.

21 RETURNS FOR CANCELLATION

To return pro rata monthly net for each uncommenced month if this insurance be cancelled either by agreement or by the operation of Clause 2 provided that a total loss of the Vessel, whether by insured perils or otherwise, has not occurred during the period of this insurance or any extension thereof.

This is a simplified Returns Clause providing only for cancellation of the insurance, either by agreement or by automatic termination under Clause 2. It will be noted that whereas under the Institute Time Clauses, Hulls the pro rata return of premium is calculated on a daily basis, under this clause the return is made only for each uncommenced month.

The following clauses shall be paramount and shall override anything contained in this insurance inconsistent therewith.

22 **WAR EXCLUSION**

In no case shall this insurance cover loss damage liability or expense caused by

22.1 war civil war revolution rebellion insurrection, or civil strife arising therefrom, or any hostile act by or against a belligerent power

22.2 capture seizure arrest restraint or detainment (barratry and piracy excepted), and the consequences thereof or any attempt thereat

22.3 derelict mines torpedoes bombs or other derelict weapons of war.

23 **STRIKES EXCLUSION**

In no case shall this insurance cover loss damage liability or expense caused by

23.1 strikers, locked-out workmen, or persons taking part in labour disturbances, riots or civil commotions

23.2 any terrorist or any person acting from a political motive.

24 **MALICIOUS ACTS EXCLUSION**

In no case shall this insurance cover loss damage liability or expense arising from

24.1 the detonation of an explosive

24.2 any weapon of war

and caused by any person acting maliciously or from a political motive.

25 **NUCLEAR EXCLUSION**

In no case shall this insurance cover loss damage liability or expense arising from any weapon of war employing atomic or nuclear fission and/or fusion or other like reaction or radioactive force or matter.

These clauses, which are expressed to be paramount, are in the same terms as the corresponding clauses in the Institute Time Clauses, Hulls 1/10/83.

7. INSTITUTE FISHING VESSEL CLAUSES

Prior to the on-going standardisation of policy forms which began in 1982, fishing vessels were customarily insured in the U.K. market upon the Trawler All Risks Clauses. As their title indicates, these clauses were generally considered to provide the kind of cover required by the U.K. fishing fleets, and there are those who genuinely regret their demise. The new form, which was introduced in 1987, retains certain of the important concessions which are of benefit to the owners of fishing vessels, while at the same time incorporating many of the standard terms which have already been reviewed in our consideration of the Institute Time Clauses, Hulls (see pages 87 to 156).

Institute Fishing Vessel Clauses 20/7/87

This insurance is subject to English law and practice.

See commentary on pages 90 to 91.

1 **NAVIGATION AND REMOVALS ASHORE**

1.1 The Vessel is covered subject to the provisions of this insurance at all times and has leave to sail or navigate with or without pilots, to go on trial trips and to assist and tow vessels or craft in distress, but it is warranted that with the exception of catch the Vessel shall not carry cargo or containers for the carriage of cargo and shall not be towed, except as is customary or to the first safe port or place when in need of assistance, or undertake towage or salvage services under a contract previously arranged by the Assured and/or Owners and/or Managers and/or Charterers. This clause 1.1 shall not exclude customary towage in connection with loading and discharging.

1.2 Any part or parts of the subject-matter insured are covered subject to the provisions of this insurance whilst ashore for the purpose of repair, overhaul or refitting, including transit from and to the Vessel.

1.3 In the event of the Vessel sailing with an intention of being (a) broken up, or (b) sold for breaking up, any claim for loss of or damage to the Vessel occurring subsequent to such sailing shall be limited to the market value of the Vessel as scrap at the time when the loss or damage is sustained, unless previous notice has been given to the Underwriters and any amendments to the terms of cover, insured value and premium required by them have been agreed. Nothing in this Clause 1.3 shall affect claims under Clauses 8, 18 or 20.

This clause is similar to Clause 1 of the Institute Time Clauses, Hulls, save for the following.

Clause 1.1 contains an additional warranty "with the exception of catch the Vessel shall not carry cargo or containers for the carriage of cargo". This is an important limitation upon the use of the vessel, and the reasons it must be strictly adhered to are pretty obvious. For one thing, fishing vessels are not designed for carriage of cargo, and the risks to which fishing vessels are exposed are hazardous enough without adding to them.

The words "with the exception of catch" make it clear that in the interpretation of this and the other clauses in the form, the fish or other seafood which has been brought on board is to be considered as a species of cargo.

Clause 1.2 is totally different from the corresponding clause in Institute Time Clauses, Hulls. Obviously a clause dealing with trading operations involving the loading or discharging of cargo from one ship to another at sea is not relevant to an insurance on a fishing ship, and the space occupied by this, the "mothership clause", is here given over to the clause extending the benefit of the insurance to "any part or parts of the subject-matter insured" whilst they are ashore or in transit for the purpose of repair, overall or refitting. This would include nets and fishing gear, even though the perils against which they are insured are limited by Clause 15.

Clause 1.3 contains, of course, no reference to the vessel "sailing with cargo".

2 **CONTINUATION**
Should the Vessel at the expiration of this insurance be at sea or in distress or at a port of refuge or of call, she shall, provided previous notice be given to the Underwriters, be held covered at a pro rata monthly premium to her port of destination.

This clause is in the same form as in the 1/10/83 text of the I.T.C. Hulls.

3 **BREACH OF WARRANTY**
Held covered in case of any breach of warranty as to locality, towage, salvage services or date of sailing, provided notice be given to the Underwriters immediately after receipt of advances and any amended terms of cover and any additional premium required by them be agreed.

This is the same as Clause 3 of the I.T.C. Hulls, except that there is no reference to a breach of warranty as to cargo or trade (for obvious reasons).

4 **TERMINATION**
This Clause 4 shall prevail notwithstanding any provision whether written typed or printed in this insurance inconsistent therewith.
Unless Underwriters agree to the contrary in writing, this insurance shall terminate automatically at the time of

4.1 change of the Classification Society of the Vessel, or change, suspension, discontinuance, withdrawal or expiry of her Class therein provided that if the Vessel is at sea such automatic termination shall be deferred until arrival at her next port or until the expiry of fifteen days, whichever shall first occur. However where such change, suspension, discontinuance or withdrawal of her Class has resulted from loss or damage covered by Clause 6 of this insurance or which would be covered by an insurance of the Vessel subject to the current Institute War and Strikes Clauses Hulls—Time such automatic termination shall only operate should the Vessel sail from her next port without the prior approval of the Classification Society

4.2 any change, voluntary or otherwise, in the ownership or flag, transfer to new management or charter on a bareboat basis, provided that if the Vessel is at sea such automatic termination shall, if required, be deferred until arrival at her next port or until the expiry of fifteen days, whichever shall first occur

4.3 requisition for title or use of the Vessel. However, in the event of requisition for title or use without the prior execution of a written agreement by the Assured, such automatic termination shall occur fifteen days after such requisition whether the Vessel is at sea or in port.

This is similar to the Termination Clause in the 1/10/83 form of the I.T.C. Hulls, except that here the deferment of the automatic termination of cover when the vessel is at sea under Clauses 4.1 and 4.2 shall not exceed fifteen days.

5 **ASSIGNMENT**

No assignment of or interest in this insurance or in any moneys which may be or become payable thereunder is to be binding on or recognised by the Underwriters unless a dated notice of such assignment or interest signed by the Assured, and by the assignor in the case of subsequent assignment, is endorsed on the Policy and the Policy with such endorsement is produced before payment of any claim or return of premium thereunder.

This is the same as Clause 5 of the I.T.C. Hulls, 1/10/83 (Clause 21 of I.T.C. Hulls, 1/11/95).

6 **PERILS**

6.1 This insurance covers loss of or damage to the subject-matter insured caused by
6.1.1 perils of the seas rivers lakes or other navigable waters
6.1.2 fire, explosion
6.1.3 violent theft by persons from outside the Vessel
6.1.4 jettison
6.1.5 piracy
6.1.6 breakdown of or accident to nuclear installations or reactors
6.1.7 contact with aircraft or similar objects, or objects falling therefrom, land conveyance, dock or harbour equipment or installation
6.1.8 earthquake volcanic eruption or lightning.
6.2 This insurance covers loss of or damage to the subject-matter insured caused by
6.2.1 accidents in loading discharging or shifting catch fuel or stores
6.2.2 bursting of boilers breakage of shafts or any latent defect in the machinery or hull
6.2.3 negligence of Master Officers Crew or Pilots
6.2.4 negligence of repairers or charterers provided such repairers or charterers are not an Assured hereunder
6.2.5 barratry of Master Officers or Crew
provided such loss or damage has not resulted from want of due diligence by the Assured, Owners or Managers.
6.3 Master Officers Crew or Pilots not to be considered Owners within the meaning of this Clause 6 should they hold shares in the Vessel.

This is the standard list of insured perils, as in Clause 6 of I.T.C. Hulls, 1/10/83, with one difference. Clause 6.2.1 covers "accidents in loading, discharging or shifting *catch fuel or stores*", the words italicised being substituted for "cargo or fuel". "Catch" takes the place of "cargo", but the inclusion of the word "stores" is a small, but welcome addition to the cover.

The Clause 6.2 proviso is in the old (1/10/83) form.

7 **POLLUTION HAZARD**

This insurance covers loss of or damage to the Vessel caused by any governmental authority acting under the powers vested in it to prevent or mitigate a pollution hazard, or threat thereof, resulting directly from damage to the Vessel for which the Underwriters are liable under this insurance, provided such act of governmental authority has not resulted from want of due diligence by the Assured, the Owners, or Managers of the Vessel or any of them to prevent or mitigate such hazard or threat. Master, Officers, Crew or Pilots not to be considered Owners within the meaning of this Clause 7 should they hold shares in the Vessel.

This is the same as Clause 7 in the I.T.C. Hulls, 1/10/83.

8 **GENERAL AVERAGE AND SALVAGE**

8.1 Any claim for general average and salvage to be on the basis of an adjustment according to the York-Antwerp Rules 1974 if so required by the Underwriters but the insured value of Hull and Machinery to be taken as the contributory value without deduction.

8.2 No claim under this Clause 8 shall in any case be allowed where the loss was not incurred to avoid or in connection with the avoidance of a peril insured against.

It is to be expected that any provision regarding general average in a policy covering vessels engaged in fishing is likely to differ from those contained in policies covering vessels trading with cargo, for a number of reasons:

— the "shape" of the common maritime adventure is different for a fishing boat than for a ship in a cargo-carrying trade;
— unless a specialised vessel (such as a factory ship) has been chartered for a period of time, it is unlikely that there will be any contractual document to regulate the position of the parties to a fishing expedition, such as is the invariable practice in the cargo trades.

When a vessel is engaged to carry cargoes, both law and practice distinguish, for the purpose of general average adjustment, between a vessel sailing in ballast, either chartered or not under charter, and a vessel with cargo. For practical purposes, the relationship of the parties to the general average will be regulated by the provisions of the bills of lading and/or charterparties, usually by the inclusion of a clause incorporating the York-Antwerp Rules.

None of this applies to a fishing expedition and so, although it lies a little outside the scope of this work, we will examine how the basic principles apply. The common maritime adventure begins when the fishing boat sails with her gear to the fishing grounds and continues whilst fishing, and on passage back to her home port until the catch is landed. For owner-operated boats, the community of interest lies in the profit to be made by the sale of the catch which is traditionally shared between the owner, the skipper and the crew. This profit cannot, of course, be quantified until the catch is sold but it is there, nonetheless, throughout the whole of the fishing expedition and comes into contribution, in accordance with the basic principles of general average, only at the end of the adventure as part of the value realised when the catch is sold.

If the fishing boat has to put into a port of refuge for the common safety during the course of the fishing expedition, it will be necessary for the purpose of the general average adjustment to determine whether or not the common maritime adventure continues after repairs have been effected to make the vessel fit for that purpose. If the vessel has catch on board, and that has to be sold at the port of refuge in order to avoid its deterioration, there is *ipso facto* a termination of the adventure. However, if the vessel had not reached the fishing grounds at the time when the accident occurred which gave rise to the necessity to put into a port of refuge or return to her home port for repairs, the question of the continuance of the adventure will be decided by determining whether, after repairs, the vessel was able to re-join the fleet at the intended fishing grounds during the same fishing season: if so, the voyage continues, and if not, then there is a *de facto* abandonment of the voyage. Although nice questions of fact are involved, the issue will not greatly affect the quantum of the claim, in view of underwriters' agreement to pay for the wages and maintenance of crew members necessarily retained during the course of average repairs, as provided in Clause 9 below.

Unless the underwriters invoke their right to have an adjustment prepared to the York-Antwerp Rules 1974, they will be obliged to recognise an adjustment prepared in accordance with the law and practice at the place where the catch is landed, or if there be no catch on board, at the place where the adventure is abandoned.[82]

That this alternative, i.e. to have the adjustment prepared in accordance with the York-Antwerp Rules, should lie in the discretion of the underwriters is somewhat surprising, since in most instances the allowances which may be made under the York-Antwerp Rules 1974 would be expected to be at least as wide, if not wider, than those available under national laws. If there is to be an option available—which is no bad thing, at least in the interest of uniformity—it might have appeared more equitable if such option were expressed to be exercisable by the assured.

However, underwriters have made an important concession by agreeing to adopt the insured value as the contributory value in any general average adjustment, without deduction on account of damage or other charges. This provision helps to avoid dispute on account of the diversity of opinion as to the market value of many fishing vessels, and considerably simplifies the process of adjustment. Corresponding concessions, waiving underwriters' customary rights to reduce certain claims in proportion to the difference between the market value and the value agreed for the purpose of the insurance, can be seen in Clauses 10.4 and 10.5.

Clause 8.2 is normal, and is found in all of the Institute Clauses.

9 **WAGES AND MAINTENANCE**
The underwriters to pay the cost of wages and maintenance of crew necessarily retained whilst the Vessel is undergoing repairs for which the Underwriters are liable under this insurance.

This clause has been taken over from the old Trawler All Risks Clauses. It was designed to alleviate the hardship experienced by owners of fishing vessels when, as a result of having to repair average damage, the owners had to pay for the crew members' wages and maintenance when there was no chance of any return for such outlay. The loss would be considerable if there was no hope of regaining the fishing grounds during the season or if the circumstances precluded any allowance in general average, e.g., when the adjustment had to be prepared in accordance with English law, or when the common maritime adventure had to be abandoned (see Clause 8 above).

82. See *Simonds* v. *White* (1824) 2 B. & C. 811, where this principle of English law is enunciated.

"crew necessarily retained"

These words mean more than "retained on board in order to assist on repairs". They include cases where the owner can show that if he did not continue to pay his crew, he would lose their services, possibly for the remainder of the fishing season.

10 DUTY OF ASSURED (SUE AND LABOUR)

10.1 In case of any loss or misfortune it is the duty of the Assured and their servants and agents to take such measures as may be reasonable for the purpose of averting or minimising a loss which would be recoverable under this insurance.

10.2 Subject to the provisions below and to Clause 12 the Underwriters will contribute to charges properly and reasonably incurred by the Assured their servants or agents for such measures. General average, salvage charges (except as provided for in Clause 10.5) collision defence or attack costs and costs incurred by the Assured in avoiding minimising or contesting liability covered by Clause 20 are not recoverable under this Clause 10.

10.3 Measures taken by the Assured or the Underwriters with the object of saving, protecting or recovering the subject-matter insured shall not be considered as a waiver or acceptance of abandonment or otherwise prejudice the rights of either party.

10.4 When expenses are incurred pursuant to this Clause 10 the liability under this insurance shall not exceed the proportion of such expenses that the amount insured hereunder bears to the value of the Vessel as stated herein.

10.5 Where a claim for total loss of the Vessel is admitted under this insurance and expenses have been reasonably incurred in saving or attempting to save the Vessel and other property and there are no proceeds, or the expenses exceed the proceeds, then the Underwriters shall pay the expenses, or the expenses in excess of the proceeds, as the case may be.

10.6 The sum recoverable under this Clause 10 shall be in addition to the loss otherwise recoverable under this insurance but shall in no circumstances exceed the amount insured under this insurance in respect of the Vessel.

This is the usual Sue and Labour clause in the form in which it appears in the I.T.C. Hulls, 1/10/83, with the following important exception:

— in Clauses 10.4 and 10.5, the amount payable by the underwriters will not be reduced in proportion to any under-insurance by reference to the market value (the difference between the market value and the agreed value for the insurance), but only in proportion to any under-subscription of the policy (the difference between the insured value and the sum insured).

11 NEW FOR OLD

Claims payable without deduction new for old.

This is the customary clause contained in the I.T.C. Hulls and other insurance forms.

12 DEDUCTIBLE

12.1 No claim arising from a peril insured against shall be payable under this insurance unless the aggregate of all such claims arising out of each separate accident or occurrence (including claims under Clauses 8, 10, 18 and 20) exceeds .... in which case this sum shall be deducted. Nevertheless the expense of sighting the bottom after stranding, if reasonably incurred specially for that purpose, shall be paid even if no damage be found. This Clause 12.1 shall not apply to a claim for total or constructive total loss of the Vessel or, in the event of such a claim, to any associated claim under Clause 10 arising from the same accident or occurrence.

12.2 Excluding any interest comprised therein, recoveries against any claim which is subject to the above deductible shall be credited to the Underwriters in full to the extent of the sum by which the aggregate of the claim unreduced by any recoveries exceeds the above deductible.

12.3 Interest comprised in recoveries shall be apportioned between the Assured and the Underwriters, taking into account the sums paid by the Underwriters and the dates when such payments were made, notwithstanding that by the addition of interest the Underwriters may receive a larger sum than they have paid.

The deductible clause is in the same terms as Clause 12 of the I.T.C. Hulls, except that, as in the Institute Time Clauses, Hulls—Port Risks, the detailed provisions relating to the number of deductibles to be applied in the event of encountering heavy weather or ice have been omitted.

13 MACHINERY DAMAGE ADDITIONAL DEDUCTIBLE

Notwithstanding any provision to the contrary in this insurance a claim for loss or damage to any machinery, shaft, electrical equipment or wiring, boiler condenser heating coil or associated pipework, arising from any of the perils enumerated in Clause 6.2.2 to 6.2.5 inclusive above or from fire or explosion when either has originated in a machinery space, shall be subject to a deductible of .... Any balance remaining, after application of this deductible, with any other claim arising from the same accident or occurrence, shall then be subject to the deductible in Clause 12.1.

The provisions of Clauses 12.2 and 12.3 shall apply to recoveries and interest comprised in recoveries against any claim which is subject to this Clause.

This Clause shall not apply to a claim for total or constructive total loss of the Vessel.

This clause does not form part of any of the other standard forms for hull insurance, although it is available for attachment to any hull policies if the underwriters so require. For the reasons why the clause came into existence, and for a commentary thereon, see pages 224 to 226 below.

14 BOTTOM TREATMENT

In no case shall a claim be allowed in respect of scraping gritblasting and/or other surface preparation or painting of the Vessel's bottom except that

14.1 gritblasting and/or other surface preparation of new bottom plates ashore and supplying and applying any "shop" primer thereto,

14.2 gritblasting and/or other surface preparation of:
the butts or area of plating immediately adjacent to any renewed or refitted plating damaged during the course of welding and/or repairs,
areas of plating damaged during the course of fairing, either in place or ashore,

14.3 supplying and applying the first coat of primer/anti-corrosive to those particular areas mentioned in 14.1 and 14.2 above,

shall be allowed as part of the reasonable cost of repairs in respect of bottom plating damaged by an insured peril.

This is the same as Clause 15 of the I.T.C. Hulls.

15 FISHING GEAR

No claim to attach hereto for loss of or damage to fishing gear unless

15.1 caused by fire lightning or violent theft by persons from outside the Vessel

15.2 totally lost as a result of the total loss of the Vessel by insured perils.

Fishing gear—particularly nets and lines—is particularly susceptible to damage from all sorts of causes, not merely from the perils insured. For this reason claims for loss or damage to fishing gear are restricted to the instances enumerated in this clause. The clause does not, however, affect the inclusion of all items of fishing gear within the insured value for the purpose of contribution to general average and/or salvage.

16 UNREPAIRED DAMAGE

16.1 The measure of indemnity in respect of claims for unrepaired damage shall be the reasonable depreciation in the market value of the Vessel at the time this insurance terminates arising from such unrepaired damage but not exceeding the reasonable cost of repairs.

16.2 In no case shall the Underwriters be liable for unrepaired damage in the event of a subsequent total loss (whether or not covered under this insurance) sustained during the period covered by this insurance or any extension thereof.

16.3 The Underwriters shall not be liable in respect of unrepaired damage for more than the insured value at the time this insurance terminates.

17 CONSTRUCTIVE TOTAL LOSS

17.1 In ascertaining whether the Vessel is a constructive total loss, the insured value shall be taken as the repaired value and nothing in respect of the damaged or break-up value of the Vessel or wreck shall be taken into account.

17.2 No claim for constructive total loss based upon the cost of recovery and/or repair of the Vessel shall be recoverable hereunder unless such cost would exceed the insured value. In making this determination, only the cost relating to a single accident or sequence of damages arising from the same accident shall be taken into account.

These clauses are the same as in I.T.C. Hulls.

18 COLLISION LIABILITY

18.1 The Underwriters agree to indemnify the Assured for any sum or sums paid by the Assured to any other person or persons by reason of the Assured becoming legally liable by way of damages for

18.1.1 loss of or damage to any other vessel or property on any other vessel

18.1.2 delay to or loss of use of any such other vessel or property thereon,

where such payment by the Assured is in consequence of the Vessel hereby insured coming into collision with any other vessel.

18.2 The indemnity provided by this Clause 18 shall be in addition to the indemnity provided by the other terms and conditions of this insurance and shall be subject to the following provisions:

18.2.1 Where the insured Vessel is in collision with another vessel and both vessels are to blame then, unless the liability of one or both vessels becomes limited by law, the indemnity under this Clause 18 shall be calculated on the principle of cross-liabilities as if the respective Owners had been compelled to pay to each other such proportion of each other's damages as may have been properly allowed in ascertaining the balance or sum payable by or to the Assured in consequence of the collision.

18.2.2 In no case shall the Underwriters' total liability under Clauses 18.1 and 18.2 exceed their proportionate part of the insured value of the Vessel hereby insured in respect of any one such collision.

18.3 The Underwriters will also pay the legal costs incurred by the Assured or which the Assured may be compelled to pay in contesting liability or taking proceedings to limit liability, with the prior written consent of the Underwriters.

EXCLUSIONS

18.4 Provided always that this Clause 18 shall in no case extend to any sum which the Assured shall pay for or in respect of

18.4.1 removal or disposal of obstructions, wrecks, cargoes or any other thing whatsoever

18.4.2 any real or personal property or thing whatsoever except other vessels or property on other vessels

18.4.3 the cargo or other property on, or the engagements of, the insured Vessel

18.4.4 loss of life, personal injury or illness

18.4.5 pollution or contamination of any real or personal property or thing whatsoever (except other vessels with which the insured Vessel is in collision or property on such other vessels).

19 SISTERSHIP

Should the Vessel hereby insured come into collision with or receive salvage services from another vessel belonging wholly or in part to the same Owners or under the same management, the Assured shall have the same rights under this insurance as they would have were the other vessel entirely the property of Owners not interested in the Vessel hereby insured; but in such cases the liability for the collision or the amount payable for the services rendered shall be referred to a sole arbitrator to be agreed upon between the Underwriters and the Assured.

These clauses which cover four-fourths collision liability, together with the customary extensions to underwriters' liability to sisterships in collision and salvage cases, are in the same form in which they appear in the Institute Time Clauses, Hulls—Port Risks.

20 PROTECTION AND INDEMNITY

20.1 The Underwriters agree to indemnify the Assured for any sum or sums paid by the Assured to any other person or persons by reason of the Assured becoming legally liable, as owner of the Vessel, for any claim, demand, damages and/or expenses, where such liability is in consequence of any of the following matters or things and arises from an accident or occurrence during the period of this insurance:

20.1.1 loss of or damage to any fixed or movable object or property or other thing or interest whatsoever, other than the Vessel, arising from any cause whatsoever in so far as such loss or damage is not covered by Clause 18

20.1.2 any attempted or actual raising, removal or destruction of any fixed or movable object or property or other thing, including the wreck of the Vessel, or any neglect or failure to raise, remove, or destroy the same

20.1.3 liability assumed by the Assured under contracts of customary towage for the purpose of entering or leaving port or manoeuvring within the port during the ordinary course of trading

20.1.4 loss of life, personal injury, illness or payments made for life salvage

20.1.5 (a) hospital medical and burial expenses of Master Officers or Crew

(b) repatriation expenses of Master Officers or Crew (other than wages, remuneration in the nature of wages, or any expenses which ensue from the termination of an agreement, sale of the Vessel or any other act of the Assured).

20.2 The Underwriters agree to indemnify the Assured for any of the following arising from an accident or occurrence during the period of this insurance:

20.2.1 the additional cost of fuel, insurance, wages, stores, provisions and port charges reasonably incurred solely for the purpose of landing from the Vessel sick or injured persons or stowaways, refugees, or persons saved at sea

20.2.2 additional expenses brought about by the outbreak of infectious disease on board the Vessel or ashore

20.2.3 fines imposed on the Vessel, on the Assured, or on any Master Officer crew member or agent of the Vessel who is reimbursed by the Assured, for any act or neglect or breach of any statute or regulation relating to the operation of the Vessel, provided that the Underwriters shall not be liable to indemnify the Assured for any fines which result from any act neglect failure or default of the Assured their agents or servants other than Master Officer or crew member

20.2.4 the expenses of the removal of the wreck of the Vessel from any place owned, leased or occupied by the Assured

20.2.5 legal costs incurred by the Assured, or which the Assured may be compelled to pay, avoiding, minimising or contesting liability with the prior written consent of the Underwriters.

EXCLUSIONS

20.3 Notwithstanding the provisions of Clauses 20.1 and 20.2 this Clause 20 does not cover any liability cost or expense arising in respect of:

20.3.1 any direct or indirect payment by the Assured under workmen's compensation or employers' liability acts and any other statutory or common law, general maritime law or other liability whatsoever in respect of accidents to or illness of workmen or any other persons employed in any capacity whatsoever by the Assured or others in on or about or in connection with the Vessel or her cargo, materials or repairs

20.3.2 liability assumed by the Assured under agreement expressed or implied in respect of death or illness of or injury to any person employed under a contract of service or apprenticeship by the other party to such agreement

20.3.3 punitive or exemplary damages, however described

20.3.4 passengers

20.3.5 catch, fishing gear or other things or interests whatsoever on board the insured Vessel or the engagements of the insured Vessel but this Clause 20.3.5 shall not exclude any claim in respect of the extra cost of removing catch or property from the wreck of the Vessel

20.3.6 property, owned by builders or repairers or for which they are responsible, which is on board the Vessel

20.3.7 liability arising under a contract or indemnity in respect of containers, equipment, fuel or other property on board the Vessel and which is owned or leased by the Assured

20.3.8 cash, negotiable instruments, precious metals or stones, valuables or objects of a rare or precious nature, belonging to persons on board the Vessel, or non-essential personal effects of any Master, Officer or crew member

20.3.9 fuel, insurance, wages, stores, provisions and port charges arising from delay to the Vessel while awaiting a substitute for any Master, Officer or crew member

20.3.10 fines or penalties arising from overloading or illegal fishing

20.3.11 pollution or contamination of any real or personal property or thing whatsoever

20.3.12 general average, sue and labour and salvage charges, salvage, and/or collision liability to any extent that they are not recoverable under Clauses 7, 11 and 13 by reason of the agreed value and/or the amount insured in respect of the Vessel being inadequate.

20.4 The indemnity provided by this Clause 20 shall be in addition to the indemnity provided by the other terms and conditions of this insurance.

20.5 Where the Assured or the Underwriters may or could have limited their liability the indemnity under this Clause 20 in respect of such liability shall not exceed Underwriters' proportionate part of the amount of such limitation.

20.6 In no case shall the Underwriters' liability under this Clause 9 in respect of each separate accident or occurrence or series of accidents arising out of the same event, exceed their proportionate part of the insured value of the Vessel.

20.7 PROVIDED ALWAYS THAT

20.7.1 Prompt notice must be given to the Underwriters of every casualty event or claim upon the Assured which may give rise to a claim under this Clause 20 and of every event or matter which may cause the Assured to incur liability costs or expense for which he may be insured under this Clause 20.

20.7.2 the Assured shall not admit liability for or settle any claim for which he may be insured under this Clause 20 without the prior written consent of the Underwriters.

Protection and indemnity risks are added in virtually the same terms as those contained in the Institute Protection and Indemnity Clauses, Hulls—Time 20/7/87, with the following variations:

- by Clause 20.1.5 this insurance will additionally reimburse the assured for any amounts paid in respect of his liabilities for hospital, medical and burial expenses of the crew, and also for their repatriation expenses in certain circumstances;
- on the other hand, by Clause 20.3.4 liability to passengers is excluded.

Similarly, where the P. & I. Clauses generally refer to "cargo", this clause refers to catch and fishing gear.

21 **NOTICE OF CLAIM AND TENDERS**

21.1 In the event of accident whereby loss or damage may result in a claim under this insurance, notice shall be given to the Underwriters prior to survey and also, if the Vessel is abroad, to the nearest Lloyd's Agent so that a surveyor may be appointed to represent the Underwriters should they so desire.

21.2 The Underwriters shall be entitled to decide the port to which the Vessel shall proceed for docking or repair (the actual additional expense of the voyage arising from compliance with the Underwriters' requirements being refunded to the Assured) and shall have a right of veto concerning a place of repair or a repairing firm.

21.3 The Underwriters may also take tenders or may require further tenders to be taken for the repair of the Vessel. Where such a tender has been taken and a tender is accepted with the approval of the Underwriters, an allowance shall be made at the rate of 30% per annum on the insured value for time lost between the despatch of the invitations to tender required by Underwriters and the acceptance of a tender to the extent that such time is lost solely as the result of tenders having been taken and provided that the tender is accepted without delay after receipt of the Underwriters' approval.

Due credit shall be given against the allowance as above for any amounts recovered in respect of fuel and stores and wages and maintenance of the Master Officers and Crew or any member thereof, including amounts allowed in general average, and for any amounts recovered from third parties in respect of damages for detention and/or loss of profit and/or running expenses, for the period covered by the tender allowance or any part thereof.

Where a part of the cost of the repair of damage other than a fixed deductible is not recoverable from the Underwriters the allowance shall be reduced by a similar proportion.

21.4 In the event of failure to comply with the conditions of this Clause 21, a deduction of 15% shall be made from the amount of the ascertained claim.

This clause is in the same terms as in the Institute Time Clauses, Hulls, 1/10/83.

22 **DISBURSEMENTS WARRANTY**

Warranted that no insurance is or shall be effected to operate during the currency of this insurance by or for account of the Assured, Owners, Managers or Mortgagees on:

22.1 disbursements, commissions or similar interests, P.P.I., F.I.A. or subject to any other like term,

22.2 excess or increased value of hull and machinery however described.

Provided always that a breach of this warranty shall not afford the Underwriters any defence to a claim by a Mortgagee who has accepted this insurance without knowledge of such breach.

It will be observed that this warranty is in much more relaxed terms than in any other form of hull insurance.

23 **RETURNS FOR LAY-UP AND CANCELLATION**

23.1 To return as follows

23.1.1 Pro rata monthly net for each uncommenced month if this insurance be cancelled by agreement or by the operation of Clause 4.

23.1.2 For each period of 30 consecutive days the Vessel may be laid up in a port or in a lay-up area provided such port or lay-up area is approved by the Underwriters (with special liberties as hereinafter allowed)

(1) .... per cent net not under repair

(2) .... per cent net under repair.

If the Vessel is under repair during part only of a period for which a return is claimable, the return shall be calculated pro rata to the number of days under (1) and (2) respectively.

23.2 PROVIDED ALWAYS THAT

23.2.1 a total loss of the Vessel, whether by insured perils or otherwise, has not occurred during the period covered by this insurance or any extension thereof

23.2.2 in no case shall a return be allowed when the Vessel is lying in exposed or unprotected waters, or in a port or lay-up area not approved by the Underwriters but, provided the Underwriters agree that such non-approved Lay-up area is deemed to be within the vicinity of the approved port or lay-up area, days during which the Vessel is laid up in such non-approved lay-up area may be added to days in the approved port or lay-up area to calculate a period of 30 consecutive days and a return shall be allowed for the proportion of such period during which the Vessel is actually laid up in the approved port or lay-up area

23.2.3 loading or discharging operations or the presence of catch on board shall not debar returns but no return shall be allowed for any period during which the Vessel is being used for the storage of catch or for lightering purposes

23.2.4 in the event of any amendment of the annual rate, the above rates of return shall be adjusted accordingly

23.2.5 in the event of any return recoverable under this Clause 23 being based on 30 consecutive days which fall on successive insurances effected for the same Assured, this insurance shall only be liable for an amount calculated at pro rata of the period rates 23.1.2(1) and/or (2) above for the number of days which come within the period of this insurance and to which a return is actually applicable. Such overlapping period shall run, at the option of the Assured, either from the first day on which the Vessel is laid up or the first day of a period of 30 consecutive days as provided under 23.1.2(1), (2) or 23.2.2 above.

It will be observed that the underwriters agree to pay pro rata monthly returns if the insurance be cancelled by the operation of Clause 4 (automatic termination), as well as when the insurance is cancelled by agreement. This right is not granted by Clause 22 of the Institute Time Clauses, Hulls, although the wording of the two clauses is identical in all other respects.

24 **WAR EXCLUSION**

In no case shall this insurance cover loss damage liability or expense caused by

24.1 war civil war revolution rebellion insurrection, or civil strife arising therefrom, or any hostile act by or against a belligerent power

24.2 capture seizure arrest restraint or detainment (barratry and piracy excepted), and the consequences thereof or any attempt thereat

24.3 derelict mines torpedoes bombs or other derelict weapons of war.

25 **STRIKES EXCLUSION**

In no case shall this insurance cover loss damage liability or expense caused by

25.1 strikers, locked-out workmen, or persons taking part in labour disturbances, riots or civil commotions

25.2 any terrorist or any person acting from a political motive.

26 **MALICIOUS ACTS EXCLUSION**

In no case shall this insurance cover loss damage liability or expense arising from

26.1 the detonation of an explosive

26.2 any weapon of war

and caused by any person acting maliciously or from a political motive.

27 **NUCLEAR EXCLUSION**

In no case shall this insurance cover loss damage liability or expense arising from any weapon of war employing atomic or nuclear fission and/or fusion or other like reaction or radioactive force or matter.

These are the usual exclusions for war, strikes and associated risks.

8. INSTITUTE YACHT CLAUSES

As we advance into a leisure society, the insurance of yachts is an expanding business. The term "yacht" may cover anything from a single-handed sailing dinghy to what are in effect privately-owned cruise ships. It is immediately evident that the drafting of a set of insurance conditions appropriate to every kind of yacht is no mean feat. The way that this has been achieved is to put together a set of clauses based upon the standard perils, but subject to all the exclusions and reservations which could reasonably be required by a prudent underwriter, whatever kind of yacht is insured, and in whatever situation the yacht may be, for example, in commission or laid up. This gives the Institute Yacht Clauses the appearance of having been drafted in a restricted manner, but it is common practice for an assured, through his broker, to request the deletion of inappropriate clauses, and yacht underwriters, many of whom are keen yachtsmen themselves, are usually willing to accommodate their assured in this respect. Indeed, some yacht underwriters offer their own conditions of insurance which differ in many respects from the standard form, while retaining some of its provisions.

Institute Yacht Clauses 1/11/85

1 **VESSEL**
Vessel means the hull, machinery, boat(s), gear and equipment, such as would normally be sold with her if she changed hands.

The yacht to be insured will, of course, have been described by the assured, and likewise a value will have been declared for her, in the negotiations leading up to the placing of the insurance. When the assured is required to provide this and other relevant information on a proposal form, the information must be true; if it is not, and is "material" in the sense that it would influence an underwriter in the assessment of the risk, then the insurer is entitled to avoid the contract of insurance—see section 18 of the Marine Insurance Act 1906. For second-hand yachts of modest value, the value declared is very much a material fact for most yacht underwriters, and the proposer is frequently asked to declare how much he paid for the yacht and where he bought it. Even if not specifically asked for in the proposal form, a yacht-owner would be well advised to furnish the fullest possible information as to the subject-matter for which he requires insurance, such as the amount he has paid for improvements and new equipment since he bought the yacht, and any boats or other special equipment to be included in the insurance.

"Gear and equipment". For a sailing yacht, these words are generally taken to include everything above the deck, including masts, spars, sails and rigging.

"Such as would normally be sold with her if she changed hands". The main purpose of these words is to exclude from the cover any personal effects or equipment which the owner would consider to be his personal property, such as a pair of binoculars or even a hand-held compass. In practice, cover against

loss of personal effects is frequently included by endorsement on the policy at a separate valuation.

2 **IN COMMISSION AND LAID UP**

2.1 The Vessel is covered subject to the provisions of this insurance

2.1.1 while in commission at sea or on inland waters or in port, docks, marinas, on ways, gridirons, pontoons, or on the hard or mud or at place of storage ashore, including lifting or hauling out and launching, with leave to sail or navigate with or without pilots, to go on trial trips and to assist and to tow vessels or craft in distress, or as is customary, but it is warranted that the Vessel shall not be towed, except as is customary or when in need of assistance, or undertake towage or salvage services under a contract previously arranged by Owners, Masters, Managers or Charterers

2.1.2 while laid up out of commission as provided for in Clause 4 below, including lifting or hauling out and launching, while being moved in shipyard or marina, dismantling, fitting out, overhauling, normal maintenance or while under survey (also to include docking and undocking and periods laid up afloat incidental to laying up or fitting out and with leave to shift in tow or otherwise to or from her lay-up berth but not outside the limits of the port or place in which the Vessel is laid up) but excluding, unless notice be given to the Underwriters and any additional premium required by them agreed, any period for which the Vessel is used as a houseboat or is under major repair or undergoing alteration.

2.2 Notwithstanding Clause 2.1 above the gear and equipment, including outboard motors, are covered subject to the provisions of this insurance while in place of storage or repair ashore.

This clause grants the assured fairly wide operational liberties, such as normally would be required during the two periods of coverage:

(*a*) whilst the yacht is in commission, and
(*b*) whilst the yacht is laid up out of commission.

Normally these two periods are agreed in advance before the insurance attaches, and are then set out in a schedule to the policy. See Clause 4 below.

Periods when the vessel is under a "major repair" or undergoing alteration are excluded, as is any time when the yacht is "used as a houseboat", unless the underwriters are approached in advance for their agreement.

"*Used as a houseboat*" means more than use by the assured as a permanently fitted-out residence; it also includes use by the crew as living accommodation during a period of lay-up—see *The "Moonacre"*.[83]

3 **NAVIGATING AND CHARTER HIRE WARRANTIES**

3.1 Warranted not navigating outside the limits stated in the Schedule to the policy or, provided previous notice be given to the Underwriters, held covered on terms to be agreed.

3.2 Warranted to be used solely for private pleasure purposes and not for hire charter or reward, unless specially agreed by the Underwriters.

4 **LAID UP WARRANTY**

Warranted laid up out of commission as stated in the Schedule to the policy, or held covered on terms to be agreed provided previous notice be given to the Underwriters.

The navigation limits and the periods when the vessel is respectively in commission and laid up are all matters which will clearly affect the underwriter in his assessment of the risk, and consequently these aspects have to be declared, either in the proposal form or otherwise, before attachment of the policy. These clauses, as also Clause 3.2 relating to the use of the yacht only for private pleasure purposes, are also in the form of warranties, breach of

83. *Sharp* v. *Sphere Drake Insurance p.l.c.* [1992] 2 Lloyd's Rep. 501.

which by the assured will entitle the underwriters to avoid the policy. However, if the assured changes his plans during the currency of the policy, e.g., by undertaking a voyage which would take the yacht outside the previously agreed navigating limits and/or extend the period in commission, he will be held covered on terms to be agreed provided he gives previous notice to the underwriters. If he wishes to charter out his yacht to others, he is not prohibited from doing so provided that he obtains underwriters' agreement to this course.

5 **SPEED WARRANTY**

5.1 Warranted that the maximum designed speed of the Vessel, or the parent Vessel in the case of a Vessel with boat(s), does not exceed 17 knots.

5.2 Where the Underwriters have agreed to delete this warranty, the conditions of the Speedboat Clause 19 below shall also apply.

This is not a "warranty" in the same sense as the word is used in Clauses 3 and 4. The effect of Clause 5.1 is that if the yacht has a maximum designed speed in excess of 17 knots, the insurance does not attach. However, as the speed of the vessel is one of the matters which must be declared prior to attachment of the risk, the underwriters will almost certainly require the terms of the Speedboat Clause 19 to apply, and in this event the speed warranty will be deleted.

6 **CONTINUATION**

Should the Vessel at the expiration of this insurance be at sea or in distress or at a port or place of refuge or of call, she shall, provided prompt notice be given to the Underwriters, be held covered at a premium to be agreed and anchored or moored at her next port of call in good safety.

This clause is similar to the Continuation Clause contained in the Institute Time Clauses, Hulls, 1/10/83, (see page 94), save that the period of extension will end when the yacht is anchored or moored at her next port of call in good safety.

7 **ASSIGNMENT**

No assignment of or interest in this insurance or in any moneys which may be or become payable thereunder is to be binding on or recognised by the Underwriters unless a dated notice of such assignment or interest signed by the Assured, and by the assignor in the case of subsequent assignment, is endorsed on the policy and the policy with such endorsement is produced before payment of any claim or return of premium thereunder.

This clause is the same as Clause 5 in the Institute Time Clauses, Hulls, 1/10/83 (see page 150).

8 **CHANGE OF OWNERSHIP**

This Clause 8 shall prevail notwithstanding any provision whether written typed or printed in this insurance inconsistent therewith.

8.1 Should the Vessel be sold or transferred to new ownership, or, where the Vessel is owned by a company, should there be a change in the controlling interest(s) of the company, then, unless the Underwriters agree in writing to continue the insurance, this insurance shall become cancelled from the time of such sale transfer or change and a pro rata daily net return of premium be made calculated on the premium charged for the in commission and/or laid up period.

8.2 If however the Vessel shall have left her moorings or be at sea at the time of sale or transfer such cancellation shall if required by the Assured be suspended until arrival at port or place of destination.

All the standard hull forms provide that cover will cease in the event of change of ownership. In the forms covering trading vessels, the relative provision forms part of the Termination Clause, for example, Clause 5.2 of the Institute Time Clauses, Hulls, 1/11/95. By the introductory words in bold print, the clause overrides anything written, typed or printed in the policy to the contrary. However, if the yacht has left her moorings or is at sea at the time of the sale or transfer, the assured is entitled to defer the cancellation of the policy until the yacht has reached her destination.

9 **PERILS**

Subject always to the exclusions in this insurance

9.1 this insurance covers loss of or damage to the subject-matter insured caused by

9.1.1 perils of the seas rivers lakes or other navigable waters

9.1.2 fire

9.1.3 jettison

9.1.4 piracy

9.1.5 contact with dock or harbour equipment or installation, land conveyance, aircraft or similar objects or objects falling therefrom

9.1.6 earthquake volcanic eruption or lightning

9.2 and, provided such loss or damage has not resulted from want of due diligence by the Assured Owners or Managers, the insurance covers

9.2.1 loss of or damage to the subject-matter insured caused by

9.2.1.1 accidents in loading, discharging or moving stores, gear, equipment, machinery or fuel

9.2.1.2 explosions

9.2.1.3 malicious acts

9.2.1.4 theft of the entire Vessel or her boat(s), or outboard motor(s) provided it is securely locked to the Vessel or her boat(s) by an anti-theft device in addition to its normal method of attachment, or, following upon forcible entry into the Vessel or place of storage or repair, theft of machinery including outboard motor(s), gear or equipment

9.2.2 loss of or damage to the subject-matter insured, *excepting motor and connections (but not strut shaft or propeller) electrical equipment and batteries and connections,* caused by

9.2.2.1 latent defects in hull or machinery, breakage of shafts or bursting of boilers (excluding the cost and expense of replacing or repairing the defective part broken shaft or burst boiler)

9.2.2.2 the negligence of any person whatsoever, but excluding the cost of making good any defect resulting from either negligence or breach of contract in respect of any repair or alteration work carried out for the account of the Assured and/or the Owners or in respect of the maintenance of the Vessel,

9.3 this insurance covers the expense of sighting the bottom after a stranding, if reasonably incurred specially for that purpose, even if no damage be found.

The named perils are much the same as in the policy forms covering commercial vessels, but the following differences may be noted:

— The perils of explosion and theft are transferred to section 2 of the Clause, and are subject to the exercise of due diligence by the assured, owners or managers. The reason is obvious. Private yachts are, regrettably, particularly exposed to these hazards: explosion, because without due care in the operation of the gas system, bottled gas may escape and, being heavier than air, collect in the bilges to form an ever-present explosion hazard; theft, because yachts are frequently unattended for long periods of time. The coverage for theft is therefore considerably circumscribed: see Clause 9.2.1.4 for the precise provisions.

— The perils of latent defects in hull or machinery, and of negligence of any person whatsoever are covered, but claims for loss or damage to "motor and connections (but not strut shaft or propeller) electrical equipment and batteries and connections" are excluded. In accordance with the accepted construction of the Inchmaree Clause, damage to the defective part is also excluded.

It is to be noted that the cover provided for loss or damage caused by latent defects *does not* extend to latent defects in gear or equipment. Thus, damage caused by the fall of a mast due to a failure through latent defect in some part of the standing rigging will not be recoverable under the policy.

— There is an exclusion in the cover provided for damage caused by the negligence of repairers, the effect of which is to limit the recoverable claim to the damage which is *consequential* upon the defect caused by such negligence, i.e., excluding the cost of repair or replacement of the part rendered defective by that negligence. This exclusion does not, however, operate if the repairers were carrying out work for the underwriters' account, i.e., for average repairs.

10 EXCLUSIONS

No claim shall be allowed in respect of any

10.1 outboard motor dropping off or falling overboard

10.2 ship's boat having a maximum designed speed exceeding 17 knots, unless such boat is specially covered herein and subject also to the conditions of the Speedboat Clause 19 below, or is on the parent Vessel or laid up ashore

10.3 ship's boat not permanently marked with the name of the parent Vessel

10.4 sails and protective covers split by the wind or blown away while set, unless in consequence of damage to the spars to which sails are bent, or occasioned by the Vessel being stranded or in collision or contact with any external substance (ice included) other than water

10.5 sails, masts, spars or standing and running rigging while the Vessel is racing, unless the loss or damage is caused by the Vessel being stranded, sunk, burnt, on fire or in collision or contact with any external substance (ice included) other than water

10.6 personal effects

10.7 consumable stores, fishing gear or moorings

10.8 sheathing, or repairs thereto, unless the loss or damage has been caused by the Vessel being stranded, sunk, burnt, on fire or in collision or contact with any external substance (ice included) other than water

10.9 loss or expenditure incurred in remedying a fault in design or construction or any cost or expense incurred by reason of betterment or alteration in design or construction

10.10 motor and connections (but not strut shaft or propeller) electrical equipment and batteries and connections, where the loss or damage has been caused by heavy weather, unless the loss or damage has been caused by the Vessel being immersed, but this Clause 10.10 shall not exclude loss or damage caused by the Vessel being stranded or in collision or contact with another vessel, pier or jetty.

This is a fairly wide set of exclusions, some of which apply to the kinds of loss or damage to which a yacht is particularly susceptible and which an assured might have difficulty in proving were occasioned by insured perils.

Clause 10.4 is an example, and in fact the wording of this clause is based upon an old custom of Lloyd's which for 200 years or more has governed the adjustment of claims for sails split by the wind or blown away while set.

Clause 10.10 is a modern extension of the same principle.

11 LIABILITIES TO THIRD PARTIES

This Clause only to apply when a sum is stated for this purpose in the Schedule to the policy

11.1 The Underwriters agree to indemnify the Assured for any sum or sums which the Assured shall become legally liable to pay and shall pay, by reason of interest in the insured Vessel and arising out of accidents occurring during the currency of this insurance, in respect of

11.1.1 loss of or damage to any other vessel or property whatsoever

11.1.2 loss of life, personal injury or illness, including payments made for life salvage, caused on or near the Vessel or any other vessel

11.1.3 any attempted or actual raising, removal or destruction of the wreck of the insured Vessel or the cargo thereof or any neglect or failure to raise, remove or destroy the same.

11.2 LEGAL COSTS

The Underwriters will also pay, provided their prior written consent has been obtained,

11.2.1 the legal costs incurred by the Assured or which the Assured may be compelled to pay in contesting liability or taking proceedings to limit liability

11.2.2 the costs of representation at any coroner's inquest or fatal accident enquiry.

11.3 SISTERSHIP

Should the Vessel hereby insured come into collision with or receive salvage services from another vessel belonging wholly or in part to the same Owners or under the same management, the Assured shall have the same rights under this insurance as they would have were the other vessel entirely the property of Owners not interested in the Vessel hereby insured; but in such cases the liability for the collision or the amount payable for the services rendered shall be referred to as a sole arbitrator to be agreed upon between the Underwriters and the Assured.

11.4 NAVIGATION BY OTHER PERSONS

The provisions of this Clause 11 shall extend to any person navigating or in charge of the insured Vessel with the permission of the Assured named in this insurance (other than a person operating, or employed by the operator of, a shipyard, marina, repair yard, slipway, yacht club, sales agency or similar organisation) and who while so navigating or in charge of the Vessel shall in consequence of any occurrence covered by this Clause 11 become liable to pay and shall pay any sum or sums to any person or persons, other than to the Assured named in this insurance, but indemnity under this Clause shall inure to the benefit of the Assured and only to a person navigating or in charge of the Vessel as described above, at the written request of and through the agency of the Assured. Nothing in this extension shall increase the Underwriters' liability beyond the limitation of liability imposed by Clause 11.8 and this extension shall be subject to all other terms and warranties of this insurance.

Nothing in this Clause 11.4 shall be deemed to override the provisions of Clause 3.2 above.

11.5 REMOVAL OF WRECK EXTENSION

This insurance also to pay the expenses, after deduction of the proceeds of the salvage, of the removal of the wreck of the insured Vessel from any place owned, leased or occupied by the Assured.

11.6 LIABILITIES SECTION EXCLUSIONS

Notwithstanding the provisions of this Clause 11 this insurance does not cover any liability cost or expense arising in respect of

11.6.1 any direct or indirect payment by the Assured under workmen's compensation or employers' liability acts and any other statutory or common law liability in respect of accidents to or illness of workmen or any other persons employed in any capacity whatsoever by the Assured or by any person to whom the protection of this insurance is afforded by reason of the provisions of Clause 11.4 above, in on or about or in connection with the Vessel hereby insured or her cargo, materials or repairs

11.6.2 any boat belonging to the Vessel and having a maximum designed speed exceeding 17 knots, unless such boat is specially covered herein and subject also to the conditions of the Speedboat Clause 19 below, or is on the parent Vessel or laid up ashore

11.6.3 any liability to or incurred by any person engaged in water skiing or aquaplaning, while being towed by the Vessel or preparing to be towed or after being towed until safely on board or ashore

11.6.4 any liability to or incurred by any person engaged in a sport or activity, other than water skiing or aquaplaning, while being towed by the Vessel or preparing to be towed or after being towed until safely on board or ashore

11.6.5 punitive or exemplary damages, however described.

11.7 WATER SKIERS LIABILITIES

Should Clause 11.6.3 and/or Clause 11.6.4 above be deleted, the liabilities mentioned in such clause(s) shall be covered hereunder, subject always to the warranties, conditions and limits of this insurance.

11.8 LIMIT OF LIABILITY

The liability of the Underwriters under this Clause 11, in respect of any one accident or series of accidents arising out of the same event, shall in no case exceed the sum stated for this purpose in the Schedule to the policy, but when the liability of the Assured has been contested with the consent in writing of the Underwriters, the Underwriters will also pay a like proportion of the costs which the Assured shall thereby incur or be compelled to pay.

In order for Clause 11 to apply, a figure has to be agreed at the time of placing the insurance, and this figure will, by Clause 11.8, be the maximum liability which underwriters will pay in respect of any one accident or series of accidents arising out of the same event. It is usual for this figure to be separately rated for premium purposes. When the terms of the insurance have been agreed, this figure will be entered in the schedule attached to the policy.

The cover provided by this clause differs from that granted under the Institute Protection and Indemnity Clauses, Hulls—Time (see pages 240 to 250) in a certain number of respects:

"By reason of interest in the insured vessel"

This expression is wider than that currently used in the Institute Protection and Indemnity Clauses, which refer to liabilities of the assured "as owner of the vessel". The words "by reason of interest in . . . " were considered in *Turner* v. *Manx Line*.[84] This case did not involve a yacht, but a "linkspan", which connected a ro-ro vessel to the quay for the purpose of loading and unloading vehicles. This was not owned by the assured (Manx Line), but was used by it in its commercial operations. It was held in the Court of Appeal that the liability of the assured did indeed arise by reason of its interest in the linkspan.

The cover granted to the assured is further extended by Clause 11.4 to cover the liabilities arising when some other person is navigating or in charge of the yacht with the assured's permission, provided that such other person is not the operator or employee of a shipyard, marina, repair yard, slipway, yacht club, sails agency or other similar organisation (which would be expected to carry its own liability insurance cover), and that the assured makes a written request to the underwriters for the benefit of this clause to be so extended.

The main areas of liabilities covered are:

Clause 11.1.1: loss of or damage to any other vessel or property.

Clause 11.1.2: loss of life, personal injury or illness, and also payments for life salvage.

Clause 11.1.3: raising, removal or destruction of the wreck of the vessel or cargo on board (an unexpected extension, this!) or liability arising from failure to do so.

Clause 11.2: legal costs incurred with the underwriters' written consent in contesting liability, taking proceedings to limit liability or for representation at an inquest or fatal accident enquiry.

On the other hand, there is a fairly wide exclusion by Clause 11.6.1 of any liability arising in respect of employees of the assured.

There are two areas in which the assured has an option for wider cover, which he must exercise at the time of placing the insurance:

— if he requires cover for liabilities arising through the use of a speedboat (i.e., a boat having a maximum designed speed exceeding 17 knots),

84. *Turner* v. *Manx Line* [1990] 1 Lloyd's Rep. 137.

such boat must be specially covered under the Speedboat Clause 19;

— if he wants cover for liabilities to or incurred by persons engaged in water sports, this must be arranged in advance.

12 **EXCESS AND DEDUCTIBLE**

12.1 No claim arising from a peril insured against shall be payable under this insurance unless the aggregate of all such claims arising out of each separate accident or occurrence (including claims under Clauses 11, 14 and 15) exceeds the amount stated for this purpose in the Schedule to the policy, in which case this sum shall be deducted. This Clause 12.1 shall not apply to a claim for total or constructive total loss of the Vessel or, in the event of such a claim, to any associated claim under Clause 15 arising from the same accident or occurrence.

12.2 Prior to the application of Clause 12.1 above and in addition thereto, deductions new for old not exceeding one-third may be made at the Underwriters' discretion in respect of loss of or damage to

12.2.1 protective covers, sails and running rigging

12.2.2 outboard motors whether or not insured by separate valuation under this insurance.

This clause is in two parts.

Clause 12.1 is based upon the deductible clause contained in all the standard hull forms, whereby the deductible figure is applied to the aggregate of all claims "arising out of each separate accident or occurrence"—as to the construction of these words, see the commentary on pages 135 to 138. The "aggregate of all claims" includes claims for salvage charges, sue and labour expenses and claims under the Protection and Indemnity Clause. The deductible is not applied to a claim for a total or constructive total loss or to any associated claim under Clause 15. The other instance normally excluded from the application of the deductible, namely a claim for the expense of sighting the bottom after a stranding, if reasonably incurred especially for that purpose, is not referred to in the context of this Clause 12: instead the customary wording has been transferred to Clause 9.3.

Clause 12.2 provides for two instances where at underwriters' discretion deductions not exceeding one-third may be made to claims for the cost of replacing outboard motors, protective covers, sails and running rigging.

13 **NOTICE OF CLAIM AND TENDERS**

13.1 Prompt notice shall be given to the Underwriters in the event of any occurrence which may give rise to a claim under this insurance, and any theft or malicious damage shall also be reported promptly to the Police.

13.2 Where loss or damage has occurred, notice shall be given to the Underwriters prior to survey and, if the Vessel is abroad, also to the nearest Lloyd's Agent so that a surveyor may be appointed to represent the Underwriters should they so desire.

13.3 The Underwriters shall be entitled to decide the port to which the Vessel shall proceed for docking or repair (the actual additional expense of the voyage arising from compliance with Underwriters' requirements being refunded to the Assured) and shall have a right of veto concerning a place of repair or a repairing firm.

13.4 The Underwriters may also take tenders or may require tenders to be taken for the repair of the Vessel.

This clause is based upon the Tender Clause contained in the Institute Time Clauses, Hulls, 1/10/83—see pages 139 to 141 for commentary.

There is however an additional requirement under the yacht clauses, namely that in the event of a theft or malicious damage the occurrence must also be promptly reported to the police.

14 SALVAGE CHARGES

Subject to any express provision in this insurance, salvage charges incurred in preventing a loss by perils insured against may be recovered as a loss by those perils.

The clause reproduces the effect of section 65 of the Marine Insurance Act 1906, by stating that salvage charges incurred in preventing a loss by perils insured against may be recovered as a loss by those perils. It is important to note that, whereas under the forms of clauses designed for vessels trading commercially claims for salvage charges will be reduced proportionately to any under-insurance, this provision does not apply here. The absence of any under-insurance provision in this context (as also in the Sue and Labour Clause) emphasises the materiality of the yacht's value in the negotiations leading up to the placing of yacht insurances.

15 DUTY OF ASSURED

15.1 In case of any loss or misfortune it is the duty of the Assured and their servants and agents to take such measures as may be reasonable for the purpose of averting or minimising a loss which would be recoverable under this insurance.

15.2 Subject to the provisions below and to Clause 12 the Underwriters will contribute to charges properly and reasonably incurred by the Assured their servants or agents for such measures. General average, salvage charges, collision defence or attack costs and costs incurred by the Assured in contesting liability covered by Clause 11.2 are not recoverable under this Clause 15.

15.3 The Assured will render to the Underwriters all possible aid in obtaining information and evidence should the Underwriters desire to take proceedings at their own expense and for their own benefit in the name of the Assured to recover compensation or to secure an indemnity from any third party in respect of anything covered by this insurance.

15.4 Measures taken by the Assured or the Underwriters with the object of saving, protecting or recovering the subject-matter insured shall not be considered as a waiver or acceptance of abandonment or otherwise prejudice the rights of either party.

15.5 The sum recoverable under this Clause 15 shall be in addition to the loss otherwise recoverable under this insurance but in no circumstances shall amounts recoverable under Clause 15.2 exceed the sum insured under this insurance in respect of the Vessel.

This clause is closely modelled upon the corresponding clause in the Institute Time Clauses, Hulls, Clause 11—Duty of Assured (Sue and Labour). Clauses 15.1, 15.2, 15.4 and 15.5 have their counterparts in Clauses 11.1, 11.2, 11.3 and 11.6 of the I.T.C., and reference may be made to the commentary on pages 131 to 135 above.

Omitted from the yacht clauses are the provisions relating to under-insurance, for the reasons already mentioned in the discussion on Clause 14, and the rather special extension of cover granted in the case of commercial vessels consequent upon the admission of a claim for a total loss.

Special to the yacht clauses is Clause 15.3, which sets out the duty of the assured to assist the underwriters should they wish to take steps to exercise their rights of subrogation against a third party.

16 UNREPAIRED DAMAGE

16.1 The measure of indemnity in respect of claims for unrepaired damage shall be the reasonable depreciation in the market value of the Vessel at the time this insurance terminates arising from such unrepaired damage, but not exceeding the reasonable cost of repairs.

16.2 In no case shall the Underwriters be liable for unrepaired damage in the event of a subsequent total loss (whether or not covered under this insurance) sustained during the period covered by this insurance or any extension thereof.

16.3 The Underwriters shall not be liable in respect of unrepaired damage for more than the insured value at the time this insurance terminates.

This is in precisely the same terms as Clause 18 of the Institute Time Clauses, Hulls—see commentary on pages 145 to 148 herein.

17 CONSTRUCTIVE TOTAL LOSS

17.1 In ascertaining whether the Vessel is a constructive total loss, the insured value shall be taken as the repaired value and nothing in respect of the damaged or break-up value of the Vessel or wreck shall be taken into account.

17.2 No claim for constructive total loss based upon the cost of recovery and/or repair of the Vessel shall be recoverable hereunder unless such cost would exceed the insured value. In making this determination, only the cost relating to a single accident or sequence of damages arising from the same accident shall be taken into account.

This is in precisely the same terms as Clause 19 of the Institute Time Clauses, Hulls—see commentary on pages 148 to 149 herein.

18 DISBURSEMENTS WARRANTY

Warranted that no amount shall be insured policy proof of interest or full interest admitted for account of the Assured, Mortgagees or Owners on disbursements, commission, profits or other interests or excess or increased value of hull or machinery however described unless the insured value of the Vessel is over £50,000 and then not to exceed 10 per cent of the total amount insured in respect of the Vessel as stated in the Schedule to the policy.

Provided always that a breach of this warranty shall not afford the Underwriters any defence to a claim by Mortgagee who has accepted this insurance without knowledge of such breach.

Normally yacht underwriters require that there should be no additional insurance on disbursements, etc. for the reasons discussed on pages 151 to 152 herein, but an exception is made in the case of yachts valued in excess of £50,000, in which case an amount up to 10 per cent of the yacht's value as stated in the policy may be separately insured in this respect.

19 SPEEDBOAT CLAUSE

WHERE THIS CLAUSE 19 APPLIES IT SHALL OVERRIDE ANY CONFLICTING PROVISIONS IN THE CLAUSES ABOVE.

19.1 **It is a condition of this insurance that when the Vessel concerned is under way the Assured named in the Schedule to the policy or other competent person(s) shall be on board and in control of the Vessel.**

19.2 No claim shall be allowed in respect of loss of or damage to the Vessel or liability to any third party or any salvage services

19.2.1 caused by or arising from the Vessel being stranded sunk swamped immersed or breaking adrift, while left moored or anchored unattended off an exposed beach or shore

19.2.2 arising while the Vessel is participating in racing or speed tests, or any trials in connection therewith.

19.3 No claim shall be allowed in respect of rudder strut shaft or propeller

19.3.1 under Clauses 9.2.2.1 and 9.2.2.2.

19.3.2 for any loss or damage caused by heavy weather, water or contact other than with another vessel, pier or jetty, but this Clause 19.3.2 shall not exclude damage caused by the Vessel being immersed as a result of heavy weather.

19.4 If the vessel is fitted with inboard machinery no liability shall attach to this insurance in respect of any claim caused by or arising through fire or explosion unless the Vessel is equipped in the engine room (or engine space) tank space and galley, with a fire extinguishing system automatically operated or having controls at the steering position and properly installed and maintained in efficient working order.

As we have already seen, this clause is available in the event that the insured vessel, or any boat insured therewith, has a maximum designed speed in excess of 17 knots. Cover is fairly severely restricted as follows:

Clause 19.2 excludes any claim for loss, damage, salvage charges or third party liability arising from certain classes of accident which may occur when the boat has been left moored or anchored unattended off an exposed beach or shore, or arising while the vessel is racing or undertaking speed trials.

Claims for loss or damage of rudder, strut, shaft or propeller will not be allowed if caused by latent defect or the negligence of anyone, nor if caused by heavy weather, water or contact, except for immersion damage as a result of heavy weather.

Clause 19.4 excludes any claim caused by or arising through fire or explosion if the boat is fitted with inboard machinery, unless a properly installed and maintained fire extinguishing system is fitted in certain locations. These locations, as set out in the clause, do not necessarily correspond with the regulations/recommendations in force in various parts of the world. Consequently, an assured having a speedboat fitted with inboard machinery is recommended to declare specifically where the fire extinguishing equipment is fitted and how it operates, in order to obtain the underwriters' agreement to the system which is actually in place.

20 CANCELLATION AND RETURN OF PREMIUM

This insurance may be cancelled by the Underwriters at any time subject to 30 days notice to the Assured or by mutual agreement, when a pro rata daily net return of premium shall be made calculated on the premium charged for the in commission and/or laid up period.

This is self-explanatory.

THE FOLLOWING CLAUSES SHALL BE PARAMOUNT AND SHALL OVERRIDE ANYTHING CONTAINED IN THIS INSURANCE INCONSISTENT THEREWITH

21 WAR EXCLUSION

In no case shall this insurance cover loss damage liability or expense caused by

21.1 war civil war revolution rebellion insurrection, or civil strife arising therefrom, or any hostile act by or against a belligerent power

21.2 capture seizure arrest restraint or detainment (barratry and piracy excepted), and the consequences thereof or any attempt thereat

21.3 derelict mines torpedoes bombs or other derelict weapons of war.

22 STRIKES AND POLITICAL EXCLUSION

In no case shall this insurance cover loss damage liability or expense caused by

22.1 strikers, locked-out workmen, or persons taking part in labour disturbances, riots or civil commotions

22.2 any terrorist or any person acting from a political motive.

23 NUCLEAR EXCLUSION

In no case shall this insurance cover loss damage liability or expense arising from

23.1 any weapon of war employing atomic or nuclear fission and/or fusion or other like reaction or radioactive force or matter

23.2 ionising radiations from or contamination by radioactivity from any nuclear fuel or from any nuclear waste from the combustion of nuclear fuel

23.3 the radioactive, toxic, explosive or other hazardous properties of any explosive nuclear assembly or nuclear component thereof.

Clauses 21 and 22 are the customary war and strikes exclusions. For consideration of what is excluded, reference should be made to Part VI of this book, where the positive cover is discussed.

The nuclear exclusion provided in Clause 23 anticipated the wider terms now incorporated in the Institute Time Clauses, Hulls, 1/11/95. See page 156.

PART IV

ADDITIONAL INSURANCES FOR SHIPOWNERS

1. HISTORICAL PERSPECTIVE

One of the oldest precepts in marine insurance, which one may think is perfectly logical, is that the subjects of the insurance will be covered for the value which they have at the commencement of the risk. In the early days, at Edward Lloyd's coffee house, the underwriter might require some proof that the value which he was being called upon to insure was realistic, and what better proof could the shipowner disclose than the bills for the amounts which he had paid for the ship, its fitting-out, and the moneys which he had disbursed in anticipation of the projected adventure.

Section 16(1) of the Marine Insurance Act 1906 restates this old rule:

> "Subject to any express provision or valuation in the policy, the insurable value of the subject-matter insured must be ascertained as follows:—
>
> (1) In insurance on ship, the insurable value is the value at the commencement of the risk, of the ship, including her outfit, provisions and stores for the officers and crew, money advanced for seamen's wages, and other disbursements (if any) incurred to make the ship fit for the voyage or adventure contemplated by the policy, plus the charges of insurance upon the whole:"

Upon this principle, that there is an insurable interest for the outlays made upon the commencement of the voyage, and upon which the shipowner expects to make a profit, it will be seen that if, during the voyage, the shipowner has to disburse additional sums by way of refitting the ship, engaging new members of the crew and taking further provisions, these outlays will also become proper subjects for insurance.

Hence the need to take out additional insurances by way of "disbursements", or, if the ship should have an enhanced value by reason of her being engaged for a special trade, upon her "increased value".

Towards the middle of the nineteenth century, it became customary to agree with the underwriters the value of the ship for the purpose of insurance, and this solved a lot of problems, in particular the amount to be settled by the underwriters in the event of a total loss. Even so, the amount of the valuation might not be adequate to indemnify the shipowner who had made substantial outlays during the course of the voyage, and consequently the shipowner was glad to have the facility of effecting further insurance, when necessary, by way of disbursements or increased value.

As to the current practice, please read on.

2. EXCESS LIABILITIES

As we have already seen when considering the main clauses, claims for salvage, general average and sue and labour charges are subject to reduction in respect of any under-insurance and cover for collision liability is limited to three-fourths of the insured value. It is therefore common practice for shipowners to take out supplementary insurances on "excess liabilities" to enable them, in the event of the vessel being under-valued in the hull policy, to obtain further coverage for the excess of any specified contributions or liabilities over and above the amounts recoverable under the hull policy.

In *Holman & Sons* v. *Merchants' Marine Insurance Company*[1] a vessel was insured under a hull policy on a valuation of £39,000. In addition, the shipowners had taken out a further policy on increased value of hull and machinery for £1,855, the risks insured including "any liability which may attach to the shipowner in consequence of the hull and machinery being valued for contribution to general average and salvage charges at more than the insured valuation" (in the hull policy). Due to the fact that the vessel was under-insured under the hull policy the shipowner was unable to recover under that policy for the full amount of the ship's contribution to salvage and general average. It was contended on behalf of the assured that they were entitled to recover the short-fall in full, up to the whole sum insured under the increased value and excess liabilities policy. It was held that the assured could only recover such proportion of the sum insured against excess liabilities as the £1,855 bore to the total excess valuation for salvage and the total excess contributory value respectively.

Some simple figures will illustrate the correct method of assessing the claim under an excess liabilities policy.

Salved Value	£10,000	on which salvage of	£2,000	is paid
Insured value in hull policy	£10,000			
Deduct — Damage	2,000			
	£8,000	pays	£1,600	
Excess value	£2,000	pays	£400	

Sum insured on Excess Liabilities £1,800 pays

$\frac{£1,800}{2,000} \times £400 =$ £360

1. (1919) 14 Asp.M.L.C. 433; 24 Com.Cas. 102; 35 T.L.R. 138.

The current clauses are:

A. Institute Time Clauses, Hulls: Excess Liabilities 1/11/95

This insurance is subject to English law and practice

1 **1.1** This insurance covers only:

1.1.1 **General Average, Salvage and Salvage Charges** recoverable under the insurances on hull and machinery but not recoverable in full by reason of the difference between the insured value of the Vessel as stated therein (or any reduced value arising from the deduction therefrom in process of adjustment of any claim which law or practice or the terms of the insurances covering hull and machinery may have required) and the value of the Vessel adopted for the purpose of contribution to general average, salvage or salvage charges, the liability under this insurance being for such proportion of the amount not recoverable as the amount insured hereunder bears to the said difference or to the total sum insured against excess liabilities if it exceed such difference.

1.1.2 **Sue and Labour Charges** recoverable under the insurances on hull and machinery but not recoverable in full by reason of the difference between the insured value of the Vessel as stated therein and the value of the Vessel adopted for the purpose of ascertaining the amount recoverable under the insurances on hull and machinery, the liability under this insurance being for such proportion of the amount not recoverable as the amount insured hereunder bears to the said difference or to the total sum insured against excess liabilities if it exceed such difference.

1.1.3 **Collision Liability (three-fourths)** recoverable under the Institute $\frac{3}{4}$ths Collision Liability and Sistership Clauses in the insurances on hull and machinery but not recoverable in full by reason of such three-fourths liability exceeding three-fourths of the insured value of the Vessel as stated therein, in which case the amount recoverable under this insurance shall be such proportion of the difference so arising as the amount insured hereunder bears to the total sum insured against excess liabilities.

1.2 The Underwriters' liability under 1.1.1, 1.1.2 and 1.1.3 separately, in respect of any one claim, shall not exceed the amount insured hereunder.

2 **RETURNS**

To return pro rata monthly net for each uncommenced month if this insurance be cancelled by agreement.

The following clauses shall be paramount and shall override anything contained in this insurance inconsistent therewith.

3 **WAR EXCLUSION**

In no case shall this insurance cover loss damage liability or expense caused by

3.1 war civil war revolution rebellion insurrection, or civil strife arising therefrom, or any hostile act by or against a belligerent power

3.2 capture seizure arrest restraint or detainment (barratry and piracy excepted), and the consequences thereof or any attempt thereat

3.3 derelict mines torpedoes bombs or other derelict weapons of war.

4 **STRIKES EXCLUSION**

In no case shall this insurance cover loss damage liability or expense caused by

4.1 strikers, locked-out workmen, or persons taking part in labour disturbances, riots or civil commotions

4.2 any terrorist or any person acting from a political motive.

5 **MALICIOUS ACTS EXCLUSION**

In no case shall this insurance cover loss damage liability or expense arising from

5.1 the detonation of an explosive

5.2 any weapon of war

and caused by any person acting maliciously or from a political motive.

6 **RADIOACTIVE CONTAMINATION EXCLUSION CLAUSE**

In no case shall this insurance cover loss damage liability or expense directly or indirectly caused by or contributed to by or arising from

6.1 ionising radiations from or contamination by radioactivity from any nuclear fuel or from any nuclear waste or from the combustion of nuclear fuel

6.2 the radioactive, toxic, explosive or other hazardous or contaminating properties of any nuclear installation, reactor or other nuclear assembly or nuclear component thereof

6.3 any weapon of war employing atomic or nuclear fission and/or fusion or other like reaction or radioactive force of matter.

As with our review of the Institute Time Clauses, Hulls, emphasis has been added to the text set out above where it differs from the wording of the 1/10/83 version. The differences are:

In Clause 1:

"recoverable under the insurances on hull and machinery but not recoverable in full . . . "

The already rather complicated wording is rendered even more convoluted by the addition of the extra words. Presumably these words were added in order to express what was previously quite clearly implied by the phrase "not recoverable in full", namely that the claim had to qualify under the terms of the hull and machinery policies, but be irrecoverable solely by reason of under-insurance.

In Clause 6:
The Radioactive Contamination Exclusion Clause takes the place of the Nuclear Exclusion Clause, or to put it another way, sub-clauses 6.1 and 6.2 were new in the 1/11/95 form.

The Exclusion Clauses generally are identical with those contained in the Institute Time Clauses, Hulls—see pages 155 to 156.

The effective part of these clauses is contained in Clause 1. Sub-clause 1.1 gives effect to the principle laid down in *Holman* v. *Merchants' Marine Insurance Company* (see page 208). Parts of the wording require special mention:

"(or any reduced value arising from the deduction therefrom in process of adjustment of any claim which law or practice or the terms of the insurances covering hull and machinery may have required)"

If the vessel's hull policy is subject to English law and practice the basis of calculating the liability is laid down in the Association of Average Adjusters Rule of Practice B33 which provides as follows:

"**B33 UNDERWRITER'S LIABILITY**

If the ship or cargo be insured for more than its contributory value, the underwriter pays what is assessed on the contributory value. But where insured for less than the contributory value, the underwriter pays on the insured value; and when there has been a particular average for damage which forms a deduction from the contributory value of the ship that must be deducted from the insured value to find upon what the underwriter contributes.

This rule does not apply to foreign adjustments, when the basis of contribution is something other than the net value of the thing insured.

That in practice, in applying the above rule for the purpose of ascertaining the liability of underwriters for contribution to general average and salvage charges, deduction shall be made from the insured value of all losses and charges for which underwriters are liable and which have been deducted in arriving at the contributory value.

In adjusting the liability of underwriters on freight for general average contribution and salvage charges, effect shall be given to Section 73 of the Marine Insurance Act, 1906, by comparing the gross and not the net amount of freight at risk with the insured value in the case of a valued policy or the insurable value in the case of an unvalued policy."

The reason for deducting from the insured value all losses and charges for which underwriters are liable and which have been deducted in arriving at the contributory value is to ensure that both figures used in the comparison have been prepared on the same basis.

"recoverable as the amount insured hereunder bears to the said difference or to the total sum insured against excess liabilities if it exceed such difference"

The words underlined are to cover the situation where there is more than one insurance against excess liabilities and the total sum insured under the policies exceeds the amount of the excess valuation. In such circumstances the sums insured are added together and each policy bears its proportionate share of any excess liability.

Clause 1.2 limits the total liability under each section of the policy, in respect of any one claim, to the amount insured.

B. Institute Time Clauses, Hulls: Disbursements and Increased Value (Total Loss only, including Excess Liabilities) 1/11/95

These clauses are designed to provide a two-fold cover:

— On disbursements and increased value, the sum insured being payable only in the event of a claim being settled on the hull policy for a total or constructive total loss, or pro rata in the event of a compromised total loss;
— On excess liabilities.

As with our review of the Institute Time Clauses, Hulls, emphasis has been added to the text set out below where it differs from the wording of the 1/10/83 version.

Clauses 1–5 Navigation; Continuation; Breach of Warranty; Classification and Termination

This insurance is subject to English law and practice

1 NAVIGATION

1.1 The subject-matter insured is covered subject to the provisions of this insurance at all times and the Vessel has leave to sail or navigate with or without pilots, to go on trial trips and to assist and tow vessels or craft in distress, but it is warranted that the Vessel shall not be towed, except as is customary or to the first safe port or place when in need of assistance, or undertake towage or salvage services under a contract previously arranged by the Assured and/or Owners and/or Managers and/or Charterers. This Clause 1.1 shall not exclude customary towage in connection with loading and discharging.

1.2 This insurance shall not be prejudiced by reason of the Assured entering into any contract with pilots or for customary towage which limits or exempts the liability of the pilots and/or tugs and/or towboats and/or their owners when the Assured or their agents accept or are compelled to accept such contracts in accordance with established local law or practice.

1.3 The practice of engaging helicopters for the transportation of personnel, supplies and equipment to and/or from the Vessel shall not prejudice this insurance.

1.4 In the event of the Vessel being employed in trading operations which entail cargo loading or discharging at sea from or into another vessel (not being a harbour or inshore craft) no claim shall be recoverable under this insurance in respect of loss of or damage to the subject-matter insured or for liability to any other vessel arising from such loading or discharging operations, including whilst approaching, lying alongside and leaving, unless previous notice that the Vessel is to be employed in such operations has been given to the Underwriters and any amended terms of cover and any additional premium required by them have been agreed.

1.5 In the event of the Vessel sailing (with or without cargo) with an intention of being (a) broken up, or (b) sold for breaking up, no claim shall be recoverable under this insurance in respect of loss or damage to the Vessel occurring subsequent to such sailing unless previous notice has been given to the Underwriters and any amendments to the terms of cover, amount insured and premium required by them have been agreed.

2 **CONTINUATION**

Should the Vessel at the expiration of this insurance be at sea and in distress or missing, she shall, provided notice be given to the Underwriters prior to the expiration of this insurance, be held covered until arrival at the next port in good safety, or if in port and in distress until the Vessel is made safe, at a pro rata monthly premium.

3 **BREACH OF WARRANTY**

Held covered in case of any breach of warranty as to cargo, locality, trade, towage, salvage services or date of sailing, provided notice be given to the Underwriters immediately after receipt of advices and any amended terms of cover and any additional premium required by them be agreed.

4 **CLASSIFICATION**

4.1 It is the duty of the Assured, Owners and Managers at the inception of and throughout the period of this insurance to ensure that

4.1.1 the Vessel is classed with a Classification Society agreed by the Underwriters and that her class within that Society is maintained

4.1.2 any recommendations requirements or restrictions imposed by the Vessel's Classification Society which relate to the Vessel's seaworthiness or to her maintenance in a seaworthy condition are complied with by the dates required by that Society.

4.2 In the event of any breach of the duties set out in Clause 4.1 above, unless the Underwriters agree to the contrary in writing, they will be discharged from liability under this insurance as from the date of the breach provided that if the Vessel is at sea at such date the Underwriters discharge from liability is deferred until arrival at her next port.

4.3 Any incident condition or damage in respect of which the Vessel's Classification Society might make recommendations as to repairs or other action to be taken by the Assured, Owners or Managers must be promptly reported to the Classification Society.

4.4 Should the Underwriters wish to approach the Classification Society directly for information and/or documents, the Assured will provide the necessary authorization.

5 **TERMINATION**

This Clause 5 shall prevail notwithstanding any provision whether written typed or printed in this insurance inconsistent therewith.

Unless the Underwriters agree to the contrary in writing, this insurance shall terminate automatically at the time of

5.1 change of the Classification Society of the Vessel, or change, suspension, discontinuance, withdrawal or expiry of her Class therein, or any of the Classification Society's periodic surveys becoming overdue unless an extension of time for such survey be agreed by the Classification Society, provided that if the Vessel is at sea such automatic termination shall be deferred until arrival at her next port. However where such change, suspension, discontinuance or withdrawal of her Class or where a periodic survey becoming overdue has resulted from loss or damage covered by Clause 6 of this insurance or which would be covered by an insurance of the Vessel subject to current Institute Time Clauses—Hulls or Institute War and Strikes Clauses Hulls—Time such automatic termination shall only operate should the Vessel sail from her next port without the prior approval of the Classification Society or in the case of a periodic survey becoming overdue without the Classification Society having agreed an extension of time for such survey,

5.2 any change, voluntary or otherwise, in the ownership or flag, transfer to new management, or charter on a bareboat basis, or requisition for title or use of the Vessel, provided that, if the Vessel has cargo on board and has already sailed from her loading port or is at sea in ballast, such automatic termination shall if required be deferred, whilst the Vessel continues her planned voyage, until arrival at final port of discharge if with cargo or at port of destination if in ballast. However, in the event of requisition for title or use without the prior execution of a written agreement by the Assured, such automatic termination shall occur fifteen days after such requisition whether the Vessel is at sea or in port.

A pro rata daily net return of premium shall be made provided that a total loss of the Vessel, whether by insured perils or otherwise, has not occurred during the period covered by this insurance or any extension thereof.

The Classification Clause (Clause 4) was new in 1995. Its terms and those of the other clauses reflect the changes made in the Institute Time Clauses, Hulls, 1/11/95. See the commentary on pages 91 to 100.

Clauses 6 and 7—Perils and Pollution Hazard

6 **PERILS**

6.1 This insurance covers total loss (actual or constructive) of the subject-matter insured caused by

6.1.1 perils of the seas rivers lakes or other navigable waters

6.1.2 fire, explosion

6.1.3 violent theft by persons from outside the Vessel

6.1.4 jettison

6.1.5 piracy

6.1.6 contact with land conveyance, dock or harbour equipment or installation

6.1.7 earthquake volcanic eruption or lightning

6.1.8 accidents in loading discharging or shifting cargo or fuel.

6.2 This insurance covers total loss (actual or constructive) of the subject-matter insured caused by

6.2.1 bursting of boilers breakage of shafts or any latent defect in the machinery or hull

6.2.2 negligence of Master Officers Crew or Pilots

6.2.3 negligence of repairers or charterers provided such repairers or charterers are not an Assured hereunder

6.2.4 barratry of Master Officers or Crew

6.2.5 contact with aircraft, helicopters or similar objects, or objects falling therefrom

provided such loss has not resulted from want of due diligence by the Assured, Owners, Managers or Superintendents or any of their onshore management.

6.3 Masters Officers Crew or Pilots not to be considered Owners within the meaning of this Clause 6 should they hold shares in the Vessel.

6.4 This insurance covers:

6.4.1 **General Average, Salvage and Salvage Charge** recoverable under the insurances on hull and machinery but not recoverable in full by reason of the difference between the insured value of the Vessel as stated therein (or any reduced value arising from the deduction therefrom in process of adjustment of any claim which law or practice or the terms of the insurances covering hull and machinery may have required) and the value of the Vessel adopted for the purpose of contribution to general average, salvage or salvage charges, the liability under this insurance being for such proportion of the amount not recoverable as the amount insured hereunder bears to the said difference or to the total sum insured against excess liabilities if it exceed such difference.

6.4.2 **Sue and Labour Charges** recoverable under the insurances on hull and machinery but not recoverable in full by reason of the difference between the insured value of the Vessel as stated therein and the value of the Vessel adopted for the purpose of ascertaining the amount recoverable under the insurances on hull and machinery, the liability under this insurance being for such proportion of the amount not recoverable as the amount insured hereunder bears to the said difference or to the total sum insured against excess liabilities if it exceed such difference.

6.4.3 **Collision Liability (three-fourths)** recoverable under the Institute $\frac{3}{4}$ths Collision Liability and Sistership Clauses in the insurances on hull and machinery but not recoverable in full by reason of such three-fourths liability exceeding three-fourths of the insured value of the Vessel as stated therein, in which case the amount recoverable under this insurance shall be such proportion of the difference so arising as the amount insured hereunder bears to the total sum insured against excess liabilities.

6.5 The Underwriters' liability under 6.4.1, 6.4.2 and 6.4.3 separately, in respect of any one claim, shall not exceed the amount insured hereunder.

7 **POLLUTION HAZARD**
This insurance covers total loss (actual or constructive) of the Vessel caused by any governmental authority acting under the powers vested in it to prevent or mitigate a pollution hazard or damage to the environment, or threat thereof, resulting directly from damage to the Vessel caused by a peril covered by this insurance, provided that such act of governmental authority has not resulted from want of due diligence by the Assured, Owners or Managers to prevent or mitigate such hazard or damage, or threat thereof. Master Officers Crew or Pilots not to be considered Owners within the meaning of this Clause 7 should they hold shares in the Vessel.

The perils insured against under sub-clauses 6.1 and 6.2, also under Clause 7, are the same as those listed in the Institute Time Clauses, Hulls, 1/11/95, but the cover is expressed to be limited to "total loss (actual or constructive)" of the vessel caused by those perils. For the commentary on the corresponding clauses in the I.T.C. Hulls, see pages 101 to 118.

Sub-clauses 6.4 and 6.5 reproduce, word for word, the effective part of the Institute Excess Liabilities form as set out and commented upon on pages 209 to 211.

Clause 8—Notice of Claim

8 **NOTICE OF CLAIM**
In the event of accident whereby loss or damage may result in a claim under this insurance, notice must be given to the Underwriters promptly after the date on which the Assured, Owners or Managers become or should have become aware of the loss or damage and prior to survey so that a surveyor may be appointed if the Underwriters so desire.
If notice is not given to the Underwriters within twelve months of that date unless the Underwriters agree to the contrary in writing, the Underwriters will be automatically discharged from liability for any claim under this insurance in respect of or arising out of such loss or damage.

This clause contains the stringent provisions regarding prompt notice which were introduced into the Institute Time Clauses, Hulls, 1/11/95 as Clause 13.1. See commentary on pages 140 to 141.

Clauses 9 and 10—Constructive and Compromised Total Losses

9 **CONSTRUCTIVE TOTAL LOSS**

9.1 In ascertaining whether the Vessel is a constructive total loss, the insured value in the insurances on hull and machinery shall be taken as the repaired value and nothing in respect of the damaged or break-up value of the Vessel or wreck shall be taken into account.

9.2 No claim for constructive total loss based upon the cost of recovery and/or repair of the Vessel shall be recoverable hereunder unless such cost would exceed the insured value in the insurances on hull and machinery. In making this determination, only the cost relating to a single accident or sequence of damages arising from the same accident shall be taken into account.

9.3 Provided that the Constructive Total Loss Clause in the current Institute Time Clauses Hulls or a clause having a similar effect is contained in the insurances on hull and machinery, the settlement of a claim for constructive total loss thereunder shall be accepted as proof of the constructive total loss of the Vessel.

9.4 Should the Vessel be a constructive total loss but the claim on the insurances on hull and machinery be settled as a claim for partial loss, no payment shall be due under this Clause 9.

10 **COMPROMISED TOTAL LOSS**
In the event of a claim for total loss or constructive total loss being settled on the insurances on hull and machinery as a compromised total loss the amount payable hereunder shall be the same percentage of the amount insured as is paid on the said insurances.

There was no change in the wording of these clauses in 1995.

Clause 9.3 states that if the Constructive Total Loss Clause in the current I.T.C. Hulls or a clause to similar effect is contained in the hull and machinery policy, the settlement of a claim for constructive total loss under the hull policy will be accepted as proof of the constructive total loss of the vessel. This clause is necessary because some policies contain entirely different provisions, or are subject to different laws or practices as to the criteria for assessing a constructive total loss. For example in several countries it is only necessary for the cost of repairs to exceed 75 per cent of the insured value in the hull policy in order to prove a constructive total loss. In such circumstances, Clause 9.3 cannot be invoked and the test to establish whether a claim under the disbursements and increased value policy has been triggered is the one laid down in Clause 9.2.

Clause 9.4 makes it clear that if the vessel is a constructive total loss, but the claim on the hull policy is settled as a claim for partial loss, no payment will be made under Clause 9. Upon initial examination it appears to be difficult to envisage circumstances where an assured would elect to claim for a partial loss when the vessel is a constructive total loss. This can happen however where, for example, the vessel is of an unusual type required for a special trade, which could not be replaced easily or at least only at a figure far in excess of the insured value. In such circumstances the assured may decide to repair and claim for a 100 per cent partial loss under the hull policy. The assured would then be unable to recover a total loss under the disbursements and increased value policy.

Clause 10 provides for the case—not at all uncommon—when a claim for a total or constructive total loss is settled under the hull policy as a "compromised" total loss for less than 100 per cent of the sum insured. In this event, the amount payable under the disbursements and increased value policy is reduced proportionately.

Clause 11—Assignment

11 **ASSIGNMENT**

No assignment of or interest in this insurance or in any moneys which may be or become payable thereunder is to be binding on or recognised by the Underwriters unless a dated notice of such assignment or interest signed by the Assured and by the assignor in the case of subsequent assignment, is endorsed on the Policy and the Policy with such endorsement is produced before payment of any claim or return of premium thereunder.

In the 1/10/83 form this was Clause 5. There was no change in the wording in 1995.

Clause 12—Returns for Lay-up and Cancellation

12 **RETURNS FOR LAY-UP AND CANCELLATION**

12.1 To return as follows:

12.1.1 pro rata monthly net for each uncommenced month if this insurance be cancelled by agreement,

12.1.2 for each period of 30 consecutive days the Vessel may be laid up in a port or in a lay-up area provided such port or lay-up area is approved by the Underwriters

(a) .... per cent net not under repair

(b) .... per cent net under repair.

12.1.3 The Vessel shall not be considered to be under repair when work is undertaken in respect of ordinary wear and tear of the Vessel and/or following recommendations in the Vessel's Classification Society survey, but any repairs following loss of or damage to the Vessel or involving structural alterations, whether covered by this insurance or otherwise shall be considered as under repair.

12.1.4 If the Vessel is under repair during part only of a period for which a return is claimable, the return shall be calculated pro rata to the number of days under 12.1.2(a) and (b) respectively.

12.2 PROVIDED ALWAYS THAT

12.2.1 a total loss of the Vessel, whether by insured perils or otherwise, has not occurred during the period covered by this insurance or any extension thereof

12.2.2 in no case shall a return be allowed when the Vessel is lying in exposed or unprotected waters, or in a port or lay-up area not approved by the Underwriters

12.2.3 loading or discharging operations or the presence of cargo on board shall not debar returns but no return shall be allowed for any period during which the Vessel is being used for the storage of cargo or for lightering purposes

12.2.4 in the event of any amendment of the annual rate, the above rates of return shall be adjusted accordingly

12.2.5 in the event of any return recoverable under this Clause 12 being based on 30 consecutive days which fall on successive insurances effected for the same Assured, this insurance shall only be liable for an amount calculated at pro rata of the period rates 12.1.2(a) and/or (b) above for the number of days which come within the period of this insurance and to which a return is actually applicable. Such overlapping period shall run, at the option of the Assured, either from the first day on which the Vessel is laid up or the first day of a period of 30 consecutive days as provided under 12.1.2(a) or (b) above.

Sub-clause 12.1.3 was new in 1995, corresponding to sub-clause 23.1.3 in the I.T.C. Hulls, 1/11/95.

Clauses 13–16—Exclusions

The following clauses shall be paramount and shall override anything contained in this insurance inconsistent therewith.

13 **WAR EXCLUSION**

In no case shall this insurance cover loss damage liability or expense caused by

13.1 war civil war revolution rebellion insurrection, or civil strife arising therefrom, or any hostile act by or against a belligerent power

13.2 capture seizure arrest restraint or detainment (barratry and piracy excepted), and the consequences thereof or any attempt thereat

13.3 derelict mines torpedoes bombs or other derelict weapons of war.

14 **STRIKES EXCLUSION**

In no case shall this insurance cover loss damage liability or expense caused by

14.1 strikers, locked-out workmen, or persons taking part in labour disturbances, riots or civil commotions

14.2 any terrorist or any person acting from a political motive.

15 **MALICIOUS ACTS EXCLUSION**

In no case shall this insurance cover loss damage liability or expense arising from

15.1 the detonation of an explosive

15.2 any weapon of war

and caused by any person acting maliciously or from a political motive.

16 **RADIOACTIVE CONTAMINATION EXCLUSION CLAUSE**

In no case shall this insurance cover loss damage liability or expense directly or indirectly caused by or contributed to by or arising from

16.1 ionising radiations from or contaminations by radioactivity from any nuclear fuel or from any nuclear waste or from the combustion of nuclear fuel

16.2 the radioactive, toxic, explosive or other hazardous or contaminating properties of any nuclear installation, reactor or other nuclear assembly or nuclear component thereof

16.3 any weapon of war employing atomic or nuclear fission and/or fusion or other like reaction or radioactive force or matter.

These are in the same form of words as in the I.T.C. Hulls, 1/11/95.

3. EXTENDED CONDITIONS

A. Institute Additional Perils Clauses, Hulls 1/11/95 (For use only with the Institute Time Clauses, Hulls 1/11/95)

Whilst it was never an Institute Clause, the forefather of the above clause, the Liner Negligence and Additional Perils Clause, was in common use from its introduction in the 1930s. Although it was included in many policies, particularly those of the major liner operators, and was subject to many differences of interpretation during its history, its wording was never tested in the courts.

With the major revision of the Institute Hull Clauses culminating in the October 1983 editions, the opportunity was taken to issue an Institute Additional Perils Clause.

The Institute Clause now reads (in its 1/11/95 version) as follows:

1 In consideration of an additional premium this insurance is extended to cover

1.1 the cost of repairing or replacing

1.1.1 any boiler which bursts or shaft which breaks

1.1.2 any defective part which has caused loss or damage to the Vessel covered by Clause 6.2.1 of the Institute Time Clauses—Hulls 1/11/95,

1.2 loss of or damage to the Vessel caused by any accident or by negligence, incompetence or error of judgement of any person whatsoever.

2 Except as provided in 1.1.1 and 1.1.2, nothing in these Additional Perils Clauses shall allow any claim for the cost of repairing or replacing any part found to be defective as a result of a fault or error in design or construction and which has not caused loss of or damage to the Vessel.

3 The cover provided in Clause 1 is subject to all other terms, conditions and exclusions contained in this insurance and subject to the proviso that the loss or damage has not resulted from want of due diligence by the Assured, Owners or Managers. Master Officers Crew or Pilots not to be considered Owners within the meaning of this Clause should they hold shares in the Vessel.

There are also versions of the Institute Additional Perils Clauses available for use with the Institute Time Clauses, Hulls, 1/10/83 and with the American Institute Hull Clauses. The only difference in wording between these two forms and the text set out above lies in sub-clause 1.1.2.

This reads in the 1/10/83 version:

1.1.2 any defective part which has caused loss or damage to the Vessel covered by Clause 6.2.2 of the Institute Time Clauses—Hulls 1/10/83

and in the version for use with the American Institute Hull Clauses:

1.1.2 any defective part which has caused loss or damage to the Vessel covered by the peril "any latent defect in the machinery or hull" as it appears in lines 79/80 of the American Institute Hull Clauses (June 2, 1977)

These are merely different ways of referring to latent defect as the cause of loss or damage in the parent clause. The coverage given—considered below—is entirely the same in each case.

"In consideration of an additional premium this insurance is extended to cover"

These words make it clear that the clause is designed to provide an extension of cover, the consideration for which is the payment of an additional premium.

"1.1 the cost of repairing or replacing

1.1.1 any boiler which bursts or shaft which breaks

1.1.2 any defective part which has caused loss or damage to the Vessel covered by Clause 6.2.1 of the Institute Time Clauses—Hulls 1/11/95"

Clause 6 of the I.T.C. Hulls, 1/11/95 provides cover against consequential loss or damage caused by, *inter alia*, bursting of boilers, breakage of shafts or any latent defect in the machinery or hull, but does not cover the cost of repairing or replacing the boiler, shaft or latently defective part (unless it was damaged as the result of the operation of one of the other insured perils). The Institute Additional Perils Clauses extend the insurance to cover the cost of repairing or replacing any boiler which has burst, any shaft which has broken or any latently defective part which has caused loss or damage covered by the parent clause. The practice is to treat these words as giving a coverage *simpliciter*—in other words to make the cost of repairing or replacing the burst boiler, broken shaft or latently defective part recoverable irrespective of cause (subject to Clause 3). The word "breakage" should be given a natural common sense meaning and a complete severance is not necessary to constitute a breakage. What constitutes bursting of a boiler has not been judicially considered in England but guidance can be gained from the American courts which have held that the discovery of fractures in a boiler is insufficient, and where because of its deteriorated condition the wall of an exhaust line gave way through the normal action of the engine exhaust this did not constitute "bursting" (*Presti* v. *Fireman's Fund Insurance Co.*[2]).

The relationship of Clause 1.1.2 of the Institute Additional Perils Clauses to its parent—Clause 6.2.2 of the I.T.C. Hulls, 1/10/83 or Clause 6.2.1 of the I.T.C. Hulls, 1/11/95—was examined briefly in *Promet Engineering* v. *Sturge (The "Nukila")*.[3] In that case Hobhouse L.J., commenting on the phrase "any defective part", said:

> "The use of the word *part* in the Additional Perils clause is normally simply to avoid the need to exclude from the indemnity to which the assured is entitled if he proves a claim under the Inchmaree clause of deducting the cost of repairing or replacing the originally defective part. For this purpose there is no need to define what is meant by the word *part.*"

2. 1972 A.M.C. 1220.

3. *Promet Engineering (Singapore) Pte. Ltd.* v. *Sturge (The "Nukila")* [1997] 2 Lloyd's Rep. 146. The facts are summarised and the case commented upon on pp. 110–111.

"1.2 loss of or damage to the Vessel caused by any accident or by negligence, incompetence or error of judgement of any person whatsoever."

The cover granted by this clause is extremely wide. The classic definition of the word "accident" is that given by Lord Lindley in *Fenton* v. *Thorley*[4]: "any unintended and unexpected occurrence which produces hurt or loss". In the light of this definition the cover granted by the Institute Additional Perils Clauses is analogous to the cover provided by an insurance against "all risks" in that fortuitous events are covered but ordinary wear and tear and inherent vice are not. By section 55 of the Marine Insurance Act 1906 "unless the policy otherwise provides, the insurer is not liable for ordinary wear and tear . . . ". It should be noted that this exclusion relates to wear and tear itself and does not deal with consequential loss and damage. Let us take an example of a pipe on a tanker which has been weakened by internal corrosion at an inaccessible elbow which, in spite of the exercise of due diligence by all concerned, is not discovered. It is submitted that the sudden failure of that pipe in service, resulting in the ingress of oil into the pump room, would constitute an "accident" and would give rise to a claim under the Institute Additional Perils Clauses for the consequential damage, the cost of replacing the worn pipe being excluded. The cover against "any accident" effectively includes all occurrences which are fortuitous from the point of view of the assured, other than those resulting from some deliberate infliction of damage.

"2 Except as provided in 1.1.1 and 1.1.2, nothing in these Additional Perils Clauses shall allow any claim for the cost of repairing or replacing any part found to be defective as a result of a fault or error in design or construction and which has not caused loss of or damage to the Vessel."

The cover against loss of or damage to the vessel caused "by negligence, incompetence or error of judgment of any person whatsoever" is qualified by Clause 2, the intention being to exclude claims for parts found to be defective but which have not resulted in any loss or damage. The intention of the clause is that parts which are or have become defective as a result of a fault or error in design or construction will only be paid for if there is a failure or breakdown in service resulting in consequential damage, and the part will not be paid for if it has been condemned in anticipation of failure or breakdown or simply found to be defective without any other damage having been caused. For example, an engine manufacturer may issue a circular advising operators of their engines that experience has shown that a particular part is prone to fatigue failure due to a combination of design factors and incorrect assembly

4. [1903] A.C. 443.

during manufacture and should be checked as a matter of priority. The cost of replacing or repairing any part found to be defective as a result of such an examination would not be covered. If, however, the part had failed in service before the manufacturer's warning had been received, the cost of its replacement would be covered. Similarly, if after the failure of a part in service, subsequent investigation proves it to have been badly designed, the cost of any improvement in the design and manufacture of the replacement part would not be recoverable under the policy. The expression "faulty design" was considered judicially in *Queensland Government Railways* v. *Manufacturers' Mutual Insurance Co.*[5] by the Supreme Court of Queensland, Australia, and on appeal to the Australian High Court.

The claim was for the cost of rebuilding piers for a bridge which was in the course of construction and had been overturned by flood waters after exceptionally heavy rain. The insurance was in a form of "Contractors All Risks policy" which provided, *inter alia*:

> " . . . this insurance shall not apply to or include:
> (vii) cost of making good faulty workmanship or construction . . .
> . . .
> (xi) loss or damage arising from faulty design and liabilities resulting therefrom".

Insurers denied liability, contending that loss was due to faulty design of the piers. It was found by the arbitrator that in the state of engineering knowledge at that time, the design of the new piers was satisfactory, but investigation following the accident showed that these piers were subject to greater transverse forces in floods than had been realised.

The judgment of the court of first instance was given by Hoare J. who found that insurers were liable. The judge said:

> "It appears to me that in their context the words 'faulty design' do imply some element of blameworthiness or negligence, which has been negatived by the arbitrator's findings. Further, having regard to the findings made by the arbitrator, it seems to me that in the state of engineering knowledge at the time, if, when the contract of insurance was made (i.e., before the tests were made to determine the precise cause of the disaster), someone had inquired of a competent engineer, 'Is the design of the piers faulty?', the answer would clearly have been, 'No'. The fact that subsequently acquired knowledge reveals that the design was not strong enough to withstand transverse forces which it is now known might be expected from a severe flood, cannot, in my opinion, on the true construction of exclusion (xi), convert a design which would at the time have been accepted by responsible and competent engineers into a 'faulty design' ".

On appeal it was held that the loss was due to faulty design, it being incorrect to limit the expression "faulty design" to cases involving personal error or non-compliance with standards which would be expected of designing

5. [1969] 1 Lloyd's Rep. 214.

engineers. The majority judgment delivered by Barwick C.J. included this passage:

> "We think it was an error [on the part of the judge in the court below] to confine 'faulty design' to the personal failure or non-compliance with standards which would be expected of designing engineers and on the part of the designing engineers responsible for piers. To design something that will not work simply because at the time of its designing insufficient is known about the problems involved and their solution to achieve a successful outcome is a common enough instance of faulty design. The distinction which is relevant is that between 'faulty', i.e. defective, design and design free from defect. . . . The exclusion is not against loss from 'negligent designing'; it is against loss from 'faulty design' and the latter is more comprehensive than the former."

A separate judgment was given by Windeyer J. who considered that the derivation of the word "fault" explains its two different meanings:

> "When used in relation to a person, a fault is a falling short in conduct or behaviour, some act or omission which, whether wilful or negligent, predicates blame."
>
> "[When] descriptive of an inanimate thing, the words 'fault' and 'faulty' have a different sense . . . they designate an objective quality of a thing. It is not up to a required standard. It is 'faulty' because it has defects, flaws, or deficiencies. . . . Dr. Johnson defined 'faulty' in this sense as meaning: 'defective, bad in any respect, not fit for the use intended.' The word can be applied not only to concrete things, but also to plans or designs to be used to produce intended results."

Clause 3 incorporates all other terms, conditions and exclusions in the insurance and specifically the due diligence provisions as they were in the 1/10/83 form of the Institute Time Clauses, Hulls. (See commentary on page 114.)

B. Institute General Average—Pollution Expenditure Clause, Hulls 1/11/95

1. Where any of the following GENERAL AVERAGE AND SALVAGE clauses are incorporated in this insurance, then the provisions of Clause 2 herein shall apply:
   - Clause 10.5 of the Institute Time Clauses—Hulls 1/11/95
   - Clause 10.5 of the Institute Time Clauses—Hull—Limited Conditions 1/11/95
   - Clause 10.6 of the Institute Time Clauses—Hull—Total Loss, General Average and $\frac{3}{4}$ths Collision Liability 1/11/95
   - Clause 8.5 of the Institute Voyage Clauses—Hulls 1/11/95
   - Clause 8.6 of the Institute Voyage Clauses—Hulls—Total Loss, General Average and $\frac{3}{4}$ths Collision Liability 1/11/95
2. In consideration of an additional premium to be agreed and provided that the contract of affreightment provides for adjustment according to the York-Antwerp Rules 1994, this insurance is extended to cover the Vessel's proportion of general average expenditure, reduced in respect of any under insurance, which is allowable under Rule XI(d) of the York-Antwerp Rules 1994 and which would be recoverable under the GENERAL AVERAGE AND SALVAGE clause of the applicable insuring conditions but for Clause 10.5.2 of the Institute Time Clauses—Hulls 1/11/95, Clause 10.5.2 of the Institute Time Clauses—Hulls—Limited Conditions 1/11/95, Clause 10.6.2 of the Institute Time Clauses—Hulls—Total Loss, General Average and $\frac{3}{4}$ths Collision Liability 1/11/95, Clause 8.5.2 of the Institute Voyage Clauses—Hulls 1/11/95, and Clause 8.6.2 of the Institute Voyage Clauses—Hulls—Total Loss, General Average and $\frac{3}{4}$ths Collision Liability 1/11/95.
3. This insurance is subject to English law and practice.

This clause was introduced shortly after its stated date of 1/11/95 in response to the criticisms levelled against hull underwriters' intention to curtail the allowances for pollution avoidance measures which can be made under the York-Antwerp Rules, 1994 when those measures form part of a general average act. See the commentary on pages 127 to 130 under the heading "The 1995 limitations on general average allowances".

Underwriters' intention was realised by the insertion of two new provisions into the General Average Clause contained in the Institute Time Clauses, Hulls, 1/11/95 and other sets of clauses deriving therefrom:

(1) in sub-clause 10.3, purporting to exclude Rule XI(d) from the application of the York-Antwerp Rules, 1994 to claims for general average when the vessel is in ballast, not under charter, and
(2) in sub-clause 10.5.2, denying any claim for "expenses or liabilities in respect of damage to the environment, or the threat of such damage, or as a consequence of the escape or release of pollutant substances from the vessel, or the threat of such escape or release".

The response of the Joint Hull Committee to the criticisms referred to above was to announce their intention to issue a supplementary clause whereby assureds could "buy back" the cover which had been removed.[6] This Pollution Expenditure Clause is the outcome.

However, the Clause does not in fact reinstate all the cover which was removed by the Institute Time Clauses, Hulls, 1/11/95 and its associated forms:

(1) The "exclusion" of Rule XI(d) still stands when the York-Antwerp Rules, 1994 are applied to claims for general average when the vessel is in ballast, not under charter. This is because the reinstatement is limited to items of expenditure allowable under Rule XI(d) which are excluded from the cover provided by the I.T.C. Hulls, 1/11/95 (or one of the associated forms) only by reason of Clause 10.5.2 (or its equivalent clause in other forms). As the "exclusion" of Rule XI(d) when the vessel is in ballast, not under charter, is a provision of Clause 10.3 of the I.T.C. Hulls, 1/11/95 it is *not* reinstated by the Institute General Average—Pollution Expenditure Clause.
(2) In any other case where Clause 10.5.2 (or its equivalent) is thought to apply, the Institute General Average—Pollution Expenditure Clause will only re-validate the suspected allowances when the general average has been adjusted in accordance with the York-Antwerp Rules, 1994 by reason of a provision to that effect contained in the

6. The present editor is advised that, up to the time of writing, the majority of hull covers in the London market with the I.T.C. Hulls, 1/11/95 include this Pollution Expenditure Clause without additional premium.

contract of affreightment. If the adjustment is properly drawn up in accordance with the York-Antwerp Rules, 1974 or any other provision, then the Pollution Expenditure Clause will not avail the shipowner, and any argument as to the suspected expenditure will have to be determined on the merits of Clause 10.5.2 of the I.T.C. Hulls, 1/11/95, or by applying the principles of equity.

C. Extensions to the subject-matter insured

In 1995, perhaps to balance the unpopular revision of the Institute Time Clauses, Hulls, re-issued that year, the Joint Hull Committee undertook the responsibility for three short forms, for attachment to the basic hull conditions, intended to extend the description of the subject-matter insured where appropriate. Each of these forms had previously been available, over a number of years, in wordings submitted by the assured or their brokers. The new forms are:

Institute Time Clauses, Hulls—Leased Equipment Clause 1/11/95

This insurance is extended to cover loss of or damage to equipment and apparatus not owned by the Assured but installed for use on the Vessel and for which the Assured has assumed contractual liability, whether such equipment or apparatus be in the nature of aids to navigation or communication or otherwise and where such loss or damage is caused by a peril insured under this insurance, subject in all other respects to its terms, conditions and exclusions. In no event shall the liability of the Underwriters exceed the lesser of the contractual liability of the Assured for loss of or damage to such equipment or apparatus or its replacement value. All such equipment and apparatus shall be included in the insured value of the Vessel.

Note the important reservation that the liability of the underwriters shall not exceed the assured's contractual liability for the leased equipment, or its replacement value, whichever is the less. This means that in examining any claim involving the leased equipment, it will be essential to call for the contract of hire in order to ascertain what the assured's contractual liability is.

Institute Time Clauses, Hulls—Passenger Equipment Clause 1/11/95

This insurance is extended to cover bar stores, equipment for passengers amusements, other stores and supplies on board the Vessel including stocks in the Vessel's shops, provided the same are owned by the Assured and do not exceed in value 5% of the insured value of the Vessel, subject in all other respects to the terms, conditions and exclusions of this insurance.

This clause is intended to be available for attachment to insurances on passenger liners, cruise vessels and passenger ferries. However, given the specialised nature of these trades, one may indeed wonder why a standard form is now displayed. Surely the experienced operators in these trades have by now evolved their own made-to-measure clauses?

Institute Time Clauses, Hulls—Parts Removed Clause 1/11/95

This insurance is extended to cover loss of or damage to parts removed from the Vessel whether such parts are ashore and/or under repair and/or in transit and where such loss or damage is caused by a peril insured under this insurance, subject in all other respects to its terms, conditions and exclusions. The Underwriters' liability for such parts removed which are covered under this clause shall not exceed 5% of the insured value of the Vessel.

If at the time of loss of or damage to the parts removed from the Vessel such parts are covered by or would be covered by any other insurance but for this clause, then this insurance shall only be excess to such other insurance.
Cover in respect of parts shall be limited to 30 days whilst removed. Period in excess of 30 days held covered at terms to be agreed provided notice be given to the Underwriters prior to the expiry of the 30 day extension.

By contrast, this is a very useful clause. Parts of the ship, particularly machinery parts, are fairly frequently taken ashore for examination and/or repair, and the question immediately to be asked in the event of their loss or damage was—do such pieces of the hull or machinery remain part of the subject-matter insured once they become detached from the ship or when they are taken ashore? Now, with this clause in place, the question does not need to be asked.

However, there are two aspects of this clause to be carefully considered:

(1) If there is a claim under this clause, it is subject "in all other respects" to the "terms, conditions and exclusions" under the insurance. This means, *inter alia*, that the claim will be subject to any deductible that may be provided for in the main body of the policy. If the insurance is subject, for example, to the Institute Time Clauses, Hulls, then nice questions may arise in determining, in the case of a continuing peril, whether one or more deductibles are to be applied under Clause 12. (See commentary on pages 135 to 137 herein.) Incidentally, the word "other" in the phrase "in all other respects" appears to be totally superfluous.

(2) The limitation expressed in the words: "Underwriters' liability for such parts removed which are covered under this clause shall not exceed 5% of the insured value of the Vessel". What does this mean? Does it mean that there is a limit on the amount of the insurance (as in the case of the Passenger Equipment Clause) for parts removed; or a limit upon the amount that can be claimed, and if so, before or after the application of the deductible?

In the opinion of the present editor, in view of the uncertainty arising from this deplorable draftsmanship, the wording of this limitation has to be interpreted in the light of all the other factors (the "matrix") governing the problem; and the only fair solution is to conclude that the net amount after application of the deductible, if any, of any claim upon the policy for loss or damage to parts removed, shall not exceed 5 per cent of the insured value.

4. ADDITIONAL DEDUCTIBLES FOR MACHINERY DAMAGE

Institute Machinery Damage Additional Deductible Clause (For use only with the Institute Time Clauses, Hulls 1/11/95)

For many years underwriters had become increasingly concerned at their worsening experience of claims which in their opinion was attributable in the main to the poor quality of personnel employed on the vessels. In 1969, with the major revision of the I.T.C. Hulls, we saw the introduction of the Negligence Co-insurance Clause (Clause 11) under which the assured became co-assurers for a proportion (10 per cent) of claims for loss of or damage to any boiler, shaft, machinery or associated equipment which was attributable in part or in whole to the negligence of Master, officers or crew. The philosophy behind the introduction of this clause was the hope that if the shipowners were made co-insurers in respect of certain crew negligence claims they would be encouraged to improve the quality of the crew, particularly engine room personnel, which they employed.

In practice the phraseology of this clause gave rise to many problems of interpretation and in the next major revision of the clauses in 1983 it was omitted from the main body of clauses, with few people lamenting its passing. Concurrently with the issue of the new I.T.C. Hulls in 1983 the Institute Machinery Damage Additional Deductible Clause was also introduced, the intention being that this should only be incorporated into policies covering vessels or fleets where factors such as the age of the tonnage and/or previous claims experience warranted its inclusion. The present clause (intended for use with the Institute Time Clauses, Hulls, 1/11/95) reads as follows:

> Notwithstanding any provision to the contrary in this insurance a claim for loss of or damage to any machinery, shaft, electrical equipment or wiring, boiler condenser heating coil or associated pipework, arising from any of the perils enumerated in Clauses 6.2.1 to 6.2.4 inclusive of the Institute Time Clauses—Hulls 1/11/95 or from fire or explosion when either has originated in a machinery space, shall be subject to the deductible amount agreed. Any balance remaining, after application of this deductible, with any other claim arising from the same accident or occurrence, shall then be subject to the deductible referred to in Clause 12.1 of the Institute Time Clauses—Hulls 1/11/95.
>
> The provisions of Clauses 12.3 and 12.4 of the Institute Time Clauses—Hulls 1/11/95 shall apply to recoveries and interest comprised in recoveries against any claim which is subject to this Clause.
>
> This Clause shall not apply to a claim for total or constructive total loss of the Vessel.

Apart from the numbering of the relevant clauses, this is the same as the 1/10/83 wording.

Like Clause 12 of the I.T.C. Hulls, the clause does not specify a figure for the additional deductible and this has to be agreed at the time of effecting the insurance and then entered into the clause.

Before the additional deductible can be applied all of the following factors must be present:

(1) The claim must be for "loss of or damage" to any of the enumerated parts of the vessel (so that it would not apply to any claim for say salvage of the vessel, necessitated by the failure of one of the designated parts).

(2) "to any machinery, shaft, electrical equipment or wiring, boiler condenser heating coil or associated pipework". It should be noted that the machinery is not limited to engine room machinery and in appropriate circumstances the additional deductible could apply to a claim for loss of or damage to deck machinery, for example winches, windlass etc.

(3) "arising from any of the perils enumerated in Clauses 6.2.1 to 6.2.4 inclusive of the Institute Time Clauses—Hulls 1/11/95 or from fire or explosion when either has originated in a machinery space". Any claim, therefore, for loss of or damage to the specified items arising from any of the perils in Clause 6.1 of the I.T.C. Hulls would not attract the additional deductible, subject to the exception of a fire or explosion originating in a machinery space.

What is a machinery space within the context of this clause? There is no agreed definition but it would almost certainly include the engine room, generator flat, steering flat and pump room. It could be argued that it also includes spaces used for the storage of machinery, e.g. forecastle and deck-house, but in the opinion of the editor this would be too wide an interpretation.

After the application of the additional deductible provided for in the clause, the balance of the claim is then subject to the deductible in the hull policies.

The provisions of Clauses 12.3 and 12.4 of the I.T.C. Hulls are imported into the clause to ensure that the treatment of any recovery and interest against any claim which has been subject to the additional deductible will be on the same basis as the main policy.

Like Clause 12 of the I.T.C. Hulls, the additional deductible does not apply to a claim for total or constructive total loss of the vessel.

Institute Machinery Damage Additional Deductible Clause (For use only with the Institute Voyage Clauses, Hulls 1/11/95)

Notwithstanding any provision to the contrary in this insurance a claim for loss of or damage to any machinery, shaft, electrical equipment or wiring, boiler condenser heating coil or associated pipework, arising from any of the perils enumerated in Clauses 4.2.1 to 4.2.4 inclusive of the Institute Voyage Clauses—Hulls 1/11/95 or from fire or explosion when either has originated in a machinery space, shall be subject to the deductible amount agreed. Any balance remaining, after application of this deductible, with any other claim arising from the same accident or occurrence, shall then be subject to the deductible referred to in Clause 10.1 of the Institute Voyage Clauses—Hulls 1/11/95.

The provisions of Clauses 10.3 and 10.4 of the Institute Voyage Clauses—Hulls 1/11/95 shall apply to recoveries and interest comprised in recoveries against any claim which is subject to this Clause.

This Clause shall not apply to a claim for total or constructive total loss of the Vessel.

This clause is for all practical purposes identical to the clause for use with the Institute Time Clauses, Hulls.

Additional Deductible Adaptation Clause

(For use whenever the Institute Machinery Damage Additional Deductible Clause and the Institute Additional Perils Clauses 1/11/95) (For use only with the Institute Time Clauses 1/11/95) are included in the same insurance

The Institute Machinery Damage Additional Deductible Clause 1/11/95 shall also apply to any claim or part thereof in respect of any machinery, shaft, electrical equipment or wiring, boiler condenser heating coil or associated pipework, where such claim or part thereof is recoverable hereunder solely by reason of the inclusion of the Institute Additional Perils Clauses—Hulls 1/11/95 in this insurance.

This clause simply applies the provisions of the Institute Machinery Damage Additional Deductible Clause to any claim recoverable under the policies solely by reason of the inclusion of the Institute Additional Perils Clauses, Hulls.

5. FREIGHT INSURANCE

Freight insurance is a complex and difficult branch of the law. When considering ships and cargoes one is dealing with tangible property. Freight, on the other hand, is far more difficult to denote and has been described as "the benefit derived by the ship-owner from the employment of his ship" (*Flint* v. *Flemyng*[7]).

Rule 16 of the Rules of Construction of the Policy (Schedule 1, Marine Insurance Act 1906) defines freight as follows:

> "The term 'freight' includes a profit derivable by a ship-owner from the employment of his ship to carry his own goods or movables, as well as freight payable by a third party, but does not include passage money."

The charterer or cargo owner may well have an insurable interest in advance freight, in so far as it is not repayable in case of loss, and this is recognised in section 12 of the Marine Insurance Act 1906. Such advances of freight are not intended to be the subject of insurance on the Institute Freight Clauses and are more properly covered as part of the valuation of the cargo.

A. Institute Time Clauses, Freight 1/11/95

This insurance is subject to English law and practice.

The effect of this provision is considered in the review of the Institute Time Clauses, Hulls (see pages 90 to 91).

1 **NAVIGATION**

1.1 The Vessel has leave to dock and undock, to go into graving dock, to sail or navigate with or without pilots, to go on trial trips and to assist and tow vessels or craft in distress, but it is warranted that the Vessel shall not be towed, except as is customary or to the first safe port or place when in need of assistance, or undertake towage or salvage services under a contract previously arranged by the Assured and/or Owners and/or Managers and/or Charterers. This Clause 1 shall not exclude customary towage in connection with loading and discharging.

1.2 This insurance shall not be prejudiced by reason of the Assured entering into any contract with pilots or for customary towage which limits or exempts the liability of the pilots and/or tugs and/or towboats and/or their owners when the Assured or their agents accept or are compelled to accept such contracts in accordance with established local law or practice.

1.3 The practice of engaging helicopters for the transportation of personnel, supplies and equipment to and/or from the Vessel shall not prejudice this insurance.

Clause 1 comprises three sub-clauses, which are similar to sub-clauses 1.1, 1.2 and 1.3 of the I.T.C. Hulls, 1/11/95 which have been considered earlier. The only difference is that in sub-clause 1.1, instead of covering the vessel "at all

7. (1830) 1 B. & Ad. 45.

times", as in the I.T.C. Hulls, the vessel is expressly given "leave to dock and undock, to go into graving dock".

The restriction on towage when in need of assistance to the "first safe port or place" has been introduced here since the 1983 form in order to bring the Hulls and Freight Clauses into line with each other.

2 **CRAFT RISK**
Including risk of craft and/or lighter to and from the Vessel.

The partial or total loss of the cargo whilst in transit to or from the vessel can result in a loss of freight to the shipowner and the risk "of craft and or lighter" is expressly covered. In these days of LASH vessels etc. these words can be of considerable importance.

3 **CONTINUATION**
Should the Vessel at the expiration of this insurance be at sea and in distress or missing, the subject-matter insured shall, provided notice be given to the Underwriters prior to the expiration of this insurance, be held covered until arrival of the Vessel at the next port in good safety, or in port and in distress until the Vessel is made safe, at a pro rata monthly premium.

This clause reflects the changes made to Clause 2 of the I.T.C. Hulls in the form of 1/11/95. See pages 94 to 95.

4 **BREACH OF WARRANTY**
Held covered in case of any breach of warranty as to cargo, trade, locality, towage, salvage services or date of sailing, provided notice be given to the Underwriters immediately after receipt of advices and any amended terms of cover and any additional premium required by them be agreed.

This is identical to Clause 3 of the I.T.C. Hulls. There was no change in 1995.

5 **CLASSIFICATION**

5.1 It is the duty of the Assured, Owners and Managers at the inception of and throughout the period of this insurance to ensure that

5.1.1 the Vessel is classed with a Classification Society agreed by the Underwriters and that her class within that Society is maintained,

5.1.2 any recommendations requirements or restrictions imposed by the Vessel's Classification Society which relate to the Vessel's seaworthiness or to her maintenance in a seaworthy condition are complied with by the dates required by that Society.

5.2 In the event of any breach of the duties set out in Clause 5.1 above, unless the Underwriters agree to the contrary in writing, they will be discharged from liability under this insurance as from the date of the breach, provided that if the Vessel is at sea at such date the Underwriters' discharge from liability is deferred until arrival at her next port.

5.3 Any incident condition or damage in respect of which the Vessel's Classification Society might make recommendations as to repairs or other action to be taken by the Assured, Owners or Managers must be promptly reported to the Classification Society.

5.4 Should the Underwriters wish to approach the Classification Society directly for information and/or documents, the Assured will provide the necessary authorization.

This clause was introduced in 1995 and is identical to Clause 4 of the I.T.C. Hulls, 1/11/95. See commentary on pages 95 to 97.

6 **TERMINATION**
This Clause 6 shall prevail notwithstanding any provision whether written typed or printed in this insurance inconsistent therewith.
Unless the Underwriters agree to the contrary in writing, this insurance shall terminate automatically at the time of

6.1 change of the Classification Society of the Vessel, or change, suspension, discontinuance, withdrawal or expiry of her Class therein, or any of the Classification Society's periodic surveys becoming overdue unless an extension of time for such survey be agreed by the Classification Society, provided that if the Vessel is at sea such automatic termination shall be deferred until arrival at her next port. However where such change, suspension, discontinuance or withdrawal of her Class or where a periodic survey becoming overdue has resulted from loss or damage covered by Clause 7 of this insurance or which would be covered by an insurance of the Vessel subject to current Institute Time

Clauses Hulls or Institute War and Strikes Clauses Hulls—Time such automatic termination shall only operate should the Vessel sail from her next port without the prior approval of the Classification Society or in the case of a periodic survey becoming overdue without the Classification Society having agreed an extension of time for such survey,

6.2 any change, voluntary or otherwise, in the ownership or flag, transfer to new management, or charter on a bareboat basis, or requisition for title or use of the Vessel, provided that, if the Vessel has cargo on board and has already sailed from her loading port or is at sea in ballast, such automatic termination shall if required be deferred, whilst the Vessel continues her planned voyage, until arrival at final port of discharge if with cargo or at port of destination if in ballast. However, in the event of requisition for title or use without the prior execution of a written agreement by the Assured, such automatic termination shall occur fifteen days after such requisition whether the Vessel is at sea or in port.

A pro rata daily net return of premium shall be made provided that a total loss of the Vessel, whether by insured perils or otherwise, has not occurred during the period covered by this insurance or any extension thereof.

This Clause 6 is in the same form as the corresponding clause in the forms of the I.T.C. Hulls, 1/11/95 which are subject to Restricted Conditions, e.g. against the risks of total loss, general average and $\frac{3}{4}$ths collision liability—see page 159. The differences between the forms of 1/11/95 and 1/10/83 are considered in the context of the basic form of Institute Time Clauses, Hulls on pages 97 to 100.

7 **PERILS**

7.1 This insurance covers loss of the subject-matter insured caused by

7.1.1 perils of the seas rivers lakes or other navigable waters

7.1.2 fire, explosion

7.1.3 violent theft by persons from outside the Vessel

7.1.4 jettison

7.1.5 piracy

7.1.6 contact with land conveyance, dock or harbour equipment or installation

7.1.7 earthquake volcanic eruption or lightning

7.1.8 accidents in loading discharging or shifting cargo or fuel.

7.2 This insurance covers loss of the subject-matter insured caused by

7.2.1 bursting of boilers breakage of shafts or any latent defect in the machinery or hull

7.2.2 negligence of Master Officers Crew or Pilots

7.2.3 negligence of repairers or charterers provided such repairers or charterers are not an Assured hereunder

7.2.4 barratry of Master Officers or Crew

7.2.5 contact with aircraft, helicopters or similar objects or objects falling therefrom

provided such loss has not resulted from want of due diligence by the Assured, Owners, Managers or Superintendents or any of their onshore management.

7.3 Masters Officers Crew or Pilots not to be considered Owners within the meaning of this Clause 7 should they hold shares in the Vessel.

8 **POLLUTION HAZARD**

This insurance covers loss of the subject matter insured caused by any governmental authority acting under the powers vested in it to prevent or mitigate a pollution hazard or damage to the environment, or threat thereof, resulting directly from a peril covered by this insurance, provided that such act of governmental authority has not resulted from want of due diligence by the Assured, Owners or Managers to prevent or mitigate such hazard or damage, or threat thereof. Masters Officers Crew or Pilots not to be considered Owners within the meaning of this Clause 8 should they hold shares in the Vessel.

Apart from the omission of the word "damage", these clauses are virtually identical to the corresponding clauses in the I.T.C. Hulls, 1/11/95—see pages 100 to 118.

9 **FREIGHT COLLISION**

9.1 It is further agreed that if the Vessel shall come into collision with any other vessel and the Assured shall in consequence thereof become liable to pay and shall pay by way of damages to any other person or persons any sum or sums in respect of the amount of freight taken into account in calculating the measure of the liability of the Assured for

9.1.1 loss of or damage to any other vessel or property on any other vessel

9.1.2 delay to or loss of use of any such other vessel or property thereon

9.1.3 general average of, salvage of, or salvage under contract of, any such other vessel or property thereon,

the Underwriters will pay the Assured such proportion of three-fourths of such sum or sums so paid applying to freight as their respective subscriptions hereto bear to the total amount insured on freight, or to the gross freight earned on the voyage during which the collision occurred if this be greater.

9.2 Provided always that:

9.2.1 liability of the Underwriters in respect of any one such collision shall not exceed their proportionate part of three-fourths of the total amount insured hereon on freight, and in cases in which, with the prior consent in writing of the Underwriters, the liability of the vessel has been contested or proceedings have been taken to limit liability, they will also pay a like proportion of three-fourths of the costs, appertaining proportionately to the freight portion of damages, which the Assured shall thereby incur or be compelled to pay;

9.2.2 no claim shall attach to this insurance:

9.2.2.1 which attaches to any other insurances covering collision liabilities

9.2.2.2 which is, or would be, recoverable in the terms of the Institute 3/4ths Collision Liability Clause if the Vessel were insured in the terms of such Institute 3/4ths Collision Liability Clause for a value not less than the equivalent in pounds sterling, at the time of commencement of this insurance, of the Vessel's limit of liability calculated in accordance with Article 6.1(b) of the 1976 Limitation Convention,

9.2.3 this Clause 9 shall in no case extend or be deemed to extend to any sum which the Assured may become liable to pay or shall pay for or in respect of:

9.2.3.1 removal or disposal, under statutory powers or otherwise, of obstructions, wrecks, cargoes or any other thing whatsoever

9.2.3.2 any real or personal property or thing whatsoever except other vessels or property on other vessels

9.2.3.3 pollution or contamination, or threat thereof, of any real or personal property or thing whatsoever (except other vessels with which the insured Vessel is in collision or property on such other vessels) or damage to the environment, or threat thereof, save that this exclusion shall not extend to any sum which the Assured shall pay for or in respect of salvage remuneration in which the skill and efforts of the salvors in preventing or minimising damage to the environment as is referred to in Article 13 paragraph 1(b) of the International Convention on Salvage, 1989 have been taken into account

9.2.3.4 the cargo or other property on or the engagements of the Vessel

9.2.3.5 loss of life, personal injury or illness.

Under several jurisdictions, of which the United States is the prime example, the limitation fund of a vessel is calculated as the sum of her value, plus her pending freight at the time of the collision. In certain circumstances, therefore, damages will be payable by the shipowner in respect of his freight and such damages may exceed the cover granted by the three-fourths collision liability clause in the hull policy. This clause is designed to cover the proportion of any such liability payable in respect of the insured freight.

"It is further agreed . . . "

These words make the Freight Collision Clause a supplemental agreement, any claim thereunder being payable in addition to any indemnity available under the rest of the policy.

" . . . that if the vessel shall come into collision with any other vessel and the Assured shall in consequence thereof become liable to pay and shall pay by way of damages to any other person or persons any sum or sums . . . "

The above wording was discussed in detail when considering Clause 8 (The Running Down Clause) contained in the I.T.C. Hulls (see page 118).

". . . in respect of the amount of freight taken into account in calculating the measure of liability of the Assured for"

To substantiate a claim under this clause evidence will be required as to how the liability of the assured was assessed and it would have to be shown quite conclusively that the amount of freight had definitely been taken into account.

Clauses 9.1.1, 9.1.2 and 9.1.3 are identical to the equivalent provisions in the I.T.C. Hulls, 1/10/83 considered in detail on pages 121 to 122.

Underwriters' liability is limited to three-fourths of the sum so paid as applying to freight, pro-rated down to take account of the ratio of the underwriters' subscriptions to the greater of:

1. the total amount insured on freight, or
2. the gross freight earned on the voyage on which the collision occurred.

The Clause 9.2 provisos

9.2.1 "liability of the Underwriters in respect of any one such collision shall not exceed their proportionate part of three-fourths of the total amount insured hereon on freight, and in cases in which, with the prior consent in writing of the Underwriters, the liability of the Vessel has been contested or proceedings have been taken to limit liability, they will also pay a like proportion of three-fourths of the costs, appertaining proportionately to the freight portion of damages, which the Assured shall thereby incur or be compelled to pay;"

Underwriter's liability is expressly limited to three-fourths of the total sum insured on freight under the policy but in addition underwriters agree to pay three-fourths of the collision costs attaching to freight, providing they have given their prior written consent to the institution of legal proceedings.

9.2.2 "no claim shall attach to this insurance:

9.2.2.1 which attaches to any other insurances covering collision liabilities

9.2.2.2 which is, or would be, recoverable in the terms of the Institute 3/4ths Collision Liability Clause if the Vessel were insured in the terms of such Institute 3/4ths Collision Liability Clause for a value not less than the equivalent in pounds sterling, at the time of commencement of this insurance, of the Vessel's limit of liability calculated in accordance with Article 6.1(b) of the 1976 Limitation Convention."

These provisions make it clear that the freight insurance is not intended to "soak up" any collision liabilities attaching to any other insurances, nor that the claim on the freight policy should be increased in some way by reason of the vessel being uninsured or inadequately insured for collision liability under the hull policy. The practical effect of this clause, therefore, is to exclude any claim which would be recoverable on the hull policies if the vessel was insured on the standard 3/4ths Collision Liability Clause on a valuation not less than the sterling equivalent of the figure for which the shipowners could calculate their limit of liability under Article 6.1(b) of the 1976 Limitation Convention. This Convention entered into force generally on 1 December 1986, following the ratification or accession of 12 countries; and since 1980 it has had the force of law in the United Kingdom by virtue of section 17 of the Merchant Shipping Act 1979. In the Convention the limits of liability are calculated in Article 6.1 on two scales:

(a) relating to loss of life or personal injury; and
(b) relating to property claims plus any claims for loss of life or personal injury left unsatisfied after applying calculation (a).

It is the (b) figure which counts for the purpose of this clause. All these figures are expressed in the Convention as "Units of Account", i.e. in Special Drawing Rights. The exclusions in Clause 9.2.3 are the customary exclusions in the 3/4ths Collision Liability Clause.

10 SISTERSHIP

Should the Vessel named herein come into collision with or receive salvage services from another vessel belonging wholly or in part to the same Owners, or under the same management, the Assured shall have the same rights under this insurance as they would have were the other vessel entirely the property of Owners not interested in the Vessel named herein; but in such cases the liability for the collision or the amount payable for the services rendered shall be referred to a sole arbitrator to be agreed upon between the Underwriters and the Assured.

This is identical to Clause 9 of the I.T.C. Hulls. See page 125.

11 GENERAL AVERAGE AND SALVAGE

11.1 This insurance covers the proportion of general average salvage and/or salvage charges attaching to freight at risk of the Assured, reduced in respect of any under-insurance.

11.2 Adjustment to be according to the law and practice obtaining at the place where the adventure ends, as if the contract of affreightment contained no special terms upon the subject; but where the contract of affreightment so provides the adjustment shall be according to the York-Antwerp Rules.

11.3 No claim under this Clause 11 shall in any case be allowed where the loss was not incurred to avoid or in connection with the avoidance of a peril insured against.

11.4 No claim under this Clause 11 shall in any case be allowed for or in respect of

11.4.1 special compensation payable to a salvor under Article 14 of the International Convention on Salvage, 1989 or under any other provision in any statute, rule, law or contract which is similar in substance

11.4.2 expenses or liabilities incurred in respect of damage to the environment, or the threat of such damage, or as a consequence of the escape or release of pollutant substances from the Vessel, or the threat of such escape or release.

11.5 Clause 11.4 shall not however exclude any sum which the Assured shall pay to salvors for or in respect of salvage remuneration in which the skill and efforts of the salvors in preventing or minimising damage to the environment as is referred to in Article 13 paragraph 1(b) of the International Convention on Salvage, 1989 have been taken into account.

Freight at the risk of the shipowner can be a contributory interest in both salvage and general average and this clause covers freight's proportion, subject to reduction to take account of any under-insurance. It should also be noted that freight can be a contributing interest in general average even when the vessel is in ballast at the time of the casualty. Rule of Practice B26 of the Association of Average Adjusters provides as follows:

> **"B26 VESSEL IN BALLAST AND UNDER CHARTER: CONTRIBUTING INTERESTS**
>
> For the purpose of ascertaining the liability of Underwriters on British policies of insurance, the following provisions shall apply—
>
> When a vessel is proceeding in ballast to load under a voyage charter entered into by the shipowner before the general average act, the interests contributing to

the general average shall be the vessel, such items of stores and equipment as belong to parties other than the owners of the vessel (e.g. bunkers, wireless installation and navigational instruments) and the freight earned under the voyage charter computed in the usual way after deduction of contingent expenses subsequent to the general average act. Failing a prior termination of the adventure, the place where the adventure shall be deemed to end and at which the values for contribution to general average shall be calculated is the final port of discharge of the cargo carried under the charter but in the event of the prior loss of the vessel and freight, or either of them, the general average shall attach to any surviving interest or interests including freight advanced at the loading port deducting therefrom contingent expenses subsequent to the general average act.

When a vessel is proceeding in ballast under a time charter alone or a time charter and a voyage charter entered into by the time charterer, the general average shall attach to the vessel and such items of stores and equipment as are indicated above. Failing a prior termination of the adventure, the adventure shall be deemed to end and the values of contribution to general average calculated at the first loading port upon the commencement of loading cargo.

When the charter to which the shipowner is a party provides for York/Antwerp Rules, the general average shall be adjusted in accordance with those Rules and British law and practice and without regard to the law and practice of any foreign port at which the adventure may terminate; and in the interpretation of Rule XI it shall be immaterial whether the extra period of detention takes place at a port of loading, call or refuge, provided that the detention is in consequence of accident, sacrifice or other extraordinary circumstance occurring whilst the vessel is in ballast.

In practice neither time charter hire, as such, nor time charterer's voyage freight shall contribute to general average."

Clauses 11.2 and 11.3 are identical to Clauses 10.2 and 10.4 of the I.T.C. Hulls, 1/11/95 which are considered on pages 126 to 127.

Clauses 11.4 and 11.5 were added in 1995. They are the equivalent of Clauses 10.5 and 10.6 of the I.T.C. Hulls, 1/11/95, which are discussed in detail on pages 127 to 130 under the heading "The 1995 limitations on general average allowances". See also the Institute General Average—Pollution Expenditure Clause, Freight, set out on page 239.

12 **FRANCHISE**

This insurance does not cover partial loss, other than general average loss, under 3% unless caused by fire, sinking, stranding or collision with another vessel. Each craft and/or lighter to be deemed a separate insurance if required by the Assured.

This is one of the few insurances still subject to a franchise. Once the franchise is attained the loss is recoverable in full. The franchise is "opened up" when the partial loss is caused by fire, sinking, stranding or collision with another vessel.

A general average loss is not subject to the franchise. The option for the assured to treat each craft and/or lighter as a separate insurance can be of benefit to the assured when the partial loss may not attain the three per cent franchise when applied to the whole, but the loss on separate craft and/or lighters may attain three per cent.

13 ASSIGNMENT

No assignment of or interest in this insurance or in any moneys which may be or become payable thereunder is to be binding on or recognised by the Underwriters unless a dated notice of such assignment or interest signed by the Assured, and by the assignor in the case of subsequent assignment, is endorsed on the Policy and the Policy with such endorsement is produced before payment of any claim or return of premium thereunder.

This clause was previously Clause 6 in the Institute Time Clauses, Freight 1/10/83. It is in exactly the same terms as Clause 5 of I.T.C. Hulls, 1/10/83 and Clause 21 of the I.T.C. Hulls, 1/11/95. See commentary on page 150.

14 MEASURE OF INDEMNITY

14.1 The amount recoverable under this insurance for any claim for loss of freight shall not exceed the gross freight actually lost.

14.2 Where insurances on freight other than this insurance are current at the time of the loss, all such insurances shall be taken into consideration in calculating the liability under this insurance and the amount recoverable hereunder shall not exceed the rateable proportion of the gross freight lost, notwithstanding any valuation in this or any other insurance.

14.3 In calculating the liability under Clause 11 all insurances on freight shall likewise be taken into consideration.

14.4 Nothing in this Clause 14 shall apply to any claim arising under Clause 16.

This was previously Clause 13 in the I.T.C. Freight, 1/10/83. There was no change in the wording in 1995.

Section 70 of the Marine Insurance Act 1906 provides as follows:

> "**70. Partial loss of freight**
>
> Subject to any express provision in the policy, where there is a partial loss of freight, the measure of indemnity is such proportion of the sum fixed by the policy, in the case of a valued policy, or of the insurable value, in the case of an unvalued policy, as the proportion of freight lost by the assured bears to the whole freight at the risk of the assured under the policy."

Clause 14.1 limits the indemnity for loss of freight to the gross freight actually lost. The method of applying Clause 14.2 is quite simple; having established the gross freight lost, this is then apportioned over all insurances on freight at the time of the loss, each policy bearing its proportionate share of the loss. Clause 14.3 places the calculation of the policies' liability for general average and salvage upon the same basis as that for a partial loss of freight. The provisions as to measure of indemnity are expressly excluded by Clause 14.4 from having any effect on a claim for total loss.

15 LOSS OF TIME

This insurance does not cover any claim consequent on loss of time whether arising from a peril of the sea or otherwise.

This clause remains unchanged in its wording.

In providing that the insurer is not liable for any loss proximately caused by delay, even though the delay may have been caused by a peril insured against, section 55(2) of the Marine Insurance Act 1906 only mentions the insurer on ship or goods and does not mention freight. The potential implications of delay were brought home to freight underwriters in the case of *Jackson* v. *Union Marine Insurance Company*.[8] In this case the vessel stranded during the ballast

8. (1873) 23 W.R. 169; 2 Asp.M.L.C. 435.

passage to a port where she was due to load a cargo. Due to the delay resulting from the casualty the charterers were entitled to throw up the charter as having been frustrated and it was held that the shipowners had therefore suffered a loss of freight by reason of the operation of an insured peril and were entitled to recover under their policy.

There then followed the case of *Inman Steamship Company Limited* v. *Bischoff*.[9] Under the charter in this case the charterers had the right to put the vessel off hire or to make such abatement by way of deduction from the freight as they should adjudge fit in the event of her becoming inefficient. This in fact is what happened when the vessel's performance was affected by perils of the seas. The shipowners who had insured "freight outstanding" under a time policy which covered, *inter alia*, perils of the seas claimed under their policy. The Court of Appeal held that the loss of freight was not caused directly by perils of the seas but by the exercise by the charterers of their discretionary powers. This judgment was unanimously approved by the House of Lords although the Law Lords gave greater emphasis to the argument that there had been no loss of freight, properly speaking, at all. One of the main points to come out in the judgments was that the position would probably have been different if there had been a stipulation in the charterparty that freight should automatically cease upon the happening of the contingencies mentioned.

This was then confirmed in the two subsequent cases of *The "Alps"*[10] and *The "Bedouin"*.[11] In both of these cases the charter-parties provided for the payment of hire/freight to cease in certain specified circumstances. It was held that in as much as the clauses in the charter-parties had been brought into operation by the immediate action of insured perils, underwriters were liable for the loss of freight/hire so caused.

The liability imposed upon underwriters as a result of the above cases was wider than they were ready to bear and the above clause was introduced to exclude all claims consequent upon loss of time, including loss of time arising from insured perils.

The clause first came before the courts in *Bensaude* v. *Thames and Mersey Marine Insurance Company Limited*.[12] The freight, which was only payable on arrival, was insured. The ship was damaged by an insured peril and as a result of the delay required for repairs, the charterers cancelled the freight contract. It was held that the claim under the freight policy was consequent upon loss of time and therefore failed.

There then followed several leading cases which can be divided in two separate categories. In *Roura and Forgas* v. *Townend*,[13] *Carras* v. *London &*

9. (1882) 31 W.R. 141; 5 Asp.M.L.C. 6.
10. (1893) 41 W.R. 527; 7 Asp.M.L.C. 337.
11. (1894) 42 W.R. 292; 7 Asp.M.L.C. 391.
12. (1897) 46 W.R. 78; 8 Asp.M.L.C. 315; 2 Com.Cas. 33.
13. (1919) 14 Asp.M.L.C. 397; 24 Com.Cas. 71; 35 T.L.R. 88.

Scottish Assurance Company[14] and *Robertson* v. *Nomikos*[15] the freight had been lost because the vessels had become constructive total losses and it was held that the loss of freight was not caused by loss of time. On the other hand, in *Atlantic Maritime* v. *Gibbon*[16] the vessel was prevented from loading by restraint of princes and the adventure was consequently frustrated. Here it was held that the claim was barred by the loss of time clause. The distinction between these two categories of cases was brought out in *Nomikos* v. *Robertson*[17]: "the exception would bar any claim whenever it is necessary for the assured to assert the lapse of time as one of the facts establishing his cause of action".

Finally, the clause came before the courts in *Naviera de Canarias S.A.* v. *Nacional Hispanica Aseguredora S.A. (The "Playa de las Nieves")*.[18] In this case it was held that the plain meaning of the clause is to exclude claims for chartered freight lost under an off-hire clause in a time charter.

For the shipowner who wishes to insure loss of hire or earnings arising from the operation of insured perils there are special insurances available, but there are no Institute Clauses for Loss of Hire and/or Earnings insurance.

16 TOTAL LOSS

16.1 In the event of the total loss (actual or constructive) of the Vessel named herein the amount insured shall be paid in full, whether the Vessel be fully or partly loaded or in ballast, chartered or unchartered.

16.2 In ascertaining whether the Vessel is a constructive total loss, the insured value in the insurances on hull and machinery shall be taken as the repaired value and nothing in respect of the damaged or break-up value of the Vessel or wreck shall be taken into account.

16.3 Should the Vessel be a constructive total loss but the claim on the insurances on hull and machinery be settled as a claim for partial loss, no payment shall be due under this Clause 16.

There was no change in this clause in 1995.

Clause 16.1 effectively makes the policy on freight an increased value insurance on the vessel. To invoke payment under the freight policy it is only necessary to show that the vessel has been an actual or constructive total loss and the assured is not put to any proof as to the amount of freight at risk at the relevant time.

Clause 16.2 lays down the "test" for establishing whether the vessel is a constructive total loss and places it on the same basis as provided for in the I.T.C. Hulls.

Clause 16.3 was introduced following the case of *Petros M. Nomikos Ltd.* v. *Robertson*.[19] In that case the policies incorporated the then Institute Time Clauses, Freight, which provided, *inter alia*, as follows:

> "5. In the event of the total loss, whether absolute or constructive of the steamer the amount underwritten by this policy shall be paid in full, whether the steamer be fully or only partly loaded or in ballast, chartered or unchartered.

14. (1936) 40 Com.Cas 288; 41 Com.Cas. 120; 52 Ll.L.Rep. 34; 53 Ll.L.Rep. 131.
15. [1938] 2 K.B. 603.
16. [1953] 1 Lloyd's Rep. 278; 2 Lloyd's Rep. 294.
17. (1939) 43 Com.Cas. 109; 59 Ll.L.Rep. 182; 61 Ll.L.Rep. 105.
18. [1976] 2 Lloyd's Rep. 80.
19. (1939) 43 Com.Cas. 109; 59 Ll.L.Rep. 182; 61 Ll.L.Rep. 105.

6. In ascertaining whether the vessel is a constructive total loss the insured value in the policies on ship shall be taken as the repair value."

After the vessel had been chartered there was an explosion and fire on board and the charter was abandoned. Although the cost of repairs exceeded the insured value in the hull and machinery policies the shipowners elected to repair and claim for a partial loss which was paid by hull underwriters. The shipowners claimed under the freight policy on ground of constructive total loss of steamer, based on Institute Time Clauses (Freight), Clause 5. The freight underwriters countered that the shipowners were not entitled to recover on the ground that there was no constructive total loss of the vessel because there had been no notice of abandonment by the shipowners. The House of Lords held that the claim under the freight policy succeeded due to the fact that the vessel was a constructive total loss within the definition of section 60 of the Marine Insurance Act 1906, notwithstanding that she was never abandoned in any sense of the word. The House of Lords held that abandonment to underwriters is not an essential ingredient of a constructive total loss, but only for a claim therefor.

17 **RETURNS FOR LAY-UP AND CANCELLATION**

17.1 To return as follows:

17.1.1 pro rata monthly net for each uncommenced month if this insurance be cancelled by agreement,

17.1.2 for each period of 30 consecutive days the Vessel may be laid up in a port or in a lay-up area provided such port or lay-up area is approved by the Underwriters

(a)................per cent net not under repair

(b)................per cent net under repair.

17.1.3 The Vessel shall not be considered to be under repair when work is undertaken in respect of ordinary wear and tear of the Vessel and/or following recommendations in the Vessel's Classification Society survey, but any repairs following loss of or damage to the Vessel or involving structural alterations, whether covered by this insurance or otherwise shall be considered as under repair.

17.1.4 If the Vessel is under repair during part only of a period for which a return is claimable, the return shall be calculated pro rata to the number of days under 17.1.2(a) and (b) respectively.

17.2 PROVIDED ALWAYS THAT

17.2.1 a total loss of the Vessel, whether by insured perils or otherwise, has not occurred during the period covered by this insurance or any extension thereof

17.2.2 in no case shall a return be allowed when the Vessel is lying in exposed or unprotected waters, or in a port or lay-up area not approved by the Underwriters

17.2.3 loading or discharging operations or the presence of cargo on board shall not debar returns but no return shall be allowed for any period during which the Vessel is being used for the storage of cargo or for lightering purposes

17.2.4 in the event of any amendment of the annual rate, the above rates of return shall be adjusted accordingly

17.2.5 in the event of any return recoverable under this Clause 17 being based on 30 consecutive days which fall on successive insurances effected for the same Assured, this insurance shall only be liable for an amount calculated at pro rata of the period rates 17.1.2(a) and/or (b) above for the number of days which come within the period of this insurance and to which a return is actually applicable. Such overlapping period shall run, at the option of the Assured, either from the first day on which the Vessel is laid up or the first day of a period of 30 consecutive days as provided under 17.1.2(a) or (b) above.

The changes made in this clause in 1995 reflect the changes made in the corresponding clause (Clause 23) in the I.T.C. Hulls, 1/11/95. See commentary on pages 152 to 155.

Clauses 18–21 Exclusions

The following clauses shall be paramount and shall override anything contained in this insurance inconsistent therewith.

18 **WAR EXCLUSION**

In no case shall this insurance cover loss damage liability or expense caused by

18.1 war civil war revolution rebellion insurrection, or civil strife arising therefrom, or any hostile act by or against a belligerent power

18.2 capture seizure arrest restraint or detainment (barratry and piracy excepted), and the consequences thereof or any attempt thereat

18.3 derelict mines torpedoes bombs or other derelict weapons of war.

19 **STRIKES EXCLUSION**

In no case shall this insurance cover loss damage liability or expense caused by

19.1 strikers, locked-out workmen, or persons taking part in labour disturbances, riots or civil commotions

19.2 any terrorist or any person acting from a political motive.

20 **MALICIOUS ACTS EXCLUSION**

In no case shall this insurance cover loss damage liability or expense arising from

20.1 the detonation of an explosive

20.2 any weapon of war

and caused by any person acting maliciously or from a political motive.

21 **RADIOACTIVE CONTAMINATION EXCLUSION CLAUSE**

In no case shall this insurance cover loss damage liability or expense directly or indirectly caused by or contributed to by or arising from

21.1 ionising radiation from or contamination by radioactivity from any nuclear fuel or from any nuclear waste or from the combustion of nuclear fuel

21.2 the radioactive, toxic, explosive or other hazardous or contaminating properties of any nuclear installation, reactor or other nuclear assembly or nuclear component thereof

21.3 any weapon of war employing atomic or nuclear fission and/or fusion or other like reaction or radioactive force or matter.

These clauses are identical to Clauses 24–27 of the Institute Time Clauses, Hulls, 1/11/95, which are considered on pages 155 to 156.

B. Institute Voyage Clauses, Freight 1/11/95

These clauses perform the same function for freight insurance as the Institute Voyage Clauses, Hulls perform for the insurance on hull and machinery. All the individual clauses, as set out in list A (except for Clause 3—the Change of Voyage Clause) are the same as in the Institute Time Clauses, Freight, 1/11/95 (correspondingly numbered as in list B):

Title of Clause	List A	List B
Navigation	1	1
Craft Risk	2	2
Perils	4	7
Pollution Hazard	5	8
Freight Collision	6	9
Sistership	7	10
General Average and Salvage	8	11

Title of Clause	List A	List B
Franchise	9	12
Measure of Indemnity	10	14
Loss of Time	11	15
Total Loss	12	16
Assignment	13	13
Exclusions for War, Strikes, Malicious Acts and Radioactive Contamination	14/17	18/21

The Institute Time Clauses, Freight, 1/11/95 are considered above—pages 227 to 238.

The only clause to be considered separately is:

Clause 3—Change of Voyage

Held covered in case of deviation or change of voyage or any breach of warranty as to towage or salvage services, provided notice be given to the underwriters immediately after receipt of advices and any amended terms of cover and any additional premium required by them be agreed.

As with any voyage insurance, the details and nature of the intended voyage are material facts which must be disclosed before the contract is concluded. This clause—the terms of which are identical to Clause 2 of the Institute Voyage Clauses, Hulls, 1/11/95—is an important amelioration of the rather stringent English law provisions as to deviation and change of voyage (see the relevant sections of the Marine Insurance Act 1906 set out on pages 172 to 174 above).

C. Institute General Average—Pollution Expenditure Clause, Freight 1/1/96

In consideration of an additional premium to be agreed, where the contract of affreightment provides for adjustment according to the York-Antwerp Rules 1994, this insurance is extended to the proportion of General Average expenditure attaching to freight at risk of the Assured, reduced in respect of any under-insurance, which is allowable under Rule XI(d) of the York-Antwerp Rules 1994 and which would be recoverable under Clause 11 of the Institute Time Clauses—Freight 1/11/95 or under Clause 8 of the Institute Voyage Clauses—Freight 1/11/95 respectively but for Clause 11.4.2 or Clause 8.4.2 therein.

This insurance is subject to English law and practice.

This is the "buy-back" clause whereby claims for the proportion of general average expenditure attaching to freight at risk can be protected against objections made to allowances in terms of Rule XI(d) of the York-Antwerp Rules, 1994 on the grounds that they are caught by the prohibition of "expenses or liabilities incurred in respect of damage to the environment" etc. However, the protection afforded by this clause will only apply when the contract of affreightment provides for adjustment of general average in accordance with the Rules of 1994.

For this prohibition generally, see the section headed "The 1995 limitations on general average allowances" on pages 127 to 130.

6. PROTECTION AND INDEMNITY RISKS

Traditionally, Lloyd's S.G. form of policy covered only the risks of loss or damage to the subject-matter insured, with the addition of general average and salvage charges; liabilities were not covered. The case which established this proposition—*De Vaux* v. *Salvador*[20]—was followed, as we have seen in connection with the Running Down Clause,[21] by a desire on the part of underwriters to fill this gap in the cover, at least in part. In the belief that, by leaving a part of this risk uninsured, they would induce shipowners to train their masters and crews to take greater care, underwriters agreed to cover the legal liabilities of their insured arising out of collision to the extent of three-fourths only.

This was not enough for cautious shipowners, who banded themselves into Protection and Indemnity Associations (very soon afterwards called "Clubs") to protect themselves against the remaining one-fourth of collision liability and also to provide a system for settling on a mutual basis other liabilities, such as those for damage to cargo, fixed objects, wreck removal and so on.

Although this is still the general pattern today, a certain number of shipowners—particularly the owners of specialist vessels—do not wish to enter their ships into one of the large P. & I. Clubs, particularly if they reckon that the liability risks to which their vessels are exposed are more restricted than the risks experienced by conventional trading ships. Hence the existence of a small but specialised market among commercial underwriters to provide P. & I. cover, and the incorporation of such cover into the Fishing Vessel Clauses and the Institute Time Clauses, Hulls—Port Risks.

Institute Protection and Indemnity Clauses, Hulls—Time 20/7/87

This insurance is subject to English law and practice.

The effect of this provision is considered in the review of the Institute Time Clauses, Hulls (see page 90).

1 **PROTECTION AND INDEMNITY**

1.1 The Underwriters agree to indemnify the Assured for any sum or sums paid by the Assured to any other person or persons by reason of the Assured becoming legally liable, as owner of the Vessel, for any claim, demand, damages and/or expenses, where such liability is in consequence of any of the following matters or things and arises from an accident or occurrence during the period of this insurance:

1.1.1 loss of or damage to any fixed or movable object or property or other thing of interest whatsoever, other than the Vessel, arising from any cause whatsoever in so far as such loss or damage is not covered by Clause 8 of the Institute Time Clauses Hulls 1/10/83 with 4/4ths substituted for 3/4ths in line nos. 80, 81, 98 and 99

1.1.2 any attempted or actual raising, removal or destruction of any fixed or movable object or property

20. (1836) 5 L.J.K.B. 134.
21. See p. 119 above.

or other thing, including the wreck of the Vessel, or any neglect or failure to raise, remove or destroy the same

1.1.3 liability assumed by the Assured under contracts of customary towage for the purpose of entering or leaving port or manoeuvring within the port during the ordinary course of trading

1.1.4 loss of life, personal injury, illness or payments made for life salvage

1.1.5 liability under Clause 1(a) of the current Lloyd's Standard Form of Salvage Agreement in respect of unsuccessful, partially successful, or uncompleted services if and to the extent that the salvor's expenses plus the increment exceed any amount otherwise recoverable under the Agreement.

1.2 The Underwriters agree to indemnify the Assured for any of the following arising from an accident or occurrence during the period of this insurance:

1.2.1 the additional cost of fuel, insurance, wages, stores, provisions and port charges reasonably incurred solely for the purpose of landing from the Vessel sick or injured persons or stowaways, refugees, or persons saved at sea

1.2.2 additional expenses brought about by the outbreak of infectious disease on board the Vessel or ashore

1.2.3 fines imposed on the Vessel, on the Assured, or on any Master Officer crew member or agent of the Vessel who is reimbursed by the Assured, for any act or neglect or breach of any statute or regulation relating to the operation of the Vessel, provided that the Underwriters shall not be liable to indemnify the Assured for any fines which result from any act neglect failure or default of the Assured their agents or servants other than Master Officer or crew member

1.2.4 the expenses of the removal of the wreck of the Vessel from any place owned, leased or occupied by the Assured

1.2.5 legal costs incurred by the Assured, or which the Assured may be compelled to pay, in avoiding, minimising or contesting liability with the prior written consent of the Underwriters.

In general, the clause provides an assured shipowner with wide protection along the lines offered by the major P. & I. Clubs. Clause 1.1 provides an indemnity for sums paid by the assured on account of his legal liability as owner of the vessel for certain classes of claim against him, whereas by Clause 1.2 the underwriters agree to indemnify the assured for certain costs, expenses and fines which the assured may have to bear in circumstances where the question of legal liability may not arise.

In Clause 1.1 we have to note:

"The Underwriters agree to indemnify the Assured for any sum or sums paid by the Assured"

As in the case of the Running Down Clause, payment by the assured is a prerequisite to a claim under this Clause 1.1.

"to any other person or persons"

There is no limitation at all upon the class of persons who may have a legal claim against the assured, provided that the liability of the assured arises in consequence of one of the matters specified in the clauses which follow.

"... by reason of the Assured becoming legally liable, as owner of the Vessel"

The nature of the liability which must attach to the assured in order to found a claim under this part of the clause differs from that which must attach to an assured under the Running Down Clause in the Hull policy in two respects:

(a) it is wider than the RDC-type liability in that it is not limited to tortious liability, i.e. that which arises "by way of damages"; but

(b) it is narrower, in that it must be a liability which attaches to the assured "as owner of the vessel".[22]

In *Rigby* v. *Sun Alliance & London Insurance Limited*[23] Mustill J., in a claim under a buildings policy, said:

> "the liability must attach to the insured 'as owner'. These words are apt to describe not the capacity of the insured or the history of the liability, but the character of the liability",

and he concluded:

> "I therefore read the . . . policy as covering any of those claims in which the status of the insured as owner of the property is an essential although not the only essential element in establishing him as the person liable in respect of the claim."

In *Chrismas* v. *Taylor Woodrow*[24] the subject-matter was a floating jack-up platform being used by demise charterers to carry a crane in connection with work for a water authority, under a contract which included a clause that on completion of the work the charterers would clear away all plant, debris etc. Owners and charterers had insured the platform with the Institute Time Clauses, Hulls—Port Risks, 20/7/87, Clause 9.1 of which is in the same terms as the Institute Protection and Indemnity Clauses, Hulls—Time. The crane fell off the platform in a storm, and the charterers claimed the expense they had incurred to remove it from the seabed.

Judge Kershaw Q.C. held that the word "owner" had to be construed in light of the fact that the assured included the charterers as well as the owners. However, it did not follow that the right construction was to treat the clause as if it read "as owner or as charterer", and the correct meaning was that "the charterer, as insured, is indemnified against any liabilities which he may be under, against which an owner would be indemnified if sued as owner". On the facts, the judge found that the charterer became liable to remove the wreck of the crane from the seabed, not in any way as charterer or because it was a charterer by demise and an owner would have been liable, but solely because of its contractual obligation to the water authority.

". . . for any claim, demand, damages and/or expenses"

This is a wider form of words than that recently considered in *P. & O. Steam Navigation Co.* v. *Youell*,[25] where the words were "legally liable to pay as

22. Under a previous form of P. & I. Clause, the corresponding words were "by reason of interest in the vessel". In *Turner* v. *Manx Line* [1990] 1 Lloyd's Rep. 137, it was held by the Court of Appeal that these words were apt to describe the interest of a lessee for his liabilities arising by contract.

23. [1980] 1 Lloyd's Rep. 359.

24. *Christmas* v. *Taylor Woodrow (The "Tayjack I")* [1997] 1 Lloyd's Rep. 407.

25. *P. & O. Steam Navigation Co.* v. *Youell* [1997] 2 Lloyd's Rep. 136.

damages". Even so, the Court of Appeal, in considering that phrase, held that once P. & O. had demonstrated that they were under a legal liability to pay, the form of compensation paid, which in some cases included refunds of passengers' fares, should not prejudice P. & O.'s right to claim under their policies.

Subject to what has been said above, the liabilities which are covered are:

(a) under Clause 1.1.1, loss or damage to any fixed or movable object etc, other than those liabilities which would fall under a four-fourths Running Down Clause;
(b) under Clause 1.1.2, for removal of wreck or obstructions of any kind, or any failure to do so. In either case, the assured is to demonstrate that he was under a legal liability to take the action concerned;
(c) under Clause 1.1.3, contractual liabilities arising out of a contract in the "customary" form for the services of tugs in port. Under the United Kingdom Standard Towage Conditions, for example, the ship accepting the services of a tug becomes legally liable for any damage sustained by the tug in performing the service, irrespective of fault;
(d) under Clause 1.1.4, for loss of life, personal injury, illness or payments made for like salvage. This is self-explanatory;
(e) under Clause 1.1.5, for any payment which the assured may have to make as owner of the vessel under Clause 1(a) (the "safety net" provisions) of the "current" Lloyd's standard form of salvage agreement (commonly known as L.O.F.).

The reference to Clause 1(a) has to do with the wording of L.O.F. 1980 under which, when salvage services rendered to a laden tanker were unsuccessful or only partially successful, the salvor was entitled to claim as against the shipowner the amount of his expenses to the extent that the same exceeded any salvage remuneration awarded for partial or incomplete services. This was the so-called "safety net" which, under an agreement between London Market Underwriters and the International Group of P. & I. Clubs, was accepted as a P. & I. responsibility.

Subsequently to the issue of these Protection and Indemnity Clauses in 1987, we have a new regime for the compensation of salvors when their salvage remuneration is insufficient to pay their expenses. This regime is contained in the International Convention on Salvage, 1989, the working provisions of which were incorporated into L.O.F. 1990. Under Article 14 of this Convention, when there has been a threat of damage to the environment and the salvage service has been unsuccessful, or succeeds only to a limited extent, the salvor will be entitled, as an exception to the "no cure—no pay" principle, to "special compensation" payable by the shipowner and funded, under an extension to the Market Agreement of 1980, by the P. & I. Clubs. The position was further strengthened by the entry into force of the Convention and the revision of Lloyd's form of salvage agreement in 1995.

In consequence of these developments, this Clause 1.1.5 needed to be revised, and this was done by the issue of an amending clause in 1991 reproduced below on pages 249 to 250.

Clause 1.2 covers a group of additional expenses customarily met by P. & I. Clubs:

(a) under Clause 1.2.1, for the deviation expenses incurred (customarily adjusted on the same basis as the cost of putting into and regaining position from a port of refuge in a general average case) for the purpose of landing sick or injured persons, stowaways, refugees or persons saved at sea;

(b) under Clause 1.2.2, for expenses incurred consequential upon an outbreak of infectious disease;

(c) under Clause 1.2.3, for fines imposed on the vessel, the assured or any crew member or agent of the vessel who is reimbursed by the assured for "any act or neglect or breach of any statute or regulation relating to the operation of the vessel". The use of the expression "relating to the operation of the vessel" and the proviso which follows in lines 27/29, place two important restrictions upon the cover provided in this clause:

— fines imposed for anything which does not have to do with the operation of the vessel, such as for the personal conduct of any member of the crew, will not be covered by this clause,

— even when the fine has to do with the operation of the vessel, there will be no recovery for a fine imposed which results from an act, neglect, failure or default of the assured or any of their servants apart from the members of the crew. Thus, if the ship or its owner is fined for its being in a poor state of maintenance, and if this was the fault of the owner's technical management, rather than the negligence of the crew, the fine will not be paid by the underwriters,

(d) under Clause 1.2.4, for expenses incurred to remove the wreck of a vessel from the assured's own property. This would not be covered under Clause 1.1.2, since the assured could not be under a legal liability to himself;

(e) by Clause 1.2.5, the underwriters agree to reimburse the assured for legal costs incurred in avoiding, minimising or contesting liability. This applies to the whole clause, not merely the sub-clauses prefixed by the numbers 1.2. However, it is essential in all cases that before incurring legal charges, the assured must approach the underwriters and obtain their written consent to the appointment of the lawyers.

EXCLUSIONS

1.3 Notwithstanding the provisions of Clauses 1.1 and 1.2 this Clause 1 does not cover any liability cost or expense arising in respect thereof:

The reason the application of these exclusions is expressed to be limited to "this Clause 1" is to avoid any ambiguity or prospective overlap in the event that the Institute P. & I. Clauses are attached to a policy covering risks of another nature.

1.3.1 any direct or indirect payment by the Assured under workmen's compensation or employers' liability acts and any other statutory or common law, general maritime law or other liability whatsoever in respect of accidents to or illness of workmen or any other persons employed in any capacity whatsoever by the Assured or others in on or about or in connection with the Vessel or her cargo materials or repairs

1.3.2 liability assumed by the Assured under agreement expressed or implied in respect of death or illness of or injury to any persons employed under a contract of service or apprenticeship by the other party to such agreement

These clauses exclude virtually every liability of the assured to his employees as well as to stevedores and repairmen, the reason being that these liabilities are expected to be insured elsewhere.

1.3.3 punitive or exemplary damages, however described

This is an attempt to counteract the growing tendency in certain of the states of the U.S.A. and elsewhere for the courts to award punitive damages, in addition to compensatory damages, simply because when a claim is defended by a person who is known to be insured, it is equally well known that insurers have deep pockets.

1.3.4 cargo or other property carried, to be carried or which has been carried on board the Vessel but this Clause 1.3.4 shall not exclude any claim in respect of the extra cost of removing cargo from the wreck of the Vessel

This clause makes explicit the absence from the cover provided by these clauses of liabilities which an assured may incur under the law of the carriage of goods by sea. This is one of the important areas customarily covered by P. & I. Clubs, where commercial market underwriters fear to tread. However, the exclusion does not apply to the cost of cargo handling in connection with claims for wreck removal under Clauses 1.1.2 and 1.2.4.

1.3.5 property, owned by builders or repairers or for which they are responsible, which is on board the Vessel

1.3.6 liability arising under a contract or indemnity in respect of containers, equipment, fuel or other property on board the Vessel and which is owned or leased by the Assured

1.3.7 cash, negotiable instruments, precious metals or stones, valuables or objects of a rare or precious nature, belonging to persons on board the Vessel, or non-essential personal effects of any Master, Officer or crew member

The nature of these exclusions is self-explanatory and go to limit the cover provided for "loss of or damage to any fixed or movable object or property or other thing of interest whatsoever" granted in Clause 1.1.1.

1.3.8 fuel, insurance, wages, stores, provisions and port charges arising from delay to the Vessel while awaiting a substitute for any Master, Officer or crew member

This clause limits the extent of the recovery which the assured can make for additional expenses arising from the injury or sickness of a crew member occurring at sea. This is quite an important area in the cover provided by most of the P. & I. Clubs, which may cover not merely the additional expenses involved in landing the sick or injured seafarer, but also his hospitalisation, repatriation and the expenses incurred engaging and sending a substitute to a ship. This clause specifically excludes the running costs of the ship incurred in port awaiting a substitute, but nothing is said, either in the positive cover or in the exclusions, as to the cost of sending a substitute to the ship. It is, however, submitted that when members of the crew have been landed and hospitalised by reason of the outbreak of an infectious disease, the "additional expenses" covered in Clause 1.2.2 will include the cost of engaging substitutes and sending them to the ship.

1.3.9 fines or penalties arising from overloading or illegal fishing

This exclusion limits the cover granted in Clause 1.2.3.

1.3.10 pollution or contamination of any real or personal property or thing whatsoever (This Clause 1.3.10 shall not exclude any amount recoverable under Clause 1.1.5)

The exclusion of liability and expenses arising from pollution or contamination is another example of an area of coverage customarily provided by P. & I. Clubs which market underwriters are not disposed to enter. The exception to this exclusion (in brackets) is probably superfluous, but has been put in for the avoidance of doubt.

1.3.11 general average, sue and labour and salvage charges, salvage, and/or collision liability to any extent that they are not recoverable by reason of the agreed value and/or the amount insured in respect of the Vessel being inadequate

Market underwriters are understandably disinclined to cover any shortfall in coverage for general average, sue and labour and salvage charges, salvage or collision liability arising by virtue of under-insurance in the policies covering hull and machinery. Some P. & I. Clubs do cover this shortfall, although this cover is often subject to a reservation that the club managers should be satisfied regarding the level of the vessel's valuation in the policies covering hull and machinery.

1.3.12 earthquake or volcanic eruption

This is a curious exclusion which applies only to these clauses and those covering Port Risks (see page 177).

1.4 PROVIDED ALWAYS THAT

1.4.1 prompt notice must be given to the Underwriters of every casualty event or claim upon the Assured which may give rise to a claim hereunder and of every event or matter which may cause the Assured to incur liability costs or expenses for which he may be insured hereunder.

1.4.2 the Assured shall not admit liability for or settle any claim for which he may be insured hereunder without the prior written consent of the Underwriters.

These clauses place the assured under an obligation to give the underwriters prompt notice of every potential claim and to allow the underwriters to decide whether or not liability should be admitted or settlement made. From a practical point of view these provisions are necessary because many of the matters covered involve mixed questions of law and fact and sometimes protracted negotiation before they are settled. When a ship is entered in a P. & I. Association for these risks, the conduct of such negotiations is usually handled by experts on the staff of the Club and the shipowner can enjoy the benefit of their advice and support. Conversely, when a shipowner buys his P. & I. coverage in the commercial market, such negotiation and advice may have to be supplied by outside experts; hence the desirability of the assured keeping his underwriters informed at all stages of the case.

2 **LIMITS**

2.1 Where the Assured or the Underwriters may or could have limited their liability the indemnity under this insurance in respect of such liability shall not exceed Underwriters' proportionate part of the amount of such limitation.

It is customary for liability cover to be restricted to the amount for which the assured can or should have limited his liability in respect of any claim falling within the insurance. Certain of the liabilities covered by Clause 1.1 may be limited under the Merchant Shipping Acts, but it appears this Clause 2.1 is framed sufficiently widely to bring in other instances of limitation, whether by foreign law, contract or otherwise. However, it is not clear how the underwriters may or could have limited their liability under Clause 1.1, since this predicates that it is only the legal liability of the assured, as owner of the vessel, which is covered.

2.2 In no case shall the Underwriters' liability under this insurance exceed their proportionate part of the amount insured hereunder in respect of each separate accident or occurrence or series of accidents arising out of the same event.

Unlike the unlimited cover granted by many P. & I. Clubs, commercial underwriters require a "cut-off" figure to be agreed when the insurance is placed, and that figure is expressed to be the amount insured which is entered in the appropriate box in the MAR form.

3 **DEDUCTIBLE**

3.1 Notwithstanding the provisions of Clause 1 no claim shall be payable under this insurance unless such claim, or the aggregate of all such claims arising out of each separate accident or occurrence, exceeds .... in which case this sum shall be deducted.

3.2 Excluding any interest comprised therein, recoveries against any claim which is subject to the above deductible shall be credited to the Underwriters in full to the extent of the sum by which the aggregate of the claim unreduced by any recoveries exceeds the above deductible.

3.3 Interest in recoveries shall be apportioned between the Assured and the Underwriters, taking into account the sums paid by the Underwriters and the dates when such payments were made, notwithstanding that by the addition of interest the Underwriters may receive a larger sum than they have paid.

The deductible clause is modelled upon that contained in the Institute Time Clauses, Hulls. A claim payable by the insurance, or the aggregate of all claims arising out of a "separate accident or occurrence" would be payable only to the extent that the deductible is exceeded. The reader is referred to pages 135 to 137 for the interpretation to be given to the words "the aggregate of all such claims arising out of each separate accident or occurrence" and to pages 138 to 139 for the treatment of recoveries under the Institute Time Clauses, Hulls, which are identical to Clauses 3.2 and 3.3 above.

4 **NAVIGATION**

The Vessel has leave to dock and undock, to go into graving dock, to sail or navigate with or without pilots, to go on trial trips and to assist and tow vessels or craft in distress, but it is warranted that the Vessel shall not be towed, except as is customary or when in need of assistance, or undertake towage or salvage services under a contract previously arranged by the Assured and/or Owners and/or Managements and/or Charterers without the prior written agreement of the Underwriters. This Clause 4 shall not exclude customary towage in connection with loading and discharging.

This version of the Navigation Clause is slightly wider than that contained in I.T.C. Hulls. For example, the coverage when the vessel is under tow or in need of assistance is not restricted to "the first safe port or place", as it is in Clause 1.1 of I.T.C. Hulls (see page 91).

5 **TERMINATION**

This Clause 5 shall prevail notwithstanding any provision whether written typed or printed in this insurance inconsistent therewith.

Unless Underwriters agree to the contrary in writing, this insurance shall terminate automatically at the time of

5.1 change of the Classification Society of the Vessel, or change, suspension, discontinuance, withdrawal or expiry of her Class therein. However where such change, suspension, discontinuance or withdrawal of her Class has resulted from loss or damage covered by Clause 6 of the Institute Time Clauses—Hulls 1/10/83 or which would be covered by an insurance of the Vessel subject to current Institute War and Strikes Clauses Hulls—Time such automatic termination shall not operate

5.2 any change, voluntary or otherwise, in the ownership or flag, transfer to new management, or charter on a bareboat basis, or requisition for title or use of the Vessel. However, in the event of requisition for title or use without the prior execution of a written agreement by the Assured, such automatic termination shall occur fifteen days after such requisition whether the Vessel is in port or at sea.

The wording in bold type emphasises that this is a clause paramount which prevails notwithstanding any contrary provision in the policy. Unless underwriters are notified and agree in writing to continue the insurance, it will terminate automatically in the same circumstances as provided in the termination clause contained in the Institute Time Clauses, Hulls—Port Risks (see commentary on page 177).

6 **BREACH OF WARRANTY**

Held covered in case of any breach of warranty as to cargo, trade, locality, towage, salvage services or date of sailing, provided notice be given to the Underwriters immediately after receipt of advices and any amended terms of cover and any additional premium required by them be agreed.

7 **ASSIGNMENT**

No assignment of or interest in this insurance or in any moneys which may be or become payable thereunder is to be binding on or recognised by the Underwriters unless a dated notice of such assignment or interest signed by the Assured, and by the assignor in case of subsequent assignment, is endorsed on the Policy and the Policy with such endorsement is produced before payment of any claim or return of premium thereunder.

These clauses are in the same terms as Clauses 3 and 21 of the Institute Time Clauses, Hulls 1/11/95 (Clauses 3 and 5 of the I.T.C. Hulls, 1/10/83)—see pages 95 and 150.

8 **DUTY OF ASSURED**

It is a condition of this insurance that the Assured and their servants and agents take such measures as may be reasonable for the purpose of averting or minimising a loss which would be recoverable under this insurance.

Unlike the versions of the Duty of Assured clause which appear in the Institute forms for ships and cargoes, the clause in this instance begins with the words "It is a condition of this insurance . . . ". Consequently, and contrary to the position which applies in hull and cargo insurances when a clause is introduced by the words "It is the duty of the Assured . . . ", a failure on the part of the assured to take such measures as a reasonable assured should have taken may entitle the underwriters to deny liability for the whole claim.[26]

Furthermore, this clause differs from the usual Duty of Assured clause in that there is no explicit reference to the obligation of the insurers to respond for the cost of such measures taken by the assured for the purpose of averting or minimising the loss. To the extent that such measures include legal costs incurred in avoiding, minimising or contesting liability, these are covered by Clause 1.2.5, provided that they are incurred with the prior written consent of the underwriters; but for the recovery of expenses other than such legal costs an assured might have to argue an implied term "in order to give business efficacy to the contract".[27]

9 **RETURNS FOR CANCELLATION**

To return pro rata monthly net for each uncommenced month if this insurance be cancelled either by agreement or by the operation of Clause 5 provided that a total loss of the Vessel, whether by insured perils or otherwise, has not occurred during the period of this insurance or any extension thereof.

This returns clause follows the other clauses introduced in 1987 by allowing a return of premium in the event of cancellation of the insurance, not only by agreement, but also when the Termination Clause (Clause 5) operates (see commentary under the Institute Time Clauses, Hulls—Port Risks on page 183 above).

10 **WAR, STRIKES, MALICIOUS ACTS AND NUCLEAR RISKS PARAMOUNT EXCLUSION**

In no case shall this insurance cover liability cost or expense arising as a result of the operation of one or more of the following perils:

10.1 war civil war revolution rebellion insurrection, or civil strife arising therefrom, or any hostile act by or against a belligerent power

10.2 capture seizure arrest restraint or detainment (barratry and piracy excepted), and the consequences thereof or any attempt thereat

10.3 derelict mines torpedoes bombs or other derelict weapons of war

10.4 strikers, locked-out workmen, or persons taking part in labour disturbances, riots or civil commotions

10.5 any terrorist or any person acting from a political motive

10.6 the use of any weapon of war, or the detonation of an explosive, by any person acting maliciously or from a political motive

10.7 any weapon of war employing atomic or nuclear fission and/or fusion or other like reaction or radioactive force or matter.

These are the same as the exclusions provided in Clauses 22–25 of the Institute Time Clauses, Hulls—Port Risks 20/7/87, although expressed in a rather more concise form of words.

Institute Protection and Indemnity Clause Amendment 1/6/91

Where any of the following sub-clauses are incorporated in this insurance they shall be deemed to be deleted

Clause 9.1.5 of the Institute Time Clauses—Hulls—Port Risks 20/7/87
Clause 10.1.5 of the Institute Time Clauses—Hulls—Port Risks including Limited Navigation 20/7/87

26. For the position under Hull and Cargo Insurances, see *The Gold Sky* [1972] 2 Lloyd's Rep. 187; *Noble Resources* v. *Greenwood* [1993] 2 Lloyd's Rep. 309, and the commentary on p. 35.

27. See *Emperor Goldmining Co. Ltd.* v. *Switzerland General Insurance Co.* [1964] 1 Lloyd's Rep. 348 and *Netherlands Insurance Co. Est. 1845* v. *Karl Ljunberg & Co.* [1986] 2 Lloyd's Rep. 19.

Clause 1.1.5 of the Protection & Indemnity Clauses—Hulls —Time 20/7/87
Clause 1.1.5 of the Protection & Indemnity Clauses—Hulls—Time 20/7/87 as incorporated into the Institute Protection & Indemnity War and Strikes Clauses—Hulls —Time 20/7/87

and the following substituted:

> liability under Clause 1(a) of Lloyd's Standard Form of Salvage Agreement 1980 in respect of unsuccessful, partially successful, or uncompleted services if and to the extent that the salvor's expenses plus the increment exceed any amount otherwise recoverable under the Agreement, also liability for special compensation payable under Article 14 of the International Convention on Salvage 1989 or under that Article as incorporated in Lloyd's Standard Form of Salvage Agreement 1990.

This amendment became necessary owing to the incorporation of Articles 13 and 14 of the International Convention on Salvage, 1989 into Lloyd's Form of Salvage Agreement (L.O.F.) 1990. Now we have L.O.F. 1995, but further amendment of this clause will not be necessary since the Convention entered into force on 1 January 1995 in the United Kingdom and on 14 July 1996 generally.

There is a brief commentary on the purpose and effect of Article 14 of the International Convention on Salvage, 1989 in the review of Clause 1.1.5 of the Institute Protection and Indemnity Clauses on pages 243 to 244.

PART V

INSURANCES FOR VARIOUS INTERESTS

1. INTRODUCTION

A contract of marine insurance is not limited so as to cover only losses occurring at sea.

Section 2(1) of the Marine Insurance Act 1906 states:

> "A contract of marine insurance may, by its express terms, or by a usage of trade, be extended so as to protect the assured against losses on inland waters or on any land risk which may be incidental to any sea voyage."

This is followed by the specific provision in section 2(2) of the Act:

> "Where a ship in course of building, or the launch of a ship, or any adventure analogous to a marine adventure, is covered by a policy in the form of a marine policy, the provisions of this Act, in so far as applicable, shall apply thereto; . . .".

Similarly, there is no limitation on the classes of person who may take out a policy of marine insurance, provided he can show that he has an insurable interest. As to this, section 5 of the Marine Insurance Act 1906 provides:

> "(1) Subject to the provisions of this Act, every person has an insurable interest who is interested in a marine adventure.
>
> (2) In particular a person is interested in a marine adventure when he stands in any legal or equitable relation to the adventure or to any insurable property at risk therein, in consequence of which he may benefit by the safety or due arrival of insurable property, or may be prejudiced by its loss, or by damage thereto, or by the detention thereof, or may incur liability in respect thereof."

It will be seen at a glance that these parameters are sufficiently wide to include, *inter alia*,

- — Insurances against the risks incidental to shipbuilding, for the protection of shipbuilders and other contractors;
- — Insurances on containers, for the benefit of container operators and others;
- — Insurances for the benefit and protection of banks and other financial institutions.

In the sections which follow, we shall examine the Institute Clauses designed specifically for the insurance of these particular risks.

2. THE INSURANCE OF SHIPBUILDERS' RISKS

Institute Clauses for Builders' Risks 1/6/88

This insurance is subject to English law and practice

For the effect of this provision, see the commentary on pages 90 to 91.

There follows a page on which a number of entries have to be made in order to identify the vessel under construction, the assured(s) under the policy, the locations(s) where the building activity is to take place and the stages of construction; see opposite.

Vessel

It is unusual for a ship to be named until the launching ceremony. For the identification of the vessel under construction, it is customary in the policy of insurance to describe her as "Newbuilding", followed by the Yard number.

Builders

The identity of the main shipbuilding contractors is a matter of prime concern to the underwriters in the placing and rating of the insurance, and of nearly equal importance are the names of the engine builders and other sub-contractors. In addition to the question of materiality in the placing of the risk, the identity of the various parties concerned with the construction of the vessel can also be important in determining who are the assured under the policy. See the commentary on *Assured* on page 261.

Builders' Yards

The locations where the main hull and various other parts of the ship are to be constructed are also to be disclosed.

Subject of Insurance

Under this heading, the various pieces of information regarding the contractors and their working locations have to be brought together, with additional information to identify the various parts and to provide a set of provisional values, based on contractors' quotations or estimates. The form provides for this information to be set out separately within two distinct periods of time:

INSTITUTE CLAUSES FOR BUILDERS' RISKS

(This insurance is subject to English law and practice)

VESSEL ....Contract or Yard No...............................

BUILDERS...

....

BUILDERS' YARDS...

....

SUBJECT OF INSURANCE

(Where more than one part of the subject-matter insured is described in Section I(A), Section I(B) or Section II below, then the respective wording of Section I(A), Section I(B) or Section II shall be applied to each part separately.)

SECTION I. Provisional Period .... from ....
but this insurance to terminate upon delivery to Owners if prior to expiry of Provisional Period.

(A) HULL and MACHINERY etc. under construction at the yard or other premises of the Builders.

Description	Contract or Yard No.	Provisionally valued at	To be built at/by

The subject-matter of this sub-section (A) is covered whilst at Builders' Yard and at Builders' premises elsewhere within the port or place of construction at which the Builders' Yard is situated and whilst in transit between such locations. The Underwriters' liability in respect of each item of this sub-section (A) which is at such locations shall attach from the time:—

(i) of inception of this Section I if such item has already been allocated to the Vessel;

(ii) of delivery to Builders of such item (if allocated) when delivered after inception of this Section I;

(iii) of allocation by Builders if allocated after inception of this Section I.

(B) MACHINERY etc. insured hereon whilst under construction by Sub-Contractors.

Description	Contract or Yard No.	Provisionally valued at	To be built at/by

The subject-matter of this sub-section (B) is covered whilst at Sub-Contractors' works and at Sub-Contractors' premises elsewhere within the port or place of construction at which the Sub-Contractors' works are situated and whilst in transit between such locations.

The Underwriters' liability in respect of each item of this sub-section (B) which is at such locations shall attach from the time:—

(i) of inception of this Section I if such item has already been allocated to the Vessel;

(ii) of delivery to the Sub-Contractors of such item (if allocated) when delivered after inception of this Section I;

(iii) of allocation by the Sub-Contractors if allocated after inception of this Section I.

The subject-matter of this sub-section (B) is also covered whilst:—

(*a*) in transit to Builders if the transit is within the port or place of construction at which the Builders' Yard is situated;

(*b*) at Builders' Yard and at Builders' premises elsewhere within the port or place of construction at which the Builders' Yard is situated and whilst in transit between such locations.

SECTION II. Provisional Period .... from ....
but this insurance to terminate upon delivery to Owners if prior to expiry of Provisional Period.

MACHINERY etc. insured hereon from delivery to Builders.

Description	Contract or Yard No.	Provisionally valued at	To be built at/by

The subject-matter of this Section II is covered whilst at Builders' Yard and at Builders' premises elsewhere within the port or place of construction at which the Builders' Yard is situated and whilst in transit between such locations. The Underwriters' liability in respect of each item of this Section II shall attach from the time of delivery to Builders.

SECTION I. This is for the period from the beginning of work at the named shipyard and covers:

(A) the hull and machinery which is under construction at the main contractor's yard or other of his premises at the same port or place and whilst in transit between such places; and
(B) machinery etc. under construction by sub-contractors at their works or other premises within the same port or place and whilst in transit between such places; also between the sub-contractors' and main contractors' yard or other premises if they are within the same port or place.

SECTION II. This covers the machinery etc. whilst at the yard or other premises of the main contractors from the time of its delivery there by sub-contractors until the completed ship is delivered to its owners.

The reason for the separation of the subject-matter is, of course, the variations in the risk as between the materials and work done on the site of the main contractor's yard and other premises, and the materials and work done by sub-contractors.

For substantial building contracts, it is quite usual and indeed desirable for all the work contracted-out to be extensively listed together with the sub-contractors' names, places of work, description and identification of all parts to be manufactured and/or supplied, all with their contract/quoted/estimated prices, a complete schedule of the same to be made available to the underwriters and up-dated as necessary. This will avoid any possible hassle over the eventual ascertainment of the insured value. (See Clause 1.)

Clause 1—Insured Value

1 **INSURED VALUE**

1.1 Whereas the value stated herein is provisional, it is agreed that the final contract price, or the total building cost plus...............................% whichever is the greater, of the subject-matter of this insurance shall be the insured value.

1.2 Should the insured value, determined as above,

1.2.1 exceed the provisional value stated herein, the Assured agree to declare to the Underwriters hereon the amount of such excess and to pay premium thereon at the full policy rates, and the Underwriters agree to accept their proportionate shares of the increase,

or

1.2.2 be less than the provisional value stated herein, the sum insured by this insurance shall be reduced proportionately and the Underwriters agree to return premium at the full policy rates on the amounts by which their respective lines are reduced.

1.3 Nevertheless, should the insured value exceed 125% of the provisional value, then the limits of indemnity under this insurance shall be 125% of the provisional value, any one accident or series of accidents arising out of the same event.

1.4 Notwithstanding the above it is understood and agreed that any variation of the value for insurance on account of a material alteration in the plans or fittings of the Vessel or a change in type from that originally contemplated does not come within the scope of this clause and such a variation requires the specific agreement of the Underwriters.

Clauses 1.1 and 1.2 provide that the insured value shall be the greater of:

— the final price under the building contract, or

— the total "building cost", i.e. what it has cost the shipyard, plus a percentage which, within reason, the yard can declare as a notional level of profit.

However, underwriters are unwilling to accept a final insured value which exceeds 125 per cent of the provisional values. This provision in sub-clause 1.3 effectively establishes a ceiling for the final insured value. Once the "final" insured value has been established, the provisional values declared under the heading "**Subject of Insurance**" will be rated up or down proportionately, with additional payments or returns of premium.

Of course, it is quite possible that in the time between agreement of the building contract and completion of the work, the owners or prospective owners may call for some change or variation in the design or equipment of the newbuilding, and where this involves a radical "change in type from that originally contemplated" or a substantial variation in value, sub-clause 1.4 requires this to be specifically agreed by the underwriters.

Clause 2—Transit

2 **TRANSIT**
Held covered at a premium to be arranged for transit not provided for in Section I or II above.

It will be appreciated from the section headed "**Subject of Insurance**" that the basic terms provided by this insurance cover the transit of parts to and from the various works and yards only to a limited degree, viz:

— under Section I(A) to and from the named builders' yard to other of the builders' premises within the port or place of construction;
— under Section I(B) to and from sub-contractors' works and premises in the same port or place, to the main builders provided that transit is totally within the port or place where the builders' yard is situated, and between the yard and the builders' other premises within the port or place of construction.

By this Clause 2 any other transportation of machinery or any other parts are held covered, but they have to be declared to the underwriters at a premium to be arranged.

Clause 3—Delayed Delivery

3 **DELAYED DELIVERY**
Held covered at a premium to be arranged in the event of delivery to Owners being delayed beyond the provisional period(s) mentioned above, but in no case shall any additional period of cover extend beyond 30 days from completion of Builders' Trials.

The construction of a ship is expected to take place within a fairly tight schedule, but in the event of some interruption or delay in the programme, this Clause 3 provides for the continuation of the risk at a premium to be arranged, but only for a maximum of 30 days. Any extension beyond that relatively short period will need to be specially negotiated.

Clause 4—Deviation or Change of Voyage

4 **DEVIATION OR CHANGE OF VOYAGE**
Held covered in case of deviation or change of voyage, provided notice be given to the Underwriters immediately after receipt of advices and any amended terms of cover and any additional premium required by them be agreed.

This Clause 4 ought logically to follow **Clause 9—Navigation** which permits the ship to proceed to sea as often as required for fitting out, docking, trials and delivery. Any variation in any of these trips which would amount to a deviation or change of voyage will be held covered provided notice is given to the underwriters immediately after receipt of advices and terms agreed, if necessary. As to what constitutes a "deviation" or "change of voyage", see the relevant sections of the Marine Insurance Act 1906 set out in the commentary on the Institute Voyage Clauses, Hulls, 1/11/95 on pages 172 to 174.

Clause 5—Perils

5 **PERILS**

5.1 SUBJECT ALWAYS TO ITS TERMS, CONDITIONS AND EXCLUSIONS this insurance is against all risks of loss of or damage to the subject-matter insured caused and discovered during the period of this insurance including the cost of repairing replacing or renewing any defective part condemned solely in consequence of the discovery therein during the period of this insurance of a latent defect. In no case shall this insurance cover the cost of renewing faulty welds.

5.2 In case of failure of launch, the Underwriters to bear all subsequent expenses incurred in completing launch.

Unlike all other Institute Clauses on Hull and Machinery, the Builders' Risks form provides, basically speaking, an "All Risks" cover subject to certain limitations. The expression "all risks of loss or damage" is more usually to be found in cargo insurances, and is commented upon herein on pages 12 to 13. In short, the expression covers every kind of accident or fortuity, including the consequences of human error, and excludes only what is inevitable and the statutory exclusions, so far as they apply.

The statutory exclusions are set out in section 55(2) of the Marine Insurance Act 1906 viz.:

"(2) In particular—

(a) The insurer is not liable for any loss attributable to the wilful misconduct of the assured, but, unless the policy otherwise provides, he is liable for any loss proximately caused by a peril insured against, even though the loss would not have happened but for the misconduct or negligence of the master or crew;

(b) Unless the policy otherwise provides, the insurer on ship or goods is not liable for any loss proximately caused by delay, although the delay be caused by a peril insured against;

(c) Unless the policy otherwise provides, the insurer is not liable for ordinary wear and tear, ordinary leakage and breakage, inherent vice or nature of the subject-matter insured, or for any loss proximately caused by rats or

> vermin, or for any injury to machinery not proximately caused by maritime perils."

In applying these provisions of the Act to an insurance on Builders' Risks, the editor's submissions are:

(1) In a policy covering "all risks of loss or damage to the subject-matter insured", the word "risk" includes the consequences of human misconduct and error,[1] and that where a shipbuilder is the assured or one of several assureds, the misconduct or negligence of his employees can be equated with the misconduct of master or crew in the case of an insurance on ship. It is otherwise in the case of *wilful* misconduct on the part of the assured, which damns the claim absolutely.[2]

(2) Unless specifically covered (which is not the case under the Institute Builders' Risks Clauses) there can be no claim for any consequences of delay in progressing or completing the building works, for example under a time penalty clause in the building contract.

(3) Having regard to the fact that the operation of building a ship is basically to do with the assembly of newly-constructed parts, it is unlikely to find instances of loss or damage due to ordinary wear and tear, inherent vice or the nature of the subject-matter insured, except in cases of latent defect or faulty design, both of which are expressly dealt with—latent defect in this Clause 5 and faulty design in Clause 8.

Clause 5.1 specifically includes not only loss or damage caused by latent defect (as is the case by Clause 6 of the Institute Time Clauses, Hulls, 1/11/95) but also the cost of repairing, replacing or renewing any defective part condemned solely on account of the discovery (during the period of the insurance) of a latent defect.

However there are two important limitations to the cover granted by this Clause 5.1:

- the loss or damage sustained or the defective part condemned must be discovered during the currency of the Builders' Risks insurance.
- No claim will be entertained for the cost of renewing faulty welding. This is a new and unpopular provision introduced in 1988, which runs contrary to the general understanding that faulty workmanship is one of the accepted risks under a Builders' Risks insurance.[3]

Clause 5.2 sets out the important undertaking whereby underwriters will bear the expense incurred in completing an unsuccessful launch.

1. See *British and Foreign Marine Insurance Co. Ltd.* v. *Gaunt* [1921] 2 A.C. 41; (1921) 7 Ll.L.Rep. 62, in which one of the underwriters' defences, rejected by the Committee, was that the loss was due to the failure of the assured's servants to take precautions to protect the goods from wet.
2. For an unsuccessful attempt by underwriters to invoke this provision to the prejudice of a claim by a co-assured, see *State of The Netherlands* v. *Youell*, discussed below in connection with Clause 15.
3. The present editor is advised that this exclusion is frequently deleted by agreement.

Clause 6—Earthquake and Volcanic Eruption Exclusion

6 **EARTHQUAKE AND VOLCANIC ERUPTION EXCLUSION**
In no case shall this insurance cover loss damage liability or expense caused by earthquake or volcanic eruption. This exclusion applies to all claims under Clauses 13, 17, 19 and 20.

This exclusion is in the same terms as are provided by the Institute Time Clauses, Hulls—Port Risks, 1/11/95.

Clause 7—Pollution Hazard

7 **POLLUTION HAZARD**
This insurance covers loss of or damage to the Vessel caused by any governmental authority acting under the powers vested in it to prevent or mitigate a pollution hazard, or threat thereof, resulting directly from damage to the Vessel for which the Underwriters are liable under this insurance, provided such act of governmental authority has not resulted from want of due diligence by the Assured, the Owners, or Managers of the Vessel or any of them to prevent or mitigate such hazard or threat. Master, Officers, Crew or Pilots not to be considered Owners within the meaning of this Clause 7 should they hold shares in the Vessel.

This clause is in the same terms as the corresponding clause in the Institute Time Clauses, Hulls, 1/10/83.

Clause 8—Faulty Design

8 **FAULTY DESIGN**
Notwithstanding anything to the contrary which may be contained in the Policy or the clauses attached thereto, this insurance includes loss of or damage to the subject-matter insured caused and discovered during the period of this insurance arising from faulty design of any part or parts thereof but in no case shall this insurance extend to cover the cost or expense of repairing, modifying, replacing or renewing such part or parts, nor any cost or expense incurred by reason of betterment or alteration in design.

This Clause 8 covers, additionally to the perils covered by Clause 5, loss or damage to the subject-matter arising from the faulty design[4] of any part or parts, provided that such consequential damage shall both occur and be discovered during the currency of the insurance. It is however important to note two limitations upon the extent of the claims recoverable when a fault in design has been discovered and rectified during the currency of the insurance:

— No part of the cost of rectification, whether by way of repairing, modifying, replacing or renewing the faultily designed part will be paid for, nor anything in the nature of alteration or improvement.
— Only physical loss or damage to the subject-matter can be claimed. This does not include, for example, the extra expense incurred in chocking up or re-aligning a line of shafting due to its vibrating excessively on account of an error in design.

4. The expression "faulty design" was considered in *Queensland Government Railways* v. *Manufacturers' Mutual Insurance Co.* [1969] 1 Lloyd's Rep. 214. See commentary on pp. 220 and 221 in connection with the Institute Additional Perils Clause.

Clause 9—Navigation

9 **NAVIGATION**

9.1 With leave to proceed to and from any wet or dry docks, harbours, ways, cradles and pontoons within the port or place of construction and to proceed under own power, loaded or in ballast, as often as required, for fitting out, docking, trials or delivery, within a distance by water of 250 nautical miles of the port or place of construction, or held covered at a premium to be arranged in the event of such distance being exceeded.

9.2 Any movement of the Vessel in tow outside the port or place of construction held covered at a premium to be arranged, provided previous notice be given to the Underwriters.

In addition to the leave to proceed where necessary within the port or place of construction, the vessel has permission to go to sea as often as required for fitting out, docking, trials and delivery, but there are two sets of circumstances which may involve payment of an additional premium:

- — if any of these trips exceed 250 nautical miles from the port or place of construction; and
- — if the ship has to be towed, in which case underwriters also require to be notified in advance.

Clause 10—Deductible

10 **DEDUCTIBLE**

10.1 No claim arising from a peril insured against shall be payable under this insurance unless the aggregate of all such claims arising out of each separate accident or occurrence (including claims under Clauses 13, 17, 19 and 20) exceeds...................................... in which case this sum shall be deducted. Nevertheless the expense of sighting the bottom after stranding, if reasonably incurred specially for that purpose, shall be paid even if no damage be found. This Clause 10.1 shall not apply to a claim for total or constructive total loss of the Vessel or, in the event of such a claim, to any associated claim under Clause 20 arising from the same accident or occurrence.

10.2 Claims for damage by heavy weather occurring during a single sea passage between two successive ports shall be treated as being due to one accident. In the case of such heavy weather extending over a period not wholly covered by this insurance the deductible to be applied to the claim recoverable hereunder shall be the proportion of the above deductible that the number of days of such heavy weather falling within the period of this insurance bears to the number of days of heavy weather during the single sea passage. The expression "heavy weather" in this Clause 10.2 shall be deemed to include contact with floating ice.

10.3 Excluding any interest comprised therein, recoveries against any claim which is subject to the above deductible shall be credited to the Underwriters in full to the extent of the sum by which the aggregate of the claim unreduced by any recoveries exceeds the above deductible.

10.4 Interest comprised in recoveries shall be apportioned between the Assured and the Underwriters, taking into account the sums paid by the Underwriters and the dates when such payments were made, notwithstanding that by the addition of interest the Underwriters may receive a larger sum than they have paid.

This is the same as Clause 12 of the Institute Time Clauses, Hulls. See commentary on pages 135 to 139.

Clauses 11 and 12—Unrepaired Damage and Constructive Total Loss

11 **UNREPAIRED DAMAGE**

11.1 The measure of indemnity in respect of claims for unrepaired damage shall be the reasonable depreciation in the market value of the Vessel at the time this insurance terminates arising from such unrepaired damage, but not exceeding the reasonable cost of repairs.

11.2 In no case shall the Underwriters be liable for unrepaired damage in the event of a subsequent total loss (whether or not covered under this insurance) sustained during the period covered by this insurance or any extension thereof.

11.3 The Underwriters shall not be liable in respect of unrepaired damage for more than the insured value at the time this insurance terminates.

12 CONSTRUCTIVE TOTAL LOSS

12.1 In ascertaining whether the subject-matter insured is a constructive total loss, the insured value shall be taken as the repaired value and nothing in respect of the damaged or break-up value shall be taken into account.

12.2 No claim for constructive total loss based upon the cost of recovery and/or repair shall be recoverable hereunder unless such cost would exceed the insured value. In making this determination, only the cost relating to a single accident or sequence of damages arising from the same accident shall be taken into account.

Apart from the omission of any reference to "wreck" in Clause 12.1, the wording of these clauses in the same as in the Institute Time Clauses, Hulls, 1/10/83 or 1/11/95. This has prompted criticism on the grounds that the wording is inappropriate:

> Clause 11. A vessel under construction, whether damaged or not, has no "market value".
> Clause 12. The concept of constructive total loss has no application to a vessel under construction, only to the ship (or other subject-matter) when it is complete.

In the opinion of the editor these criticisms are valid, and further consideration should be given to the re-drafting of these clauses in the context of the following observations:

(1) If a vessel under construction sustains damage, the question whether or not to repair will depend in the first place upon the buyer—does he want this newbuilding for his service, even though its completion will be delayed?

(2) If he does, then the claim under the Builders' Risks insurance will be based upon the cost of repairs, and the question of a constructive total loss by expense will not arise.

(3) If the buyer has grounds for rejecting the partially built and damaged vessel, the shipbuilder should, in equity, be entitled to claim for his loss based upon the value he had put into the uncompleted structure, less any proceeds he could reasonably obtain from a disposal of the damaged remains. This might in law be an actual total loss of the part of the subject-matter in fact completed at the time of the casualty, but it would not be a constructive total loss as presently defined by Clause 12.

Clause 13—General Average and Salvage

13 GENERAL AVERAGE AND SALVAGE

13.1 This insurance covers the Vessel's proportion of salvage, salvage charges and/or general average, reduced in respect of any under-insurance, but in case of general average sacrifice of the Vessel the Assured may recover in respect of the whole loss without first enforcing their right of contribution from other parties.

13.2 Adjustments to be according to the law and practice obtaining as the place where the adventure ends, as if the contract of affreightment contained no special terms upon the subject; but where the contract of affreightment so provides the adjustment shall be according to the York-Antwerp Rules.

13.3 When the Vessel sails in ballast, not under charter, the provisions of the York-Antwerp Rules, 1974 (excluding Rules XX and XXI) shall be applicable, and the voyage for this purpose shall be deemed to continue from the port or place of departure until the arrival of the Vessel at the first port or place thereafter other than a port or place of refuge or a port or place of call for bunkering only. If at any such intermediate port or place there is an abandonment of the adventure originally contemplated the voyage shall thereupon be deemed to be terminated.

13.4 No claim under this Clause 13 shall in any case be allowed where the loss was not incurred to avoid or in connection with the avoidance of a peril insured against.

The text of this clause is the same as in the Institute Time Clauses, Hulls, 1/10/83.

Once again, the wording is not particularly appropriate to a vessel under construction. However, the terms of the clause will govern any claim for general average and salvage whenever the vessel is proceeding under the restricted liberties granted by **Clause 9—Navigation**.

Clause 14—Notice of Claim

14 **NOTICE OF CLAIM**

In the event of loss damage liability or expense which may result in a claim under this insurance, prompt notice shall be given to the Underwriters prior to repair and, if the subject-matter is under construction abroad, to the nearest Lloyd's Agent so that a surveyor may be appointed to represent the Underwriters should they so desire.

This provision is a little wider than those appearing in other forms; compared with the Institute Time Clauses, Hulls, 1/10/83, for example, in place of "accident, whereby loss or damage may result", we have "loss damage liability or expense" and the notice to underwriters must be prompt.

Clause 15—Change of Interest

15 **CHANGE OF INTEREST**

Any change of interest in the subject-matter insured shall not affect the validity of this insurance.

Before considering what this clause means, we need to look at the question who may be an assured under a policy on Builders' Risks.

The Assured under a policy on Builders' Risks

Readers will have seen from the Introduction to this Part V of the book (see page 252) that there are many persons who may have an insurable interest in the building of a ship, which by section 2(2) of the Marine Insurance Act 1906 is "an adventure analogous to a marine adventure". Although it is not unknown for a shipyard to insure its own interest separately, the most common practice is for the purchaser, the shipyard and all its sub-contractors (whether named or not) to be designated as co-assured in the policy, covering their respective interests and liabilities, and also their mutual liabilities without recourse one against any other.

An insurance was effected on these terms in *State of The Netherlands* v. *Youell*.[5] Underwriters, faced with a substantial claim for the cost of re-applying

5. *State of The Netherlands* v. *Youell* [1997] 2 Lloyd's Rep. 440 (Commercial Court) and [1998] 1 Lloyd's Rep. 236 (Court of Appeal).

and re-bonding certain damaged paintwork, raised a number of defences, under the first of which they alleged that the damage was due to the wilful misconduct of either the Netherlands Navy or the shipyard. It was held in the Commercial Court that the Navy and the shipyard were not joint assured; the insurance was composite and the interests of the co-assured were several. Consequently, even if the shipyard had been guilty of wilful misconduct, this would not afford a defence to a claim brought by the Navy.

Even though the current practice will be strengthened as a result of this judgment, it remains of comfort to both shipyards and their customers that by virtue of this Change of Interest Clause, the validity of the insurance will not be affected by the transfer of interest, e.g. from shipyard to purchaser, during the currency of the policy.

Clause 16—Assignment

16 **ASSIGNMENT**

No assignment of or interest in this insurance or in any moneys which may be or become payable thereunder is to be binding on or recognised by the Underwriters unless a dated notice of such assignment or interest signed by the Assured, and by the assignor in the case of subsequent assignment, is endorsed on the Policy and the Policy with such endorsement is produced before payment of any claim or return of premium thereunder.

This clause is in the standard form for hull insurances.

Clauses 17 and 18—Collision Liability and Sistership

17 **COLLISION LIABILITY**

17.1 The Underwriters agree to indemnify the Assured for any sum or sums paid by the Assured to any other person or persons by reason of the Assured becoming legally liable by way of damages for

17.1.1 loss of or damage to any other vessel or property on any other vessel

17.1.2 delay to or loss of use of any such other vessel or property thereon

17.1.3 general average of, salvage of, or salvage under contract of, any such other vessel or property thereon,

where such payment by the Assured is in consequence of the Vessel hereby insured coming into collision with any other vessel.

17.2 The indemnity provided by this Clause 17 shall be in addition to the indemnity provided by the other terms and conditions of this insurance and shall be subject to the following provisions:

17.2.1 Where the insured Vessel is in collision with another vessel and both vessels are to blame then, unless the liability of one or both vessels becomes limited by law, the indemnity under this Clause 17 shall be calculated on the principle of cross-liabilities as if the respective Owners had been compelled to pay to each other such proportion of each other's damages as may have been properly allowed in ascertaining the balance or sum payable by or to the Assured in consequence of the collision.

17.2.2 In no case shall the Underwriters' total liability under Clause 17.1 and 17.2 exceed their proportionate part of the insured value of the Vessel hereby insured in respect of any one such collision.

17.3 The Underwriters will also pay the legal costs incurred by the Assured or which the Assured may be compelled to pay in contesting liability or taking proceedings to limit liability, with the prior written consent of the Underwriters.

EXCLUSIONS

17.4 Provided always that this Clause 17 shall in no case extend to any sum which the Assured shall pay for or in respect of

17.4.1 removal or disposal of obstructions, wrecks, cargoes or any other thing whatsoever

17.4.2 any real or personal property or thing whatsoever except other vessels or property on other vessels

17.4.3 the cargo or other property on, or the engagements of, the insured Vessel

17.4.4 loss of life, personal injury or illness

17.4.5 pollution or contamination of any real or personal property or thing whatsoever (except other vessels with which the insured Vessel is in collision or property on such other vessels).

18 SISTERSHIP

Should the Vessel hereby insured come into collision with or receive salvage services from another vessel belonging wholly or in part to the same Owners or under the same management, the Assured shall have the same rights under this insurance as they would have were the other vessel entirely the property of Owners not interested in the Vessel hereby insured; but in such cases the liability for the collision or the amount payable for the services rendered shall be referred to a sole arbitrator to be agreed upon between the Underwriters and the Assured.

These clauses are in the same form as in the Institute Time Clauses, Hulls —Port Risks, 20/7/87. They will of course only be applicable when the vessel is proceeding under the liberties granted by **Clause 9—Navigation**.

Clause 19—Protection and Indemnity

19 PROTECTION AND INDEMNITY

19.1 The Underwriters agree to indemnify the Assured for any sum or sums paid by the Assured to any other person or persons by reason of the Assured becoming legally liable, as Owner of the Vessel, for any claim, demand, damages and/or expenses, where such liability is in consequence of any of the following matters or things and arises from an accident or occurrence during the period of this insurance:

19.1.1 loss of or damage to any fixed or movable object or property or other thing or interest whatsoever, other than the Vessel, arising from any cause whatsoever in so far as such loss or damage is not covered by Clause 17

19.1.2 any attempted or actual raising, removal or destruction of any fixed or movable object or property or other thing, including the wreck of the Vessel, or any neglect or failure to raise, remove, or destroy the same

19.1.3 liability assumed by the Assured under contracts of customary towage for the purpose of entering or leaving port or manoeuvring within the port

19.1.4 loss of life, personal injury, illness or payments made for life salvage.

19.2 The Underwriters agree to indemnify the Assured for any of the following arising from an accident or occurrence during the period of this insurance:

19.2.1 the additional cost of fuel, insurance, wages, stores, provisions and port charges reasonably incurred solely for the purpose of landing from the Vessel sick or injured persons or stowaways, refugees, or persons saved at sea

19.2.2 additional expenses brought about by the outbreak of infectious disease on board the Vessel or ashore

19.2.3 fines imposed on the Vessel, on the Assured, or on any Master Officer crew member or agent of the Vessel who is reimbursed by the Assured, for any act or neglect or breach of any statute or regulation relating to the operation of the Vessel, provided that the Underwriters shall not be liable to indemnify the Assured for any fines which result from any act neglect failure or default of the Assured their agents or servants other than Master Officer or crew member

19.2.4 the expenses of the removal of the wreck of the Vessel from any place owned, leased or occupied by the Assured

19.2.5 legal costs incurred by the Assured, or which the Assured may be compelled to pay, in avoiding, minimising or contesting liability with the prior written consent of the Underwriters.

EXCLUSIONS

19.3 Notwithstanding the provisions of Clauses 19.1 and 19.2 this Clause 19 does not cover any liability cost or expense arising in respect of:

19.3.1 any direct or indirect payment of the Assured under workmen's compensation or employers' liability acts and any other statutory or common law, general maritime law or other liability whatsoever in respect of accidents to or illness of workmen or any other persons employed in any capacity whatsoever by the Assured or others in on or about or in connection with the Vessel or her cargo materials or repairs

19.3.2 liability assumed by the Assured under agreement expressed or implied in respect of death or illness of or injury to any person employed under a contract of service or apprenticeship by the other party to such agreement

19.3.3 punitive or exemplary damages, however described

19.3.4 cargo or other property carried, to be carried or which has been carried on board the Vessel but this Clause 19.3.4 shall not exclude any claim in respect of the extra cost of removing cargo from the wreck of the Vessel

19.3.5 loss of or damage to property, owned by builders or repairers or for which they are responsible, which is on board the Vessel

19.3.6 liability arising under a contract or indemnity in respect of containers, equipment, fuel or other property on board the Vessel and which is owned or leased by the Assured
19.3.7 cash, negotiable instruments, precious metals or stones, valuables or objects of a rare or precious nature, belonging to persons on board the Vessel, or non-essential personal effects of any Master, Officer or crew member
19.3.8 fuel, insurance, wages, stores, provisions and port charges arising from delay to the Vessel while awaiting a substitute for any Master, Officer or crew member
19.3.9 fines or penalties arising from overloading or illegal fishing
19.3.10 pollution or contamination of any real or personal property or thing whatsoever.
19.4 The indemnity provided by this Clause 19 shall be in addition to the indemnity provided by the other terms and conditions of this insurance.
19.5 Where the Assured or the Underwriters may or could have limited their liability the indemnity under this Clause 19 in respect of such liability shall not exceed Underwriters' proportionate part of the amount of such limitation.
19.6 In no case shall the Underwriters' liability under this Clause 19 in respect of each separate accident or occurrence or series of accidents arising out of the same event, exceed their proportionate part of the insured value of the Vessel.
19.7 PROVIDED ALWAYS THAT
19.7.1 prompt notice must be given to the Underwriters of every casualty event or claim upon the Assured which may give rise to a claim under this Clause 19 and of every event or matter which may cause the Assured to incur liability costs or expense for which he may be insured under this Clause 19
19.7.2 the Assured shall not admit liability for or settle any claim for which he may be insured under this Clause 19 without the prior written consent of the Underwriters.

This P. & I. Clause is virtually the same as in the Institute Time Clauses, Hulls—Port Risks, 20/7/87. There are, however, certain omissions:

- sub-clause 1.5, dealing with "safety net" expenses under L.O.F. 1980.
- The exclusions relating to under-insurance—underwriters agree, in effect, that the vessel is fully covered for insurance by virtue of **Clause 1—Insured Value**.

Clauses 19.5 and 19.6 are the same as Clauses 2.1 and 2.2 in the Institute P. & I. Clauses.

20 Duty of Assured Clause (Sue and Labour)

20 **DUTY OF ASSURED (SUE AND LABOUR)**
20.1 In case of any loss or misfortune it is the duty of the Assured and their servants and agents to take such measures as may be reasonable for the purpose of averting or minimising a loss which would be recoverable under this insurance.
20.2 Subject to the provisions below and to Clause 10 the Underwriters will contribute to charges properly and reasonably incurred by the Assured their servants or agents for such measures. General average, salvage charges (except as provided for in Clause 20.4) collision defence or attack costs and costs incurred by the Assured in avoiding, minimising or contesting liability covered by Clause 19 are not recoverable under this Clause 20.
20.3 Measures taken by the Assured or the Underwriters with the object of saving, protecting or recovering the subject-matter insured shall not be considered as a waiver or acceptance of abandonment or otherwise prejudice the rights of either party.
20.4 When a claim for total loss of the subject-matter insured is admitted under this insurance and expenses have been reasonably incurred in saving or attempting to save the subject-matter insured and other property and there are no proceeds, or the expenses exceed the proceeds, then this insurance shall bear its pro rata share of such proportion of the expenses, or of the expenses in excess of the proceeds, as the case may be, as may reasonably be regarded as having been incurred in respect of the subject-matter insured.
20.5 The sum recoverable under this Clause 20 shall be in addition to the loss otherwise recoverable under this insurance but shall in no circumstances exceed the amount insured under this insurance in respect of the Vessel.

The wording of this clause is virtually the same as in the Institute Time Clauses, Hulls, 1/10/83, except that the references in the I.T.C. Hulls to under-insurance are omitted, thus demonstrating once again that in the Builders' Risks Clauses the underwriters have conceded that by virtue of Clause 1 the subject-matter is fully covered for insurance.

However the extent to which this Duty of Assured Clause can be applied in the case of an insurance on Builders' Risks is somewhat doubtful. In *State of The Netherlands* v. *Youell*, referred to above, the Court of Appeal[6] held that section 78(4) of the Marine Insurance Act 1906 (which is reproduced as sub-clause .1 of the Duty of Assured Clause) could have no application to the activities of the shipbuilders in the performance of their obligations contained in the shipbuilding contract; consequently the underwriters could not raise as a defence against a claim for unsatisfactory workmanship the allegation that in this respect the shipyard (as one of the co-assured) had not taken proper steps to minimise the loss which had occurred through this faulty workmanship.

Clauses 21–24—Exclusions

The following clauses shall be paramount and shall override anything contained in this insurance inconsistent therewith.

21 **WAR EXCLUSION**

In no case shall this insurance cover loss damage liability or expense caused by

21.1 war civil war revolution rebellion insurrection, or civil strife arising therefrom, or any hostile act by or against a belligerent power

21.2 capture seizure arrest restraint or detainment (barratry and piracy excepted), and the consequences thereof or any attempt thereat

21.3 derelict mines torpedoes bombs or other derelict weapons of war.

22 **STRIKES EXCLUSION**

In no case shall this insurance cover loss damage liability or expense caused by

22.1 strikers, locked-out workmen, or persons taking part in labour disturbances, riots or civil commotions

22.2 any terrorist or any person acting from a political motive.

23 **MALICIOUS ACTS EXCLUSION**

In no case shall this insurance cover loss damage liability or expense arising from

23.1 the detonation of an explosive

23.2 any weapon of war

and caused by any person acting maliciously or from a political motive.

24 **NUCLEAR EXCLUSION**

In no case shall this insurance cover loss damage liability or expense directly or indirectly caused by or contributed to by or arising from

24.1 ionising radiations from or contamination by radioactivity from any nuclear fuel or from any nuclear waste from the combustion of nuclear fuel

24.2 the radioactive, toxic, explosive or other hazardous properties of any explosive nuclear assembly or nuclear component thereof

24.3 any weapon of war employing atomic or nuclear fission and/or fusion or other like reaction or radioactive force or matter.

The first three of these Exclusion Clauses are in the same form as their counterparts in all the Hull insurances which we have been examining. The same is not, however, the case with Clause 24—Nuclear Exclusion. Here we have a list of exclusions more extensive than are contained in the Institute Time Clauses, Hulls, 1/10/83 or the Clauses dated 20/7/87 (Port Risks,

6. [1998] 1 Lloyd's Rep. 236 at 245.

Fishing Vessels, etc.), but not yet as wide as in the Institute Time Clauses, Hulls, 1/11/95, in that sub-clause 24.2 does not refer to the contaminating properties of an explosive nuclear assembly, nor to nuclear installations other than those manufacturing explosive devices.

3. INSURANCE ON CONTAINERS

Reflecting the hybrid nature of containers, which to some people are things to be put on board a ship to be carried as cargo, and to other people form an extension of the ship for the carriage of goods, the insurance forms which cover containers contain elements extracted from the standard conditions covering both cargoes and ships. The container operator may be a shipowner, freight forwarder or a mere lessor of travelling boxes for others to use, but whatever the nature of his operation he will require an insurance which will cover all his containers, wherever they may be, and whatever their value, on the same general conditions. Hence the importance of the detailed information to be presented to the underwriters at the commencement of the risk, which will be copied into the schedule which appears at the end of the policy form (or which is attached to it), and the need for clear identification of each of the containers covered by the policy.

Two Institute forms are available: one on full conditions, and the other covering only total loss, general average, salvage, salvage charges and sue and labour.

The commentary which follows refers to the "full conditions" form.

Institute Container Clauses, Time 1/1/87

This insurance is subject to English law and practice

The effect of this provision is considered in the commentaries on both cargo clauses (page 38) and hull clauses (pages 90 to 91).

RISKS COVERED

1 This insurance covers all risks of loss of or damage to the subject-matter insured, except as provided in Clauses 4, 5, 6, 7 and 8 below. — Risks Clause

2 This insurance covers general average salvage and salvage charges, adjusted or determined according to the contract of affreightment and/or the governing law and practice, incurred to avoid or in connection with the avoidance of loss from any cause except those excluded in Clauses 5, 6, 7 and 8 or elsewhere in this insurance. For the purpose of claims for general average contribution salvage and salvage charges recoverable hereunder the subject-matter insured shall be deemed to be insured for its full contributory value. — General Average Clause

3 This insurance is extended to indemnify the Assured against such proportion of liability under the contract of affreightment "Both to Blame Collision" Clause as is in respect of a loss recoverable hereunder. In the event of any claim by shipowners under the said Clause the Assured agree to notify the Underwriters who shall have the right, at their own cost and expense, to defend the Assured against such claim. — "Both to Blame Collision" Clause

4 The Underwriters shall only be liable under Clauses 1 and 2 above for loss of or damage to the machinery of the container — Machinery Clause

4.1 when the container is a total loss (actual or constructive)

4.2 when such damage is caused by

4.2.1 fire or explosion originating externally to the machinery
4.2.2 vessel or craft being stranded grounded sunk or capsized
4.2.3 overturning derailment or other accident to land conveyance or aircraft
4.2.4 collision or contact of vessel or craft with any external object other than water
4.2.5 general average sacrifice

Clause 1—Risks Clause

The wording is the same as in Clause 1 of the Institute Cargo Clauses (A), 1/1/82.

"All risks of loss of or damage to subject-matter insured"

The meaning of these words is examined in detail on pages 12 to 14.

Clause 2—General Average Clause

The form of the words and the effect of the first paragraph of this clause is precisely the same as for Clause 2 of the Institute Cargo Clauses (A), which is the subject of commentary on pages 16 to 18.

Clause 3—"Both to Blame Collision" Clause

This is the same as Clause 3 of the Institute Cargo Clauses (A)—see page 18.

Clause 4—Machinery Clause

The effect of this clause is to restrict any claim for loss or damage sustained by the machinery (if any) of the container to claims where the container is a total loss (actual or constructive), or as regards claims for partial loss, where the damage is caused by one of the perils within the ambit of Institute Cargo Clauses (C)—see commentary on pages 39 to 42. There is a further restriction, namely that in the case of damage caused by fire or explosion, this must originate somewhere other than in the machinery itself.

EXCLUSIONS

5 In no case shall this insurance cover General Exclusion Clause
5.1 loss damage or expense attributable to wilful misconduct of the Assured
5.2 ordinary wear and tear, ordinary corrosion and rust, or gradual deterioration
5.3 mysterious disappearance, unexplained loss and loss discovered upon taking inventory
5.4 loss damage or expense caused by inherent vice or nature of the subject-matter insured
5.5 loss damage or expense proximately caused by delay, even though the delay be caused by a risk insured against (except expenses payable under Clause 2 above)
5.6 loss damage or expense arising from insolvency or financial default
5.7 loss damage or expense arising from
unseaworthiness of vessel or craft,
unfitness of vessel craft or conveyance for the safe carriage of the subject-matter insured,
where the Assured or their servants are privy to such unseaworthiness or unfitness.

6 In no case shall this insurance cover loss damage liability or expense caused by — War Exclusion Clause

6.1 war civil war revolution rebellion insurrection, or civil strife arising therefrom, or any hostile act by or against a belligerent power

6.2 capture seizure arrest restraint or detainment (barratry and piracy excepted), and the consequences thereof or any attempt thereat

6.3 derelict mines torpedoes bombs or other derelict weapons of war

6.4 confiscation nationalisation requisition or pre-emption.

7 In no case shall this insurance cover loss damage liability or expense — Strikes Exclusion Clause

7.1 caused by strikers, locked-out workmen, or persons taking part in labour disturbances, riots or civil commotion

7.2 resulting from strikes, lock-outs, labour disturbances, riots or civil commotions

7.3 caused by any terrorist or any person acting from a political motive.

8 In no case shall this insurance cover loss damage liability or expense arising from any weapon of war employing atomic or nuclear fission and/or fusion or other like reaction or radioactive force or matter. — Nuclear Exclusion Clause

Certain of these exclusions correspond with the exclusions contained in the Institute Cargo Clauses, as follows:

Exclusions per Institute Container Clauses, Time	*Exclusions per Institute Cargo Clauses*
5.1 corresponds to	4.4
5.5 corresponds to	4.5
5.7 corresponds to	5.1

For commentary see the observations under the Institute Cargo Clauses (A) on pages 19 to 23 above.

The exclusion contained in Clause 5.2 is based upon the customary exclusion provided in section 55(2)(*c*) of the Marine Insurance Act 1906. "*Ordinary corrosion and rust*" and "*gradual deterioration*" are merely symptoms or examples of ordinary wear and tear.

"5.3 mysterious disappearance, unexplained loss and loss discovered upon taking inventory"

These words reflect the general principle of law that the burden of proof is upon the assured to demonstrate that he has suffered a loss, and that under an "all risks" cover the loss or damage was caused fortuitously—see commentary on page 13.

"5.6 loss damage or expense arising from insolvency or financial default"

This clause differs from Clause 4.6 in the Institute Cargo Clauses in that the persons whose insolvency or financial default caused the loss or damage are not specified. It might be that the London market introduced this exclusion in its present form into the container clauses in order to be able to decline liability in the event of a future case on facts similar to those in *Integrated Container Services Limited* v. *British Traders Insurance Co. Limited*,[7] where

7. [1981] 2 Lloyd's Rep. 460; [1984] 1 Lloyd's Rep. 154.

container owners recovered expenses incurred under the sue and labour clause in order to secure the release of certain of their containers from the premises of their lessees who had gone bankrupt.

Except in one respect, the War, Strikes and Nuclear exclusions (Clauses 6, 7 and 8) are the same as provided in Clauses 6, 7 and 4.7 of the Institute Cargo Clauses. The difference is that in the list of "war" perils set out in Clause 6.2—"capture seizure arrest restraint or detainment"—not only are cases arising from acts of piracy excepted, but also those which arise as a consequence of barratry of the Master or crew. This means that if a ship with the assured's containers on board were seized or detained by foreign government authorities because the Master was barratrously engaged in smuggling (as was the case in *Cory* v. *Burr*[8]), the insurers would be liable to respond for the loss or for expenses incurred by the assured under the sue and labour clause to recover their containers.

SCOPE OF INSURANCE

9 Each container is covered, including whilst on deck, within the sea and territorial limits specified in the Schedule below. Breach of these limits held covered at a premium to be agreed, subject to prompt notice being given to the Underwriters. Limits Clause

10 If a container insured hereunder is sold leased or hired to a party not named as an Assured, the insurance of that container shall terminate automatically unless the Underwriters agree in writing to continue to cover. Sale or Hire Clause

This Clause 10 shall prevail notwithstanding any provision whether written, typed or printed in this insurance inconsistent therewith.

An alternative heading to Clauses 9 and 10 might be PROMPT NOTICE. Clause 10 clearly implies that when the container owner leases or hires out a number of containers for their commercial operation, both the owner and the operator must be co-assured under the policy. Any change in this arrangement, such as a sub-lease, must be notified to the underwriters with a request for their written agreement to continue the cover, otherwise the insurance of the containers involved will be terminated. The operator will be the person who will have knowledge of the containers' destinations under the fixtures which he arranges with his cargo customers, and Clause 9 requires him to give prompt notice to the underwriters if any of these destinations should lie outside the geographical limits declared when the insurance is placed and noted in the schedule to the policy.

CANCELLATION

11 This insurance may be cancelled by either the Underwriters or the Assured giving 30 days' notice (such cancellation becoming effective on the expiry of 30 days from midnight of the day on which notice of cancellation is issued by or to the Underwriters). Cancellation Clause

11.1 In the event of cancellation by the Underwriters, they shall allow pro rata daily net return of premium to the Assured.

11.2 In the event of cancellation by the Assured, the Underwriters shall allow such return of premium as may be agreed.

30 days' notice is required if either the underwriters or the assured wish to cancel the policy.

8. (1883) 5 Asp.M.L.C. 109.

ASSIGNMENT

12 No assignment of or interest in this insurance or in any moneys which may be or become payable hereunder is to be binding on or recognised by the Underwriters unless a dated notice of such assignment or interest signed by the Assured, and by the assignor in the case of subsequent assignment, is endorsed on the Policy and the Policy with such endorsement is produced before payment of any claim or return of premium thereunder. *Assignment Clause*

This clause is in the same terms as Clause 21 of the Institute Time Clauses, Hulls—see page 150.

CLAIMS

13 In order to recover under this insurance the Assured must have an insurable interest in the subject-matter insured at the time of the loss. *Insurable Interest Clause*

14 In the event of accident whereby loss or damage may result in a claim under this insurance, prompt notice shall be given to the Underwriters or, if the container is abroad, to the nearest Lloyd's Agent so that a surveyor may be appointed to represent the Underwriters should they so wish. *Notice of Claim Clause*

15 Where a claim is payable under this insurance for a container which is damaged but is not a total loss, the measure of indemnity shall not exceed the reasonable cost of repairing such damage. *Partial Loss and Deductible Clause*

15.1 The Underwriters only to be liable for the excess of the deductible specified in the Schedule below in respect of each container any one accident or series of accidents arising from one event but this deductible shall not apply to

15.1.1 total loss (actual or constructive)

15.1.2 general average salvage or salvage charges

15.1.3 charges incurred under Clause 18 below.

15.2 In respect of each container the Underwriters shall not be liable

15.2.1 in respect of unrepaired damage for more than the insured value at the time this insurance terminates

15.2.2 for unrepaired damage in the event of a subsequent total loss (whether or not covered by this insurance) sustained during the period covered by this insurance or any extension thereof.

16 **16.1** In ascertaining whether a container is a constructive total loss, the insured value of that container shall be taken as the repaired value and nothing in respect of the damaged or scrap value shall be taken into account. *Constructive Total Loss Clause*

16.2 No claim for constructive total loss based upon the cost of recovery and/or repair of a container shall be recoverable hereunder unless such cost would exceed the insured value of that container. In making this determination, only the cost relating to a single accident or sequence of damages arising from the same accident shall be taken into account.

The Insurable Interest Clause (Clause 13) is in the same terms as Clause 11.1 of the Institute Cargo Clauses—see page 30.

The Notice of Claim is similar to Clause 10.1 as it was in the Institute Time Clauses, Hulls, 1/10/83, and it is to be observed that, once again, the Container form requires that the notice be given promptly.

Clause 15 deals with the measure of indemnity for partial losses and the application of the deductible applying to each container (and set out in the schedule to the policy).

By section 56(1) of the Marine Insurance Act 1906, a partial loss is defined as any loss which is not a total loss. Partial losses therefore include claims for general average, salvage and salvage charges, as well as particular average. Unlike the deductible clause contained in all Institute Hull Clauses (see in particular Clause 12 of the Institute Time Clauses, Hulls—see page 135) which applies the deductible to the aggregate of all claims, the deductible under the container clauses applies only to claims for particular average (damage to a container which does not amount to a total loss). Thus, claims for total loss of a container, general average, salvage, salvage charges and charges under the sue and labour clause are paid without deduction. It is also of interest that the London market has, for the container clauses only, abandoned the expression "the aggregate of all claims arising out of each separate accident or occurrence" in favour of "any one accident or series of accidents arising from one event", perhaps for the benefit of container operators unfamiliar with the intricacies of hull claims adjustment.

Other simplified rules of adjustment are set out in Clause 15:

- the measure of indemnity for particular average shall not exceed the reasonable cost of repairs;
- the underwriters' liability in respect of unrepaired damage to any one container shall not exceed its insured value,

nor shall there be any claim for unrepaired damage to any one container in the event of its becoming a total loss during the period of the insurance.

Clause 16, dealing with constructive total loss, contains provisions based upon the equivalent clause in the Institute Time Clauses, Hulls.

BENEFIT OF INSURANCE

17 This insurance shall not inure to the benefit of any carrier or bailee other than the Assured. — *Not to Inure Clause*

This is similar to Clause 15 of the Institute Cargo Clauses.

MINIMISING LOSSES

18 It is the duty of the Assured and their servants and agents in respect of loss recoverable hereunder — *Duty of Assured (Sue and Labour) Clause*

18.1 to take such measures as may be reasonable for the purpose of averting or minimising such loss, and

18.2 to ensure that all rights against carriers, bailees or other third parties are properly preserved and exercised

and the Underwriters will, in addition to any loss recoverable hereunder, reimburse the Assured for any charges properly and reasonably incurred in pursuance of these duties.

19 Measures taken by the Assured or the Underwriters with the object of saving, protecting or recovering the subject-matter insured shall not be considered as a waiver or acceptance of abandonment or otherwise prejudice the rights of either party. — *Waiver Clause*

The Duty of Assured Clause (Clause 18) is also referred to under its old title of the Sue and Labour Clause. It is in the same terms as Clause 16 of the Institute Cargo Clauses. See the commentary on pages 34 to 37.

Clause 19 (the Waiver Clause) is in the same terms as in all the standard forms for both cargoes and hulls.

IT IS A CONDITION OF THIS INSURANCE THAT EACH CONTAINER BEARS CLEAR MARKS OF IDENTIFICATION.

This is self-explanatory.

There then follows in the printed form a Schedule setting forth an identification of the insured containers, the sea and territorial limits covered by the insurance, the names of the oversea vessels on which containers will be carried (where this is relevant) and the amount of the deductible to be applied under Clause 15, viz.:

SCHEDULE

<table>
<tr><td colspan="3">Subject-Matter Insured</td><td>Sea and Territorial Limits</td></tr>
<tr><td>Type & Size</td><td>Identification Marks</td><td>Value</td><td>(which are deemed to include normal flying routes between points within these Sea and Territorial Limits)</td></tr>
<tr><td colspan="3"></td><td>Oversea Vessels</td></tr>
<tr><td colspan="3">Deductible</td><td></td></tr>
<tr><td colspan="4">or as per schedule attached</td></tr>
</table>

4. MORTGAGEES' INTEREST INSURANCE

Banks and other institutions providing ship finance require insurance protection just as much as any other entrepreneur.

The insurable interest of a mortgagee bank is defined in section 14(1) of the Marine Insurance Act 1906.

> "Where the subject-matter insured is mortgaged, the mortgagor has an insurable interest in the full value thereof, and the mortgagee has an insurable interest in respect of any sum due or to become due under the mortgage."

The mortgagee's initial requirement is for cover against the perils customarily insured by the shipowners' hull policies and the risks normally covered by the shipowners' P. & I. entry. Theoretically he can obtain this cover in three different ways:

1. By effecting a separate insurance to cover his own interest;
2. So far as the hull insurances are concerned, to effect the policies in

such a way that both the shipowners' and the mortgagee's interests are covered as co-assured[9]; or

3. By requiring the mortgagor shipowner to assign the hull policies and P. & I. entry in his favour. This is frequently achieved by endorsements on the shipowners' policies and Club entries noting the interest of the mortgagee.

A mortgagee to whom a policy has been assigned can bring an action under his own name, but he is under a distinct disadvantage: he can be thwarted by any defence which the underwriters would have been entitled to raise as against the original assured.[10] Thus if the shipowner has been guilty of wilful misconduct in regard to the loss,[11] non-disclosure of a material fact,[12] a breach of the duty of utmost good faith[13] or breach of warranty,[14] an innocent mortgagee suing under the assignment will find the insurers able to plead that the shipowner's turpitude had discharged them from liability.

A mortgagee suing as original assured is on a slightly better wicket. In these circumstances, provided that he can demonstrate his innocence, the fact that the shipowner has been guilty of "wilful misconduct"[15] will not of itself bar his claim on the policy. However, since 1924 a mortgagee insured on standard hull conditions has been unable to recover his loss in any case where the ship has been scuttled, since in that year the House of Lords decided in the leading case of *Samuel* v. *Dumas*[16] that a loss by sea water which has been deliberately let into a ship is not a loss by perils of the sea, on account of the absence of the element of fortuity. More than any other factor, this case demonstrated to the providers of ship finance the need for some kind of protection against the risk of misconduct on the part of their customers.

Since World War II there have been a number of different forms of Mortgagees' Interest Insurance, none of which have been totally satisfactory. After relying for a number of years on brokers' wordings or foreign forms,[17] the London insurance market eventually issued an Institute form of Mortgagees' Interest Clauses in May 1986. For reasons which will appear in the commentary, the 1986 form did not impress its prospective clients, and we have had to wait until 1997 for a form which deserves to succeed.

9. As envisaged by s. 14(2) of the Marine Insurance Act 1906.

10. Marine Insurance Act 1906, s. 50(2).

11. *Continental Illinois National Bank* v. *Alliance Assurance Co. Ltd. (The "Captain Panagos D.P.")* [1986] 2 Lloyd's Rep. 470.

12. *Pickersgill & Sons* v. *London & Provincial I.C.L.* [1912] 3 K.B. 614.

13. *Black King Shipping Corp.* v. *Massie (The "Litsion Pride")* [1985] 1 Lloyd's Rep. 437.

14. *Bank of Nova Scotia* v. *Hellenic Mutual War Risks Assn. (The "Good Luck")* [1988] 1 Lloyd's Rep. 514; [1995] 2 Lloyd's Rep. 191 (H.L.).

15. Marine Insurance Act 1906, s. 55(2)(*a*).

16. *Samuel* v. *Dumas* [1924] A.C. 431; (1924) 18 Ll.L.Rep. 211.

17. Notably the Swedish form criticised by Lloyd L.J. in *Schiffshypotekenbank Lübeck* v. *Compton ("The Alexion Hope")* [1988] 1 Lloyd's Rep. 311.

Institute Mortgagees' Interest Clauses, Hulls 1/3/97

This insurance is subject to English law and practice

The effect of this provision is considered in the commentary appearing on pages 90 to 91.

A. Recital

A. RECITAL

Whereas the Assured has entered into a loan agreement commensurate with which the Assured holds certain collateral security including a first mortgage on the Mortgaged Vessel and endorsements of its interests on the Owners' Policies and Club Entries.

Now it is agreed as follows:

These introductory words point to one of the major differences between the form of 1/3/97 and the previous form of 1986. The 1986 form was designed on the premise that the insured bank would enter into an open contract with the insurer, by which all the ships mortgaged to the bank would be declared. This "all or nothing" basis for insurance did not, generally speaking, commend itself to the banks. Mortgagees' Interest Insurance does not come cheap, and most ship finance institutions would prefer to separate their portfolios between the "good risk" clients they could trust not to defraud their insurers and the not-so-good boys on whose ships a Mortgagees' Interest Insurance was desirable. This approach is the one adopted for the 1/3/97 form, which is drafted on the basis of a separate insurance on each named individual vessel. Of course, if a bank wants to include all its mortgaged vessels on one open cover, it is free to do so, and no doubt special terms can be negotiated.

The Recital assumes that the assured holds a first mortgage on the insured vessel, and indeed there is a warranty to this effect (Clause 4.3). Consequently if the assured has a mortgage of lower priority, this must be declared at the time of placing the risk, and the policy endorsed accordingly.

Clause 1—Insuring Clause

1 INSURING CLAUSE

1.1 This insurance will indemnify the Assured for loss resulting from loss of or damage to or liability of the Mortgaged Vessel which, in the absence of an Insured Peril set out in Clause 2.1 below, would prima facie be covered by the Owners' Policies and Club Entries, and not excluded therein, but in respect of which there is subsequent non-payment (or reduced payment which is approved in advance by the Underwriters hereon) by any of the underwriters of Owners' Policies and Club Entries as a result of any Insured Peril, **provided always that such Insured Peril occurs or exists without the privity of the Assured.**

1.2 The indemnity payable hereunder shall be

1.2.1 the amount of the Assured's Net Loss and any amounts recoverable under Clause 6 herein, collectively not exceeding the Sum Insured on the Mortgaged Vessel, or

1.2.2 the amount of the unrecoverable claim or part thereof under any of the Owners' Policies and Club Entries

whichever is the lesser amount.

1.3 All the above is subject to the Definitions, Exclusions, Warranties and Conditions below.

In its first paragraph this clause summarises the purpose and effect of the insurance. A loss, damage or liability would *prima facie* be covered by the Owners' Policies and Club Entries (as defined in Clause 2.2) if it were not for a defence based upon the assured's misconduct. These instances of the shipowner's or ship manager's misconduct are set out in Clause 2.1, where they are defined as the "Insured Perils" under the Mortgagees' Interest Insurance.

The words "and not excluded therein" were added to the clause in 1997, presumably to make it doubly clear that the risks specifically excluded by the Owners' Policies and Club Entries cannot found a claim upon the Mortgagees' Interest Insurance—but how could they? The addition appears to the present editor to be superfluous.

There is also the important proviso in bold type that the Insured Peril relied upon by the mortgagee must "occur or exist without the privity of the [mortgagee] assured". In this context, as in others, it must be borne in mind that "Privity" includes "blind-eye" knowledge as well as actual privity.[18]

The second paragraph of the Insuring Clause sets out the indemnity payable. This is the lesser of:

- the mortgagee's actual Net Loss (as defined in Clause 2.3) *plus* any claim under the Duty of Assured (Sue and Labour) Clause, the total not exceeding the sum insured;
- the claim (or part of the claim) which is not recoverable under any of the Owners' Policies and Club Entries.

As a matter of construction, although the words "not exceeding the sum Insured" appear only in sub-clause 1.2.1, their effect is to form an upper limit to the claim, on whichever basis it is put forward.

It is also to be noted that, contrary to the 1986 form and to the usual canons of indemnity, a claim under the Sue and Labour Clause can be made only to the extent that it, together with the mortgagee's net loss, falls within the sum insured. See also Clause 6.5.

Clause 2—Definitions

2 **DEFINITIONS**

2.1 **Insured Perils**

2.1.1 Avoidance of the Owners' Policies and Club Entries or any of them by the underwriters thereof on the grounds of a misrepresentation or non-disclosure of any material circumstance, whether such misrepresentation or non-disclosure arises from the assured thereunder or any of such assured's insurance agents or insurance brokers,

2.1.2 breach of any statutory provision or any express or implied promissory warranty or condition, including without limitation

2.1.2.1 breach of any implied warranty of seaworthiness or legality,

2.1.2.2 breach of Section 39(5) of the Marine Insurance Act of 1906,

2.1.2.3 breach of trading warranties contained in any of the Owners' Policies and Club Entries,

2.1.2.4 breach of any warranty or condition in any of the Owners' Policies and Club Entries in respect of the classification of the Mortgaged Vessel by the Classification Society or any failure to comply with the recommendations of such Society to the extent required by such warranty or condition,

2.1.2.5 breach of any warranty or condition in any of the Owners' Policies and Club Entries which requires compliance with any condition survey, structural survey or P&I Club survey requirements and pursuant to which clauses underwriters deny a claim,

18. See commentary on s. 39(5) of the Marine Insurance Act 1906 on p. 115.

2.1.2.6 breach of any warranty condition in any of the Owners' Policies and Club Entries in respect of the ownership, flag, management or charter on a bareboat basis of the Mortgaged Vessel,

2.1.3 failure by the assured under the hull and machinery policy or the owners, managers or superintendents of the vessel or any of their onshore management to exercise due diligence in respect of any loss or damage to the Mortgaged Vessel where such failure to exercise due diligence entitles the underwriters of the owner's hull and machinery policy to deny a claim otherwise recoverable thereunder,

2.1.4 any deliberate or fraudulent casting away of or damage to the Mortgaged Vessel,

2.1.5 avoidance of a claim under any of the Owners' Policies and Club Entries or of any of the Owners' Policies and Club Entries by reason of breach of the duty of good faith in respect of such claim, or

2.1.6 the operations of any applicable provision in any of the Owners' Policies and Club Entries which provides for a time limitation on the presentation of claims,

2.1.7 in the event of the total loss of the Mortgaged Vessel, the final judgment or award of the courts or arbitration tribunal agreed to have jurisdiction under the express terms of Owners' Policies and Club Entries (or in the event of there being no such express terms the competent court) following a contested hearing whereby the Owners' claim is not recoverable under either Owners' hull and machinery or war risks policies on the ground that the loss has not been proved to have been proximately caused by a peril insured under those policies and is not otherwise excluded from payment by an exclusion or other provision therein.

2.2 **Owners' Policies and Club Entries**—means hull and machinery policies on terms equivalent to or wider than the current Institution Time Clauses, Hulls or American Institute Hull Clauses, (if taken, increased value policies on terms equivalent to Institute Time Clauses—Hull Disbursements and Increased Value (Total Loss Only and Excess Liabilities) or American Institute Increased Value and Excess Liabilities Clauses), War risks on terms equivalent to current Institute War and Strikes Clauses Hulls—Time and full protection and indemnity risks on conditions equivalent to the rules of a P&I Club that is a member of the International Group of P&I Associations.

2.3 **Net Loss**—means the Assured's loss under the loan agreement to the extent secured by mortgage on the Mortgaged Vessel net of any amounts recovered or recoverable under all security arrangements contained in or collateral to the loan including but not limited to all mortgages (whether on vessels insured hereunder or on other vessels), liens, any floating and fixed charges, security interests, guarantees, insurance policies and pledges.

2.4 **Mortgaged Vessel**—means the vessel mortgaged to the Assured which is listed on the schedule attached hereto.

2.1 Insured Perils

In contrast with all previous forms of Mortgagees' Interest Insurance, the 1/3/97 Clauses set out a full list of the Insured Perils, i.e. a complete catalogue of the sins of omission and commission which will damn any claim under the "*Owners' Policies and Club Entries*" and consequently trigger a claim on the Mortgagees' Interest Insurance. Also included by sub-clause 2.1.7 is a reference to that class of case such as *The "Popi M"*[19] where the owner fails in his claim on his (the owner's) policies solely because he is unable to meet the burden of proving that the ship was lost by insured perils.

2.2 Owners' Policies and Club Entries

There is a small but significant change from the 1986 form. The hull and machinery policy may now be on terms "*equivalent to or wider than the current [forms mentioned]*", i.e. Institute Time Clauses, Hulls, 1/11/95 or American Institute Hull Clauses (2 June 1977) and their associated Disbursements/ Increased Value clauses. This allows for cases where the mortgagor shipowners have insured their vessels on other hull conditions, provided they are

19. *The "Popi M"* [1985] 2 Lloyd's Rep. 1 (H.L.).

at least as wide as the forms mentioned. As observed in "Part III—Marine Hull Forms", the Institute Time Clauses, Hulls, 1/10/83, although no longer "current", remain very popular and are certainly as wide, if not wider than the 1/11/95 form.

However, taking into account that the list of perils in Clause 2.1 is drafted with specific English law situations in mind, the present editor would not recommend using this form of Mortgagees' Interest Insurance in conjunction with an insurance on hull and machinery which is subject to a foreign law or jurisdiction.

As to the Owners' Club Entries, it is to be noted that the Club's conditions must be "*equivalent to*" those of a member of the International Group of P. & I. Associations.

2.3 Net Loss

The main point here is that in computing the amount payable by this insurance, the assured bank has to give credit against the amount outstanding under the loan agreement for all recoveries available under other securities it may hold, including security on other vessels forming part of the loan agreement.

2.4 Mortgaged Vessel

Provision is made for the name(s) of the ship(s) mortgaged to the assured to be listed on a schedule attached to the policy.

Clause 3—Exclusions

3. **EXCLUSIONS**

In no case shall this policy cover:

3.1 any loss or expense arising from or as a result of

3.1.1 the relevant Owners' Policies and Club Entries, having been terminated or cancelled or cover suspended or non-payment of claims by the underwriters or insurance brokers thereof due to non-payment of premiums or calls.

3.1.2 insolvency or financial default of any of the underwriters of the Owners' Policies and Club Entries,

3.1.3 inability of any party to transmit funds,

3.1.4 any fluctuation in exchange rates,

3.1.5 the operation of any franchise deductible or provision for self-insurance,

3.2 loss or damage directly or indirectly caused by or contributed to by or arising from:

3.2.1 ionising radiation from or contamination by radioactivity from any nuclear fuel or from any nuclear waste or from combustion of nuclear fuel,

3.2.2 the radioactive, toxic, explosive or other hazardous or contaminating properties of any nuclear installation, reactor or other nuclear assembly or nuclear component thereof,

3.2.3 any weapon of war employing atomic or nuclear fission and/or fusion or other like reaction or radioactive force or matter.

This clause falls into two parts:

— Clause 3.1 excludes specifically any loss or expense as a result of the termination or cancellation of the Owners' Policies and/or Club Entries by reason of non-payment of premiums or calls; also as a result of the insolvency or financial default on the part of the original underwriters, or other purely financial risks.

— Clause 3.2 is based upon the Radioactive Contamination Exclusion Clause of 1990, as contained in Institute Time Clauses, Hulls, 1/11/95—see page 156 herein.

Clause 4—Warranties

4 **WARRANTIES**

It is warranted in respect of the Mortgaged Vessel that:

4.1 Owners' Policies and Club Entries have been taken out and, except as a result of the occurrence or existence of an Insured Peril without the privity of the Assured, shall be maintained throughout the currency of this insurance for an insured value and limit of liability not less than the amount insured hereunder or the amount of the outstanding loan to the extent secured by the Mortgaged Vessel,

4.2 each of the Owners' Policies and Club Entries endorsed to the extent of the Assured's interest, and

4.3 the Assured has procured and registered a valid first mortgage.

The first and most important of these warranties requires the mortgagee bank to ensure that the Owners' Policies and Club Entries are in place *and are maintained in place* throughout the currency of the Mortgagees' Interest Insurance, the only excepting circumstance being the occurrence of one of the Insured Perils (defaults of the shipowner) without the privity of the bank, of course. This imposes a serious duty on the bank continually to monitor the position with regard to the Owners' Policies and Club Entries, a duty which it is well-nigh impossible to perform unless the bank is kept continuously *au courant* with the manner in which the shipowner performs his obligations (a) to pay premiums and (b) to demonstrate good faith in his dealings with his underwriters. In the past it has been suggested that one way to tackle the problem is for the mortgagee bank to employ the same insurance broker as his shipowner client; now it is virtually standard practice for the bank, as a condition of the loan agreement, to require the mortgagor shipowner to obtain a Letter of Undertaking from his broker whereby he (the broker) undertakes to advise the bank of any occurrence which might jeopardise the maintenance of the insurance. As regards the Club Entry, where generally speaking no broker is involved, it is the Club which provides the Letter of Undertaking.[20]

The warranty in sub-clause 4.2 requires that the Owners' Policies and Club Entries are endorsed to the extent of the bank's interest.

By sub-clause 4.3 the bank warrants that it has procured and registered a valid first mortgage. If the bank holds a mortgage of lesser priority, it may still be possible to arrange mortgagees' interest insurance, in which case this warranty must be deleted.

20. For a case where a bank successfully relied upon a Letter of Undertaking in order to recover its financial loss see *Bank of Nova Scotia* v. *Hellenic Mutual War Risks Assn. (The "Good Luck")* [1988] 1 Lloyd's Rep. 514; [1995] 2 Lloyd's Rep.191 (H.L.).

Clause 5—Change of Ownership or Control

5 **CHANGE OF OWNERSHIP OR CONTROL**

This insurance will terminate automatically at the time the Assured becomes or is aware of or privy to any change of:

5.1 Classification Society or of change, suspension, discontinuance, withdrawal or expiry of the Mortgaged Vessel's class within that Society,

5.2 ownership, flag, management or control of the Mortgaged Vessel,

unless the Assured gives prompt notice of such change in writing, and agrees to pay an additional premium, if required, and Owners' Policies and Club Entries are maintained.

By reason of this clause the assured bank has also to keep a wary eye on the ownership, flag, management and control of the mortgaged vessel; also (under the 1/3/97 clauses) on the continuance of the vessel's entry in her classification society, since in the event of a change in the situation which becomes known to the assured bank, or to which the bank is privy, the underwriters have the right to invoke the automatic termination of the insurance. The assured bank can however avoid this "automatic termination" if it is able to give prompt notice—whatever that may mean—of the event in question and an assurance that the Owners' Policies and Club Entries remain in force.

Clause 6—Duty of Assured (Sue and Labour)

6 **DUTY OF ASSURED (SUE AND LABOUR)**

6.1 The Assured shall report in writing to the Underwriters any circumstances which may give rise to a claim under this insurance within 30 days of the Assured's knowledge of such circumstances and shall thereafter keep the Underwriters fully informed of all developments.

6.2 It is the duty of the Assured and their servants and agents to take such measures as may be reasonable for the purpose of averting or minimising a loss which would be recoverable under this insurance.

6.3 The Underwriters will reimburse charges properly and reasonably incurred by the Assured their servants or agents for such measures except for legal costs and expenses incurred by the Assured in relation to any claim under Owners' Policies and Club Entries which shall only be reimbursed in accordance with clause 6.4 herein.

6.4 Subject to the condition precedent that the Mortgaged Vessel is entered in a Freight, Demurrage and Defence Club covering the cost of the owner proceeding against the Owners' Policies and Club Entries, the Underwriters will reimburse those legal costs and expenses incurred by the Assured in pursuing the non-paying Owners' Policies and Club Entries not otherwise recoverable as part of the Net Loss but only where the Assured can demonstrate to the satisfaction of the Underwriters that it has made every reasonable effort to compel the owner to pursue the non-paying Owners' Policies and Club Entries. This policy shall not pay for legal costs and expenses incurred by the Assured in monitoring the claim against the Owners' Policies and Club Entries.

6.5 Any amounts payable under this clause shall be included within and shall not be additional to the Sum Insured.

6.6 Measures taken by the Assured or the Underwriters with the object of averting or minimising a loss which would be recoverable under this insurance shall not be considered as a waiver or acceptance of a claim or otherwise prejudice the rights of either party.

Clauses 6.2, 6.3 and 6.6 set forth the customary requirement that the assured shall take such measures as may be reasonable to avert or minimise a loss, that the underwriters will reimburse the assured for the cost of such measures and that neither party shall be prejudiced thereby.

Clause 6.1 places the assured under an additional duty to report in writing to the underwriters any circumstances which may give rise to a claim under the insurance within 30 days of its coming to the assured's notice, and thereafter to keep the underwriters informed of developments. This is a new provision, along the lines of the "further and better information" provisions of Institute Time Clauses, Hulls, 1/11/95, and it could cause bankers some hardship. It will certainly keep their insurance departments on their toes.

Clause 6.4 permits the assured bank to claim the legal costs and expenses incurred in pursuing its claim as assignee on the Owners' Policies and Club Entries, but only in rather limited circumstances, viz: that the mortgaged vessel is entered in a Freight, Demurrage and Defence Club and that the bank has done its utmost to compel the owner to obtain the support of the F., D. & D. Club in pursuing its claim against the non-paying policies and/or Club entries.

Clause 6.5 is the joker in the pack. For reasons which are certainly not clear to the present editor, underwriters have for the first time ever reversed the long-standing and time-honoured rule whereby Sue and Labour charges are payable in addition to the sum insured on the policy.

Clause 7—Claims

7 **CLAIMS**

7.1 The Assured shall prove a claim under this insurance by:

7.1.1 demonstrating to the satisfaction of the Underwriters that by reason of the perils insured under clause 2.1 there is no reasonable prospect of the Owners and/or Assured succeeding in the claim against the underwriters of the Owners' Policies and Club Entries, or

7.1.2 in the event of disagreement between the Underwriters and the Assured by either referring the issue to a sole arbitrator in London to be agreed upon between the Underwriters and the Assured or on final court judgment or arbitration award delivered in favour of the underwriters of Owners' Policies and Club Entries.

7.2 The Underwriters shall pay any claim hereunder within 3 months of the date that both the claim is proved in accordance with Clause 7.1 and Net Loss is established.

In the earliest forms of Mortgagees' Interest Insurance written in the London market, non-payment by the underwriters subscribing Owners' Policies and/or Club Entries was deemed to have taken place only when "a final Court judgment [was] delivered in favour of those underwriters", or (in the case of the 1986 form) at such earlier time as the assured could demonstrate to the satisfaction of the M.I.I. underwriters that there was no reasonable prospect of success against the owners' policies.

Now, under the 1/3/97 form, the reference to "final court judgment" has mercifully been transferred to sub-clause 7.1.2 which provides for alternative solutions to be applied only in the event of disagreement between the M.I.I. underwriters and the assured. These alternatives are:

— arbitration by a sole arbitrator to be agreed, or
— final court judgment or arbitration award against the owners' insurers.

By Clause 7.2 the M.I.I. underwriters are bound to pay within three months of the claim being proved (as above) and the bank's Net Loss (see Clause 2.3) being established.

Clause 8—Subrogation

8 **SUBROGATION**

8.1 Upon payment to the Assured of a claim hereunder, the Underwriters shall be subrogated to all the rights and remedies of the Assured in respect of such payment.

8.2 It is a condition of this insurance that any payments by the Underwriters shall not be applied by the Assured in or towards discharge or satisfaction of the amount of the outstanding indebtedness.

Clause 8.1 is a straightforward re-statement of the principle of subrogation which underlies all contracts of insurance.

Clause 8.2 is designed to prevent a bank from paying over to its client any part of the recovery which it makes from its underwriters.

Clause 9—Effect of Under Insurance

9 **EFFECT OF UNDER INSURANCE**

If the loan amounts are not fully insured hereunder at the time of loss, then the indemnity payable hereunder including any sue and labour amounts shall be reduced in proportion to the under insurance.

This clause provides for the amount recoverable (including any claim payable under the Sue and Labour Clause) to be reduced pro-rata in the event of the loan amounts not being fully insured at the time of the loss.

Clause 10—Automatic Termination

10 **AUTOMATIC TERMINATION**

10.1 Cover hereunder for loss of or damage to or liability of a Mortgaged Vessel shall terminate in respect of those risks covered by the War and Strikes Clauses of the Mortgaged Vessel

10.1.1 AUTOMATICALLY upon the outbreak of war (whether there be a declaration of war or not) between any of the following

United Kingdom, United States of America, France, the Russian Federation, the People's Republic of China

10.1.2 AUTOMATICALLY in respect of a Mortgaged Vessel in the event of that Mortgaged Vessel being requisitioned either for title or use

10.1.3 7 days after the Underwriters of the Owner's War Risks Insurances or any of them have given notice of cancellation unless such War Risks Insurances have been reinstated prior to or from the expiry of such notice and any new rate of premium and amendments to terms, conditions or warranties, if any, have been agreed, or

10.1.4 7 days after the Underwriters hereon have given notice of cancellation in respect of such risks.

10.2 Cancellation in accordance with Clauses 10.1.3 and 10.1.4 shall become effective on the expiry of 7 days from midnight on the day on which the notice of cancellation is given. The Underwriters agree however to reinstate this insurance subject to agreement between the Underwriters and the Assured prior to the expiry of such notice of cancellation as to new rate of premium and/or conditions and/or warranties.

This clause applies only to those risks covered by the War and Strikes policies taken out on the insured vessel. The effect of the clause is similar to the Termination Clause contained in the Institute War and Strikes Clauses, Hulls —Time (Clause 5 in the 1/10/83 form or Clause 6 in the 1/11/95 form); see page 314.

PART VI

WAR AND STRIKES RISKS FORMS

1. HISTORICAL PERSPECTIVE

From men of war to the terrorists of today

If we look at the list of perils which by Lloyd's form of policy the underwriters were "contented to bear and do take upon us in this voyage", we find that prominence is given to the warlike and hostile acts which might befall the adventure. Those perils were:

> " . . . of the seas, *men of war*, fire, *enemies, pirates, rovers, thieves*, jettisons, *letters of mart and countermart, surprisals, takings at sea, arrests, restraints, and detainments of all Kings, Princes and people, of what nation, condition, or quality so ever*, barratry of the Master and Mariners, and of all other perils, losses, and misfortunes, that have or shall come to the hurt, detriment, or damage of the said goods and merchandises, and ship, etc., or any part thereof". (Emphasis added by the editor)

After reading this list it is not difficult to appreciate how hazardous a maritime adventure was in the days when Lloyd's form of policy was evolving, and how much of that hazard arose from the hostile acts of men. Of course, in those days every merchantman was armed, and the gunner was as important a member of the crew as the boatswain. Even so, a heavily laden merchantman was no match, either in sailing ability or fire power, for a man of war or a pirate cutter, and many were the losses which underwriters had to bear from these causes in the seventeenth and eighteenth centuries.

During the Napoleonic Wars both England and France came to appreciate the economic dimension of the conflict, and it was about this time that underwriters, wishing to exempt themselves from the consequences of economic blockade, began to insert into their policies of insurance the "free of capture and seizure" clause (or the F.C. & S. Clause, as it came to be known). Merchants who wanted this cover had to take out a separate insurance to cover the risks excluded by the F.C. & S. Clause, which would, of course, be rated separately by the underwriters prepared to run these risks, according to the best available intelligence as to the strength of the enemy's blockade.

During the American Civil War it became common to add to the F.C. & S. warranty " . . . all consequences of hostilities".[1] By the time of the First World War, the standard form of the F.C. & S. Clause had been extended to exclude the consequences, not only of hostilities, but also "war-like operations whether before or after declaration of war".

During both the First and Second World Wars, the ships requisitioned by the United Kingdom Government were engaged under charter-parties by which the Government bore the risks excluded by the F.C. & S. Clause, so that, in effect, the Government was the war risk underwriter for those vessels.

Many were the law cases finely argued as a result of casualties occurring during both World Wars, in order to decide whether or not the losses occurred "in consequence of hostilities or war-like operations". This line of legal authority culminated in the well-known case of *The "Coxwold"*, in which the House of Lords held that the stranding of the vessel near a dimmed light, whilst steaming on a course set by the naval officer in charge of a convoy, was the consequence of a war-like operation. This decision was considered by many to have upset the balance between marine and war risk underwriters, to the extent that the F.C. & S. Clause should be further revised. This was done, and the form of words in use from 1943, and for some forty years thereafter, read as follows:

> "Warranted free of capture, seizure, arrest, restraint or detainment, and the consequences thereof or of any attempt thereat; also from the consequences of hostilities or warlike operations, whether there be a declaration of war or not; but this warranty shall not exclude collision, contact with any fixed or floating object (other than a mine or torpedo), stranding, heavy weather or fire unless caused directly (and independently of the nature of the voyage or service which the vessel concerned or, in the case of a collision, any other vessel involved therein, is performing) by a hostile act by or against a belligerent power; and for the purpose of this warranty 'power' includes any authority maintaining naval, military or air forces in association with a power. Further warranted free from the consequences of civil war, revolution, rebellion, insurrection, or civil strife arising therefrom, or piracy."

It has to be observed that the reinstatement of the risks excluded by the F.C. & S. Clause, if this is all that is undertaken by the war risks policy, merely reverts to the cover granted by Lloyd's S.G. form. It does not enlarge the risks in any way. In order to meet this, it became usual for war risk insurances to express the cover granted in two different ways, viz.:

— the risks excluded by the F.C. & S. Clause, and
— the "positive" cover.

An example of a clause providing such positive cover was:

1. As to the meaning of this term, see *Ionides* v. *Universal Marine Insurance Co.* (1863) 10 Jur. (N.S.) 18, and the remarks of Lord Wright in *Yorkshire Dale Steamship Co. Ltd* v. *Minister of War Transport (The "Coxwold")* (1942) 73 Ll.L.Rep. 1.

"This insurance covers loss of or damage to the property hereby insured caused by—
(a) hostilities, warlike operations, civil war, revolution, rebellion, insurrection or civil strife arising therefrom;
(b) mines, torpedoes, bombs or other engines of war."

The new clauses introduced in 1982 and 1983 have done away with all this convoluted draftsmanship. The risks covered by the War Clauses are described in new terms. Gone entirely are "the consequences of hostilities or warlike operations", and so, at a stroke, all the law cases and learned commentaries dealing with the interpretation of those words have become merely of academic interest.

To complete our historical review, insurance is now available to cover loss or damage caused by terrorists—although, rather oddly so far as cargo insurances are concerned, the cover is provided not under the War Clauses, but under the Strikes Clauses. So, before looking at the clauses in detail, we note that, for reasons which will shortly appear, there are separate forms for War Risks and for Strikes Risks so far as goods are concerned, whereas for hulls both War and Strikes Risks are covered under the same policy form.

2. CARGO INSURANCES

The reason, in the London insurance market, that insurances on goods are covered by different forms for war risks and for strikes risks is something of an anomaly. This is because of an agreement between various underwriters in the London market relating to transit insurances, called the "Waterborne Agreement", whereby underwriters in the marine market will not in general cover war risks in respect of goods on land. Thus the Transit Clause, which regulates the duration of the risk, differs according to the risks which are covered.

This distinction does not apply to the covers available for hulls and for freight.

A. INSTITUTE WAR CLAUSES (CARGO) 1/1/82

RISKS COVERED

The risks covered by this form are set out in Clauses 1 and 2.

Clause 1—Risks Clause

1 This insurance covers, except as provided in Clauses 3 and 4 below, loss of or damage to the subject-matter insured caused by
1.1 war civil war revolution rebellion insurrection, or civil strife arising therefrom, or any hostile act by or against a belligerent power
1.2 capture seizure arrest restraint or detainment, arising from risks covered under 1.1 above, and the consequences thereof or any attempt thereat
1.3 derelict mines torpedoes bombs or other derelict weapons of war.

"war"

"War" involves the employment of force between states or entities having, at least *de facto*, the characteristic of a state. In some respects the fact that a state of war has been declared may be significant, for example by rendering illegal the voyage by a ship carrying goods belonging to the declared enemy—see *British & Foreign Marine Insurance Co.* v. *Sanday.*[2] As Lord Wrenbury said in that case:

> "A declaration of war by the Sovereign is a political or executive act, done by virtue of his prerogative, which creates a state of war. A state of war is a lawful state, and is one in which every subject of his Majesty becomes an enemy of the nation against which war is declared."

However, a declaration of war is no longer (if it ever was) an essential ingredient: an undeclared war may exist *de facto* between sovereign states, as it can between quasi-sovereign entities. For example, the invasion of China by Japanese armies in 1937 was held in *Kawasaki K.K.K.* v. *Bantham Steamship Co.*[3] to amount to an outbreak of war within a clause of a charter-party entitling the shipowner to cancel the charter, even though there was no declaration of war and both countries continued to maintain diplomatic relations with each other.

In comparison with the old forms of war risk clauses, the term "war" by itself may be narrower than "hostilities", but not greatly so. As Lord Atkinson said in *Britain Steamship Co.* v. *The King*[4]: "hostilities connotes the idea of belligerents, properly so called, enemy nations at war with one another". Accordingly, when "war" is considered together with the other perils listed in this Clause 1.1, the total effect is probably much the same as "consequences of hostilities" under the old form of words, as construed by the English courts.[5]

"civil war", "revolution", "rebellion", "insurrection"

In the context of a commercial contract, such as a policy of marine insurance, these expressions bear their ordinary "business" meaning.[6]

"Civil war" denotes the state of hostilities between different sections or groups in the same state, each exercising at least quasi-governmental authority. During the Spanish Civil War, in a case involving the requisition of trawlers and the confiscation of their gear by an organised body known as the "Basque Militia", the House of Lords concluded that the loss of the trawlers and their gear was proximately caused by "civil war", and it was said that "the word

2. (1916) 21 Com.Cas. 154.
3. (1939) 44 Com.Cas. 170.
4. [1921] 1 A.C. 99.
5. See the interesting discussion on the interpretation of the word "consequences" in *Templeman on Marine Insurance*, 5th edn., at p. 172, and the cases there cited.
6. *National Oil Co. of Zimbabwe* v. *Sturge* [1991] 2 Lloyd's Rep. 281, *per* Saville J.

'war' in a policy of insurance includes civil war unless the context makes it clear that a different meaning should be given to the word".[7]

In inverse order the words "revolution", "rebellion" and "insurrection" suggest a rising scale in the development of civil disorder. In an American case involving the hijacking of an airliner by two avowed members of the Popular Front for the Liberation of Palestine,[8] counsel and the court agreed that if the loss had not been caused by an "insurrection", then it could not have been caused by a rebellion or a revolution. In that case it was held that the word "insurrection" meant a violent uprising by a group or movement acting for the specific purpose of overthrowing the constituted government and seizing its powers.

"Rebellion" and "revolution" are terms so similar that one may need to go to a dictionary to ascertain what distinction there is between them. The *Universal English Dictionary* offers the following:

> "Rebellion:—A state of organised armed and open resistance against the authority and Government or Sovereign of the country to which one is in allegiance; distinguished from Civil War, usually by the smaller number of the rebels."
>
> "Revolution:—Complete subversion of established political authority and establishment of a new form of government; overthrow of existing political conditions."

One is tempted to sum this up by saying that a rebellion becomes a revolution at the moment it becomes successful.

In *National Oil Co.* v. *Sturge*, Saville J. observed that "rebellion" and "insurrection" also have somewhat similar meanings to each other, but he categorised them thus: "each means an organised and violent internal uprising in a country with, as a main purpose, the object of trying to overthrow or supplant the government of that country, though 'insurrection' denotes a lesser degree of organisation and size than 'rebellion' ".

"civil strife arising therefrom"

These words cover civil strife or unrest which arises in consequence of any of the preceding risks. They have to be contrasted with "riots or civil commotions", for which cover is provided in the Institute Strikes Clauses (Cargo). In practice the dividing line may be hard to find between civil strife arising from an insurrection and a civil commotion which does not. It is submitted that the factor which would bring the loss within the War Clauses is the existence of an intent on the part of the rebels or insurrectionists to overthrow the established government. So in the case of loss or damage by looters, one would have to enquire into the reason for the breakdown of law and order, and if that had

7. *Pesquarias y Secaderos de Bacalao de Espana* v. *Beer* (1949) 82 Ll.L.Rep. 501.
8. *Pan American World Airways Inc.* v. *The Aetna Casualty & Surety Co.* [1975] 1 Lloyd's Rep. 77.

arisen, say in consequence of a severe bombing attack by an enemy or an attempt by a group of people to overthrow the government, the loss would fall under the War Clauses.

"any hostile act by or against a belligerent power"

These words are a great deal narrower than the words which they replace, "hostilities or warlike operations", on the interpretation of which so much legal energy had been expended in past years. They are probably narrower even than "hostilities" alone, since to bring a claim within these words it would have to be shown:

(a) that the loss or damage had been proximately caused by an act (that is to say, some action on the part of somebody),
(b) which was "hostile" (which may or may not involve a question of intent),
(c) directed either by or against a "power" which is "belligerent".

"Power" includes a state and probably also an entity exercising quasi-governmental authority.

"Belligerent" has not yet been defined in this context. The expression has two possible meanings, one restricted, and one much wider. A restricted definition is provided in the *Dictionary of English Law*: " . . . carrying on war according to the law of nations". In vernacular usage, the term probably applies to anyone engaged in armed conflict.

However, the use of the words "by or against" does ensure that the property of neutrals which are subject to armed attack either by the forces of a State at war, or of one in opposition to it, is protected by the clause.

"1.2 capture seizure arrest restraint or detainment, arising from risks covered under 1.1 above, and the consequences thereof or any attempt thereat"

"capture" and "seizure"

In *Cory* v. *Burr*[9] Lord Fitzgerald said:

> "In the construction of this warranty [the F.C. & S. Clause] it is observable that capture and seizure do not mean the same thing. 'Capture' would seem properly to include every act of seizing or taking by an enemy or belligerent. 'Seizure' seems to be a larger term than 'capture', and goes beyond it, and may reasonably be interpreted to embrace every act of taking forcible possession, either by a lawful authority, or by overpowering force."

In that case, a ship was seized by the Spanish Revenue Authorities because the

9. (1883) 5 Asp.M.L.C. 109.

Master was barratrously engaged in smuggling. The House of Lords held that this was a "seizure" in terms of the F.C. & S. clause. It is, however, to be noted that a loss of cargo from the same cause would not give rise to a claim under the present Institute War Clauses (Cargo), since the seizure would not have arisen from one of the risks covered under Clause 1.1

"arrest", "restraint" or "detainment"

In Lloyd's form of policy these perils were described by the words "arrests, restraints and detainments of all Kings, Princes, and people, of what nation, condition or quality so ever . . . ". In the Rules for Construction of Policy contained in the Marine Insurance Act 1906, Rule 10 states "the term 'arrests, etc. of Kings, Princes and people' refers to political or executive acts, and does not include a loss caused by riot or by ordinary judicial process".

It is settled law that the arrest or restraint does not have to be accompanied by force. In *British & Foreign Marine Insurance Co.* v. *Sanday*,[10] goods insured under a policy covering war risks were held to be a constructive total loss by "restraint of Princes", when, being loaded on a British ship, they were diverted from their original destination (Hamburg) and taken to a port in the United Kingdom, in consequence of the declaration of war between Great Britain and Germany. As Lord Atkinson said, "the declaration carries with it all the force of a law prohibiting intercourse with the enemy save with licence of the Sovereign. It has the executive forces of the Crown behind it to enforce obedience to it."

Likewise, in *Miller* v. *Law Accident Insurance Co.*,[11] the restraint consisted merely of a general decree of the Argentine Government prohibiting the landing of cattle from the United Kingdom at any Argentine port: " . . . the issuing of the decree . . . was an act of State and comes within the words within the body of the policy . . . ".

"arising from risks covered under 1.1 above"

These are new words of qualification which limit the cover in respect of capture, etc. to instances which arise as a result of the war or "war-like" perils listed in Clause 1.1. For example, in the cases referred to above, it will be seen that in *Sanday*'s case the restraint arose from the declaration of war, whereas in *Miller*'s case the restraint had nothing to do with war or any of the risks now covered in Clause 1.1.

10. (1916) 21 Com.Cas. 154.
11. (1903) 8 Com.Cas. 161.

"and the consequences thereof or any attempt thereat"

In the previous forms of the F.C. & S. and War Risks Clauses these words appeared in juxtaposition to "capture, seizure, arrest, restraint or detainment", which risks they qualify and expand. Despite their now being separated by the intervening phrase "arising from etc . . . " they should receive the same interpretation.

"1.3 derelict mines torpedoes bombs or other derelict weapons of war"

These words replace "mines, torpedoes, bombs or other engines of war", which were the words appearing in previous forms of War Risks Clauses. The word "derelict" has presumably been added in order to reverse the effect of the decision in *Costain-Blankevoort (U.K.) Dredging Co.* v. *Davenport*,[12] in which it was held that damage sustained by a dredger which sucked up ammunition which had been dumped after the end of the Second World War was not the consequence of a "warlike operation".

So, if derelict engines of war are within the cover granted by the Institute War Clauses, can it be said that all loss or damage caused by an active engine of war will also be covered, as was the case under the previous clauses? Alas, this appears not to be so. On the contrary, it appears to be necessary to enquire by whom or on whose orders the mine was sown, the torpedo fired or the bomb thrown. If that arose in the course of a war or as a result of one of the "war-like" perils listed in Clause 1.1, the claim will be covered by the War Clauses; conversely, if the weapon had been discharged in the course of a civil commotion (not amounting to an insurrection) or, say, by a terrorist, then, as we shall see, there will be a claim under the Institute Strikes Clauses.

Clause 2—General Average Clause

2 This insurance covers general average and salvage charges, adjusted or determined according to the contract of affreightment and/or the governing law and practice, incurred to avoid or in connection with the avoidance of loss from a risk covered under these clauses.

This clause is very similar to the General Average Clause contained in the Institute Cargo Clauses (A), (B) and (C), but it must be observed that the cover is, of course, limited to general average and salvage charges incurred in order to avoid a loss which would fall within the War Clauses.

An interesting old case[13] illustrates a general average sacrifice made in order to avoid a loss by capture. The Master of a ship being pursued by an enemy extinguished the ship's lights at nightfall, and instead placed a light upon

12. (*The "Nassau Bay"*) [1979] 1 Lloyd's Rep. 395.
13. Cited in Emerigon, *Des Assurances et des Contrats a La Grosse*, c. xii, s. 41, p. 606.

the masthead of the ship's boat, which he set adrift in a different direction: the enemy chased the empty boat, and the ship got away.

For the meaning of the words "adjusted or determined according to the contract of affreightment and/or the governing law and practice", see the commentary under Clause 2 of the Institute Cargo Clauses (A), above on pages 17 and 18.

EXCLUSIONS

The exclusions are contained in Clauses 3 and 4.

Clause 3—General Exclusions Clause

3 In no case shall this insurance cover

3.1 loss damage or expense attributable to wilful misconduct of the Assured

3.2 ordinary leakage, ordinary loss in weight or volume, or ordinary wear and tear of the subject-matter insured

3.3 loss damage or expense caused by insufficiency or unsuitability of packing or preparation of the subject-matter insured (for the purpose of this Clause 3.3 "packing" shall be deemed to include stowage in a container or liftvan but only when such stowage is carried out prior to attachment of this insurance or by the Assured or their servants)

3.4 loss damage or expense caused by inherent vice or nature of the subject-matter insured

3.5 loss damage or expense proximately caused by delay, even though the delay be caused by a risk insured against (except expenses payable under Clause 2 above)

3.6 loss damage or expense arising from insolvency or financial default of the owners managers charterers or operators of the vessel

3.7 any claim based upon loss of or frustration of the voyage or adventure

3.8 loss damage or expense arising from any hostile use of any weapon of war employing atomic or nuclear fission and/or fusion or other like reaction or radioactive force or matter.

The first six of these exclusions correspond with the exclusions contained in Institute Cargo Clauses, as follows:

Exclusions per Institute War Clauses (Cargo) and Institute Strikes Clauses (Cargo)		*Exclusions per Institute Cargo Clauses (A), (B) and (C)*
3.1	corresponds to	4.1
3.2		4.2
3.3		4.3
3.4		4.4
3.5		4.5
3.6		4.6

For commentary, see the observations under the Institute Cargo Clauses (A) on pages 19 to 22 above.

Exclusions which do not appear in the Institute Cargo Clauses

"3.7 any claim based upon loss of or frustration of the voyage or adventure"

In the words of Lord Wright, this clause was "undoubtedly invented from a desire to abrogate the effect of *Sanday*'s case where only the adventure was affected by the peril, the goods being unaffected". *Sanday*'s case[14] is commented upon on page 289, and it will be remembered that the declaration of war operated to make the adventure *ipso facto* illegal; in other words, the restraint frustrated that adventure.

The clause will also have the effect of excluding such a claim as arose in the case of *Rodocanochi* v. *Elliott*.[15] In that case goods were insured from the Far East to the United Kingdom, with an overland transit through France. The goods got as far as Paris at about the time when that city became invested by the Prussian army in 1870, with the result that it became impossible to remove the goods from Paris and send them on to their destination. It was held that their detention within Paris was brought about "by the immediate and direct action of the German army", and since "this was not a mere retardation of the voyage, but a breaking up of the whole adventure" the assured was entitled to abandon the goods to the underwriters and claim for a constructive total loss.

However, the words of Clause 3.7 do *not* mean that any claim which involves the loss or frustration of the voyage or adventure will be excluded. The exception applies only to claims which are "*based upon*" such loss or frustration, that is to say, such claims as, in the absence of the exclusion, would only be recoverable by virtue of a loss or frustration of the voyage. So, in a set of test cases which were taken to the House of Lords in 1941, it was held that when goods on board a number of German ships were diverted from their voyages by the actions of the German captains obeying the orders of their Government, there was a physical restraint upon the goods as well as a loss of adventure.[16] Lord Wright said: "What happened here was that the master, being in possession of the goods as a carrier . . . seized them in the sense that he ceased to hold them as carrier and changed the character of his possession by taking and controlling them as agent for the German Government . . . ". Thus, despite the inclusion of the "frustration clause" in the War Risk insurances, the owners of the goods were able to recover for their loss in each case.

"3.8 loss damage or expense arising from any hostile use of any weapon of war employing atomic or nuclear fission and/or fusion or other like reaction or radioactive force or matter"

The wording of this clause differs from the atomic/nuclear weapon exclusion contained in the Institute Cargo Clauses, Institute Strikes Clauses (Cargo) and other similar forms, but only by the inclusion of the one additional word "hostile". This would seem to suggest that a loss by a "non-hostile" use of such a weapon, such as by its explosion whilst being deployed by friendly

14. (1916) 21 Com.Cas. 154.
15. (1874) 2 Asp.M.L.C. 399.
16. *Middows Ltd.* v. *Robertson* and other cases (H.L.) (1941) 70 Ll.L.Rep. 173.

forces, would result in a claim for which underwriters under the Institute War Clauses (Cargo) would respond.

Clause 4—Unseaworthiness and Unfitness Exclusion Clause

4 4.1 In no case shall this insurance cover loss damage or expense arising from
unseaworthiness of vessel or craft,
unfitness of vessel craft conveyance container or liftvan for the safe carriage of the subject-matter insured,
where the Assured or their servants are privy to such unseaworthiness or unfitness, at the time the subject-matter insured is loaded therein.
4.2 The Underwriters waive any breach of the implied warranties of seaworthiness of the ship and fitness of the ship to carry the subject-matter insured to destination, unless the Assured or their servants are privy to such unseaworthiness or unfitness.

The wording of the clause and its effect is the same as Clause 5 of the Institute Cargo Clauses (A), (B) and (C). See commentary on page 23.

DURATION

Clause 5—Transit Clause

5 5.1 This insurance
5.1.1 attaches only as the subject-matter insured and as to any part as that part is loaded on an oversea vessel
and
5.1.2 terminates, subject to 5.2 and 5.3 below, either as the subject-matter insured and as to any part as that part is discharged from an oversea vessel at the final port or place of discharge,
or
on expiry of 15 days counting from midnight of the day of arrival of the vessel at the final port or place of discharge,
whichever shall first occur;
nevertheless,
subject to prompt notice to the Underwriters and to an additional premium, such insurance
5.1.3 reattaches when, without having discharged the subject-matter insured at the final port or place of discharge, the vessel sails therefrom,
and
5.1.4 terminates, subject to 5.2 and 5.3 below, either as the subject-matter insured and as to any part as that part is thereafter discharged from the vessel at the final (or substituted) port or place of discharge,
or
on expiry of 15 days counting from midnight of the day of re-arrival of the vessel at the final port or place of discharge or arrival of the vessel at a substituted port or place of discharge, whichever shall first occur.
5.2 If during the insured voyage the oversea vessel arrives at an intermediate port or place to discharge the subject-matter insured for on-carriage by oversea vessel or by aircraft, or the goods are discharged from the vessel at a port or place of refuge, then, subject to 5.3 below and to an additional premium if required, this insurance continues until the expiry of 15 days counting from midnight of the day of arrival of the vessel at such port or place, but thereafter reattaches as the subject-matter insured and as to any part as that part is loaded on an on-carrying oversea vessel or aircraft. During the period of 15 days the insurance remains in force after discharge only whilst the subject-matter insured and as to any part as that part is at such port or place. If the goods are on-carried within the said period of 15 days or if the insurance reattaches as provided in this Clause 5.2
5.2.1 where the on-carriage is by oversea vessel this insurance continues subject to the terms of these clauses,
or
5.2.2 where the on-carriage is by aircraft, the current Institute War Clauses (Air Cargo) (excluding sendings by Post) shall be deemed to form part of this insurance and shall apply to the on-carriage by air.
5.3 If the voyage in the contract of carriage is terminated at a port or place other than the destination agreed therein, such port or place shall be deemed the final port of discharge and such insurance terminates in accordance with 5.1.2. If the subject-matter insured is subsequently reshipped to the

original or any other destination, then *provided notice is given to the Underwriters before the commencement of such further transit and subject to an additional premium*, such insurance reattaches

5.3.1 in the case of the subject-matter insured having been discharged as the subject-matter insured and as to any part as that part is loaded on the on-carrying vessel for the voyage;

5.3.2 in the case of the subject-matter not having been discharged, when the vessel sails from such deemed final port of discharge;

thereafter such insurance terminates in accordance with 5.1.4.

5.4 The insurance against the risks of mines and derelict torpedoes, floating or submerged, is extended whilst the subject-matter insured or any part thereof is on craft whilst in transit to or from the oversea vessel, but in no case beyond the expiry of 60 days after discharge from the oversea vessel unless otherwise specially agreed by the Underwriters.

5.5 *Subject to prompt notice to Underwriters, and to an additional premium if required*, this insurance shall remain in force within the provisions of these Clauses during any deviation, or any variation of the adventure arising from the exercise of a liberty granted to shipowners or charterers under the contract of affreightment.

(For the purpose of Clause 5
"arrival" shall be deemed to mean that the vessel is anchored, moored or otherwise secured at a berth or place within the Harbour Authority area. If such a berth or place is not available, arrival is deemed to have occurred when the vessel first anchors, moors or otherwise secures either at or off the intended port or place of discharge
"oversea vessel" shall be deemed to mean a vessel carrying the subject-matter from one port or place to another where such voyage involves a sea passage by that vessel)

This clause, although it appears to be extremely complicated, says little more than that the risk does not attach until the goods are loaded on to the overseas steamer and does not extend beyond 15 days after arrival of the vessel at the final port or place of discharge. Furthermore, if there is a discharge of the goods at an intermediate port or place (even a port or place of refuge), the assured can obtain continuation of the cover (under this insurance) only on payment of an additional premium if required.

The same applies in the event that the contract of carriage is terminated at a port or place other than the destination named in the bill of lading or charter-party. The provision in Clause 5.3 is in this respect to be contrasted with the terms of Clause 9 of the Institute Cargo Clauses—see page 28.

Re-attachment of the insurance is provided for:

— after discharge at an intermediate port or place, on loading into either the original or a forwarding vessel;
— after discharge at a port or place where the contract of carriage is terminated, on reshipment to an on-carrying vessel, but only if notice is given to the underwriters "before the commencement of such further transit" and subject to an additional premium. It is not entirely clear what is intended by the words "before the commencement of such further transit". However, if it had been intended to mean prior to reshipment, it would have been much simpler to say so, and it is therefore submitted by the editor that the words employed imply that the notice is to be given before the on-carrying vessel sails.

Clause 5.4 provides for an extension of the risks of "mines and derelict torpedoes, floating or submerged" whilst the goods are on craft in transit to or from the ocean steamer: in transit to the ocean steamer there is no limitation on the period of extension, but the period of extension whilst in transit from the ocean steamer to destination will not extend beyond 60 days after discharge from the ocean steamer unless the underwriters specially agree. It is to be noted that the risks for which this extension of time is granted are not precisely the same as the perils listed in Clause 1.3.

Clause 5.5 is more stringent than the corresponding clause in the Institute Cargo Clauses (Clause 8.3), and requires prompt notice to be given to the underwriters, and payment of an additional premium if required, for continuation of the cover in the event of a deviation or any variation of the adventure arising from the exercise of the liberty granted to the carrier under the contract of affreightment.

Clause 6—Change of Voyage Clause

6 Where, after attachment of this insurance, the destination is changed by the Assured, *held covered at a premium and on conditions to be arranged subject to prompt notice being given to the Underwriters.*

This clause is the same as Clause 10 in the Institute Cargo Clauses and, like that clause, it is considerably more restricted than its predecessor which, subject to prompt notice and an additional premium, held the assured covered in the event of a change of voyage by the shipowner or carrier—see pages 28 and 29.

Clause 7

7 **Anything contained in this contract which is inconsistent with Clauses 3.7, 3.8 or 5 shall, to the extent of such inconsistency, be null and void.**

This clause is printed in bold type to draw attention to it. It is of the type of clause called a "Clause Paramount" which is intended to prevail notwithstanding anything to the contrary. The protected clauses are exclusions 3.7 and 3.8, and also the Transit Clause (Clause 5), variation of the terms of which would breach the "Waterborne Agreement".

CLAIMS

Clause 8—Insurable Interest Clause

8 **8.1** In order to recover under this insurance the Assured must have an insurable interest in the subject-matter insured at the time of the loss.

8.2 Subject to 8.1 above, the Assured shall be entitled to recover for insured loss occurring during the period covered by this insurance, notwithstanding that the loss occurred before the contract of insurance was concluded, unless the Assured were aware of the loss and the Underwriters were not.

This clause is the same as Clause 11 in the Institute Cargo Clauses. See commentary on page 30.

Clause 9—Increased Value Clause

9 **9.1** If any Increased Value insurance is effected by the Assured on the cargo insured herein the agreed value of the cargo shall be deemed to be increased to the total amount insured under this insurance and all Increased Value insurances covering the loss, and liability under this insurance shall be in such proportion as the sum insured herein bears to such total amount insured.

In the event of claim the Assured shall provide the Underwriters with evidence of the amounts insured under all other insurances.

9.2 **Where this insurance is on Increased Value the following clause shall apply:**
The agreed value of the cargo shall be deemed to be equal to the total amount insured under the primary insurance and all Increased Value insurances covering the loss and effected on the cargo by the Assured, and liability under this insurance shall be in such proportion as the sum insured herein bears to such total amount insured.
In the event of claim the Assured shall provide the Underwriters with evidence of the amounts insured under all other insurances.

This clause is the same as Clause 14 in the Institute Cargo Clauses. See commentary on page 34.

Clause 10—Not to Inure Clause

10 This insurance shall not inure to the benefit of the carrier or other bailee.

This is the standard clause found in all cargo insurances.

Clause 11—Duty of Assured Clause

11 It is the duty of the Assured and their servants and agents in respect of loss recoverable hereunder
11.1 to take such measures as may be reasonable for the purpose of averting or minimising such loss, and
11.2 to ensure that all rights against carriers, bailees or other third parties are properly preserved and exercised
and the Underwriters will, in addition to any loss recoverable hereunder, reimburse the Assured for any charges properly and reasonably incurred in pursuance of these duties.

This clause is in the same terms as Clause 16 of the Institute Cargo Clauses. However, it has to be borne in mind that underwriters will only reimburse the assured under this insurance for expenses incurred under this clause "in respect of loss recoverable hereunder", that is to say, in connection with a claim brought about by one of the "war perils" listed in Clause 1.

As to the clause generally, see the commentaries on pages 34 to 37 and 48.

Clause 12—Waiver Clause

12 Measures taken by the Assured or the Underwriters with the object of saving, protecting or recovering the subject-matter insured shall not be considered as a waiver or acceptance of abandonment or otherwise prejudice the rights of either party.

This is the same as Clause 17 in the Institute Cargo Clauses. See commentary on page 37.

AVOIDANCE OF DELAY

Clause 13—Reasonable Despatch Clause

13 It is a condition of this insurance that the Assured shall act with reasonable despatch in all circumstances within their control.

This is the same as Clause 18 in the Institute Cargo Clauses. It is of considerable antiquity and its purpose is self-evident.

LAW AND PRACTICE

Clause 14—English Law and Practice Clause

14 This insurance is subject to English law and practice.

This clause appears in all the new standard forms of cargo insurance. See commentary on page 38.

There then follows the Note which appears at the foot of all the standard forms for cargo insurances (also reviewed on page 38):

NOTE:—It is necessary for the Assured when they become aware of an event which is "held covered" under this insurance to give prompt notice to the Underwriters and the right to such cover is dependent upon compliance with this obligation.

B. INSTITUTE STRIKES CLAUSES (CARGO) 1/1/82

RISKS COVERED

The risks covered by this form are set out in Clauses 1 and 2.

Clause 1—Risks Clause

1 This insurance covers, except as provided in Clauses 3 and 4 below, loss of or damage to the subject-matter insured caused by
- **1.1** strikers, locked-out workmen, or persons taking part in labour disturbances, riots or civil commotions
- **1.2** any terrorist or any person acting from a political motive.

"strikers, locked-out workmen, or persons taking part in labour disturbances"

These words, it is submitted, have to be construed in the ordinary everyday sense in which they are understood. If this is correct, then perhaps the daily newspapers will provide us with a better illustration of the risks covered by these words than would be available from any academic analysis of them.

Conversely, it would seem from the recent case of *Athens Maritime Enterprises Corporation* v. *Hellenic Mutual War Risks Association*[17] that the term "riots" has to be construed as a term of art. Following previous authority, the learned judge in that case adopted the definition of a riot set out in *Field* v. *The Receiver of Metropolitan Police*,[18] which was as follows:

"In order to constitute a riot five elements are necessary—
1. A number of persons not less than three;
2. A common purpose;
3. Execution or inception of the common purpose;
4. An intent on the part of the number of persons to help one another, by force if necessary, against any person who may oppose them in the execution of the common purpose;

17. (*The "Andreas Lemos"*) [1982] 2 Lloyd's Rep. 483.
18. [1907] 2 K.B. 853, *per* Phillimore J. at p. 860.

5. Force or violence, not merely used in and about the common purpose, but displayed in such a manner as to alarm at least one person of reasonable firmness and courage."

This highly technical definition has not commended itself to the courts in the United States of America. In *Pan American World Airways Inc.* v. *The Aetna Casualty and Surety Co.* the U.S. Court of Appeals, without deciding the matter, remarked that, in accordance with some of the authorities, a common law riot must be accompanied by tumult or commotion, and that there was also a respectable body of opinion that in insurance policies the term "riot" takes its meaning from common speech, in the sense of a tumultuous assembly of a multitude of people.

While noting the tendency to divergence between the opinions expressed in recent cases in England and the United States of America, it must be borne in mind that this insurance is, by Clause 14, subject to English law and practice, and consequently for the purpose of interpreting the word "riots" in this insurance, the rule in *Field's case* will, for the time being, prevail.

"civil commotions"

In a recent case it was held that a civil commotion need not involve a revolt against the Government, but there must be disturbances with sufficient cohesion to prevent them from being the work of a "mindless mob".[19] At the same time it was recognised that a "civil commotion" borders very closely on an "insurrection", but in the case referred to, the learned judge was not obliged to make this distinction. If such a borderline case were to arise under the terms of the Institute Strikes Clauses (Cargo), the distinction would have to be made, the more particularly since "insurrection" is specifically excluded under Clause 3.10.

"1.2 Any terrorist or any person acting from a political motive"

These words replace the rather vague expression which appeared in the previous clauses, namely "persons acting maliciously".

"terrorist"

One may be tempted to believe that anyone may recognise a terrorist from his actions, particularly in today's climate of "terrorist" activities. There have been recent cases involving loss and damage caused by terrorists,[20] but, unfortunately from the point of view of legal definition, the word "terrorist"

19. *Spinney's* v. *Royal Insurance* [1980] 1 Lloyd's Rep. 406, *per* Mustill J.
20. For example, see *Pan American World Airways Inc.* v. *The Aetna Casualty & Surety Co.* [1975] 1 Lloyd's Rep. 77.

did not appear in the policy conditions, either as a peril insured or excluded.

"any person acting from a political motive"

This covers the phenomenon of the "gentle terrorist", who does not wish to do anyone any harm, but wishes merely to demonstrate his objection to somebody or editor has some cause by doing some physical damage to some property associated with the object of his objection. The editor has some knowledge of this class of case, having dealt with claims for damage to a ship and her cargo on board caused by a refugee group having placed a bomb against the side of the ship.

Clause 2—General Average Clause

2 This insurance covers general average and salvage charges, adjusted or determined according to the contract of affreightment and/or the governing law and practice, incurred to avoid or in connection with the avoidance of loss from a risk covered under these clauses.

In order to constitute a claim under these clauses, the general average act or the salvage service must be performed with the object of avoiding a loss from one of the perils insured in Clause 1. For general observations on the subject of general average and salvage, and the meaning of the words "adjusted or determined" and "according to the contract of affreightment and/or the governing law and practice", see the commentary under the Institute Cargo Clauses (A) on pages 17 and 18.

EXCLUSIONS

The exclusions are contained in Clauses 3 and 4.

Clause 3—General Exclusions Clause

3 In no case shall this insurance cover

3.1 loss damage or expense attributable to wilful misconduct of the Assured

3.2 ordinary leakage, ordinary loss in weight or volume, or ordinary wear and tear of the subject-matter insured

3.3 loss damage or expense caused by insufficiency or unsuitability of packing or preparation of the subject-matter insured (for the purpose of this Clause 3.3 "packing" shall be deemed to include stowage in a container or liftvan but only when such stowage is carried out prior to attachment of this insurance or by the Assured or their servants)

3.4 loss damage or expense caused by inherent vice or nature of the subject-matter insured

3.5 loss damage or expense proximately caused by delay, even though the delay be caused by a risk insured against (except expenses payable under Clause 2 above)

3.6 loss damage or expense arising from insolvency or financial default of the owners managers charterers or operators of the vessel

3.7 loss damage or expense arising from the absence shortage or withholding of labour of any description whatsoever resulting from any strike, lockout, labour disturbance, riot or civil commotion

3.8 any claim based upon loss of or frustration of the voyage or adventure

3.9 loss damage or expense arising from the use of any weapon of war employing atomic or nuclear fission and/or fusion or other like reaction or radioactive force or matter

3.10 loss damage or expense caused by war civil war revolution rebellion insurrection, or civil strife arising therefrom, or any hostile act by or against a belligerent power.

The first six of these exclusions (Clauses 3.1–3.6 inclusive) are the same as those which appear in the Institute Cargo Clauses (A) (B) and (C). See the commentary on pages 19 to 22.

Clause 3.7 is specific to the Strikes Clauses. The same words appeared in previous forms, and they make it clear that, while the insurance will pay for loss or damage caused by the violent behaviour of strikers, the underwriters will not respond for any claim which arises merely from the withdrawal of the strikers' labour. So, for example, if workmen, about to shift goods from the quay into a warehouse, are called out on strike, and as a result the goods left on the quayside sustain damage in consequence of their exposure to the elements, this is not such a loss or damage as is covered by the policy.

Exclusion 3.8 is common to both the War Clauses and the Strikes Clauses. For commentary see pages 291 to 292.

Exclusion 3.9 is one which appears in all Institute Clauses for cargo. See page 22.

Exclusion 3.10 is designed to take out the claims which would be covered by the Institute War Clauses. The meaning of the words in this exclusion is examined on pages 285 to 288, but it may be noted again how fine is the dividing line between a "civil commotion", the consequences of which are covered by the Institute Strikes Clauses, and an "insurrection", or civil strife arising from an insurrection, which is excluded from the Strikes Clauses but covered in the War Clauses. As stated above, it appears that the distinction lies in the motive of the insurgents. If their objective is the overthrow of the Government or some part of the established order, the claim will fall on the War Clauses, and if not, it will lie under the Strikes Clauses.

Clause 4—Unseaworthiness and Unfitness Exclusion Clause

4 4.1 In no case shall this insurance cover loss damage or expense arising from
unseaworthiness of vessel or craft,
unfitness of vessel craft conveyance container or liftvan for the safe carriage of this subject-matter insured,
where the Assured or their servants are privy to such unseaworthiness or unfitness, at the time the subject-matter insured is loaded therein.

4.2 The Underwriters waive any breach of the implied warranties of seaworthiness of the ship and fitness of the ship to carry the subject-matter insured to destination, unless the Assured or their servants are privy to such unseaworthiness or unfitness.

This clause is in the same terms as Clause 5 of the Institute Cargo Clauses. See commentary on page 23.

DURATION

Clauses 5, 6 and 7—Duration of the Risk, Termination of the Contract of Carriage and Change of Destination

5 5.1 This insurance attaches from the time the goods leave the warehouse or place of storage at the place named herein for the commencement of the transit, continues during the ordinary course of transit and terminates either

5.1.1 on delivery to the Consignees' or other final warehouse or place of storage at the destination named herein,
5.1.2 on delivery to any other warehouse or place of storage, whether prior to or at the destination named herein, which the Assured elect to use either
5.1.2.1 for storage other than in the ordinary course of transit or
5.1.2.2 for allocation or distribution,
or
5.1.3 on the expiry of 60 days after completion of discharge overside of the goods hereby insured from the oversea vessel at the final port of discharge,
whichever shall first occur.
5.2 If, after discharge overside from the oversea vessel at the final port of discharge, but prior to termination of this insurance, the goods are to be forwarded to a destination other than that to which they are insured hereunder, this insurance, whilst remaining subject to termination as provided for above, shall not extend beyond the commencement of transit to such other destination.
5.3 This insurance shall remain in force (subject to termination as provided for above and to the provisions of Clause 6 below) during delay beyond the control of the Assured, any deviation, forced discharge, reshipment or transhipment and during any variation of the adventure arising from the exercise of a liberty granted to shipowners or charterers under the contract of affreightment.

6 If owing to circumstances beyond the control of the Assured either the contract of carriage is terminated at a port or place other than the destination named therein or the transit is otherwise terminated before delivery of the goods as provided for in Clause 5 above, then this insurance shall also terminate *unless prompt notice is given to the Underwriters and continuation of cover is requested when the insurance shall remain in force, subject to an additional premium if required by the Underwriters*, either
6.1 until the goods are sold and delivered at such port or place, or, unless otherwise specially agreed, until the expiry of 60 days after arrival of the goods hereby insured at such port or place, whichever shall first occur,
or
6.2 if the goods are forwarded within the said period of 60 days (or any agreed extension thereof) to the destination named herein or to any other destination, until terminated in accordance with the provisions of Clause 5 above.

7 Where, after attachment of this insurance, the destination is changed by the Assured, *held covered at a premium and on conditions to be arranged subject to prompt notice being given to the Underwriters.*

These clauses are the same as Clauses 8, 9 and 10 in the Institute Cargo Clauses. See pages 25 to 29. Contrast, however, the restricted duration clauses which apply in the Institute War Clauses (Cargo) which are the subject of commentary on pages 294 to 295.

CLAIMS

Clause 8—Insurable Interest Clause

8 8.1 In order to recover under this insurance the Assured must have an insurable interest in the subject-matter insured at the time of the loss.
8.2 Subject to 8.1 above, the Assured shall be entitled to recover for insured loss occurring during the period covered by this insurance, notwithstanding that the loss occurred before the contract of insurance was concluded, unless the Assured were aware of the loss and the Underwriters were not.

This is the same as Clause 11 in the Institute Cargo Clauses. See page 30.

Clause 9—Increased Value Clause

9 9.1 If any Increased Value insurance is effected by the Assured on the cargo insured herein the agreed value of the cargo shall be deemed to be increased to the total amount insured under this insurance and all Increased Value insurances covering the loss, and liability under this insurance shall be in such proportion as the sum insured herein bears to such total amount insured.

In the event of claim the Assured shall provide the Underwriters with evidence of the amounts insured under all other insurances.

9.2 **Where this insurance is on Increased Value the following clause shall apply:**

The agreed value of the cargo shall be deemed to be equal to the total amount insured under the primary insurance and all Increased Value insurances covering the loss and effected on the cargo by the Assured, and liability under this insurance shall be in such proportion as the sum insured herein bears to such total amount insured.

In the event of claim the Assured shall provide the Underwriters with evidence of the amounts insured under all other insurances.

This clause is the same as Clause 14 in the Institute Cargo Clauses. See page 34.

BENEFIT OF INSURANCE

Clause 10—Not to Inure Clause

10 This insurance shall not inure to the benefit of the carrier or other bailee.

This is the same as Clause 15 in the Institute Cargo Clauses.

MINIMISING LOSSES

Clause 11—Duty of Assured Clause

11 It is the duty of the Assured and their servants and agents in respect of loss recoverable hereunder

11.1 to take such measures as may be reasonable for the purpose of averting or minimising such loss, and

11.2 to ensure that all rights against carriers, bailees or other third parties are properly preserved and exercised

and the Underwriters will, in addition to any loss recoverable hereunder, reimburse the Assured for any charges properly and reasonably incurred in pursuance of these duties.

While this clause is in the same terms as Clause 16 in the Institute Cargo Clauses, it has to be noted that the right of the assured to recover for the expenses reasonably incurred in averting or minimising a loss is restricted to those instances where the loss or damage averted or minimised has arisen, or would have arisen in consequence of the perils listed in Clause 1.

Bills of lading are frequently claused in such a way as to grant the shipowner or carrier a liberty to avoid calling at a strike-bound port and instead to discharge cargo at an alternative port where labour is working. This would constitute a permitted variation of the adventure under the contract of affreightment, and thus, by Clause 5.3, the insurance would remain in force without the assured having to give notice to the underwriters (as would be the case, under Clause 7, if it were the assured himself who had changed the destination). If, consequent upon the exercise of that liberty, the shipowner or carrier claims the extra cost of proceeding to the alternative port and discharging the cargo there, as a special charge on the goods concerned, will this be recoverable from the underwriters insuring those goods under the Institute Strikes Clauses (Cargo)?

It is submitted that the answer depends upon the conditions in the strike-bound port. If the withdrawal of labour is peaceful, then all that has been averted is a loss of time, and the assured's claim would be caught by exclusion 3.7 (see above). However, if there was such a condition of unrest in the strike-bound port that there was a real risk of loss or damage occurring in consequence of a "civil commotion" then the editor submits that a claim can properly be brought under this Clause 11 for the extra cost involved in diverting the cargo.

Clause 12—Waiver Clause

12 Measures taken by the Assured or the Underwriters with the object of saving, protecting or recovering the subject-matter insured shall not be considered as a waiver or acceptance of abandonment or otherwise prejudice the rights of either party.

This is the same as Clause 17 in the Institute Cargo Clauses.

Clause 13—Reasonable Despatch Clause

13 It is a condition of this insurance that the Assured shall act with reasonable despatch in all circumstances within their control.

This is the same as Clause 18 in the Institute Cargo Clauses.

Clause 14—English Law and Practice Clause

14 This insurance is subject to English law and practice.

This is the same as Clause 19 in the Institute Cargo Clauses. See commentary on page 38.

Under this is printed:

NOTE:—It is necessary for the Assured when they become aware of an event which is "held covered" under this insurance to give prompt notice to the Underwriters and the right to such cover is dependent upon compliance with this obligation.

This is the note which appears at the foot of all Institute Clauses covering goods. See the observations on page 38.

C. WAR AND STRIKES FORMS FOR PARTICULAR COMMODITIES

Appropriate forms have been created for the commodity trades by marrying the special terms agreed with those trades (see examples and commentary on pages 50 to 79) with the Institute War Clauses and the Institute Strikes Clauses.

Up to the time of writing, the following forms have been issued in their new (post 1/1/82) format:

Institute War Clauses (Commodity Trades)	5/9/83
Institute War Clauses (FOSFA Trades)	1/7/85
Institute Strikes Clauses (Coal)	1/10/82
Institute Strikes Clauses (Bulk Oil)	1/2/83
Institute Strikes Clauses (Commodity Trades)	5/9/83
Institute Strikes Clauses (Jute)	1/1/84
Institute Strikes Clauses (Natural Rubber)	1/1/84
Institute Strikes Clauses (FOSFA Trades)	1/7/85
Institute Strikes Clauses (Frozen Food)	1/1/86
Institute Strikes Clauses (Frozen Meat)	1/1/86
Institute Strikes Clauses (Timber Trade Federation)	1/4/86

D. INSTITUTE ADDITIONAL EXPENSES CLAUSES (CARGO—WAR RISKS) 1/7/85

This insurance is only to cover additional expenses incurred in consequence of War Risks, and only to the extent and subject to the conditions set forth in the following clauses:—

1 In the event of interruption or frustration of the voyage or adventure by arrests, restraints, detainment or acts of Kings, Princes and Peoples in prosecution of hostilities or by blockades or other warlike operations, whether there be a declaration of war or not, and whether by a belligerent or otherwise, or by reason of the exercise by the carrier of any liberty granted by any "War Risks" clause in the contract of affreightment, and the goods being discharged at a port other than the port of destination specified in this insurance or, where a country or district is specified in this insurance as the destination of the voyage, being discharged outside the limits of such country or district, the Underwriters shall pay (subject to the limit stated below) their proportion of additional expenses (including additional marine and war risk premiums and duty, if any) reasonably incurred by the Assured, in consequence of such interruption or frustration and discharge, for landing and/or warehousing charges and/or for transhipment to original destination or for returning the goods to the point of origin of the shipment or for transhipping to a substituted destination.

2 The additional expenses for returning the goods to the point of origin of the shipment or for transhipping to a substituted destination referred to in Clause 1 shall be considered reasonably incurred only if

2.1 the approval thereto of the Underwriters hereon has been first obtained, or

2.2 the sum for which the goods could have been sold there at the time the decision to transport the goods was made, less all necessary charges incurred in transporting the goods, including duty, if any, *exceeds* the sum which could have been realised by a sale at the place where the voyage or adventure was interrupted or frustrated, less duty, if any, which would have become payable in event of sale there, *and is not less than* the sum which could have been realised at some other place to which the Assured might reasonably have sent the goods, less all necessary charges which would have been incurred in transporting the goods, including duty, if any.

3 Subject to the provisions of Clause 2, if the goods are returned to the point of origin of the shipment or transhipped to a substituted destination, and the sum realised or which could be realised there, by the sale of the goods, exceeds the sum insured hereunder, the Underwriters' liability hereunder for additional expenses in respect of transport and duty shall be limited to the amount by which the said additional expenses incurred exceed the difference between the sum realised or which could be realised by the sale of the goods and the sum insured hereunder.

4 This insurance does not cover any expenses

4.1 incurred as a result of physical damage to vessel or cargo,

4.1.1 which may be recoverable under Marine or War Risk insurances on the goods, or

4.1.2 which may not be recoverable under such insurances by a reason of insufficiency of the sum insured thereunder,

4.2 incurred subsequent to and in consequence of prohibition by the Government of the United Kingdom or of any of its Allies whereby the Assured is prevented from removing the goods from the port or place or country of discharge.

5 Warranted that the goods are covered by insurance against War Risks and against Marine Risks to an extent not less than the cover provided by the Institute Cargo Clauses (C).

6 Risk to commence at times of sailing and it is warranted that when the vessel sails the contract of carriage provides for discharge of the goods at the destination named in this insurance.

7 Where the vessel has the option under the contract of carriage to discharge the goods at any specified port or ports, or any port or ports in a specified range, no liability shall arise hereunder by reason of discharge at any such port or ports.

8 Underwriters shall not be liable for
8.1 warehousing charges after a period of six months,
8.2 any expenses incurred more than twelve months after the goods were discharged unless the goods were in course of being forwarded, returned or transhipped to a substituted destination, before the expiry of the said twelve months.
9 Unless otherwise agreed the sum insured hereunder shall be that for which the goods are insured against Marine Risks or the C.I.F. value whichever be the greater. The sum insured by this insurance shall be the limit of liability hereunder.
10 Warranted that the goods are not at any time during the voyage, the property of any government or of any person, firm or corporation (including those domiciled in neutral territory) who are alien enemies of the United Kingdom or its Allies.
11 This insurance excludes loss damage or expense arising from any hostile use of any weapon of war employing atomic or nuclear fission and/or fusion or other like reaction or radio-active force or matter.
12 This insurance is subject to English law and practice.

These Clauses re-instate (albeit in a restricted fashion) the cover which is removed from the Institute War Clauses (Cargo) by Exclusion 3.7, otherwise known as the "Frustration Clause". That clause reads: "In no case shall this insurance cover any claim based upon loss of or frustration of the voyage or adventure"; see pages 291 and 292 for a commentary thereon.

Clause 1 sets out the reinstated cover in general terms, although some of the later clauses impose certain quite important restrictions. To summarise the overall effect:

1. There has to be an interruption or frustration of the voyage (Clause 1);
   - in consequence of an "arrest, restraint or detainment or [other] act of Kings, Princes and [or] Peoples in prosecution of hostilities or by blockades or other warlike operations"—this form of words resurrects some of the archaic phraseology abandoned in the "quiet revolution" of 1982, although Clause 1 specifically provides for their application whether the perpetrator is or is not a belligerent and whether or not there has been a declaration of war;
   - alternatively, the interruption or frustration may come about by reason of the exercise by the carrier of a liberty granted by a "War Clause" in the contract of carriage (the clause says "contract of affreightment" but this phrase is no longer considered accurate in this context).

2. The cargo has to be discharged from the carrying ship at a port other than the port of destination specified in the insurance, or if a country or district is specified as the destination, then outside that country or district (Clause 1); but where the contract of carriage has given the carrier the option to discharge within a specified range, the discharge of cargo within that range will not give rise to any claim under this insurance (Clause 7).

3. If these conditions are satisfied, the underwriters will pay the additional expenses reasonably incurred by the assured for "landing and/or warehousing charges and/or for transhipment" to original destination or (subject to a test of reasonableness) to a substituted destination or a return to the place of shipment.

If the assured opts to return the goods to their place of origin, or to attempt to obtain a better price by forwarding them to a substituted destination, he must first obtain the underwriters' approval, or alternatively demonstrate after the event that his claim for the cost of forwarding was reasonable by reference to the rather complicated formula set out in sub-clause 2.2. The effect of this formula is that if *either (x)* the amount for which the goods could have been sold at the place of interruption of the voyage, less duty, if any, *or (y)* the amount realisable at some alternative destination, net of the cost of forwarding, including duty, if any, *exceeds (z)* the amount for which the goods could have been sold at either the point of origin or at the substituted destination (depending on the basis of the claim), computed at the time the decision was taken to forward, less the cost of forwarding, including duty, if any, then the claim will (presumably) be discounted by the difference, i.e. *(z) minus the greater of (x) or (y)*.

On the other hand, as provided by Clause 3, if the assured, by returning the goods to their point of origin or forwarding them to a substituted destination, was able (or could have been able) to realise on sale a sum greater than the sum insured, i.e. make a "profit", then his claim for forwarding expenses and duty, if any, will be reduced by that amount.

These are, however, only minor criticisms. The major flaw in these Additional Expenses Clauses, as seen from the point of view of a cargo assured, is that they do not provide for the case where by reason of the restraint the assured has lost possession of his goods and is unlikely to recover them within a reasonable time. These are the very circumstances which would give rise to a claim for a constructive total loss, as provided by section 60(2)(i) of the Marine Insurance Act 1906, were it not for the Frustration Clause in the Institute War Clauses (Cargo).

Clauses 4, 5, 6, 8, 9, 10 and 11 contain various self-explanatory warranties and exclusions, which further reduce the attractiveness of this so-called additional cover.

3. HULL INSURANCES

INSTITUTE WAR AND STRIKES CLAUSES, HULLS—TIME 1/11/95

This form combines war risks and strikes risks in one document.

In common with all Hull forms, the following words appear in the heading: "This insurance is subject to English law and practice". See pages 90 and 91 for the editor's observations on these words.

Clause 1—Perils

1 Subject always to the exclusions hereinafter referred to, this insurance covers loss of or damage to the Vessel caused by

1.1 war civil war revolution rebellion insurrection, or civil strife arising therefrom, or any hostile act by or against a belligerent power

1.2 capture seizure arrest restraint or detainment, and the consequences thereof or any attempt thereat
1.3 derelict mines torpedoes bombs or other derelict weapons of war
1.4 strikers, locked-out workmen, or persons taking part in labour disturbances, riots or civil commotions
1.5 any terrorist or any person acting maliciously or from a political motive
1.6 confiscation or expropriation.

Clause 1.1 lists the war and war-like risks in the same words as appear in the Institute War Clauses (Cargo), and the observations made on pages 286 to 288 apply equally to them.

Clause 1.2 is however wider than the corresponding clause in the Institute War Clauses (Cargo), in that the perils of capture, seizure, arrest, restraint or detainment are not limited to those which arise in consequence of the war and war-like risks set out in Clause 1.1. Subject therefore to the exclusions, and particularly those set out in Clauses 5.1.2, 5.1.3, 5.1.4 and 5.1.5 (see below), a seizure, arrest or restraint exercised in time of peace by the political or executive arm of a Government or power will be covered, equally with such acts performed in war or war-like circumstances.

Clause 1.3 is the same as in the Institute War Clauses (Cargo). See commentary on page 290.

Clause 1.4 is the same as Clause 1.1 in the Institute Strikes Clauses (Cargo). See pages 297 to 298.

Clause 1.5 retains the risk of loss or damage by persons "acting maliciously", and adds, by way both of clarification and expansion, the risks of loss or damage caused by a terrorist or a person acting from a political motive. The cover is therefore wider than that provided in the Cargo Clauses.

"*Maliciously*" means "out of spite, or ill-will", and as an insured peril it may well overlap with acts performed with a political motivation or in the course of a civil commotion. Sabotage is a malicious act. So are many acts of barratry, but as barratry is one of the perils insured under the Institute Time Clauses, Hulls, a loss from this cause will be excluded from the War and Strikes cover by reason of Clause 5.3 of the Institute War and Strikes Clauses, Hulls—Time, unless the act of barratry involved the detonation of an explosive, in which event it would be excluded from the marine risks cover by virtue of Clause 26 of the Institute Time Clauses, Hulls, 1/11/95.

"1.6 confiscation or expropriation"

These seemingly "new" perils do not appear to the editor to be wider than the kind of political or executive acts of a Government or a power which, under Rule 10 for the Rules for Construction of Policy contained in the Marine Insurance Act 1906, are comprehended within the words "arrests, restraints and detainments of all Kings, Princes and People . . . " as they appeared in Lloyd's form of policy. However, whether listed in the Institute War and Strikes Clauses, Hulls—Time merely for clarification or by way of expansion of the perils insured, it is to be noted that they were not among the listed perils in the old forms of War and Strikes Clauses for Hulls, neither do they appear in the current Institute War Clauses (Cargo).

A dictionary definition of "confiscation" is:

> "Appropriation to the public treasury (by way of penalty)", with the additional colloquial meaning of "legal robbery with the sanction of the ruling power".

"Expropriation" suggests an executive act of dispossession, not necessarily by way of a penalty.

Clause 2—Incorporation

2 **INCORPORATION**

The Institute Time Clauses—Hulls 1/11/95 (including 3/4ths Collision Liability amended to 4/4ths) except Clauses 1.4, 2, 3, 4, 5, 6, 12, 22.1.8, 23, 24, 25, 26 and 27 are deemed to be incorporated in this insurance in so far as they do not conflict with the provisions of these clauses.

Held covered in case of breach of warranty as to towage or salvage services provided notice be given to the Underwriters immediately after receipt of advices and any additional premium required by them be agreed.

The first part of this clause incorporates the relevant provisions of the Institute Time Clauses—Hulls, particularly those relating to general average and salvage, sue and labour charges[21] and the clauses dealing with the adjustment of claims, namely Clauses 14, 15, 16, 17, 18, 19 and 20. It is to be noted that in one respect the cover granted by the Institute War and Strikes Clauses, Hulls—Time is wider than provided in the Institute Time Clauses. This is in respect to collision liability, which is granted in full (4/4ths) under the War and Strikes Clauses, whereas it is normal to limit the cover to 3/4ths in the insurances covering marine risks. So, for example, if a ship insured with the Institute War and Strikes Clauses is taken over by a party of hijackers acting for a political motive and, whilst under their control, collides with and does damage to another vessel, then any collision liability which attaches to the owner of the ship (in spite of his temporary dispossession) will be met in full.

The second part of this Clause 2 holds the assured covered in the event of a breach of warranty as to towage or salvage services, with the usual proviso regarding notice and the payment of any additional premium. By implication therefore, breaches of warranty as to cargo, trade, locality and date of sailing will not be held covered.

Clause 3—Detainment

In the event that the Vessel shall have been the subject of capture seizure arrest restraint detainment confiscation or expropriation, and the Assured shall thereby have lost the free use and disposal of the Vessel for a continuous period of 12 months then for the purpose of ascertaining whether the Vessel is a constructive total loss the

21. For a review of the cases relating to the payment of a ransom or other sum of money demanded by a captor or foreign government for the release of the insured vessel, see *Royal Boskalis Westminster N.V.* v. *Mountain* [1997] L.R.L.R. 523 at pp. 612, 621 and 635.

Assured shall be deemed to have been deprived of the possession of the Vessel without any likelihood of recovery.

This is an important new clause and requires some explanation.

By section 60(2) of the Marine Insurance Act 1906, there is a constructive total loss where, *inter alia*, the assured is deprived of the possession of his ship by a peril insured against, and it is unlikely that he can recover it. On the outbreak of the war between Iraq and Iran, a number of ships were trapped in the Shatt-al-Arab by the outbreak of hostilities, and even those which were physically able to sail were prohibited from so doing by the Iraqi authorities. While clearly subject to restraint, underwriters questioned whether the assured had been deprived of the possession of their ships, and if they had, whether they were likely or unlikely to recover them. A test case, *The "Bamburi"*[22] was selected for the arbitration of a judge arbitrator, who found in favour of the claimants. In his reasons, the arbitrator dealt with the following points:

1. Was the detention of the vessel proximately caused by perils insured?

The arbitrator found that the order preventing the vessel from sailing emanated from an executive organ of the Government of Iraq, and that this constituted a "restraint of princes". It was not a mere restriction on navigation.

However, the arbitrator considered that if there had been no restraint or detainment by the Iraqi Government, he would not have been able to find that the vessel's detention constituted a loss by "hostilities or war-like operations", merely an apprehension of loss by those perils.

2. Have the owners been deprived of possession?

The arbitrator held that it was irrelevant to this question that the owners continued to receive payment of hire during the first year that the vessel was detained. There was a real distinction between physical loss of use and financial loss of reward.

The arbitrator found that the owners had been wholly deprived of the "free use and disposal" of the ship. He made a lengthy review of the law in order to deal with the challenge that the deprivation of "free use and disposal" was the right test to apply to answer this question, and concluded that although the "loss of the adventure" theory (which still holds good in the case of a policy of insurance on goods) had been discarded at least by 1857 as regards claims on policies of insurance on ship, the "free use and disposal" test was still correct.

22. [1982] 1 Lloyd's Rep. 312.

3. Was it "unlikely" that the owners could recover the vessel (within a reasonable time)?

It was not disputed that the words "within a reasonable time" are implicit in section 60(2)(i)(*a*) of the 1906 Act—see *Polurrian Steamship Co.* v. *Young.*[23]

The arbitrator judged that a reasonable time in a case of this sort would be 12 months from the notice of abandonment, without taking into account any period before the notice.

This Clause 3 summarises the effect of the arbitrator's decision, and lays down the sensible rule that where the assured has lost the free use and disposal of the vessel for a continuous period of 12 months, then it shall be deemed to be a constructive total loss.

In a recent book, some uncertainty was expressed regarding the interpretation of this clause.[24] For the avoidance of doubt, the present editor would submit the following propositions:

(a) the clause does not affect the time when the cause of action arises, which is retrospective to the event giving rise to the loss, i.e. when the capture, seizure, etc. takes effect[25];
(b) the clause does not remove the need for the assured to give notice of abandonment in order to claim for a constructive total loss;
(c) the assured remains entitled (and at the same time he is under a duty) to give notice of abandonment "with reasonable diligence after receipt of reliable information of the loss".[26]

In other words, an assured cannot be criticised for giving notice of abandonment as soon as the information in his hands shows that his ship has been captured or detained and that from his point of view it appears unlikely that he will recover her. If the underwriters decline the abandonment they will agree to put the assured in the same position as if a writ had been issued on that day. Thereafter the assured will be entitled to succeed in his claim for a constructive total loss in either of the following circumstances:

(i) if within 12 months it can be shown by examination of all the available evidence that the assured has been deprived of possession and it is unlikely that he can recover the vessel; or
(ii) if a period of 12 months has elapsed during the whole of which the assured has lost the "free use and disposal" of the vessel.

23. (1915) 19 Com.Cas. 143; 20 Com.Cas. 152.
24. Gotthard Gauci, "Constructive Total Losses" in *The Modern Law of Marine Insurance* (1996).
25. *Bank of America National Trust* v. *Chrismas (The "Kyriaki")* [1993] 1 Lloyd's Rep. 137.
26. Marine Insurance Act 1906, s. 62(3).

Clause 4—Notice of Claim and Tenders

4 **NOTICE OF CLAIM AND TENDERS**
In the event of accident whereby loss or damage may result in a claim under this insurance, notice must be given to the Underwriters promptly after the date on which the Assured, Owners or Managers become or should have become aware of the loss or damage and prior to survey so that a surveyor may be appointed if the Underwriters so desire.
If notice is not given to Underwriters within twelve months of that date unless the Underwriters agree to the contrary in writing, the Underwriters will be automatically discharged from liability for any claim under this insurance in respect of or arising out of such accident or the loss or damage.

The text set out here is exactly the same as the new Clause 13.1 in the Institute Time Clauses, Hulls, 1/11/95. As this provision was new in 1995 and is considerably more stringent than the one it replaces (see commentary on page 140) it has to be assumed that its reproduction here is deliberate, in order to emphasise its importance. The remainder of Clause 13 of the Institute Time Clauses, Hulls, 1/11/95, which refers to the taking of tenders for repairs, is not set out in the War and Strikes Risks form, although it applies by virtue of the Incorporation Clause.

Clause 5—Exclusions

5 **EXCLUSIONS**
This insurance excludes
5.1 loss damage liability or expense arising from
5.1.1 the outbreak of war (whether there be a declaration of war or not) between any of the following countries:
United Kingdom, United States of America, France, the Russian Federation, the People's Republic of China
5.1.2 requisition, either for title or use, or pre-emption
5.1.3 capture seizure arrest restraint detainment confiscation or expropriation by or under the order of the government or any public or local authority of the country in which the Vessel is owned or registered
5.1.4 arrest restraint detainment confiscation or expropriation under quarantine regulations or by reason of infringement of any customs or trading regulations
5.1.5 the operation of ordinary judicial process, failure to provide security or to pay any fine or penalty or any financial cause
5.1.6 piracy (but this exclusion shall not affect cover under Clause 1.4),
5.2 loss damage liability or expense directly or indirectly caused by or contributed to by or arising from
5.2.1 ionising radiations from or contamination by radioactivity from any nuclear fuel or from any nuclear waste or from the combustion of nuclear fuel
5.2.2 the radioactive, toxic, explosive or other hazardous or contaminating properties of any nuclear installation, reactor or other nuclear assembly or nuclear component thereof
5.2.3 any weapon of war employing atomic or nuclear fission and/or fusion or other like reaction or radioactive force or matter,
5.3 loss damage liability or expense covered by the Institute Time Clauses—Hulls 1/11/95 (including 3/4ths Collision Liability Clause amended to 4/4ths) or which would be recoverable thereunder but for Clause 12 thereof,
5.4 any claim for any sum recoverable under any other insurance on the Vessel or which would be recoverable under such insurance but for the existence of this insurance,
5.5 any claim for expenses arising from delay except such expenses as would be recoverable in principle in English law and practice under the York-Antwerp Rules 1994.

The major difference between the present clause and the Exclusions listed in the 1/10/83 form consists in the new wording for the nuclear and radioactive contamination exclusion in sub-clause 5.2. This excludes "loss damage liability or expense directly or indirectly caused by or contributed to by or arising from . . . ", a form of words no doubt designed to create a kind of paramount exclusion.

Although renumbered and to some extent re-worded (the Russian Federation being substituted for the Soviet Union), the other exclusions remain as they were before.

Clause 5.1.1 excludes any claim arising from the outbreak of war involving any two or more of the major powers. In this event the insurance is also automatically terminated by virtue of Clause 6.2.

Clause 5.1.2 excludes "requisition or pre-emption". *"Requisition"* means a demand for use in military service. *"Pre-emption"* is understood to have something of the same meaning in the United States of America. In either case it is presumed that the owner will lose possession only for a temporary period of time, and will have the vessel returned to him by the requisitioning authority when it is no longer required. It is also to be noted that requisition is one of the events which brings about the automatic termination of the insurance.

Clause 5.1.3 excludes the perils of capture, seizure etc. (including confiscation or expropriation) by the government or a public or local authority of the country in which the vessel is owned or registered. It was a supposed rule of English law that a marine insurance policy subject to that law would not cover the risk of British capture, on the grounds of public policy. Since the House of Lords held to the contrary in *British and Foreign Marine Insurance Co.* v. *Sanday*,[27] albeit that this was a case involving cargo, it has been necessary to make some specific exclusion in the policy to revert to what was understood to be the traditional position.

Clause 5.1.4 excludes arrest etc. (including confiscation or expropriation) arising in three circumstances. Two of these, under quarantine regulations, and by reason of infringement of any customs regulations, were excluded under the previous forms of War and Strikes Clauses, but the exclusion of claims arising by reason of infringement of "trading regulations" was new in 1983.

The exclusion relating to infringement of customs regulations has been considered in two cases. In *Panamanian Oriental Steamship Corporation* v. *Wright*[28] the Court of Appeal held that the ship had been confiscated under Vietnamese regulations which provided for that penalty in the event of breach of customs regulations. Not so straightforward was the case of *The "Wondrous"*.[29] In that case one of the questions for decision was whether the detention of the vessel waiting for customs clearance (which on the evidence would not have been granted owing to non-payment of port dues and other

27. (1916) 21 Com.Cas. 154.
28. (*The "Anita"*) [1971] 1 Lloyd's Rep. 487.
29. *Ikerigi Cia Naviera* v. *Palmer (The "Wondrous")* [1991] 1 Lloyd's Rep. 400; [1992] 2 Lloyd's Rep. 56.

charges) was excluded "by reason of infringement of any customs . . . regulations". In the Commercial Court Hobhouse J. held that just as the words "restraint" and "detainment" have to be given a wide commercial interpretation (see, for example, *The "Bamburi"*), the exclusion must be read in the same way. In the Court of Appeal Lloyd L.J. agreed with this view; Nourse L.J. likewise, but with evident reluctance, whereas McCowan L.J. was of the view that, as the vessel never attempted to leave the port without paying, there was no actual infringement. In the opinion of the present editor, the interpretation of McCowan L.J. is to be preferred to that of his judicial colleagues.

Clause 5.1.5 excludes "the operation of ordinary judicial process, failure to provide security or to pay any fine or penalty or any financial cause". So far as these circumstances are mainly those which would justify the vessel being placed under civil arrest at the suit of an aggrieved party, these exclusions may be considered, at any rate so far as English law is concerned, as merely declaratory. However, in *The "Wondrous"* the words "any financial cause" were held to be wider than "financial default" (the words which appear in the Institute Cargo Clauses—see page 22), and to cover the non-payment of dues and charges by parties other than the assured. Thus if a ship be detained in port on the order of the authorities because the cargo interests have failed to provide a guarantee for financial reasons, the exception will apply.

Since piracy has been accepted again by underwriters in the British insurance markets as a marine risk, it is necessary in order to avoid duplication to exclude it from the list of war perils, and this is achieved by Clause 5.1.6. However, as has been noted in our review of the Institute Time Clauses —Hulls (see page 155), Clause 25 of those clauses excludes claims arising from riots or civil commotions which are of course covered by the Institute War and Strikes Clauses (Clause 1.4) as we have observed above. The traditional English law definition of "riot" (see pages 297 to 298) recently approved in the case of *The "Andreas Lemos"*[30] is sufficiently wide to cover some (although not all) acts of piracy—hence the need for the words (in Clause 5.1.6) to limit the exclusion of piracy to those cases which do not also constitute a "riot".

Clause 5.3 is inserted in order to avoid any duplication of cover with the Institute Time Clauses—Hulls.

Clause 5.4 is designed to prevent any claim falling upon the policy containing the Institute War and Strikes Clauses which can or could be recovered under any other insurance on the vessel. In the event of there being such a duplication of cover, it is intended that the other insurance should pay on a "first loss" basis.

Clause 5.5 is the usual clause excluding any claim for expenses arising from delay, except when allowable in general average.

30. See n. 17.

Clause 6—Termination

6 **TERMINATION**

6.1 This insurance may be cancelled by either the Underwriters or the Assured giving 7 days notice (such cancellation becoming effective on the expiry of 7 days from midnight of the day on which notice of cancellation is issued by or to the Underwriters). The Underwriters agree however to reinstate this insurance subject to agreement between the Underwriters and the Assured prior to the expiry of such notice of cancellation as to new rate of premium and/or conditions and/or warranties.

6.2 Whether or not such notice of cancellation has been given this insurance shall TERMINATE AUTOMATICALLY

6.2.1 upon the outbreak of war (whether there be a declaration of war or not) between any of the following countries:

United Kingdom, United States of America, France, the Russian Federation, the People's Republic of China

6.2.2 in the event of the Vessel being requisitioned, either for title or use.

6.3 In the event either of cancellation by notice or of automatic termination of this insurance by reason of the operation of this Clause 6, or of the sale of the Vessel, pro rata net return of premium shall be payable to the Assured.

This was Clause 5 in the 1/10/83 form.

Clause 6.1 permits either party to give the other seven days' notice before the cancellation becomes effective. The underlying intention of the clause is to enable underwriters to vary the rate of premium and/or the conditions of the insurance in the event of a serious change of circumstances relating to war risks in the vessel's likely trading area.

The second part of the clause relates to the reinstatement of the insurance if underwriters and the assured can agree to the new terms within the period of the seven days' notice. Prior to 1983, the period of notice used to be 14 days, so it must be assumed that reinstatement negotiations are much less protracted than they used to be.

Clause 6.2 relating to automatic termination is self-explanatory, but it is to be noted that in contrast with the form of 1/10/83, the hostile detonation of a nuclear weapon anywhere in the world is no longer an event giving rise to the automatic termination of the insurance.

There is also an important caution at the foot of the clauses, which reads as follows:

This insurance shall not become effective if, subsequent to its acceptance by the Underwriters and prior to the intended time of its attachment, there has occurred any event which would have automatically terminated this insurance under the provisions of Clause 6 above.

This is also self-explanatory.

4. INSURANCES ON FREIGHT

INSTITUTE WAR AND STRIKES CLAUSES, FREIGHT—TIME 1/11/95

This insurance is subject to English law and practice.

Clause 1—Perils

Subject always to the exclusions hereinafter referred to, this insurance covers

1.1 loss (total or partial) of the subject-matter insured caused by

1.1.1 war civil war revolution rebellion insurrection, or civil strife arising therefrom, or any hostile act by or against a belligerent power
1.1.2 capture seizure arrest restraint or detainment, and the consequences thereof or any attempt thereat
1.1.3 derelict mines torpedoes bombs or other derelict weapons of war
1.2 loss (total or partial) of the subject-matter insured arising from loss of or damage to the Vessel caused by
1.2.1 strikers, locked-out workmen, or persons taking part in labour disturbances, riots or civil commotions
1.2.2 any terrorist or any person acting maliciously or from a political motive
1.2.3 confiscation or expropriation.

This clause appears in both the 1/10/83 and 1/11/95 forms of the Institute War and Strikes Clauses, Freight.

It will be noted that, whereas the list of perils covered is the same as appears in the Institute War and Strikes Clauses, Hulls—Time, there is an important difference in the manner of their operation. Any loss of freight, whether total or partial, caused by war or the "war-like" perils listed in sub-clauses 1.1.1, 1.1.2 and 1.1.3 will be responded for under this insurance. Contrarily, the "strikes" risks covered by sub-clauses 1.2.1, 1.2.2 and 1.2.3 will only be paid for when the loss of freight, whether total or partial, arises from loss of or damage to the ship caused by those perils.

The reason for this limitation is not at all clear to the editor. To take an example, if goods which the shipowner has contracted to carry are destroyed by persons taking part in a labour disturbance whilst they are on the quayside awaiting shipment:

- the owner of the cargo will suffer a loss which is covered by the Institute Strikes Clauses (Cargo), whereas
- the shipowner, who bears the risk of freight, will not be entitled to receive any freight in respect of the goods which he has contracted to carry, but this loss will not be covered under the Institute War and Strikes Clauses, Freight—Time.

Likewise any loss of freight which is at the shipowner's risk "until right and true delivery", which the shipowner may suffer in consequence of a loss of cargo caused by "strikes" perils during the voyage and before delivery of the cargo, falls outside the scope of this insurance.

Clause 2—Incorporation

The Institute Time Clauses—Freight 1/11/95 except Clauses 2, 3, 4, 5, 6, 7, 12, 17, 18, 19, 20 and 21 are deemed to be incorporated in this insurance in so far as they do not conflict with the provisions of these clauses.
Held covered in case of breach of warranty as to towage or salvage services provided notice be given to the Underwriters immediately after receipt of advices and any additional premium required by them be agreed.

It will be appreciated that the incorporation of the Institute Time Clauses, Freight is far from complete. The risk of craft and/or lighter to and from the vessel (Clause 2 of the Institute Time Clauses, Freight) is not included, there is no Continuation Clause and the circumstances in which the assured will be held covered in case of breach of warranty are limited to instances when towage or salvage services are provided by the ship, subject to the usual proviso regarding notice and payment of any additional premium required by the underwriters.

On the other hand the Franchise Clause contained in the Institute Time Clauses, Freight is not incorporated in the War and Strikes Clauses, and consequently when there has been a partial loss of freight caused by the war and strikes perils insured under these clauses, the claim will be paid irrespective of percentage.

Clause 3—Detainment

In the event that a claim for a constructive total loss of the Vessel is paid on the war risks insurance of the Vessel under Clause 3 (Detainment) of the Institute War and Strikes Clauses—Hulls—Time 1/11/95 or the Institute War and Strikes Clauses—Hulls—Voyage 1/11/95 as a result of the loss of the free use and disposal of the Vessel for a continuous period of 12 months due to capture, seizure, arrest, restraint, detainment, confiscation or expropriation whilst this insurance is in force, the amount insured hereunder shall be paid in full less any claims otherwise arising during the said period of 12 months which have been paid or are recoverable hereunder or under insurances subject to the Institute Time Clauses—Freight 1/11/95 and/or the Institute Voyage Clauses—Freight 1/11/95 and any recoveries made in respect of the said period.

This is in similar terms to the corresponding clause in the 1/10/83 form.

The general effect of this clause is that if the assured has lost the "free use and disposal" of the vessel for a continuous period of 12 months due to capture, seizure, arrest, restraint, detainment, confiscation or expropriation during the currency of the insurance, a claim which is met by the war risks insurance on the ship will be followed for the full amount of the insurance subscribed on the War and Strikes Risks Clauses, Freight. Of course, if any interim payments have been made for losses payable by the War and Strikes Clauses, Freight, they will be deducted in arriving at the overall settlement under this clause.

Clause 4—Exclusions

This insurance excludes

4.1 loss (total or partial) or expense arising from

4.1.1 the outbreak of war (whether there be a declaration of war or not) between any of the following countries:

United Kingdom, United States of America, France, the Russian Federation, the People's Republic of China

4.1.2 requisition, either for title or use, or pre-emption

4.1.3 capture seizure arrest restraint detainment confiscation or expropriation by or under the order of the government or any public or local authority of the country in which the Vessel is owned or registered

4.1.4 arrest restraint detainment confiscation or expropriation under quarantine regulations or by reason of infringement of any customs or trading regulations

4.1.5 the operation of ordinary judicial process, failure to provide security or to pay any fine or penalty or any financial cause

4.1.6 piracy (but this exclusion shall not affect cover under Clause 1.2.1),

4.2 loss (total or partial) or expense directly or indirectly caused by or contributed to by or arising from

4.2.1 ionising radiations from or contamination by radioactivity from any nuclear fuel or from any nuclear waste or from the combustion of nuclear fuel

4.2.2 the radioactive, toxic, explosive or other hazardous or contaminating properties of any nuclear installation, reactor or other nuclear assembly or nuclear component thereof

4.2.3 any weapon of war employing atomic or nuclear fission and/or fusion or other like reaction or radioactive force or matter,

4.3 loss (total or partial) or expense covered by the Institute Time Clauses—Freight 1/11/95 or which would be recoverable thereunder but for Clause 12 thereof,

4.4 any claim (not being a claim recoverable under the Institute War and Strikes Clauses Freight—Voyage 1/11/95) for any sum recoverable under any other insurance on the subject-matter insured or which would be recoverable under such insurance but for the existence of this insurance,

4.5 loss proximately caused by delay or any claim for expenses arising from delay except such expenses as would be recoverable in principle in English law and practice under the York-Antwerp Rules 1994,

4.6 any claim based upon loss of or frustration of any voyage or adventure.

The wording of this clause was altered in 1995 in the same manner as the Exclusions Clause in the Institute War and Strikes Clauses, Hulls—Time. See commentary on pages 311 to 313, and in particular the exclusions in Clauses 4.1.4 and 4.1.5 (corresponding to 5.1.4 and 5.1.5 in the I.W. & S. Clauses, Hulls), which were considered in the context of freight insurance in *The "Wondrous"*.[31]

Clauses 4.3 and 4.4 exclude any claim which would be recoverable either under the Institute Time Clauses, Freight, or any other insurance upon freight, except for claims recoverable in the event that the insurances on freight for War and Strikes risks are supplemented by a voyage insurance on similar terms.

Clause 4.5 is in rather different terms from the corresponding clause which appears in the Institute War and Strikes Clauses, Hulls—Time. Expenses arising from delay are not covered, except for a contribution payable in general average to detention expenses admissible under the York-Antwerp Rules. In addition, the insurance excludes any loss of freight proximately caused by delay, and this reflects the fact that losses of freight due to this cause are not payable under the policies of insurance covering marine risks (see Clause 15 of the Institute Time Clauses, Freight: "any claim consequent on loss of time")[32]; nor may they be admitted in general average (see Rule C of the York-Antwerp Rules).

Clause 4.6, which excludes any claim based upon loss of or frustration of any voyage or adventure, has its counterpart in the Institute War and Strikes Clauses for Cargo. The clause was considered in *Atlantic Maritime Co. Inc.* v. *Gibbon*.[33] In this case the ship was chartered to load a cargo at a Chinese port, which happened to be in the hands of the Communist forces at the time of the Chinese Civil War. Whilst waiting in that port, the Master received a warning from an officer of the Government forces that he should leave the port on account of the dangers which would threaten his ship in the event of a Government attack. The Master took heed of this warning; the vessel sailed from the port, and the judges in the Court of Appeal held that the contract to be performed under the charter-party was frustrated. Although the judges were not unanimous as to whether there had been a "restraint of Princes",

31. See n. 29 above.
32. See commentary on pp. 234–236.
33. [1953] 2 Lloyd's Rep. 294.

they all agreed that the claim, if any, was caught by the "Frustration Clause".

Clause 5—Termination

5.1 This insurance may be cancelled by either the Underwriters or the Assured giving 7 days notice (such cancellation becoming effective on the expiry of 7 days from midnight of the day on which notice of cancellation is issued by or to the Underwriters). The Underwriters agree however to reinstate this insurance subject to agreement between the Underwriters and the Assured prior to the expiry of such notice of cancellation as to new rate of premium and/or conditions and/or warranties.

5.2 Whether or not such notice of cancellation has been given this insurance shall TERMINATE AUTOMATICALLY

5.2.1 upon the outbreak of war (whether there be a declaration of war or not) between any of the following countries:

United Kingdom, United States of America, France, the Russian Federation, the People's Republic of China

5.2.2 in the event of the Vessel being requisitioned, either for title or use.

5.3 In the event either of cancellation by notice or of automatic termination of this insurance by reason of the operation of this Clause 5, or of the sale of the Vessel, pro rata net return of premium shall be payable to the Assured.

This clause is in the same terms as Clause 6 of the Institute War and Strikes Clauses, Hulls—Time, commented upon on page 314.

There then appears the caution:

This insurance shall not become effective if, subsequent to its acceptance by the Underwriters and prior to the intended time of its attachment, there has occurred any event which would have automatically terminated this insurance under the provisions of Clause 5 above.

This is also the same as in the Institute War and Strikes Clauses, Hulls—Time.

INDEX

Bold *entries refer to clauses set out in full and detailed discussion on those clauses*